SAP PRESS e-books

Print or e-book, Kindle or iPad, workplace or airplane: Choose where and how to read your SAP PRESS books! You can now get all our titles as e-books, too:

- By download and online access
- For all popular devices
- And, of course, DRM-free

Convinced? Then go to **www.sap-press.com** and get your e-book today.

Getting Started with ABAP®

SAP PRESS is a joint initiative of SAP and Rheinwerk Publishing. The know-how offered by SAP specialists combined with the expertise of Rheinwerk Publishing offers the reader expert books in the field. SAP PRESS features first-hand information and expert advice, and provides useful skills for professional decision-making.

SAP PRESS offers a variety of books on technical and business-related topics for the SAP user. For further information, please visit our website: *www.sap-press.com*.

Paul Hardy
ABAP to the Future
2015, 727 pages, hardcover
ISBN 978-1-4932-1161-6

James Wood, Joseph Rupert (2nd edition)
Object-Oriented Programming with ABAP Objects
2015, 470 pages, hardcover
ISBN 978-1-4932-993-5

Puneet Asthana, David Haslam
ABAP 7.4 Certification Guide—SAP Certified Development Associate
2015, 663 pages, paperback
ISBN 978-1-4932-1212-5

Schneider, Westenberger, Gahm
ABAP Development for SAP HANA
2013, 609 pages, hardcover
ISBN 978-1-59229-859-4

Brian O'Neill

Getting Started with ABAP®

Publishing

Bonn • Boston

Editor Hareem Shafi
Acquisitions Editor Kelly Grace Weaver
Copyeditor Melinda Rankin
Cover Design Graham Geary
Photo Credit Shutterstock.com: 267106544/© designspace, 245028052/© GuoZhongHua
Layout Design Vera Brauner
Production Nicole Carpenter
Typesetting SatzPro, Krefeld (Germany)
Printed and bound in the United States of America, on paper from sustainable sources

ISBN 978-1-4932-1242-2

© 2016 by Rheinwerk Publishing, Inc., Boston (MA)
1st edition 2016

Library of Congress Cataloging-in-Publication Data
O'Neill, Brian (Computer programmer), author.
Getting started with ABAP / Brian O'Neill.
pages cm
Includes index.
ISBN 978-1-4932-1242-2 (print : alk. paper) -- ISBN 1-4932-1242-7 (print : alk. paper) -- ISBN 978-1-4932-1244-6 (print and ebook : alk. paper) -- ISBN 978-1-4932-1243-9 (ebook) 1. ABAP/4 (Computer program language) 2. Databases. I. Title.
QA76.73.A12O54 2015
005.13'3--dc23
2015030307

All rights reserved. Neither this publication nor any part of it may be copied or reproduced in any form or by any means or translated into another language, without the prior consent of Rheinwerk Publishing, 2 Heritage Drive, Suite 305, Quincy, MA 02171.

Rheinwerk Publishing makes no warranties or representations with respect to the content hereof and specifically disclaims any implied warranties of merchantability or fitness for any particular purpose. Rheinwerk Publishing assumes no responsibility for any errors that may appear in this publication.

"Rheinwerk Publishing" and the Rheinwerk Publishing logo are registered trademarks of Rheinwerk Verlag GmbH, Bonn, Germany. SAP PRESS is an imprint of Rheinwerk Verlag GmbH and Rheinwerk Publishing, Inc.

All of the screenshots and graphics reproduced in this book are subject to copyright © SAP SE, Dietmar-Hopp-Allee 16, 69190 Walldorf, Germany.

SAP, the SAP logo, ABAP, BAPI, Duet, mySAP.com, mySAP, SAP ArchiveLink, SAP EarlyWatch, SAP NetWeaver, SAP Business ByDesign, SAP BusinessObjects, SAP BusinessObjects Rapid Mart, SAP BusinessObjects Desktop Intelligence, SAP BusinessObjects Explorer, SAP Rapid Marts, SAP BusinessObjects Watchlist Security, SAP BusinessObjects Web Intelligence, SAP Crystal Reports, SAP GoingLive, SAP HANA, SAP MaxAttention, SAP MaxDB, SAP PartnerEdge, SAP R/2, SAP R/3, SAP R/3 Enterprise, SAP Strategic Enterprise Management (SAP SEM), SAP StreamWork, SAP Sybase Adaptive Server Enterprise (SAP Sybase ASE), SAP Sybase IQ, SAP xApps, SAPPHIRE NOW, and Xcelsius are registered or unregistered trademarks of SAP SE, Walldorf, Germany.

All other products mentioned in this book are registered or unregistered trademarks of their respective companies.

Contents at a Glance

Part I The Foundation

1	The History of SAP Technologies	21
2	Creating Your First Program	37
3	Creating Data Dictionary Objects	97
4	Accessing the Database	149
5	Storing Data in Working Memory	183
6	Making Programs Modular	217
7	Creating a Shopping Cart Example	261

Part II Finishing Touches

8	Working with Strings and Texts	299
9	Working with Dates, Times, Quantities, and Currencies	329
10	Error Handling	363

Appendices

A	Preparing your Development Environment	395
B	Modern UI Technologies	431
C	Other Resources	439
D	The Author	443

Dear Reader,

Learning a language is an ambitious undertaking. Fluency comes with dedication, hard work, and a good teacher. Luckily, programming languages aren't as complex as French or Spanish, and don't take nearly as long to learn. Even better, you have a superb instructor in the form of Brian O'Neill, who has poured every ounce of teacherly skill he possess into the pages of this book.

Getting Started with ABAP offers you the ABCs of ABAP programming, beginning with the very basics of ABAP and building a firm foundation in syntax, data types, variables, operations, data dictionaries, and more. As you follow along you will gain the skills needed to develop your own program, and then enhance that program with techniques such as modularization, string manipulation, and text symbol application. Sample code and detailed screenshots will help guide you as you make your way through the book. By the end, you will have gained a full understanding of all basic ABAP language concepts and will be ready to tackle your own programming projects head-on!

What did you think about *Getting Started with ABAP*? Your comments and suggestions are the most useful tools to help us make our books the best they can be. Please feel free to contact me and share any praise or criticism you may have.

Thank you for purchasing a book from SAP PRESS!

Hareem Shafi
Editor, SAP PRESS

Rheinwerk Publishing
Boston, MA

hareems@rheinwerk-publishing.com
www.sap-press.com

Contents

Introduction 15

PART I The Foundation

1 The History of SAP Technologies 21

From R/1 to S/4 HANA 21
Navigating an ABAP System 23
    Overview of the ABAP Screen in SAP GUI 23
    Overview of ABAP Screen in SAP NWBC 27
    Overview of ABAP Screen in SAP Fiori 27
ABAP System Landscapes 28
    Client/Server Architecture 28
    Background Jobs 29
    Sandbox, Dev, QA, PRD 31
    Finding the Version of a System in SAP GUI 33
The Limitations of Backward Compatibility 34
Summary 36

2 Creating Your First Program 37

Hello, World! 37
    Creating a New Program with Eclipse 37
    Creating a New Program in Transaction SE80 40
    Writing a "Hello, World!" Program 44
Data Types 46
    The Data Keyword 46
    Numeric Data Types 47
    Character Data Types 49
    Inline Data Declarations 51
Arithmetic and Basic Math Functions 52
    Arithmetic Operations 52
    Math Functions 54
Flow Control 56
    IF Statements 56
    CASE Statements 59

DO Loops	60
WHILE Loops	60
Formatting Code	61
Comments	63
Common Commenting Mistakes	64
Using Comments while Programming	64
Classic Selection Screen Programming	65
SELECTION-SCREEN	66
BLOCK	67
PARAMETER	69
SELECT-OPTIONS	72
Selection Texts	74
Program Lifecycle	75
AT SELECTION-SCREEN	75
START-OF-SELECTION	76
Debugging Basics	76
Program to Debug	77
Breakpoints in Eclipse	79
Breakpoints in the SAP GUI	83
Watchpoints in Eclipse	88
Watchpoints in SAP GUI	91
Tying It All Together	92
The Problem	93
The Solution	94
Summary	95

3 Creating Data Dictionary Objects — 97

What Is a Data Dictionary?	97
What Is a Database?	97
Data Elements	99
Entity Relationship Diagrams	100
Database Normalization	101
Relationships in ERDs	103
The Flight Data Model	105
Flight Example ERD	105
Creating and Editing Tables	108
Viewing the Flight Table Configuration	109

Viewing the Flight Data	116
Setting Up the Flights Example	118
Creating an Append Structure	119
Creating a Custom Transparent Table	122
Data Elements	130
Viewing the S_BOOK_ID Data Element	130
Creating a New Data Element	133
Domains	135
Viewing the BOOLEAN Domain	136
Creating a New Domain	138
Documentation	140
Maintenance Dialogs	141
Structures and Table Types	143
Creating Structures	143
Creating Table Types	145
Summary	146

4 Accessing the Database 149

SQL Console in Eclipse	149
SELECT Statements	151
Basic SELECT Statements	151
SELECT SINGLE	153
SELECT...UP TO n ROWS	155
SELECT...WHERE	155
INSERT	156
MODIFY/UPDATE	158
DELETE	159
INNER JOIN	160
LEFT OUTER JOIN	163
FOR ALL ENTRIES IN	165
With SELECT Options	167
New Open SQL	169
Table Locks	170
Viewing Table Locks	172
Creating Table Locks	174
Setting Table Locks	175
Performance Topics	179

9

Obsolete Database Access Keywords 180
    SELECT…ENDSELECT 181
    Short Form Open SQL 181
Summary 181

5 Storing Data in Working Memory 183

Using ABAP Data Dictionary Data Types 183
    Data Types 183
    Creating Your Own Structures 185
    Field Symbols 186
Standard Table 188
    Defining Standard Tables 188
    READ TABLE 190
    LOOP AT 193
    Inserting Rows in a Standard Table 195
    Changing Rows of a Standard Table 196
    Deleting Rows of a Standard Table 197
Sorted Table 199
    Defining Sorted Tables 199
    Inserting, Changing, and Deleting Sorted Rows 200
    BINARY SEARCH 202
    DELETE ADJACENT DUPLICATES FROM 204
Hashed Table 205
    Defining Hashed Tables 205
    Reading Hashed Tables 206
    Inserting, Changing, and Deleting Hashed Table Rows 207
Which Table Should Be Used? 208
Updating ABAP Data Dictionary Table Type 210
Copying Table Data 212
Displaying Data from Working Memory 213
Obsolete Working Memory Syntax 214
    WITH HEADER LINE 215
    OCCURS 215
    Square Brackets ([]) 215
    Short Form Table Access 215
Summary 216

6 Making Programs Modular 217

Separation of Concerns 217
Introduction to Object-Oriented Programming 220
    What Is an Object? 221
    Modularizing with Object-Oriented Programming 222
Structuring Classes 223
    Implementation vs. Definition 223
    Creating Objects 224
    Public and Private Sections 225
    Class Methods 226
    Importing, Returning, Exporting, and Changing 230
    Constructors 236
    Recursion 237
    Inheritance 239
Global Classes 241
    How to Create Global Classes in Eclipse 242
    How to Create Global Classes in Transaction SE80 243
    Using the Form-Based View in Transaction SE80 245
Obsolete Modularization 249
    Function Modules 249
    Form Subroutines 257
Summary 258

7 Creating a Shopping Cart Example 261

The Design 262
    The Database 263
    The Global Class 263
    The Access Programs 264
Database Solution 266
    Data Elements 266
    Transparent Tables 271
Accessing the Database Solution 280
Creating Classic Screens for the Solution 286
    Product Maintenance Program 286
    Shopping Cart Maintenance Program 290
Summary 295

PART II Finishing Touches

8 Working with Strings and Texts 299

String Manipulation 299
    String Templates 299
    String Functions 302
Text Symbols 304
    Creating Text Symbols 304
    Translating Text Symbols 309
Translating Data in Tables 311
Obsolete Strings and Text 316
Updating the Shopping Cart Example 316
    Applying Text Symbols 316
    Updating the Database 319
    Using the Translation Table 324
Summary 327

9 Working with Dates, Times, Quantities, and Currencies 329

Dates 329
    Date Type Basics 330
    Factory Calendars 331
    Datum Date Type 335
    System Date Fields 336
    Date-Limited Records 336
Times 337
    Calculating Time 338
    Timestamps 338
    SY-UZEIT (System Time vs. Local Time) 341
Quantities 341
    Data Dictionary 342
    Converting Quantities 344
Currencies 345
    Data Dictionary 346
    Converting Currencies 347
Updating the Shopping Cart Example 348
    Updating the Database 349

	Updating the Global Class	356
	Updating the ABAP Programs	358
Summary		361

10 Error Handling 363

SY-SUBRC		363
Message Classes		364
	Displaying a Message Class	364
	Creating a Message Class	367
	Using the MESSAGE Keyword	368
Exception Classes		372
	Unhandled Exceptions	373
	TRY/CATCH Statements	378
	Custom Exception Classes	381
Obsolete Exceptions		386
	Non-Class-Based Exceptions	386
Updating the Shopping Cart Example		389
Summary		392

Appendices 393

A	Preparing your Development Environment	395
B	Modern UI Technologies	431
C	Other Resources	439
D	The Author	443

Index 445

Introduction

Thank you for picking up this book and making the decision to increase your knowledge of ABAP! You will find this book to be detailed and easy-to-follow, with numerous working code examples and step-by-step instructions supported by screenshots. After reading this book, you will have a basic understanding of the new and old aspects of the ABAP language and will be able to write a working program that reads and updates the connected database in a modern ABAP style. You also will be able to identify and support programs written in an older ABAP style and update them as necessary.

All SAP topics are a journey, not a destination. This book will be a great first step, but you will need to continue your learning after you reach its end as well. At the end of the book, you will find a number of recommend resources that you can use to stay on top of the latest ABAP developments and provide an introduction to some additional technologies to grow your skills further.

Audience

In order to begin reading this book, you do not need any prior knowledge about ABAP, programming, or any SAP products.

The target audience for this book is new developers who have never programmed in any language before and developers who have programmed in a language other than ABAP. For the latter group, we point out key differences and similarities between ABAP and other languages throughout the book.

With that said, nondevelopers can get a lot out of this book as well. If you are someone who works in a support organization and needs to test and debug code, this book will help you to get a better understanding of the ABAP language and cover everything you need to know in order to debug ABAP code.

If you are a nondeveloper who manages developers, you may find that this book demonstrates how much the ABAP language has changed over the years.

Structure of This Book

The book is broken up into 10 chapters and three appendices. We will describe each of the chapters and their objectives in this section.

Chapter 1 is for readers who are new to the world of SAP and working with ABAP-based systems. It will talk about the history of SAP as a company and the history of the ABAP language. We will also cover some concepts that are important to know before working on an SAP ABAP-based system.

In **Chapter 2**, We'll introduce the ABAP programming language and cover everything you need to know to build a working, simple ABAP program. We will cover the basic building blocks of programming here and conclude by building a program that utilizes basic programming logic concepts.

Chapter 3 will introduce the ABAP data dictionary, the central repository for data used in all ABAP-based SAP systems. The data dictionary allows you to manage definitions for all object types (tables, views, types, domains, lock objects, etc.) used in ABAP programs and SAP components. We will explain how to create data dictionary objects using hands-on examples.

Now that you know how to create data dictionary objects, **Chapter 4** will cover how to access the data stored in the database using OpenSQL commands. We'll use working code examples to introduce OpenSQL.

In **Chapter 5**, we'll cover how to use internal tables for storing data in working memory. You'll learn how to use internal tables to store and process data retrieved from databases via hands-on examples and working programs.

ABAP programs should be modular, meaning that their components can be separated and recombined in different ways. In **Chapter 6**, We will explain how to achieve basic modularization in ABAP programs using object-oriented programming with hands-on examples and working programs.

Chapter 7 will summarize everything that has been covered so far in the book to create a shopping cart application. This application will include creating data dictionary objects, accessing those objects, and using logic to process the data.

In **Chapter 8**, we will cover how to manipulate strings and use text symbols in ABAP code. We'll also cover the basics of using strings and text to translate an ABAP program into another language. You'll also update the shopping cart program from Chapter 7 to use multiple languages.

Chapter 9 will cover the basics of working with dates, times, quantities, and currencies in code and data dictionary objects. We'll also cover how to convert these data types as needed. You'll then update the shopping cart example again to use quantities and currencies.

In **Chapter 10**, you'll learn various methods of error handling and how and when to cleanly handle errors without causing an exception to occur on a user's screen. You'll then add this error handling to the shopping cart example.

If you need to set up the ABAP editor in Eclipse or have never used the ABAP workbench inside ABAP systems, **Appendix A** will cover how to set up a development environment and introduce the different ABAP integrated development environments (IDEs).

Appendix B will introduce some additional user-interface technologies. These are out of scope for this book, but are great next steps for your ABAP learning journey.

Appendix C will cover some additional resources to continue your ABAP learning journey.

PART I
The Foundation

The History of SAP Technologies

As an ABAP developer, it's helpful to learn the basic history of SAP as a company to better understand where the ABAP language has come from and where it's going. In this chapter, we will cover the history of SAP as a company, its flagship SAP ERP product, and its new SAP HANA platform. We will also cover how the history of ABAP can affect how you write and support ABAP programs.

From R/1 to S/4 HANA

In 1972, five former IBM employees formed a company that they called *Systemanalyse und Programmentwicklung* (System Analysis and Program Development) or SAP for short. The technology used to run the system allowed it to run in real time instead of relying on mainframe programs that had to run at a scheduled time. Beginning with accounting, the company developed different modules while working with their different customers, and these modules became the R/1 system, R standing for real time.

R/1 system

The next evolution was R/2, which was released in 1979; by 1982, the company had more than 250 customers in Germany, Austria, and Switzerland and 100 employees. By 1992, R/3 was released as a client/server application that could run on UNIX systems; the company had 3,157 employees, and half of its revenue was generated outside of Germany. To help support the high demand of R/3 implementations by customers, SAP added independent consulting companies as *logo partners*. By 1994, R/3 was also released for Windows NT and gained SAP's partner IBM as a new customer.

R/2 system

Throughout the 1990s, SAP benefitted greatly from the business process reengineering IT movement. SAP ERP promised to make companies run more efficiently by ditching multiple unconnected legacy systems and processes in favor of a single solution running

SAP ERP

best practice processes. Some customers implemented an SAP ERP system to remove legacy systems that were tainted with the Y2K bug, threating the future of their business in the new millennium.

E-commerce
In 1999, SAP embraced e-commerce with its mySAP.com portfolio, which combined e-commerce solutions with the R/3 SAP ERP solution, followed by purchasing TopTier, a corporate portals company that turned into SAP's Java-based enterprise portals solution.

SAP NetWeaver
In 2004, the first version of SAP NetWeaver was released, and SAP pursued a service-oriented architecture (SOA) product strategy. The next big change to the SAP ERP system would be the release of SAP Business Suite 7 in 2009.

SAP HANA
The next major shift for SAP occurred in 2010 with the release of a new in-memory, column-oriented relational database system: SAP HANA (for *Hasso's New Architecture*), named after SAP founder Hasso Plattner. Soon after, SAP announced support for its business warehouse product on SAP HANA, followed by support for its entire business suite of products (SAP ERP, SAP CRM, etc.).

S/4 HANA
In 2015, SAP released the latest version of its SAP ERP solution, called S/4 HANA. The S in *S/4* stands for *simple* and promises a simpler configuration experience, a simpler user interface based on HTML5 called SAP Fiori, and a simpler database design that combines transactional processing with analytical processing. With the SAP Fiori user experience, an SAP system can be accessed from a phone, tablet, or desktop device.

Today, SAP's products have evolved greatly since the early beginnings of R/1. They are being hosted on-premise and in the cloud, integrated with other SAP solutions and non-SAP solutions on-premise and in the cloud, and accessed by more types of devices than ever before. Running these different applications, including S/4 HANA, still requires the ABAP language. Over the years, the ABAP language has had to evolve to keep up with the latest technological trends, resulting in drastic changes and upgrades to the ABAP language.

ABAP
SAP's portfolio also contains non-ABAP systems and systems from companies that were purchased as SAP became the very large company it is today. For those systems, ABAP still will play a role when

interfacing with a central, ABAP-based SAP ERP, SAP CRM, or other ABAP-based system.

As an ABAP developer, it's important to know how much things have changed over the years for SAP ERP and other products. The history of SAP affects the history of the system that you'll be working on. Before working on an ABAP system, find out the history of that system, when the system was implemented, and how it was supported since implementation. Later in this chapter, we will talk more about how the history of a system can affect you as an ABAP developer.

Navigating an ABAP System

There are multiple ways to work with an SAP NetWeaver system. You may use SAP GUI, SAP NetWeaver Business Client (NWBC), or even an SAP Fiori app. In this section, we will briefly cover these three user interfaces for the SAP NetWeaver system. In this book, you will primarily use SAP GUI or the Eclipse integrated development environment (IDE) when accessing the SAP NetWeaver system and ABAP programs.

ABAP clients

Overview of the ABAP Screen in SAP GUI

SAP GUI (graphical user interface) is the traditional interface for accessing ABAP-based systems and is still used in many systems by administrators and power users, even if most users access the system using SAP NWBC or some other method. Figure 1.1 shows the initial screen you'll see when logging into SAP GUI.

SAP GUI

Figure 1.1 The Initial Screen in SAP GUI

Transactions · When using an ABAP system, most users' interaction is through the use of a transaction. A *transaction* is a program that represents some sort of business process, such as create order, display order or change order.

Figure 1.2 shows the system toolbar, located on the top of the screen. These options will not change when accessing the system.

Figure 1.2 System Toolbar

SAP GUI toolbar · The check mark and textbox to its right are used to access specific transactions in the system by entering a transaction code (SE80 for example). To the right of the textbox are SAVE, BACK, EXIT, and CANCEL buttons, which can be used when executing an ABAP program. Next to the right are PRINT, FIND, and FIND NEXT buttons, followed by buttons for navigating up and down on the screen.

The next button allows you to create a new session. *Sessions* are similar to opening up a second browser when accessing a website. The number of sessions that can be opened at once may be limited by system settings. Next to that is a button to create a desktop shortcut to open SAP GUI and enter the transaction you're currently accessing.

The question mark button will provide some basic help for accessing the system, and the screen button will provide options for the SAP GUI itself.

SAP GUI application toolbar · Below the system toolbar is the application toolbar, which will change for each application you use. Let's cover some of the basic options for the menu screen, as shown in Figure 1.3.

Figure 1.3 Initial SAP GUI Screen Application Toolbar

The first two buttons let you toggle between the user menu ▣ and SAP menu ▣. The user menu is generated based on roles assigned to the logged-in user, allowing only the transactions to which the user has access to be revealed. The SAP menu will display all of the transactions in the system regardless of whether or not the user has the authority to access them.

The third button displayed ▣ is used to access the SAP Business Workplace, where messages can be displayed and created. This may be used as part of the workflow functionality.

The next set of buttons are used to CREATE, DELETE, and EDIT favorite transactions ▣ ▣ ▣. To add a favorite, select the transaction from the menu and click on the leftmost of these three buttons. This will add the transaction to the list of favorites shown at the top of the screen in Figure 1.4.

In Figure 1.4, you can see the FAVORITES menu list and the full SAP MENU, a collection of folders that can be expanded to reveal transactions for the system. Also in Figure 1.4 the ABAP EDITOR transaction is highlighted.

SAP GUI favorites menu

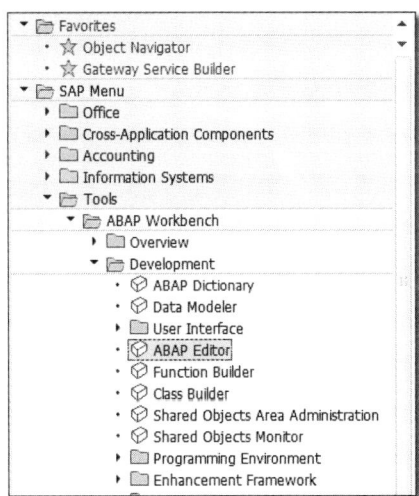

Figure 1.4 SAP GUI Favorites and SAP Menu

SAP GUI developer user menu

You can see the much shorter USER MENU in Figure 1.5. The user menu will display different options depending on the user's roles, whereas the SAP menu will show the same options for all users.

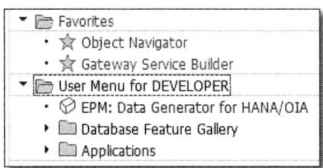

Figure 1.5 The SAP GUI User Menu Display

SAP GUI system information

At the bottom of the SAP GUI, some additional information (shown in Figure 1.6) can be toggled between hidden and displayed by selecting the arrow on the left. Some basic information about the system you are connecting to is displayed. In Figure 1.6, A4H is the system ID, 1 is the session, and 001 is the client. In addition, ABAPCI is the application server name, and INS indicates that insert is toggled on; the lock icon indicates whether the secure network connection (SNC) is being used. In Figure 1.6, the lock is unlocked meaning that SNC is not being used.

Figure 1.6 System Information in SAP GUI

You can also click the down arrow to display different information in the first section of the toolbar. The different options are shown in Figure 1.7. Selecting PROGRAM will display the program name, which can be useful for ABAP developers trying to find the name of a program to update.

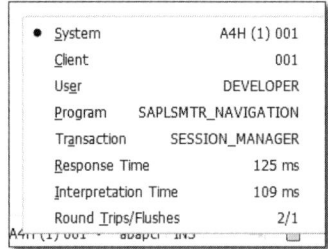

Figure 1.7 Additional System Information Options from the Toolbar

Overview of ABAP Screen in SAP NWBC

You can enter SAP NWBC via the client application or by entering Transaction NWBC in the system toolbar shown in Figure 1.2 and then pressing [Enter]. If you access SAP NWBC through the transaction, it will open in your default web browser.

SAP NetWeaver Business Client

SAP NWBC can be configured via user roles, which will affect what options are displayed to the user. If a user has multiple user roles, they may be able to select a relevant one in a screen like the one shown in Figure 1.8.

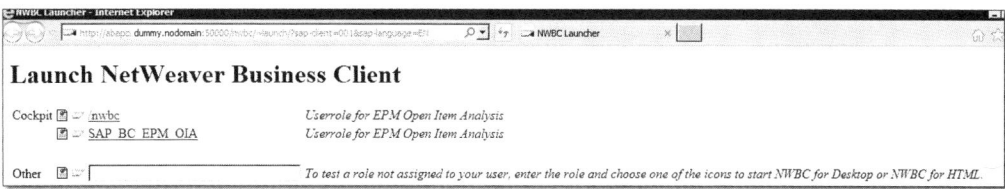

Figure 1.8 Choosing a Cockpit Based on Assigned SAP NWBC Roles

Once inside, SAP NWBC will look similar to the image shown in Figure 1.9. SAP NWBC is highly customizable through a user's assigned roles and can contain transactions written for SAP GUI or for the web (including SAP Screen Personas, Web Dynpro, and SAP Fiori).

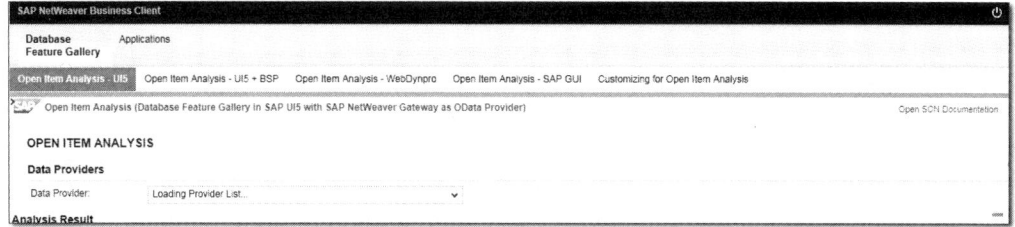

Figure 1.9 An Example SAP NWBC Screen

Overview of ABAP Screen in SAP Fiori

SAP Fiori is a collection of HTML5-based applications that use the SAPUI5 JavaScript framework and the SAP Fiori theme. Many SAP-provided apps require an SAP HANA backend, which allows for analytical as well as transactional processing. SAP Fiori apps are grouped by function as tiles in the Launchpad screen shown in Figure 1.10.

SAP Fiori

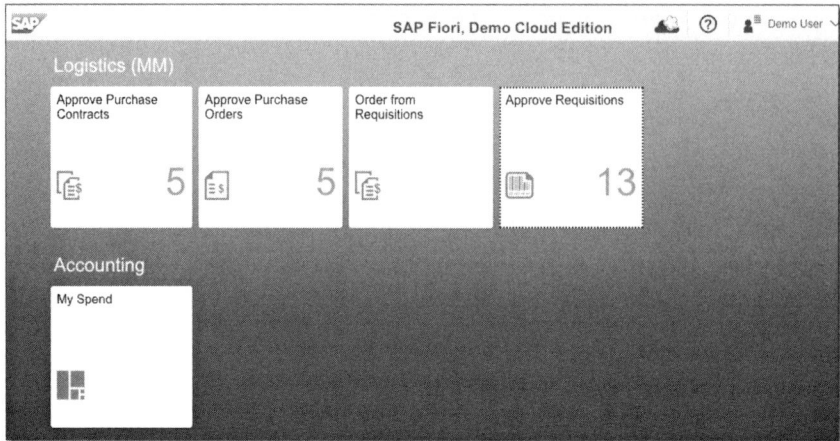

Figure 1.10 Example of the SAP Fiori Launchpad

While the SAP Fiori interface is written with HTML5 and JavaScript, it still relies on an ABAP backend to interface with the database and process the data.

ABAP System Landscapes

ABAP system technical architecture

In this section, we will cover the technical architecture of ABAP systems and review some technical topics that are important to understand as an ABAP developer.

Built in to every ABAP system is version control and a transport management system that allows developers and system configurators to make changes in a development system and then move those exact changes into different environments.

SAP BASIS

The technical system setup is typically completed by an SAP BASIS team, which is an SAP-ism for system administrator. The term *basis* comes from the name of the technical module of an ABAP system.

Client/Server Architecture

ABAP systems follow a client/server architecture (see Figure 1.11). This means that the ABAP code that you write will execute centrally on the ABAP server that the user accesses though one of the clients discussed in the previous section.

ABAP System Landscapes   1

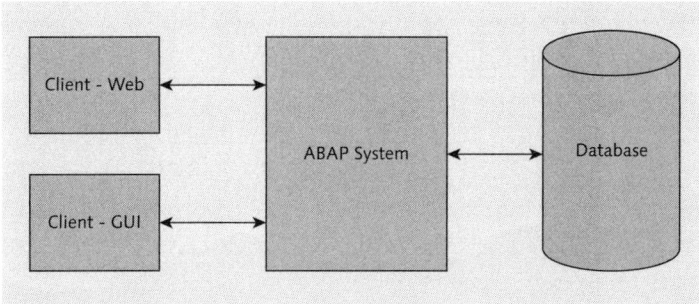

Figure 1.11 Overview of Client/Server Architecture

The server will work with a database; prior to the release of S/4 HANA, it could be one of many types of database. In S/4 HANA, customers will need to host their solution on the SAP HANA database. It's possible to host systems prior to S/4 HANA on an SAP HANA database as well.

When we are using the term client in the above section, we are talking about a client used to access the system. Within the ABAP system, there is another definition of client. A *client* in an ABAP system is used to separate system data. Most tables in an ABAP will have a common key for client. As a result, a company could have a client for their North American business and another client for the European business. While the ABAP programs would be the same in both clients, users in each business would only be able to see data in their own client, almost as if there were two separate systems running the same programs. When setting up an ABAP system, client dependent configuration allows for the system to act slightly different depending on the client that the user is using. With that said, the client setup is dependent on the company using the system and having multiple clients is not a requirement.

Client

Background Jobs

Even though the R/3 system has long promised real-time transaction processing, scheduled program execution—typically called *background jobs*—has also always been present. The need for background jobs is reduced in S/4 HANA by performing analysis instantly on transactional data.

29

Sometimes, programs are run as background jobs because they consume a great of deal of time, such as a mass change program that may take a long time to update all relevant records. In other cases, programs are run as background jobs because they need to be executed at a certain time, such as a program that issues payroll checks.

Programs that take a long time can be selected to run in the background by an SAP GUI user by selecting PROGRAM • EXECUTE IN BACKGROUND after entering selection options for an ABAP program.

Program status
You can view the status of a program that is being executed in the background by entering Transaction SM37 (see Figure 1.12), where the JOB NAME and USER NAME textboxes are set to * to select all of the jobs for the given date.

Execute
When you click on the EXECUTE button shown in Figure 1.12, you will see a list of jobs, some information about them, and their statuses. Figure 1.13 shows a large list of different jobs that have successfully run, listed with a status of FINISHED. Some jobs also show a status of RELEASED, meaning that they are scheduled to run in the future.

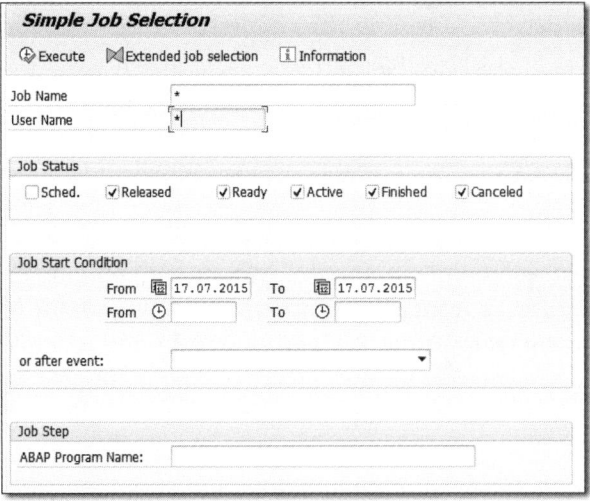

Figure 1.12 Transaction SM37 Selection page

ABAP System Landscapes

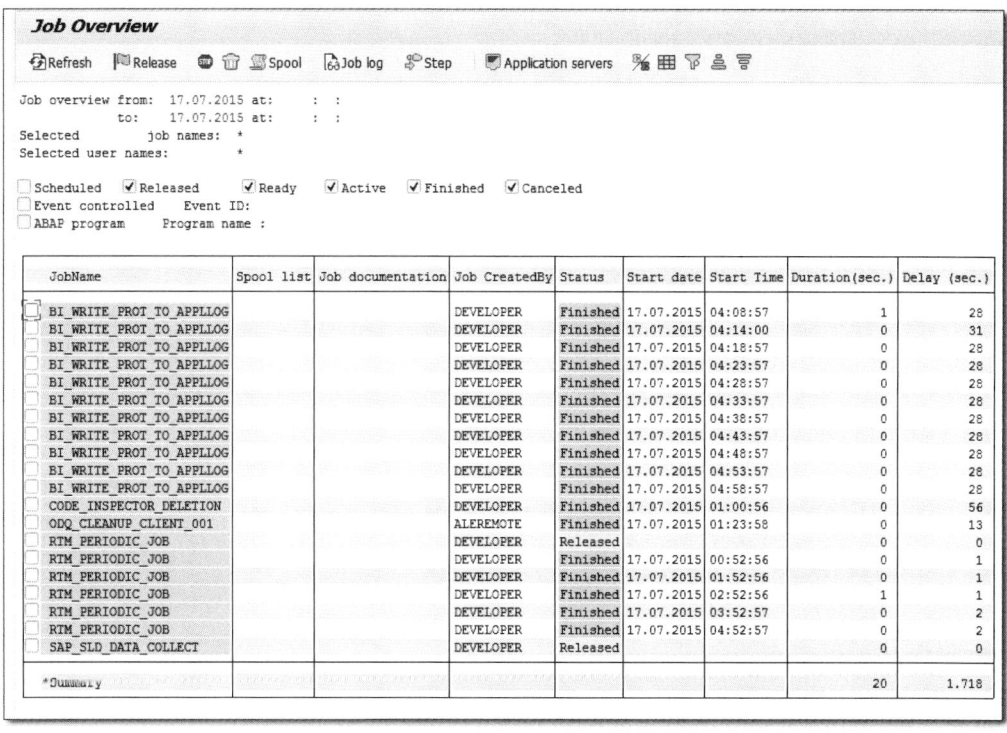

Figure 1.13 A List of Background Jobs from Transaction SM37

Sandbox, Dev, QA, PRD

In a typical ABAP system implementation, customers will have at least the sandbox, development, quality assurance, and production environments. As a developer, you will make changes solely in the development environment and then move those changes to other systems.

The exact configuration of a system will depend on the needs and IT processes of the company that implemented the system. At the very minimum, you should be making changes in a development system and testing them in a QA system before moving them to a production environment.

System configuration

The different systems are connected via the SAP Transport Management System (TMS). System configuration or program changes are moved across the system landscape using *transports*, collections of changes associated with the user who made them. You can view your

SAP TMS

system's SAP TMS configuration by entering Transaction STMS and clicking on the TRANSPORT ROUTES button highlighted in Figure 1.14.

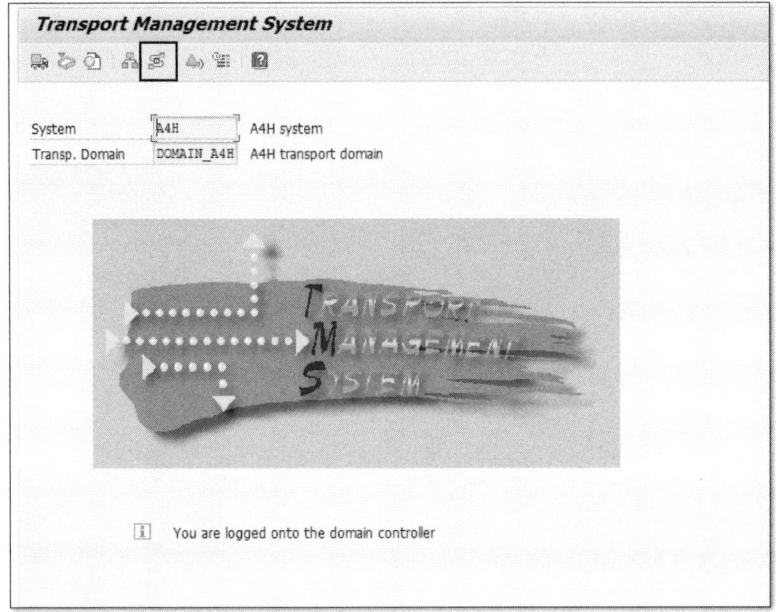

Figure 1.14 Transaction STMS

From there, you will see all of your connected systems, similar to what is shown in Figure 1.15.

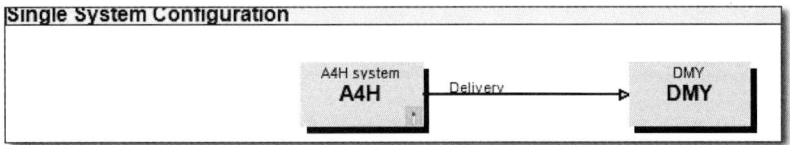

Figure 1.15 Example TMS Configuration Showing Two Connected Systems

Transaction STMS   After making your relevant changes, you can release them using Transaction STMS or from within the Eclipse IDE. Contact your SAP BASIS team to determine the exact steps to follow for your company's processes.

Throughout the book, we'll recommend keeping changes locally on a development or sandbox environment. You don't need to transport changes in order to execute or test them.

Finding the Version of a System in SAP GUI

Updates in any technical environment are expected. Some features of the ABAP language may not be available in your ABAP version, so it's important to note what version of the SAP NetWeaver Application Server you're currently running. You can do this by accessing your system using SAP GUI and selecting SYSTEM • STATUS from the top menu bar.

SAP NetWeaver version check

In the SYSTEM STATUS popup, you will see a lot of information about your system, including a high-level product version. Click on the highlighted button shown in Figure 1.16 to see the version details.

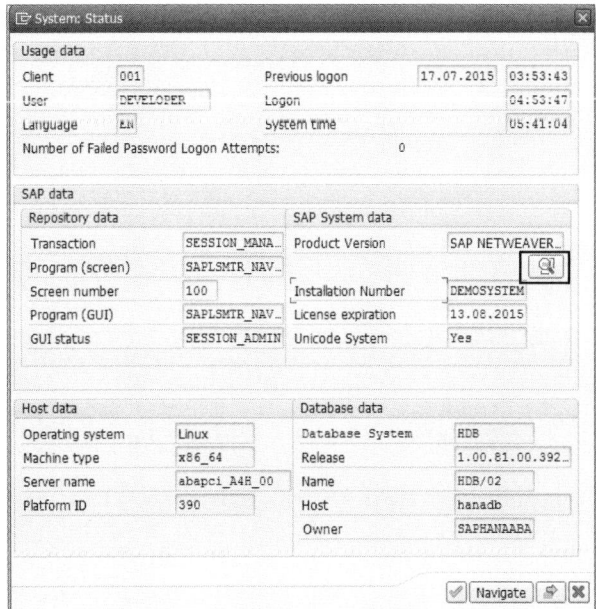

Figure 1.16 SAP GUI System Status Popup

In the INSTALLED SOFTWARE popup, you will be able to see all of the components installed on your system. The first component listed

Installed components

33

should be the SAP_BASIS component, which indicates the version of your base system, including the version of the underlying ABAP language. The RELEASE column indicates the version, and the SP-LEVEL column indicates the support package level. In Figure 1.17, you can see that the highlighted SAP_BASIS component is version 740 with support package 8. Throughout the book, we will cover recent changes in ABAP 7.4 SP8, but will also provide examples that run in older systems.

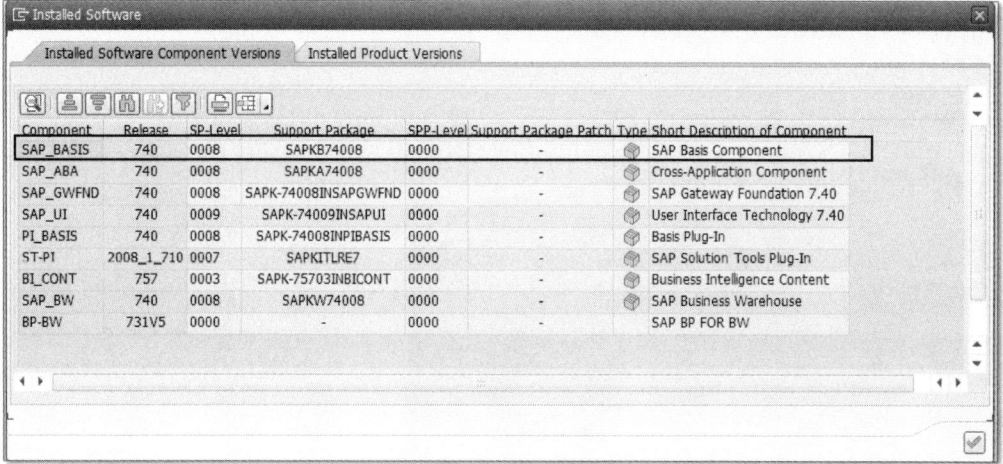

Figure 1.17 Installed Software Popup

In a full environment, you may see more components for the different modules installed to run the environment. This is where you can see the version for any installed module.

The Limitations of Backward Compatibility

The ABAP language has a lot of history; it's evolved greatly since its early beginnings and continues to evolve on a regular basis. However, with every update to the ABAP language, all language keywords are still supported, even if they are marked as obsolete. This creates some interesting advantages and challenges for any ABAP developer.

ABAP code updates

ABAP is backward compatible so that customers are not forced to update existing code every time that they decide to update their system. However, this does not mean that customers *should not* update their code. System updates can include new functionality that makes custom-written ABAP code unnecessary. It's always better to rely on standard code when possible, because it will be covered by the SAP support agreement.

The reality is that many SAP customers do not review their code after upgrading and rely on old ABAP programs that were written when the system was implemented and were never updated to utilize modern ABAP. That's why throughout this book, we will cover not only the modern way to write ABAP programs but also some common obsolete keywords and syntax.

An unexpected side effect of supporting obsolete code is that it's possible for developers to write obsolete code without receiving a warning from the compiler. If developers never update their skills, they won't know that their coding standards are out of date. At a 2011 TechEd presentation, the writer of SAP's ABAP technical documentation, Horst Keller, described this problem in terms of an ABAP developer having one year of experience 10 times instead of 10 years of experience.

Obsolete code support

Just as you reviewed the history of SAP as a company, it's important to review the history of the implementation that you're working on, even if you're a consultant working on the system for only a few months. Does the company review its custom ABAP code during every system update? Are there a few old programs that continually break down that have never been revisited? If you ever have to work on an old program that was never updated, at what point do you rewrite it in a modern fashion instead of continually trying to fix it? The answers to those questions can result in IT baggage, which can complicate IT projects.

Understanding your system implementation

In today's IT environment, budgets can greatly affect policy related to maintaining ABAP systems for any company. Old, problematic ABAP programs are considered technical debt and it will only become more expensive to fix them later instead of now. However, if there's no time or budget to fix such issues, then it may seem easier to worry about them at a later time. As a developer, it's important to recognize

Technical Debt

1 The History of SAP Technologies

these scenarios and make appropriate recommendations for when old programs need to be replaced.

Modern ABAP syntax

As a result of starting your ABAP journey with this book, you should be able to recognize these types of behaviors and update obsolete code using modern ABAP syntax. It's also important to continue to learn and stay up-to-date with the latest changes in the ABAP language, which you can expect to happen regularly. It's easy to do things the same way you were taught over and over, but a savvy developer will always continue learning. In Appendix C, you will find some resources to help you keep up with the latest updates to the ABAP language.

Summary

In this chapter, we covered the history of SAP as a company from its early beginnings to the large company that it is today. We also introduced some different ways to access an ABAP system, from SAP GUI and the SAP NetWeaver Business Client to SAP Fiori.

Next, we addressed some technical details about how an ABAP landscape is created and how different systems are connected, allowing you to move your changes through a system landscape and ensure that proper testing is completed before making changes to an ABAP system.

Finally, we talked about some of the issues and concerns that arise from a backward compatible programming language. Having this understanding is an important to becoming the best ABAP programmer possible.

In the next chapter, you'll jump into the ABAP language and start writing real ABAP code.

Creating Your First Program

Congratulations, it's time to begin programming! This chapter is written for people who have never programmed before, but will still be useful for those of you who have some programming experience in a language other than ABAP. You'll begin by learning to program a favorite called "Hello, World!" (which will test that your system is up and running), and the chapter will conclude with a program that is able to take input from a user, process that input, and produce some output.

If you need to set up a demo environment or get some familiarity with the ABAP integrated development environment or IDE, go to Appendix A before starting this chapter. We recommend using ABAP development tools (ABAP for Eclipse) as your IDE for this book, but we will also include instructions for the older SE80 IDE.

Hello, World!

The first ABAP program will be the simplest possible. A "Hello, World!" program is used as a common introduction to all programming languages and simply outputs the words "Hello, World!" The real point of this program is to ensure that your SAP system is set up correctly and that you will be able to follow along with the rest of the book. In the following sections, we walk you through the steps to create your first program.

Creating a New Program with Eclipse

You should have Eclipse installed with the ABAP development tools and have an ABAP project created. If Eclipse isn't set up, take a look at Appendix A, which covers all of the required steps to set up your Eclipse environment.

Eclipse perspectives

If you're using the Eclipse-based ABAP development tools, make sure that you're in the ABAP perspective by selecting WINDOW • OPEN PERSPECTIVE • ABAP. If ABAP is not an option, select WINDOW • OPEN PERSPECTIVE • OTHER…, and select ABAP from the perspective options, as shown in Figure 2.1.

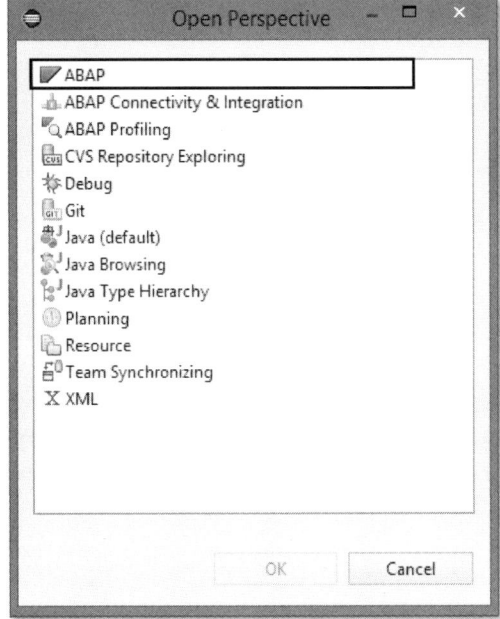

Figure 2.1 Selecting the ABAP Perspective

The other ABAP-related perspectives in the list are out of the scope of this book; we'll only be using the ABAP perspective for development and the DEBUG perspective for debugging.

Creating a new ABAP program

Now that you're in the ABAP perspective, open your project from within Project Explorer. Right-click the project name and select NEW • ABAP PROGRAM (Figure 2.2).

Hello, World!

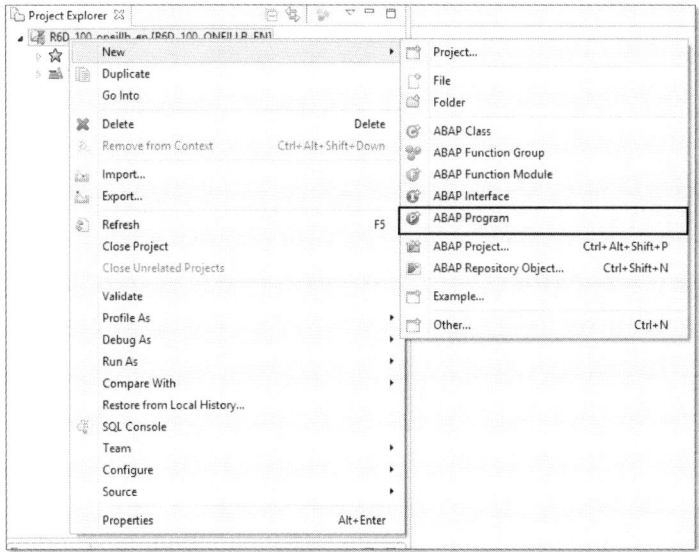

Figure 2.2 Creating a New ABAP Program

In the NEW ABAP PROGRAM wizard popup, enter "$TMP" in the PACKAGE field and select the checkbox for ADD TO FAVORITE PACKAGES if it is not disabled; if it is, then it's already a favorite. The $TMP package is used for local development that won't be transported to other systems. You typically use a package created for your own project.

New program attributes in Eclipse

Next, enter "Z_HELLO_WORLD" (Figure 2.3) in the NAME field and "Hello World Program" in the DESCRIPTION field, and click FINISH.

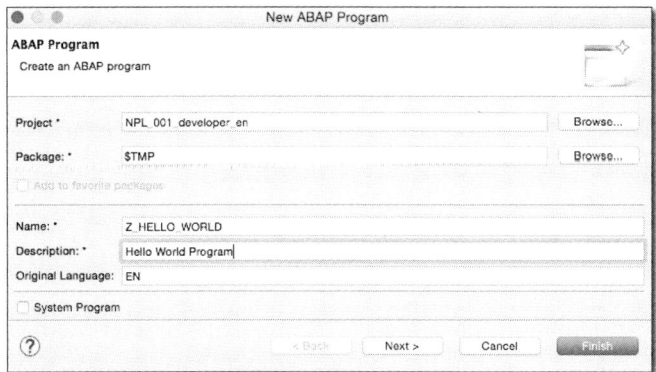

Figure 2.3 New ABAP Program Wizard in Eclipse

39

Finding your program in Eclipse

You've now created your first program in Eclipse! You will see your "Hello, World!" program listed under PROJECT • FAVORITE PACKAGES • $TMP • SOURCE LIBRARY • PROGRAMS. An ABAP editor window will open for your new program with a line declaring the program by using the REPORT keyword followed by the program name (Figure 2.4).

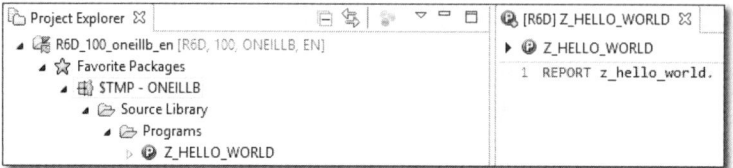

Figure 2.4 The "Hello, World!" Program Created in Eclipse

Creating a New Program in Transaction SE80

If you are using Transaction SE80 as your ABAP IDE, select PROGRAM from the dropdown in the center of the left side of the screen, type "Z_HELLO_WORLD" in the textbox below it, and press Enter (Figure 2.5).

Figure 2.5 Creating a New Program in Transaction SE80

You will be prompted with a popup asking if you want to create the program Z_HELLO_WORLD; click the YES button (Figure 2.6).

A new popup (Figure 2.7) allows you to set the name of the program. Leave it as Z_HELLO_WORLD, and leave the CREATE WITH TOP INCLUDE box unchecked.

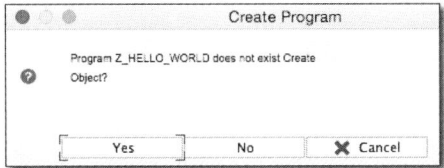

Figure 2.6 Create Program Popup in Transaction SE80

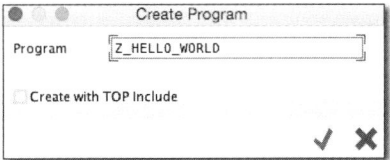

Figure 2.7 Second Create Program Popup in Transaction SE80

In the PROGRAM ATTRIBUTES popup, change the TITLE to "Hello World Program" and ensure the TYPE is EXECUTABLE PROGRAM. You can leave the rest of the options set to their defaults, as shown in Figure 2.8. You should refer to your own company's development standards when determining if the other attributes described in Table 2.1 are required; if your company does not require values to be entered in these attributes, we recommend avoiding them.

New program attributes in SE80

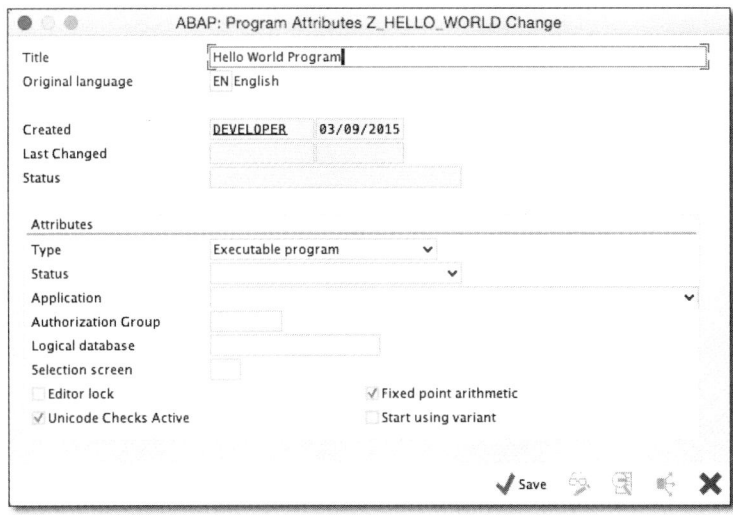

Figure 2.8 Program Attributes Popup when Creating a Program in Transaction SE80

Attribute	Definition
STATUS	Indicates whether the program is a system, test, or production program. We recommend leaving this blank or selecting CUSTOMER PRODUCTION PROGRAM. A system program cannot be debugged.
APPLICATION	A SAP module that is required for your program. This selection does not affect your program; it's just informational.
AUTHORIZATION GROUP	Authorization groups can be used to limit access to your application to a specific group. However, this is not the only way to restrict access to your program, and you should follow the preferred method for your company. Authorization groups are used to restrict access to other SAP objects and tables as well.
LOGICAL DATABASE	Logical databases are an obsolete way of accessing a predefined view of the database.
SELECTION SCREEN	This obsolete option lets you choose a selection screen tied to a given logical database.
EDITOR LOCK	This option will prevent anyone besides the creator from making changes to the program. We recommend never turning this lock on; long after your development is complete, someone else may need to update or enhance your code, and this restricts them from making changes.
UNICODE CHECKS ACTIVE	This option should always be turned on, even if you have a non-Unicode system. This check will prevent you from writing non-Unicode-compliant code that won't run if you move to a Unicode-compliant system or are already on a Unicode-compliant system.
FIXED POINT ARITHMETIC	This option should always be checked; otherwise, you can lose data stored as fractions.
START USING VARIANT	This option should typically be unchecked. It requires a variant (a prepopulated selection for running a report) for the program to be started.

Table 2.1 Program Attributes Definitions

Click the SAVE button to create the program.

Finally, select a package (Figure 2.9). Enter "$TMP" as the package or click the LOCAL OBJECT button, and click the SAVE button.

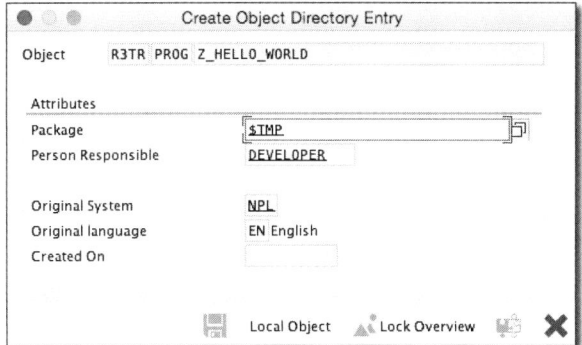

Figure 2.9 Selecting a Package in Transaction SE80

Now, you should see your program listed in the bottom half of the left side of the screen. Double-click the program name to open it, and click the EDIT button to begin making changes (Figure 2.10).

Changing your program in SE80

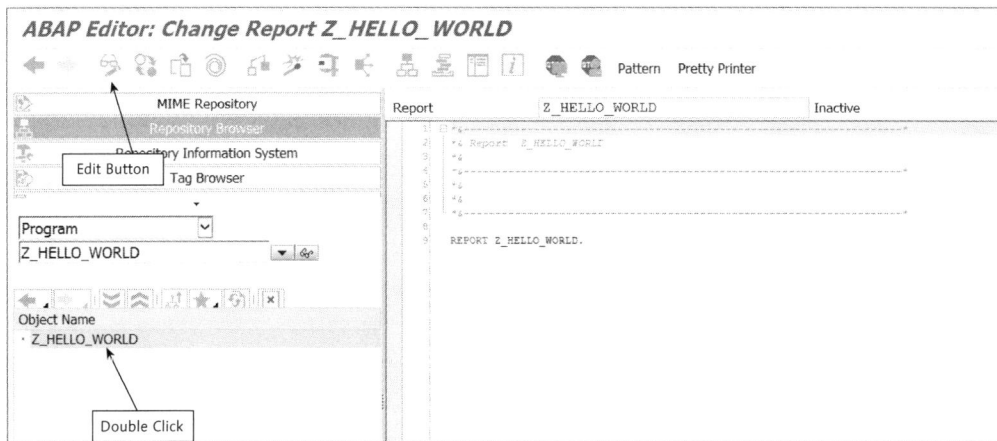

Figure 2.10 The "Hello, World!" Program in Transaction SE80

Creating Your First Program

 Updating IDE Settings in Transaction SE80

If you are using Transaction SE80 as your preferred ABAP IDE, make sure you update your editor settings to greatly improve your experience.

You can do this by going to UTILITIES • SETTINGS • ABAP EDITOR • EDITOR and ensuring that FRONT-END EDITOR (NEW) is selected.

Writing a "Hello, World!" Program

Now, you're ready to add code! In ABAP, you can output text to the screen using the keyword WRITE. Older ABAP programs used WRITE as the main interface with users, but when writing an SAP GUI program today, you should use the ALV grid instead, which is covered in Chapter 5. Enter the code shown in Listing 2.1 into your ABAP IDE to create your first ABAP program.

```
PROGRAM Z_HELLO_WORLD.
WRITE 'HELLO WORLD'.
```
Listing 2.1 Basic "Hello, World!" Program

Basic ABAP syntax This simple program demonstrates the basic syntax of the ABAP language (diagrammed in Figure 2.11). Each line begins with an ABAP keyword, such as REPORT or WRITE, followed by a value, and ending with a period. Also notice that strings are created using single quotes (') and not double quotes ("). Double quotes are used to create comments, which is covered later in this chapter.

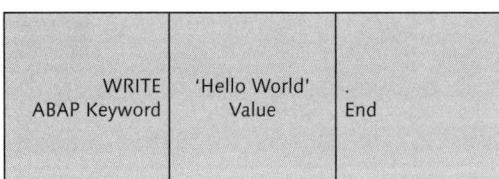

Figure 2.11 Basic ABAP Syntax Breakdown

Activating ABAP programs Next, you need to activate the program. When editing any ABAP code, the program will be inactive until you activate it, meaning that the most recently activated version will be run until you activate a new one. The buttons to activate and run your program from Transaction SE80 and Eclipse are shown in Figure 2.12.

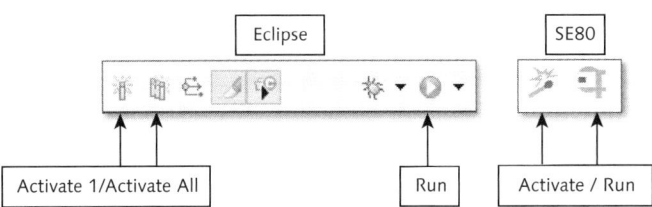

Figure 2.12 Activate and Run Buttons

Now, run the program by pressing [F8] or by clicking the RUN PROGRAM button in your IDE and you will see the result as shown in Figure 2.13.

Executing an ABAP program

Figure 2.13 The Output from a Successful Run of Z_HELLO_WORLD

Now that you've created your basic "Hello, World!" program, let's discuss the concept of *chained statements*. Chaining statements allows you to send multiple values to a single ABAP keyword. The ABAP keyword must be suffixed with a colon, and each value must be separated by a comma. Each value can then be on a new line or the same line. Try this with your "Hello, World!" program using the code in Listing 2.2.

Chained statements

```
REPORT Z_HELLO_WORLD.
WRITE: 'Hello World',
       'Here I am!'.
```
Listing 2.2 Hello World with Chained Statements

A chained statement is processed in the same way as calling the same ABAP keyword twice, but it removes redundant text, making your code easier to read. The example shown in Listing 2.3 uses chained statements, but places them on the same line, which is somewhat more difficult to read. Listing 2.4 shows the "Hello, World!" program without chained statements. Both Listing 2.3 and Listing 2.4 have the same result as Listing 2.2, but Listing 2.2 is neater and easier to read.

```
WRITE: 'Hello World', 'Here I am!'.
```
Listing 2.3 Hello World with Chained Statements on the Same Line

```
WRITE 'Hello World'.
WRITE 'Here I am!'.
```
Listing 2.4 Hello World without Chained Statements

Now that you're familiar with how to create your first program, we're going to change topics and discuss how to add data and logic to your application.

Data Types

In ABAP, one of the first actions you typically take is defining variables that will store the data you use. Such variables represent locations in memory where data will be stored. The data could be numeric, such as an integer (123), or alphabetic, such as a character (a) or string of characters (abc). In the following sections, we will walk you through the process of creating variables and cover the different types of variables that you'll use.

The Data Keyword

Variables in ABAP

Variables are defined with the DATA keyword followed by the name of the variable and then the TYPE keyword followed by the data type. The following example creates a variable called d_variable of type i:

```
DATA d_variable TYPE i.
```

Initial values

When creating a new variable, it is given an *initial* value. New data variables do not get a *null* value as you may have seen in other languages. The initial value of ld_variable is 0 since it's a numeric data type. You can create a variable and give it a value using the optional VALUE keyword.

```
DATA d_variable TYPE i VALUE 123.
```

Chaining variables

By adding a colon after the keyword DATA, you can chain multiple variable definitions together. In the example in Listing 2.5, you create two variables, one called ld_variable and the other called ld_other_variable. ld_variable has no value set, so it will have an initial value of 0; `ld_other_variable` will have a value of `'Hello World'`. The rest of the section will cover the various types used in ABAP.

```
DATA: d_variable       TYPE i,
 d_other_variable TYPE string VALUE 'Hello World'.
```
Listing 2.5 Chained Data Declarations Example

 ABAP Variable Naming

ABAP is not a case-sensitive language, meaning the compiler sees no difference between, for example, `D_variable` and `d_variable`. This is why it's common to separate words using an underscore instead of using CamelCase, which you may have seen in other programming languages.

You will also notice that each variable name begins with `d` (meaning global data). This is based on my company's naming conventions. Each company may have its own naming standards; make sure you contact the lead ABAP developer to find those standards before starting work on a new project. We will cover the difference between global and local variables in Chapter 6.

All variables should be created in the beginning of an ABAP program, except when using inline data declarations (described later in the chapter). This way there is a single place to find the variable definition in case we need to change them.

Where to define variables

Numeric Data Types

The basic data types are the simplest building blocks for any program. Let's start with the numeric data types listed in Table 2.2. Some data types are marked with a *; we want to avoid using these when possible because they have a very limited number range.

Data Type	Description
b*	Byte: one-byte integer
s*	Short: two-byte integer
i	Integer: four-byte integer
p	Packed number
decfloat16	Decimal floating point number with 16 places

Table 2.2 Basic Numeric Data Types

Data Type	Description
decfloat34	Decimal floating point number with 34 places
f*	Binary floating point number with 17 decimal places

Table 2.2 Basic Numeric Data Types (Cont.)

Integer data types

Integer types (b, s, i) will hold any *whole number*; well, almost any whole number. Avoid the byte (b) and short (s) integer types, because they were created to use less memory when being used. The integer range for a byte is 0 to 255, a short is -32,768 to 32,767, and an integer is -2,147,483,648 to 2,147,483,647. In the ancient days of computing, programmers used the smaller data types for performance reasons or due to memory limitations. Luckily, today dinosaurs no longer roam the world and memory is much cheaper, so you can use the larger i data type. For example:

```
DATA: ld_integer TYPE i VALUE 200.
```

Decimal data types

The packed (p), decimal floating point (decfloat16, decfloat34), and binary floating point (f) data types hold *decimal numbers*, and each works a little differently.

Packed numbers

Packed numbers allow you to define the number of decimal places (up to 14) in the number, and the value stored will be rounded when assigned. If no decimal value is defined, it will be treated as an integer. This is a go-to data type for handling data such as distances or money, for which you want values to have only a limited number of decimal places. In the below example, the resulting value would be 3.12.

```
DATA: ld_packed TYPE p DECIMALS 2 VALUE '3.115'.
```

 Warning

Calculations with packed numbers are slower than the other numeric data types, because they have to be evaluated on a software level instead of on a hardware level.

Decimal floating point numbers

Introduced in ABAP 7.02, decimal floating point numbers (decfloat16 and decfloat34) can be used when you need more precision in your calculations or when you need to work with numbers that are outside of the range for i. decfloat16 allows for 16 decimal places of precision, and decfloat34 allows for 34 decimal places of precision. In the example below, the resulting value would be 3.115.

```
DATA: ld_decfloat TYPE decfloat16 VALUE '3.115'
```

Decimal floating point numbers are stored as a decimal value multiplied by 10 to some power. They are called decimal floating points because the decimal will float depending on the power of 10. This also allows for a higher range than an integer, but decfloat16 uses the same amount of memory as an integer (i).

Binary floating point (f) numbers work similarly to decimal floating point numbers but can run calculations faster.

Binary floating point numbers

 Warning

Binary floating point numbers may produce some unpredictable rounding errors and should be avoided if possible. See the ABAP documentation in Transaction ABAPDOCU for the specific rounding errors that can occur.

In the below binary floating point example, the resulting value would be 3.115.

```
DATA: ld_float TYPE f VALUE '3.115'
```

Character Data Types

Character-based data types are listed in Table 2.3. The c data type is marked with a * because we want to avoid this when using multiple characters, because it can only hold a defined number of characters, unlike a string which can hold any number of characters.

Data Type	Description
c*	Any fixed amount of alphanumeric characters
string	A variable length of alphanumeric characters
n	A fixed length of numeric characters

Table 2.3 Basic Character Data Types

Data Type	Description
d	A date in the form yyyymmdd
t	A time in the form hhmmss

Table 2.3 Basic Character Data Types

Character data type

The character (c) data type is used to store a fixed amount of up to 262,143 alphanumeric characters. The number of characters is defined using the LENGTH keyword. If no length is provided, it is treated as a single character. If you are unsure of how many characters you will need, use a string (described in the next paragraph) instead. An example using a character data type with a fixed length and with a single character is shown below.

```
DATA: d_chars        TYPE c LENGTH 5 VALUE 'fiver',
      ld_single_char TYPE c VALUE 'A'.
```

String data type

A string (string) data type is used to hold any number of characters, and its length will change automatically as its value changes. In the example below, the variable d_string will hold the 'Hello World', without having to declare a length.

```
DATA: d_string TYPE string VALUE 'Hello World'.
```

Numeric text data type

A numeric text (n) data type works just like the character (c) data type, except it only allows for numeric characters. This data type is useful when working with IDs that have leading zeros, such as 00005543. If you use an integer data type with such an ID, then the leading zeros will be dropped, but they will be preserved in a numeric text data type. In the example below, the value of d_num will be 00005543. The leading zeros are added because the length is larger than the supplied number.

```
DATA: d_num TYPE n LENGTH 8 VALUE 5543.
```

Date data type

A date (d) data type is used to store any date. The first four characters are the year, the next two represent the month, and the last two represent the day. This means that the month and day should always be two characters each. For example, January 2nd, 2015, would be represented as 20150102. We will cover more details about working with dates in Chapter 9. In the below example, the d_date variable is being created with the date of November 1st 2015.

```
DATA: d_date TYPE d VALUE '20151101'.
```

A time (t) data type is used to store any time. The first two characters are the hour (based on a 24-hour clock), the second two characters are the minutes, and the last two characters are the seconds. Just as with dates, a single digit hour, minute, or second should have a leading zero (more details about working with time can be found in Chapter 9). In the example below, the variable d_time is being created with the time 8:15:22 in the morning.

Time data type

```
DATA: d_time TYPE t VALUE '081522'.
```

Inline Data Declarations

Inline data declarations are new as of ABAP 7.4 SP2. This means that instead of defining variables in the beginning of the program with a specific type, you can define them when they are needed and not specify the type that the data will be. The variable is still hard-typed to a specific data type, meaning that it can't start as an integer and then change to a string, for example. The data type is inferred based on how the variable is used when it is declared. In the below example, d_integer is created as an integer, which is inferred because we said that it is equal to a whole number.

Inline data declarations

```
DATA(d_integer) = 10.
```

> **Note**
>
> There are no spaces inside the parentheses.

The example above could also be completed without using inline data declarations using the code below.

```
DATA: d_integer TYPE integer.
d_integer = 10.
```

Use caution when declaring inline data declarations. In the example, we used a whole number, which inferred the variable to be created as an integer. This could cause rounding problems if we later wanted to add data that was a decimal floating point.

Inline data declaration caution

The benefits of using inline data declarations is that you can make programs smaller and more readable while saving time by not having to jump to the top of the program to add more data declarations. We will cover other uses of inline data declarations throughout the book.

Arithmetic and Basic Math Functions

Now that you've learned how to declare variables and assign them initial values, let's cover some basic calculations that you can perform with those variables.

Arithmetic Operations

Assigning a value

To assign a value into a variable you've already declared, use the variable name, followed by the equals sign, and then the value as shown in the example below.

```
DATA: ld_integer TYPE i.
ld_integer = 3.
```

`ld_integer` now holds the value 3.

 Obsolete Syntax

> The keyword `MOVE` is another way to assign values to variables. This method should never be used, but you may see it when supporting older ABAP-based systems. For example:
>
> `MOVE: 3 TO ld_integer.`
>
> This obsolete syntax is a relic of the past, when COBOL was another popular language. Using it and other obsolete syntax will make your code more verbose and harder for others to understand quickly.

List of operations

The value on the right-hand side of the equation can be a number or an arithmetic calculation. Table 2.4 lists ABAP's arithmetic operations. If you have experience in other languages, you will notice that +=, -= and ++ are not valid operations in ABAP.

Operation	Description
+	Addition
-	Subtraction

Table 2.4 Arithmetic Operations

Operation	Description
*	Multiplication
/	Division
DIV	Division with no remainder
MOD	Remainder of a division operation
**	Raise to the power of the right-hand number

Table 2.4 Arithmetic Operations (Cont.)

When using arithmetic operations, the order of operations is applied, meaning that calculations in parenthesis are completed first, followed by exponents, multiplication, addition, and lastly, subtraction. As a result, if you look at the two examples below, the first result will be 600, while the second result will be 303. This is because the operations within the parenthesis were completed first. Don't forget to assign the result to an appropriate variable, as we did with `ld_result` in the example below.

Order of operations

```
DATA: ld_result TYPE decfloat16.
ld_result = ( 3 + 3 ) * ( 10 * 10).
ld_result = 3 + 3 * 10 * 10.
```

 Whitespace in ABAP

Unlike some other programming languages, whitespace is important to the ABAP compiler. This means you must always enter a space after the opening parenthesis, before the closing parenthesis, and between each arithmetic operation. You will see this need for whitespace in other areas as well.

Bad: (3*3)

Good: (3 * 3)

All division-based operations divide the number on the left by the number on the right. Dividing by zero will cause the program to crash. We will cover how to prevent that from happening using flow control later in the chapter. There are three different types of division operations, in the first, shown below, the value of `d_result` will be

Division based operations

3.33 followed by repeating threes. The / operation will complete basic division.

```
DATA: d_result TYPE decfloat16
ld_result = 10 / 3.
```

In the next example, the value of `d_result` will be 3 because the `DIV` operation will complete the division and drop any remainders.

```
d_result = 10 DIV 3.
```

In the final example below, the value of `d_result` will be 1 because the `MOD` operation will only return the remainder of 10 divided by 3.

```
d_result = 10 MOD 3.
```

Exponent operations

The `**` operation raises the number on the left to the power of the number on the right; therefore, the result of the following operation is 1,000:

```
DATA: d_result TYPE decfloat16.
ld_result = 10 ** 3.
```

Calculations with variables

Everything up to this point has used hardcoded numbers in the calculations, but we can also use other variables within the arithmetic operation. An example using variables in an arithmetic operation is shown below, where we use the variables `ld_ten` and `ld_three` instead of the numbers 10 and 3.

```
DATA: d_ten TYPE decfloat16 VALUE 10,
      d_three TYPE i VALUE 3.
d_result = d_ten ** d_three.
```

We can also use the variable which is storing the result as a variable in the arithmetic operation. In the example below, we are incrementing the value of `d_result` by 1.

```
d_result = d_result + 1.
```

Math Functions

In addition to the basic math operations, ABAP provides other numerical functions to make your life easy when working with numbers. The syntax is function(argument) when using math functions. In the below example, the function is `abs` and the argument is `-10` and the result would be the absolute value of -10, which is 10.

```
abs( -10 ).
```

Table 2.5 lists out all of the various math functions that are available in ABAP.

Math functions

Function	Result
abs	Returns the absolute value of the argument
sign	Returns the sign of the argument
ceil	Returns the argument rounded to the next highest number
floor	Returns the argument rounded to the next lowest number
trunc	Returns only the integer, dropping any decimal values
frac	Returns only the decimal values of the argument
ipow	Takes two arguments and raises the base argument to the power of the expression

Table 2.5 Math Function

The below example uses the `abs` function, which will return the absolute value of the argument, which in this case would be 10.

```
abs( -10 ).
```

The next example uses the `sign` function, which will return the sign of the argument, which in this case would be -.

sign function

```
sign( -10 ).
```

The following example uses the `ceil` function, which will return the result of rounding the argument up, which in this case would be 2.

ceil function

```
ceil( 1.4 ).
```

The below example uses the `floor` function, which will return the result of rounding the argument down, which in this case would be 1.

floor function

```
floor( 1.6 ).
```

The next example uses the `trunc` function, which will return only the integer value of the argument, dropping any decimal values which in this case would be 1.

trunc function

```
trunc( 1.6 ).
```

frac function	The following example uses the `frac` function, which will return the decimal values of the argument, dropping any integer values, which in this case would be 6. `frac( 1.6 ).`
ipow function	The `ipow` function can be used in place of `**` and in many cases has better performance than using `**`. Unlike the other math functions, `ipow` takes two arguments: `base` and `exp`. The function will raise the base to the power of the exp. In the example below, 10 is raised to the power of 3, which would return 1000. `ipow( base = 10 exp = 3 ).`

Variables in math functions	Just as with the arithmetic functions, you can use either numbers or variables as the arguments in any of the math functions. The example below uses a variable with the abs function and will set the value of `d_result` to 10.
	
	`DATA: d_value TYPE i VALUE -10,`
	`      d_result TYPE i.`
	`d_result = abs( d_value ).`

Flow Control

Now that you've created variables and completed some sort of calculation against those variables, we will cover how to add some basic binary logic to our program in the following sections.

IF Statements

An `IF` statement evaluates whether a certain condition is true or false. If that condition is true, the code within the statement will execute; otherwise, it will continue.

A condition is evaluated using one or more of the operators in Table 2.6.

Operator	Description
=	Equal: true if both values are equal to each other
<>	Not equal: true if both values do not equal each other

Table 2.6 IF Statement Operators

Operator	Description
<	Less than: true if the number on the left is less than the number on the right
>	Greater than: true if the number on the left is greater than the number on the right
<=	Less equal: true if the number on the left is less than or equal to the number on the right
>=	Greater equal: true if the number on the left is greater than or equal to the number on right
BETWEEN n AND n1	Between: true if the number on the left is between n and n1

Table 2.6 IF Statement Operators (Cont.)

You can test the operators from Table 2.6 by modifying your "Hello, World!" program to test for a condition. The code to execute when the IF statement is true must be between the IF and ENDIF keywords:

IF statement example

```
DATA: d_test TYPE i.
d_test = 1.
IF d_test = 1.
    WRITE: 'Hello World'.
ENDIF.
```

As long as the value of d_test is 1, you'll see "Hello World" printed on the screen.

```
DATA: d_test TYPE i.
d_test = 0.
IF d_test = 1.
    WRITE: 'Hello World'.
ENDIF.
```

You also can combine multiple operators using the AND and OR keywords. For AND, *both operators* must return true before the code within the IF statement will run. For OR, *only one of the operators* has to return true for the code in the IF statement to run. In the following example, 'Hello World' will not be written to the screen because, d_test is not equal to both 0 and 1.

AND/OR IF statements

```
DATA: d_test TYPE i.
d_test = 1.
IF d_test = 0 AND d_test = 1.
```

57

```
        WRITE: 'Hello World'.
ENDIF.
```

In the next example, "Hello World" will be written to the screen because d_test is equal to 0 OR 1.

```
DATA: d_test TYPE i.
d_test = 1.
IF d_test = 0 OR d_test = 1.
    WRITE: 'Hello World'.
ENDIF.
```

IF paranthesis Just as with the arithmetic calculations, we can use parentheses to create more complex IF statements. Parentheses group IF statement tests together; those IF statements can be combined with an AND or OR, as in the following example, where we test if d_test is 0 and 1 or if d_test is 0 or 1. Since d_test is 0 or 1, 'Hello World' is written to the screen.

```
DATA: d_test TYPE i.
d_test = 1.
IF ( d_test = 0 AND d_test = 1 ) OR
   ( d_test = 0 OR d_test = 1 ).
    WRITE: 'Hello World'.
ENDIF.
```

ELSE When the initial condition is evaluated as false, you can add the ELSE keyword, which will run the code within the ELSE and ENDIF keywords when the test for IF is false. In the below example, 'ELSE' would be written to the screen, because the value of d_test is not between 5 and 10, causing the code under the ELSE to be executed.

```
DATA: d_test TYPE i.
d_test = 1.
IF d_test BETWEEN 5 AND 10
    WRITE: 'Hello World'.
ELSE.
    WRITE: 'ELSE'.
ENDIF.
```

ELSEIF You may want to evaluate multiple conditions before utilizing the ELSE statement, which is a case in which the ELSEIF keyword can be useful. ELSEIF will only evaluate its condition if the IF/ELSEIF before it was evaluated as false. In Listing 2.6, even though ELSEIF d_test = 1 was true, it wasn't evaluated because the test before it was found to be true, so 'ELSEIF' was written to the screen.

```
DATA: d_test TYPE i.
d_test = 1.
IF d_test BETWEEN 5 AND 10
    WRITE: 'Hello World'.
ELSEIF d_test > 0.
    WRITE: 'ELSEIF'.
ELSEIF d_test = 1.
 WRITE: 'ELSEIF 1'.
ELSE.
    WRITE: 'ELSE'.
ENDIF.
```
Listing 2.6 ELSEIF d_test = 1 Not Evaluated

CASE Statements

A CASE statement works like an IF statement, except that the CASE statement will always evaluate *only one variable* and *only uses the equal to condition*. The CASE statement uses the keyword WHEN to evaluate the variable against a value and WHEN OTHERS to handle any value that was not caught by the existing tests. The example shown in Listing 2.7 will write '1' to the screen and not execute any of the other WRITE commands.

CASE

```
DATA: d_test TYPE i.
d_test = 1.
CASE d_test.
    WHEN 0.
        WRITE: '0'.
    WHEN 1.
        WRITE: '1'.
    WHEN 2.
        WRITE: '2'.
    WHEN OTHERS.
        WRITE: 'Others'.
ENDCASE.
```
Listing 2.7 Will Output 1 Because WHEN 1 Evaluated as True

Also, as with IF statements, you can use OR to evaluate multiple values. The example in Listing 2.8 will write 'found' to the screen because the value of d_test is 0 or 1.

Using OR with CASE

```
DATA: d_test TYPE i.
d_test = 1.
CASE d_test.
    WHEN 0 OR 1.
        WRITE: 'found'.
```

```
        WHEN 2.
           WRITE: '2'.
        WHEN OTHERS.
           WRITE: 'Others'.
ENDCASE.
```
Listing 2.8 Will Write Found Because 1 Evaluated as 0 OR 1

DO Loops

DO   Using the keyword DO, you can execute a block of code any number of times. Define the number of times by adding a number and the keyword TIMES. The block of code that will run is between DO and ENDDO. In the following example, the code within the loop will be executed 5 times and the number 5 will be written to the screen.

```
DATA: ld_test TYPE i VALUE 0.
DO 5 Times.
    ld_test = ld_test + 1.
ENDDO.
WRITE: ld_test.
```

 Infinite Loops

Loops can be very powerful, but also can cause a program to get in a never-ending or infinite loop. DO...ENDO without defining the number of times to run will run until the EXIT keyword is executed.

Using the EXIT keyword within a loop can get ugly, so I recommend using a WHILE loop, unless you only need to define the number of times something is to be run using DO.

WHILE Loops

WHILE   A WHILE loop works like a DO loop, but instead of indicating a number of times that the loop content is to be run, it indicates a condition that will cause the loop to stop. Any operation condition that is valid in an IF statement will be valid for the WHILE loop. In the example below, the code within the loop will be executed until the value of d_test is no longer less than 5. As a result, the number 5 will be written to the screen since 5 is not less than 5.

```
DATA: ld_test type i VALUE 0.
WHILE ld_test < 5.
    ld_test = ld_test + 1.
```

```
ENDWHILE.
WRITE: ld_test.
```

 Booleans in ABAP

A Boolean is something that can be true or false, represented in many languages as a single-bit data type that can be 0 or 1, 0 meaning false and 1 meaning true.

ABAP Booleans are a single character and treat 'X' as true and an empty character ' ' as false. When working with Booleans, it is best to use the Boolean data objects abap_true and abap_false.

In ABAP, the following statement would use the abap_true to evaluate whether it's true:

```
IF true_variable = abap_true.
```

Boolean is an ABAP data type and can be assigned true/false values using abap_true and abap_false:

```
DATA: ld_boolean TYPE boolean.
ld_boolean = abap_true.
```

Formatting Code

So far in this book, you may have noticed that anytime we use keywords in a program, they're in all caps, whereas other words are all lowercase. Although you could remember to do this while programming, it's easy to forget. Also, within every IF statement, the code has always been indented to indicate that it's running under some condition listed above.

Luckily, you can easily run a formatter from within Eclipse (or Transaction SE80) to format your code. First, you need to configure the formatter to set keywords as uppercase and identifiers as lowercase.

In Eclipse, right-click your project, and select PROPERTIES. Then, go to ABAP DEVELOPMENT • EDITORS • SOURCE CODE EDITORS • FORMATTER and select KEYWORDS UPPERCASE, IDENTIFIERS LOWERCASE in the dropdown. Also, make sure that the checkbox for INDENT SOURCE CODE is checked. The result should match Figure 2.14 exactly.

Formatting settings for Eclipse

2 Creating Your First Program

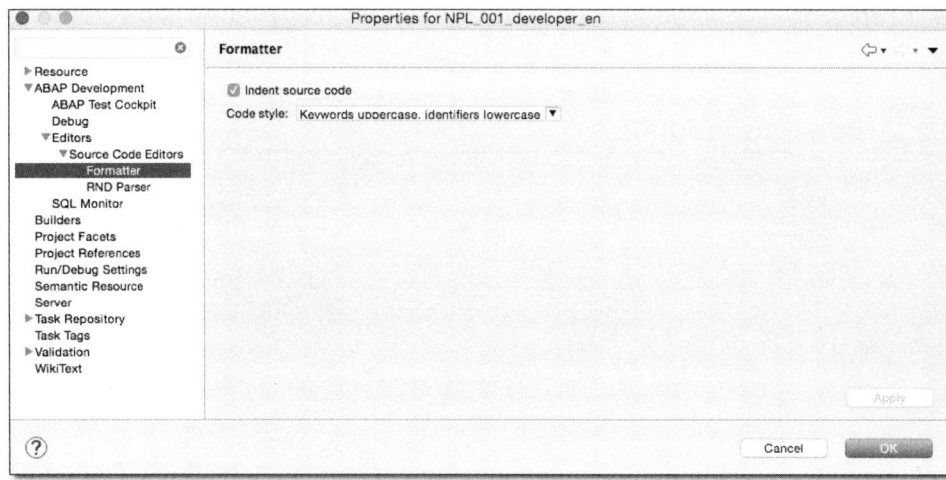

Figure 2.14 Formatter Settings in Eclipse

Formatting in Eclipse

Next, from the Eclipse menu, click SOURCE • FORMAT to format the entire program or SOURCE • FORMAT BLOCK to format a block of selected text. You will notice the changes take effect immediately.

Formatting settings for Transaction SE80

If you are a Transaction SE80 user, go to UTILITIES • SETTINGS • ABAP EDITOR • PRETTY PRINTER; select the checkboxes for INDENT and UPPERCASE/LOWERCASE and the radio button for KEYWORD UPPERCASE. The result should match Figure 2.15.

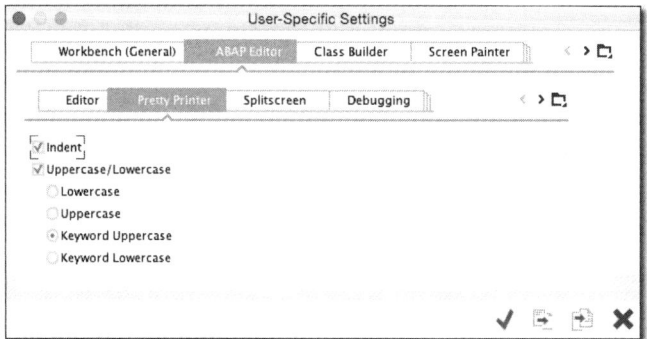

Figure 2.15 Formatter Settings in Transaction SE80

Formatting in Transaction SE80

Next, you can click the pretty button in the Transaction SE80 toolbar. You will notice that your code is updated immediately.

Formatting your source code helps to make it easier to read for yourself or a developer who may need to debug it in a different environment. Indenting can also be a huge help when trying to look through your code. Formatting only takes a second, so get into the habit of doing it regularly when working on projects.

Why should you format code?

When declaring multiple variables, you'll notice that the automatic formatter does not help much. You may prefer to line up the declarations so that the TYPE keyword is all in one line, as in the example below, but this is not automated by Eclipse or Transaction SE80.

Manual formatting

```
DATA: ld_var       TYPE i,
      ld_variable  TYPE i,
      ld_other_var TYPE i.
```

Comments

Now that you've learned some ABAP basics, you're ready to learn how to comment your code. The ABAP comment keywords (Table 2.7), designate anything typed on their lines as not relevant for the compiler. This gives comments two powerful uses:

> They can be used to leave notes for future programmers who will use your code.

> They're tools for troubleshooting code that isn't working.

Keyword	Description
"	Comments entire line after symbol
*	Comments entire line (must be first character)

Comment keywords

Table 2.7 Types of Comments

It is important to remember that when writing any program, you're not writing it for yourself, but for the person who is supporting it. A change to a program that you wrote might not be required for years after you wrote it, by which time a new developer may not be able to get in touch with you to discuss your code. As a result, it's important to leave good comments that can help explain what is happening in your code.

Why should you leave comments in your code?

Good comments are measured in quality, not quantity, and good code will need fewer comments than bad code. When someone looks at your code, you want the comments to explain something that doesn't make a lot of sense or something that might be complicated to someone who was not in any design session.

Common Commenting Mistakes

Unnecessary comments

A common commenting mistake is to add comments that are unnecessary. In the following example, you already know that you're declaring data, because the keyword DATA is there. Also, the program contains a meaningful variable name, so you already know that ld_title is a title. The related comments don't add anything to the program.

```
PROGRAM Z_COMMENTS.
"Declare Data
DATA: d_title TYPE string. "title
```

Useful comments

Here's an example of a more useful comment:

```
...
"All totals must be multiplied by 5 due to local regulations
d_total = d_total * 5.
WRITE: d_total.
```

You get some total and multiply it by 5. Someone looking at this code the first time may wonder why he's multiplying the total by 5, so I included an explanation using comments that explains that some regulations require the results to be multiplied by 5.

Using Comments while Programming

Debugging with comments

Sometimes, you may think you have a really good idea for how something could work, but might need to go another direction. Comments allow you to set code aside and try it another way. Then, you can easily go back to earlier code if needed, without having to work with your source control system.

```
...
"d_total + 5.
d_total + 6.
...
```

You can easily comment some code by entering a " or * at the beginning of that line of code, then test. Next you can comment the second line of code, and test again. This is why there are some great features in your handy IDE to comment out multiple lines at once. You can do this in Eclipse by selecting SOURCE • ADD COMMENT (or [Ctrl]+[5]), which will comment out all of your highlighted code. In Transaction SE80, you can comment out multiple lines of code by selecting UTILITIES • BLOCK/BUFFER • INSERT COMMENT (or [Ctrl]+[<] to comment and [Ctrl]+[>] to uncomment).

Classic Selection Screen Programming

So far, you've created a program that uses variables to store data and then uses arithmetic and flow control to process those variables. Many times, the values that you need to process come from the database, a user, or (more likely) both. You'll learn how to get data from the database in Chapter 4; for now, we'll cover how to get data from the user.

There are multiple ways to interface with users in ABAP-based systems, and Appendix B covers them briefly. The simplest way is through classic selection screen programming, which we'll cover here. Whether you use this method or one of the more modern interfaces depends on the user experience strategy of the company you work for. The basic keywords of classic selection screen programming are shown below in Table 2.8. We will explain each of these in more details throughout this section.

Keyword	Description
SELECTION-SCREEN	Defines a screen
PARAMETER	Gets input for a single variable from the user
SELECT-OPTIONS	Gets a range of data from the user
BLOCK	Used to organize the different input items on the screen

Selection screen keywords

Table 2.8 Classic Selection Screen Keywords

In the selection screen flow, you ask the user for some input, process that input, and provide results. This process could be used to complete a query and display the results or to complete some actions

Selection screen flow

65

using the data that you find. This is different than a module pool program that may have multiple screens that the user completes in order to complete an entire transaction.

SELECTION-SCREEN

You can gather data from the user using the PARAMETER and SELECT-OPTIONS keywords, but those keywords must be contained inside a SCREEN or a within a BLOCK inside a screen. Screens are given a unique number to distinguish them from one another. Every ABAP program contains a standard screen 1000 when created. Figure 2.16 illustrates the relationship between a screen, a block, and input.

Selection screen hierarchy

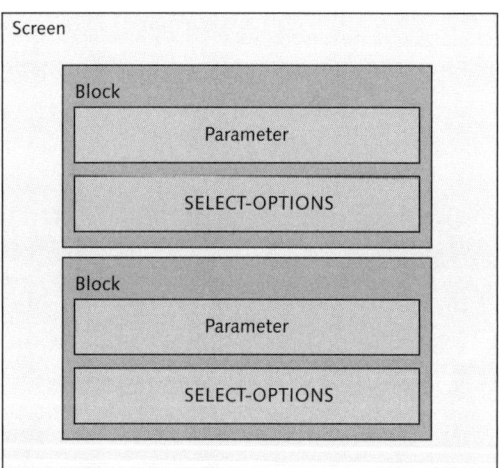

Figure 2.16 Diagram of Selection Screen Hierarchy

If you want to create additional screens to use in addition to the default screen 1000, you can do so with the BEGIN OF SCREEN keyword. You can then call your screen using the CALL SELECTION-SCREEN keyword. Because the default screen is always 1000, your new screen will not be called unless you specifically call it. In Listing 2.9, you can see that a new screen is defined with an id of 2000.

```
SELECTION-SCREEN BEGIN OF SCREEN 2000.
    PARAMETER p_input TYPE string.
SELECTION-SCREEN END OF SCREEN 2000.
CALL SELECTION-SCREEN 2000.
```
Listing 2.9 Define a New Selection Screen

BLOCK

The BLOCK is used to organize the input elements within the selection screen. If you start your ABAP program with a BLOCK, that BLOCK will be added to screen 1000. A block can have any alphanumeric name, unlike the screen, which can only have a numeric identifier. Blocks can be reused across multiple screens in an ABAP program. Some additional BLOCK options are listed in Table 2.9.

Organize input elements

Option	Description
WITH FRAME	Adds a frame around the input options inside of the block
WITH FRAME TITLE <title>	Adds a title to the top of the block
NO INTERVALS	Removes the second input box from SELECT-OPTIONS within the block to make the entire block have a smaller width.

Table 2.9 Additional Options for the BLOCK Keyword

Using BLOCK with WITH FRAME and WITH FRAME TITLE adds a professional look to your program. WITH FRAME TITLE requires the use of a text symbol; text symbols are defined within the program.

Creating text symbols is not currently a feature in Eclipse, so you have to open your program in the GUI editor. In Eclipse, right-click your program name from Project Explorer, select OPEN IN SAP GUI, and the ABAP editor will open in the main window. Within the GUI (Transaction SE80), select GOTO • TEXT ELEMENTS • TEXT SYMBOLS. Click the EDIT button, add "001" as the symbol ID and "Enter Your Selection Below" for the text, and click [Enter]. The current length (LNGTH) and max length (MAX.) fields will be automatically populated to the number of characters that you added (Figure 2.17).

Text symbols

Anytime you need to change your text, you can always increase the max length. You'll need to activate changes to text symbols. You'll learn more about text symbols in Chapter 8.

Creating Your First Program

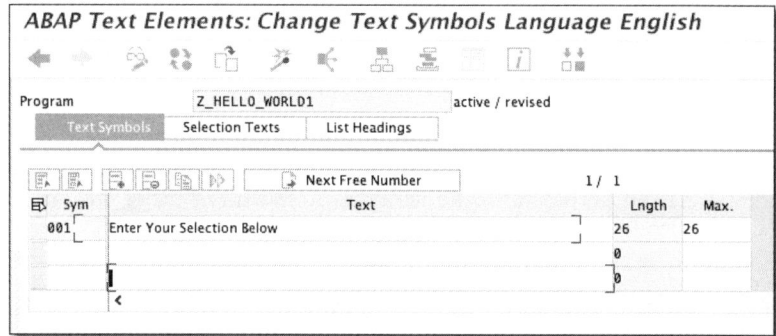

Figure 2.17 The Maintain Text Symbols Screen

Selection screen frame

Figure 2.18 shows a selection screen without a frame, and Figure 2.19 shows a selection screen with a frame and title using the text symbol that you just created. You can see how only two lines of code can make the selection screen look much more professional.

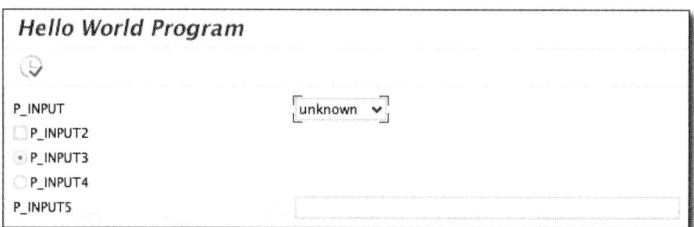

Figure 2.18 Input Options without a Frame

The code to create the screen in Figure 2.18 is shown below in Listing 2.10:

```
SELECTION-SCREEN BEGIN OF BLOCK selection.
     PARAMETER:
        p_input  TYPE boolean AS LISTBOX VISIBLE LENGTH 10,
        p_input2 TYPE boolean AS CHECKBOX,
        p_input3 TYPE boolean RADIOBUTTON GROUP grp,
        p_input4 TYPE boolean RADIOBUTTON GROUP grp,
        p_input5 TYPE string.
SELECTION-SCREEN END OF BLOCK selection.
```
Listing 2.10 Creating a Selection Screen Block

Figure 2.19 is created using the code in Listing 2.11. Notice the highlighted `SELECTION-SCREEN` code, which provides the frame title with the text symbol as discussed earlier in the section.

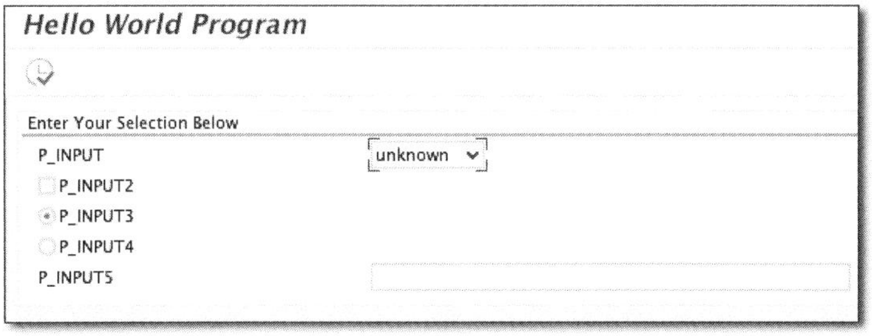

Figure 2.19 Input Options with a Frame

```
SELECTION-SCREEN BEGIN OF BLOCK selection WITH FRAME TITLE
text-001.
    PARAMETER:
        p_input  TYPE boolean AS LISTBOX VISIBLE LENGTH 10,
        p_input2 TYPE boolean AS CHECKBOX,
        p_input3 TYPE boolean RADIOBUTTON GROUP grp,
        p_input4 TYPE boolean RADIOBUTTON GROUP grp,
        p_input5 TYPE string.
SELECTION-SCREEN END OF BLOCK selection.
```
Listing 2.11 Selection Screen Example

PARAMETER

Now that you know how to organize the input controls using screens and blocks, it's time to cover the actual input controls, beginning with the `PARAMETER` keyword. The parameter keyword will take a single input from a user and save the input in a `PARAMETER` variable. An example parameter is shown below, where the user will see a textbox and will be able to enter any text in that textbox. We can then access the parameter `p_input` just like we do any other variable.

```
PARAMETER: p_input TYPE string.
```

The parameter variable names must be eight characters in length or less. Table 2.10 provides a list of parameter options that give the parameters some additional functionality.

Parameter options

Option	Effect
OBLIGATORY	User cannot execute the program until a value is entered.
DEFAULT	Set a default value for the parameter.
AS CHECKBOX	Parameter is set as a checkbox that will return ABAP_TRUE or ABAP_FALSE when selected or not selected.
RADIOBUTTON GROUP group	Works like a checkbox, but will only allow one parameter to be selected within a defined group.
AS LISTBOX VISIBLE LENGTH n	Will create a dropdown selection for all possible options for the parameter data type. The dropdown list width is defined by n.

Table 2.10 Selection Screen Parameter Options

You can add the OBLIGATORY option to prevent the user from running the program without entering a value:

PARAMETER: p_input TYPE string **OBLIGATORY**.

Parameters can also be given a default value by adding the DEFAULT keyword with a value:

```
PARAMETER:
    p_input TYPE string OBLIGATORY DEFAULT 'SOME TEXT'.
```

 Case-Insensitive Input

Any parameters entered by the user will be converted to all uppercase when passed to your program.

We can then use the parameter options from Table 2.10 to provide a user-friendly interface, as shown in Figure 2.20.

The code in Listing 2.12 shows the code used to demonstrate the different parameter options shown in Figure 2.20.

```
SELECTION-SCREEN BEGIN OF BLOCK selection WITH FRAME TITLE
    text-001.
    PARAMETER:
        p_input  TYPE boolean AS LISTBOX VISIBLE LENGTH 10,
        p_input2 TYPE boolean AS CHECKBOX,
```

```
       p_input3 TYPE boolean RADIOBUTTON GROUP grp DEFAULT 'X',
       p_input4 TYPE boolean RADIOBUTTON GROUP grp,
       p_input5 TYPE string OBLIGATORY.
SELECTION-SCREEN END OF BLOCK selection.
```
Listing 2.12 Different Options for the PARAMETER Keyword

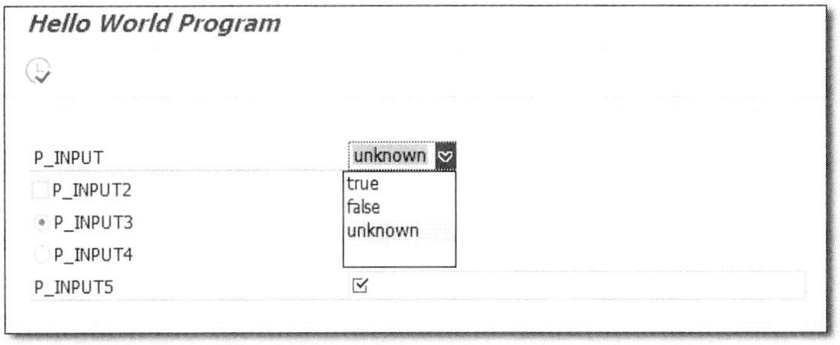

Figure 2.20 Parameter Options Example

The options within the list box are provided from the data type being used. You'll learn how to create your own data types in Chapter 3.

When radio buttons are used, only one radio button per group can be selected at a time, but it's possible for the user to click EXECUTE on the selection screen without any radio button selected. For this reason, you want to set one button as selected by default. To do so, set the default value to 'X':

Default radio buttons

```
PARAMETER:
    p_radio TYPE boolean RADIOBUTTON GROUP grp DEFAULT 'X'.
```

The radio button group identifier can be any four characters, and you can create multiple groups of radio buttons by changing that identifier:

Radio button groups

```
PARAMETER: p_radio  TYPE boolean RADIOBUTTON GROUP grp,
           p_radio2 TYPE boolean RADIOBUTTON GROUP grp,
           p_radio3 TYPE boolean RADIOBUTTON GROUP grp2,
           p_radio4 TYPE boolean RADIOBUTTON GROUP grp2.
```

Let's update the "Hello, World!" program to take input from the user and write that input out on the screen. Include a block with a frame title to make your selection screen look more professional (Listing 2.13).

Updating "Hello, World!"

Creating Your First Program

```
REPORT Z_HELLO_WORLD.
SELECTION-
SCREEN BEGIN OF BLOCK selection WITH FRAME TITLE text-001.
    parameter p_input TYPE string.
END OF BLOCK selection.
WRITE: p_input.
```
Listing 2.13 Program to Output Any Data Entered by the User

 Boolean Parameters

Always use checkboxes or radio buttons when trying to get a Boolean response from a user. Otherwise, you're expecting the user to enter "X" into a textbox to indicate true, which can be very confusing.

SELECT-OPTIONS

The `SELECT-OPTIONS` keyword allows for the user to select from a range of options. This keyword comes in handy when you need to access data from a database, which we'll cover in Chapter 4. Selection options are stored in an internal table, which we will cover working with more in Chapter 5. For now, we'll explain how to use a selection option to gather input from a user.

SELECT-OPTIONS data types

Unlike `PARAMETER`, `SELECT-OPTIONS` requires a variable based on a database table in order to define what options are available to be selected. (You'll learn more about these database-based data types in Chapter 4). Figure 2.21 shows that you can enter a range of values as well as see possible options that can be selected by the user. All of this is enabled with only one line of code!

The code used to create what we see in Figure 2.21 is shown below in Listing 2.14. The select options are shown in bold. Notice that the `ld_airport` variable is of type `sairport-id`, meaning that it uses the `id` column of the `sairport` table.

```
DATA: ld_airportid TYPE sairport-id.
SELECTION-SCREEN BEGIN OF BLOCK selection
    SELECT-OPTIONS: so_air FOR ld_airportid.
END OF BLOCK selection.
```
Listing 2.14 SELECT-OPTIONS Syntax

Classic Selection Screen Programming

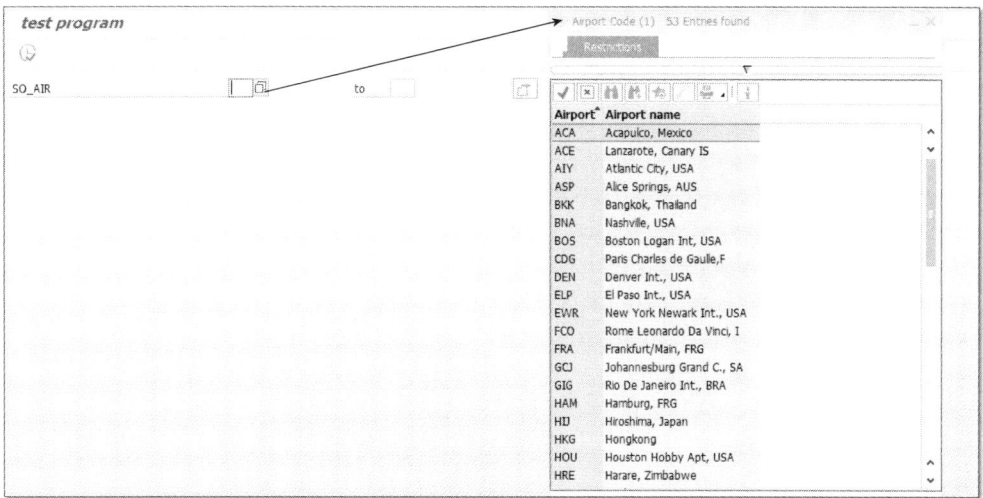

Figure 2.21 Select Options with Options from Database Values

You can see all of the options that users have by clicking on the button to the right of a highlighted field. They can choose a single value or a range of values, or even exclude a single value or range of values. You can also add additional options, such as greater than or less than, through the button to the left of the textbox within the multiple selection screen (Figure 2.22).

Select-options value ranges

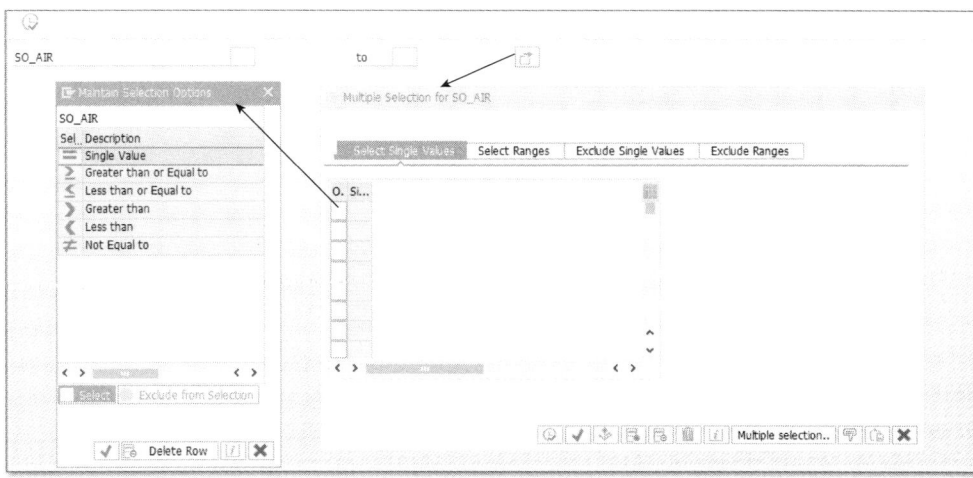

Figure 2.22 Additional Options within the Selection Options

Selection Texts

The parameter and selection option variable names that you choose may make sense to you as the developer, but they may not make sense to users. Apply better descriptions to your parameters and selection options by selecting GOTO • TEXT ELEMENTS • SELECTION TEXTS (If you are using ABAP in Eclipse, you'll need to right-click your program in the PROJECT EXPLORER view and select OPEN WITH SAP GUI). On this screen, you'll see any parameters and selection options that you have defined, and you can add any text description that you want as shown in Figure 2.23.

Dictionary descriptions

You can also select the DICTIONARY REF. checkbox for any definitions based on a database data type to get the database type description, as shown in the second parameter in Figure 2.23. In Figure 2.24 you can see that HELLO STRING is displayed in the first parameter and AIRPORT CODE is displayed in the second parameter.

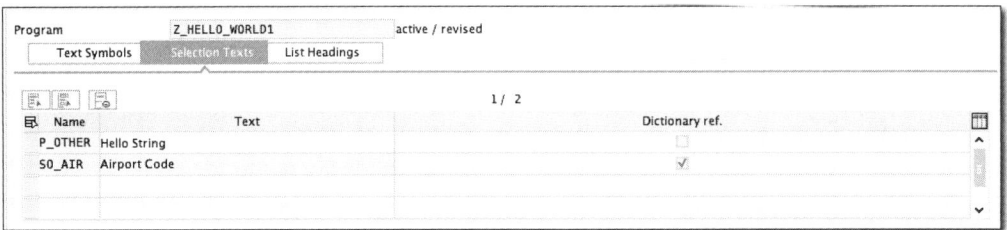

Figure 2.23 Adding Selection Texts

Figure 2.24 Selection Screen with Selection Texts

 Advanced Classic Dynpro Programming

A topic out of the scope of this book is some of the advanced Dynpro programming techniques. ABAP comes with a WYSIWYG Dynpro editor, but your company may have a user experience strategy based on ABAP Web Dynpro or SAPUI5. Take time to learn what is most relevant to your company. SAP recommends ABAP Web Dynpro or SAPUI5 as a modern solution.

Program Lifecycle

When working with classic ABAP programs, you can use a lifecycle event to trigger code. Using these events is not always necessary, but they may be needed to handle some basic UI functions in your program.

For the purposes of this book, the most important thing to remember is that the order of the events is the same order as shown in Table 2.11. We are going to focus on the AT SELECTION-SCREEN and START-OF-SELECTION events.

Event	Description
LOAD-OF-PROGRAM	This event is triggered once before your program is loaded into memory.
INITIALIZATION	This event is called before any selection screens are processed.
AT SELECTION-SCREEN	This event is associated with specific options on the screen and can be used for enforcing validations and providing custom options for the user to select.
START-OF-SELECTION	This event is triggered after the user has completed the selection screen and pressed the EXECUTE button.

Program lifecycle events

Table 2.11 ABAP Program Lifecycle Events

AT SELECTION-SCREEN

This event is very useful in classic ABAP selection screens; it allows you to validate user entries before executing the rest of your code. Let's take the "Hello, World!" program from Listing 2.8 and add a validation in Listing 2.15 to throw an error if the user does not enter "HELLO WORLD". Remember, the text entered will always be converted to uppercase.

```
REPORT z_hello_world.
SELECTION-SCREEN BEGIN OF BLOCK selection
  WITH FRAME TITLE text-001.
PARAMETER p_input TYPE string.
SELECTION-SCREEN END OF BLOCK selection.
```

```
AT SELECTION-SCREEN.
  IF p_input <> 'HELLO WORLD'.
    MESSAGE e000(38) WITH 'Invalid Entry'.
  ENDIF.
START-OF-SELECTION.
  WRITE: p_input.
```
Listing 2.15 Display an Error when HELLO WORLD Is Not Entered

When executing the code in Listing 2.15, if we enter some text for p_input that is not "HELLO WORLD", we will see the error displayed in Figure 2.25. We will cover error messages in Chapter 10. For now, note that you can use MESSAGE e000(38) WITH followed by some text to display an error message.

Figure 2.25 Invalid Entry Error

The AT SELECTION-SCREEN code in Listing 2.15 will be executed until the START-OF-SELECTION event is defined.

START-OF-SELECTION

The START-OF-SELECTION event is optional to use if no other events are defined, because it's the default event that will begin executing your code. However, if another event is defined in your program (such as in Listing 2.15), then you will need to add the START-OF-SELECTION event to indicate the end of the code block for the other event. If an error is thrown in the AT SELECTION-SCREEN event, then the code in the START-OF-SELECTION event will not be executed.

Debugging Basics

Before you can really start writing ABAP code, you need to learn how to debug it. In ABAP and any programming language, *debugging* is the art of finding out what went wrong in your application. Sometimes, even the simplest of applications may have an issue, which is why this book covers debugging as soon as possible so that you can use it while trying to understand why your applications are not working.

Debugging can be very powerful not only when trying to resolve an issue, but also when trying to understand how a program works. Debugging allows you to watch what the system does as it executes your code. A *breakpoint* allows you to pause the execution of a program so that you can inspect what's going on. When debugging, you can pause the program and allow it to move one line at a time while you inspect any variables.

Breakpoint

It's possible to set breakpoints that stop for other users, but for now, you'll be creating session breakpoints that will only affect your session, which means you don't need to worry about interrupting other users on the system.

A *watchpoint* works much like a breakpoint but will only pause the program when a certain condition is met. That condition can be when a variable's value changes to anything or when a variable changes to a particular value. Watchpoints can save you a ton of time when you just need to find where a variable is being set to a strange number. That location could be deep inside of a loop, and perhaps you don't want to spend time going through one loop at a time.

Watchpoint

The following sections cover debugging in both the SAP GUI and in eclipse. To follow along, we'll provide a program that you can debug, which uses concepts already covered in this chapter.

Program to Debug

The provided program (Listing 2.16) is a basic calculator. It uses two parameters and radio buttons for various functions. The selected radio button function will indicate which math function to execute.

Basic calculator program

```
REPORT z_sample1.
DATA: d_result TYPE decfloat16.

SELECTION-SCREEN BEGIN OF BLOCK selection WITH FRAME.
PARAMETER:
    p_val1   TYPE decfloat34,
    p_add    TYPE boolean RADIOBUTTON GROUP grp DEFAULT 'X',
    p_subt   TYPE boolean RADIOBUTTON GROUP grp,
    p_multi  TYPE boolean RADIOBUTTON GROUP grp,
    p_divide TYPE boolean RADIOBUTTON GROUP grp,
    p_power  TYPE boolean RADIOBUTTON GROUP grp,
    p_val2   TYPE decfloat34.
SELECTION-SCREEN END OF BLOCK selection.
```

```
AT SELECTION-SCREEN.
  IF p_divide = abap_true AND p_val2 = 0.
    MESSAGE e000(38) WITH 'Cannot divide by zero'.
  ENDIF.

START-OF-SELECTION.
  IF p_add = abap_true.
    d_result = p_val1 + p_val2.
  ELSEIF p_subt = abap_true.
    d_result = p_val1 - p_val2.
  ELSEIF p_multi = abap_true.
    d_result = p_val1 * p_val2.
  ELSEIF p_divide = abap_true.
    d_result = p_val1 / p_val2.
  ELSEIF p_power = abap_true.
    d_result = ipow( base = p_val1 exp = p_val2 ).
  ENDIF.
  WRITE: d_result.
```
Listing 2.16 Sample Program for Debugging

Tip

Getting a syntax error when using the ipow function? You might be on an older version of ABAP. Try p_val1 ** p_val2, instead.

The ipow math function was added to the ABAP language as of ABAP 7.40 SP2.

Before you start debugging the program, let's review what's happening here.

Selection screen

First, you have the classic SELECTION-SCREEN, which is declared with a BLOCK using the keyword WITH FRAME to make it look professional. Next, you use the PARAMETER: keyword to declare seven parameters chained with a comma. The chaining is allowed because of the colon after PARAMETER.

Data validation

Next, you have data validation using the AT SELECTION-SCREEN event, for which you use an IF statement to check if you're using both the divide function and a zero for your second value; if you are, the program will throw an error message that will stop the execution of code.

Data processing

Next, you have data processing using the START-OF-SELECTION event, for which a series of IF and ELSEIF commands determines which function is used. When these commands determine the function, they will then run the calculation and store the result in `d_result`.

Finally, the program outputs the value for `d_result` by writing it on the screen.

Data output

Breakpoints in Eclipse

Setting breakpoints is easy. You need to set the breakpoint on any line of executable code; you cannot set a breakpoint on any whitespace or code for which variables are being declared. Start by creating a break point on this line of code:

```
IF p_divide = abap_true AND p_val2 = 0.
```

To create a breakpoint in Eclipse, double-click the left side of the screen, just to the left of the line number. If successful, you'll see a small circle like the one shown in Figure 2.26.

Creating a breakpoint

```
14   AT SELECTION-SCREEN.
 15    IF p_divide = abap_true AND p_val2 = 0.
 16      MESSAGE e000(38) WITH 'Cannot divide by zero'.
 17    ENDIF.
```

Figure 2.26 Breakpoint Set at Line 15

To test the breakpoint, click the RUN PROGRAM button or press [F8], enter some data, and then click EXECUTE or press [F8]. The first time you do this, you'll prompted by Eclipse to confirm that you want to switch to the DEBUGGER perspective. If you see this popup, click YES and also click the REMEMBER MY DECISION checkbox so that you do not see the same popup next time you debug.

Testing a breakpoint

In the DEBUGGER perspective, you'll see your code in the center area of the screen. You can actually make changes to your code in this area, but they won't be active during this debug session. You will also notice that the line of code with your breakpoint is highlighted, and a small arrow appears over your breakpoint (Figure 2.27).

Changing code in the debugger perspective

```
14   AT SELECTION-SCREEN.
 15    IF p_divide = abap_true AND p_val2 = 0.
 16      MESSAGE e000(38) WITH 'Cannot divide by zero'.
 17    ENDIF.
```

Figure 2.27 Code View with a Breakpoint Set

Additional Ways to Set and Remove Breakpoints

In Eclipse, you can also set a breakpoint by selecting RUN • TOGGLE BREAKPOINT or RUN • TOGGLE LINE BREAKPOINT. You can also disable all breakpoints by selecting RUN • SKIP ALL BREAKPOINTS. This will preserve the breakpoints you set but not pause the program when you get there, and you can turn them back on by selecting RUN • SKIP ALL BREAKPOINTS again.

You can also delete all of your breakpoints by selecting RUN • REMOVE ALL BREAKPOINTS.

Debug actions — Step the debugger forward using [F5]; you'll see the arrow and green highlighted line move to the START-OF-SELECTION line. Using the STEP INTO function [F5], follow the program into the next line of code. The STEP OVER function [F6] will follow the program into the next line of code but will run any deeper functions, such as a method in a class (covered in Chapter 6), without pausing, unlike the step into function, which will step into that method and pause right away. The STEP RETURN function [F7] will run the rest of the code in a deeper function and pause when it exits the deeper function. When you're done debugging, you can use the RESUME function [F8] to let the program run until the next breakpoint or the terminate function to stop the debugging session. You can find the buttons for the above mentioned debugger functions in the debugging toolbar shown in Figure 2.28.

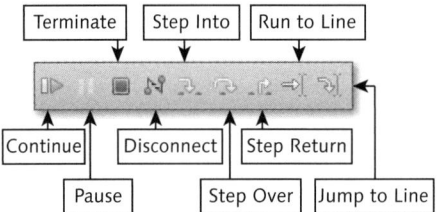

Figure 2.28 The Debugging Toolbar

Toolbar functions — Some additional buttons on the toolbar include the following: the PAUSE button, which will pause an actively running program; the TERMINATION button, which will stop the program running; the DISCONNECT button, which will disconnect the debugger from your code; the RUN TO LINE button, which will run the code normally up to the point where you have placed the cursor; and the JUMP TO LINE button, which will skip all of the code between what's currently being run and where your cursor is.

Below the toolbar on the left side of the screen is the *execution stack* pictured in Figure 2.29. You won't see much while running the debugging sample program, but this is useful when debugging complex programs or standard programs. Note the [SYSTEM] indicator in Figure 2.29, which lets you know that those programs in the stack are being used by the system, not your program.

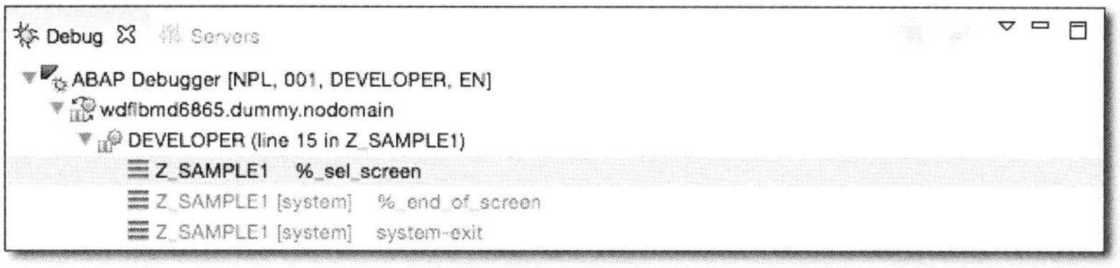

Execution stack

Figure 2.29 Program Execution Stack

You'll revisit the program execution stack after writing more complex programs.

On the top-right side of the screen, you can see the VARIABLES selection, pictured in Figure 2.30. If you expand the GLOBALS selection, you can see all of the variables that you created. You can also change the value of your variables here by selecting the VALUE column and entering a new value.

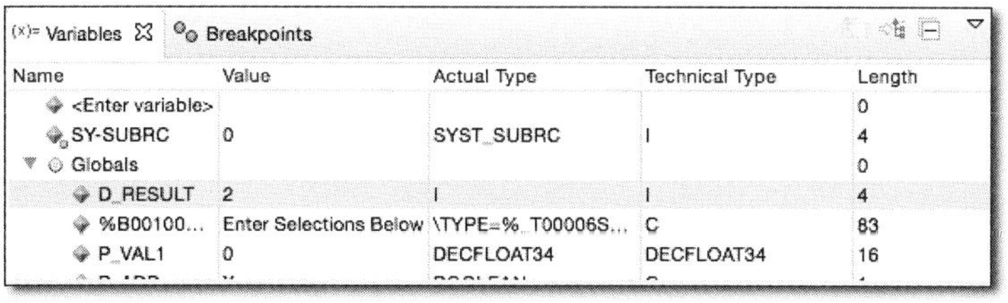

Variables view

Figure 2.30 The Variables Window

From the VARIABLES window, you should see a tab for BREAKPOINTS. Click it to view some breakpoint options and a list of all of your breakpoints (Figure 2.31).

Breakpoints view

Creating Your First Program

Figure 2.31 The Breakpoints Window in the Eclipse Debugger Perspective

If you uncheck any breakpoint, then that breakpoint will be set as inactive, meaning that your code will not stop at that point. You can make it active again by rechecking it. You also can select the RESTRICT TO RUNNING DEBUGGERS checkbox, which will make your breakpoint only valid for the current program you're debugging. If you select that checkbox, then if you launch another program that would hit your breakpoint, it would ignore your breakpoint, because you already have a running debug session.

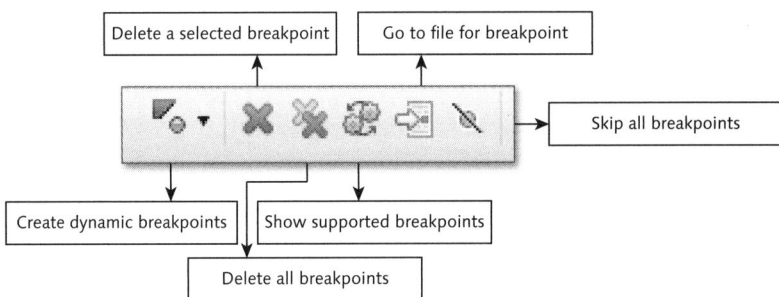

Figure 2.32 The Breakpoint Toolbar

Breakpoint toolbar options

You have a few options on the breakpoint toolbar shown in Figure 2.32. The first one allows you to create dynamic breakpoints, which will stop every time a certain ABAP command is run. For example, if you know a message is thrown before something goes terribly wrong, then you can have a breakpoint set for every time the MESSAGE keyword is used. Making dynamic breakpoints is easy in Eclipse, because the IDE provides a popup in which you can search for the ABAP command that you want to cause the program to pause (Figure 2.33).

The next button in the toolbar shown in Figure 2.32 is the DELETE SELECTED BREAKPOINT button, which will remove a breakpoint selected the breakpoint list below the toolbar. This is followed by the DELETE ALL BREAKPOINTS button, which removes all of the breakpoints.

Debugging Basics

Figure 2.33 Select Dynamic Breakpoint Statement

The next button is the SHOW SUPPORTED BREAKPOINTS button, which resembles a gear. This button is used to display only breakpoints for the language in which you are working. Therefore, if you have another project in Eclipse with breakpoints, you will only see the ABAP ones.

The GO TO FILE FOR BREAKPOINT button is pretty useful, especially if you have breakpoints across multiple programs. It will take you to the exact line of code where a selected breakpoint was set. Finally, the SKIP ALL BREAKPOINTS toolbar button will make all of your breakpoints inactive.

Now that you know how to step through your program, set breakpoints, and change variables, practice those tasks a few times with the sample calculator program. Next, we'll cover how to debug ABAP programs in the SAP GUI. Even if your primary IDE is Eclipse, you should still learn how to debug in the GUI in case you're unable to use Eclipse in a given ABAP system; plus, there are a few advanced debugger features (not covered in this book) that are only available in the GUI debugger.

Breakpoints in the SAP GUI

Before you begin debugging in the SAP GUI, make sure your settings have the new debugger selected. You can check this by entering

Debugging settings

Transaction SE80 and then selecting UTILITIES • SETTINGS • ABAP EDITOR • DEBUGGING; there, ensure that NEW DEBUGGER is selected. The new debugger is easier to use than the classic debugger and has many more features.

 Why Is the Classic Debugger Still Loading?

The new debugger uses one of your available sessions, whereas the classic debugger does not. For that reason, if you start a debug session in the GUI and it loads the classic debugger even though you updated your settings, just close an open session, and then you can switch to the new debugger by selecting DEBUGGING • SWITCH TO NEW ABAP DEBUGGER.

Also, ensure that the SESSION BREAKPOINT ACTIVE IMMEDIATELY checkbox is selected. This option will make sure that your breakpoint is set, even if you are already running a program that would hit that breakpoint. Without this option, you would have to exit the program and return to it to have your breakpoint active. Your settings should match what is shown in Figure 2.34.

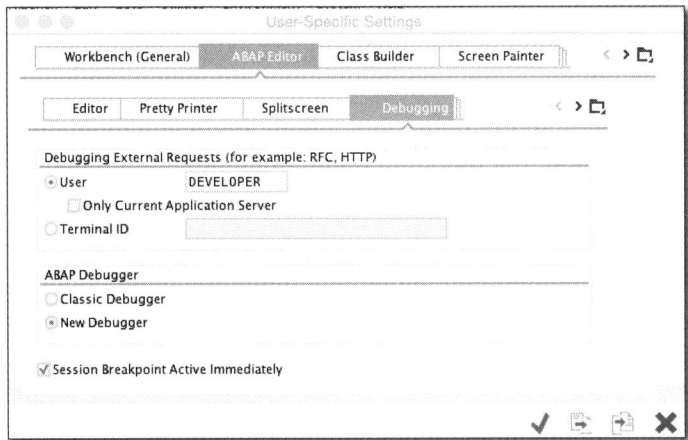

Figure 2.34 The ABAP Editor Settings within SAP GUI

Creating breakpoints

Now, let's start debugging! You can create a breakpoint by double-clicking to the left of the line numbers inside of the ABAP editor workspace on any line of executable code. Create a breakpoint on the following line of code:

```
IF p_divide = abap_true AND p_val2 = 0.
```

You'll see that the line will turn red, and a red stop sign with a screen will appear (Figure 2.35).

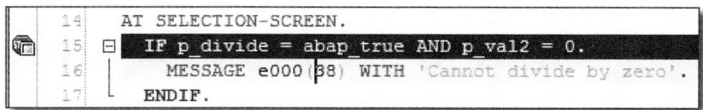

Figure 2.35 Setting a Breakpoint in Transaction SE80

You can also set a breakpoint by clicking one of the breakpoint buttons in the ABAP editor toolbar (Figure 2.36).

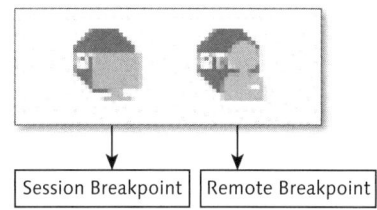

Figure 2.36 SAP GUI Breakpoint Buttons

A *session breakpoint* is set when you double-click to the left of your code; it will pause code that you are running in your current session. A *remote breakpoint* will pause code for a selected user's session, which can be through an RFC or HTTP connection. You can choose the user that you want the remote breakpoint to be activated for by going to UTILITIES • SETTINGS • ABAP EDITOR • DEBUGGING, where you can add any username in the USER textbox.

Types of breakpoints

Now that you have a session breakpoint set, you can test it by pressing F8 to start the program. Then, press F8 from the selection screen to execute the program, and the ABAP debugger will start up and pause the program as soon as your breakpoint is hit.

Testing a breakpoint

When your breakpoint is hit and the program pauses, you can see the line of code where the program stopped, indicated by the small arrow pointing at your code as shown in Figure 2.37. The code that you see can't be edited from this view, but you can see the whole program in the main ABAP screen.

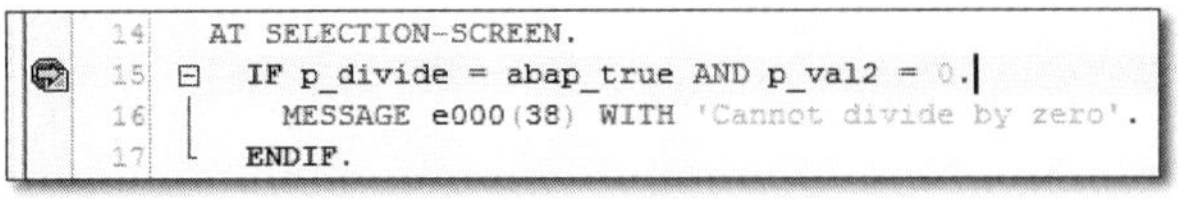

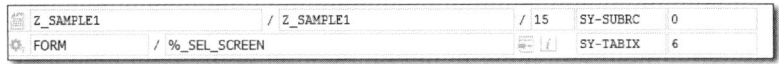

Figure 2.37 The Debugger Pausing on a Line of Code

Debugger information

At the top of the screen, you can see some information about the code you're debugging. This can be useful when debugging large and complex programs. Figure 2.38 shows that you're in the selection screen for program Z_SAMPLE1. You can also see the values for `sy-subrc` and `sy-tabix`, which will be covered in more detail later in this book.

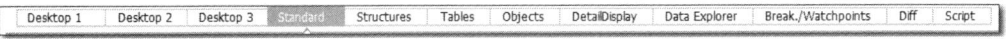

Figure 2.38 Debugging Location Information in the ABAP Debugger

Views and display

The ABAP debugger provides multiple customizable views, such as Desktop 1, Desktop 2, and Desktop 3 as shown in Figure 2.39. You can switch between these views by clicking on the appropriate tab at the top of the screen. Each view will still be the same code, but will show different information. The last tab, SCRIPT, is for running ABAP debugger scripts, which is out of scope for this book.

Figure 2.39 Different Tabs of the SAP GUI Debugger

ABAP and screen stack

The ABAP AND SCREEN STACK display in the standard view (Figure 2.40) will show what programs were called to get to where we are. You'll revisit the stack when you write more complex programs; for now, you can see that there are a lot of system programs involved in creating your selection screen.

Below the stack display in the STANDARD tab is the VARIABLE view, shown in Figure 2.41. By default, the VARIABLE view is blank; you can type in a variable or double-click a variable in your source code to see its value. You can also see a list of variables available from the LOCALS or GLOBALS tab. When you enter a variable name in the VARIABLES 1 or VARIABLES 2 tab, you'll see the value of the variable and can edit the value by clicking the EDIT button. Try looking up a variable and changing the value in your debugger.

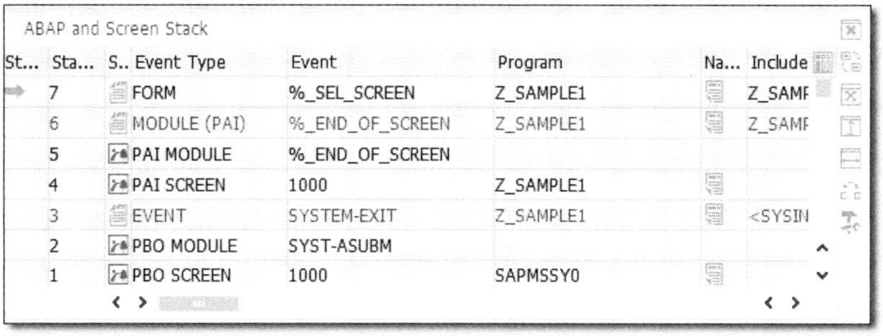

Figure 2.40 The ABAP and Screen Stack Display in the SAP GUI Debugger

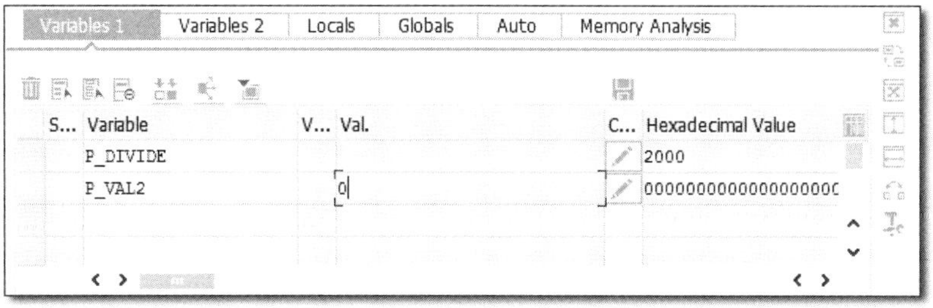

Figure 2.41 Displaying Variables in the ABAP Debugger

Now that you're familiar with viewing your ABAP code and the values within your variables, the next step is to learn how to step your code forward. A few shortcuts and a toolbar shown in Figure 2.42 help you handle stepping through your code: Click [F5] or press the STEP INTO button to execute the next line of code. This means that if a method or function outside of your program is hit, you'll go into that method or function and continue debugging, unlike the STEP OVER button or [F6], which will step over any method or function. Stepping over a method or function means that the code will still run, but the debugger will not pause the program again until it is done. Next, the RETURN button or [F7] will cause the debugger to pause as soon as it returns from a method or function. Finally, CONTINUE or [F8] will let the code continue until another breakpoint is hit. The corresponding buttons are displayed in Figure 2.42.

Step through code

2 Creating Your First Program

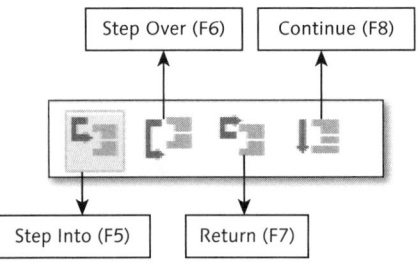

Figure 2.42 ABAP Debugger Toolbar

As you step the program forward, you'll see the arrow move around the program. Debugging like this is a great way to learn how a certain program works.

Watchpoints in Eclipse

Now that you've learned about breakpoints, let's dive into watchpoints. Breakpoints will pause your program every time that a particular line of code is reached, whereas a watchpoint will only pause when a watched variable's value changes. This can be useful when trying to figure out why a variable has a certain value.

Watchpoint scope — Watchpoints will only look at the variable in your current program, so if your program passes the variable on to another program or class, it will not be watching for changes in that other program.

Watchpoints are created after you're already in a debugging session, so open your debugging sample program and create a breakpoint on the line of code where you check whether the user is dividing by zero. Next, run the program, set it to calculate 10 plus 10, and click EXECUTE.

Once your breakpoint is hit, highlight the variable for d_result, right-click it, and select SET WATCHPOINT as shown in Figure 2.43. If you get some sort of error message, make sure d_result is selected.

You'll see a popup alert letting you know that a watchpoint was created for your variable. This popup is unnecessary, so we recommend that you select the DO NOT SHOW AGAIN checkbox shown in Figure 2.44.

Debugging Basics

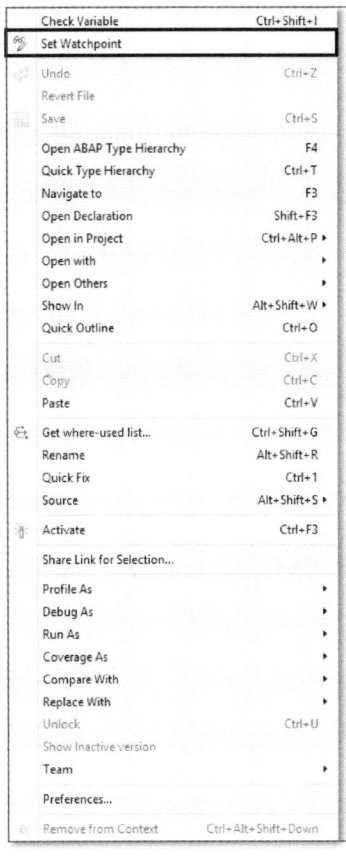

Figure 2.43 Right-Click options with Set Watchpoint Highlighted

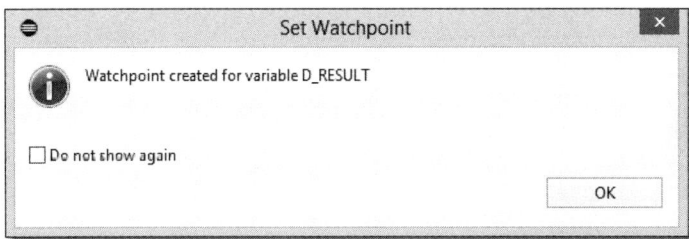

Figure 2.44 Set Watchpoint Popup

You'll see the new watchpoint listed under the VARIABLES tab. If you expand the watchpoint, you'll see a recent value and current value

Variables tab

displayed. You can now continue your program, and you should see it pause as soon as the `d_result` variable changes.

When the variable value changes, the watchpoint will pause the program. The new value will be displayed as the current value, and the old value will be displayed as the recent value (Figure 2.45).

Name	Value	Actual Type	Technical Type
\<Enter variable\>			
SY-SUBRC	0	SYSUBRC	I
▷ Globals			
▲ Watchpoint D_RESULT Values			
Recent Value	0	DECFLOAT16	DECFLOAT16
Current Value	20	DECFLOAT16	DECFLOAT16

Figure 2.45 Watchpoint Details in the Variables Table

Breakpoints tab In the BREAKPOINTS tab, you'll also see your new watchpoint added. You can uncheck the watchpoint to deactivate it, just as with a breakpoint.

Watchpoint conditions Sometimes when you're debugging, you don't want to see every time a variable changes, but you want to see when a variable changes to a specific value. In this scenario, use watchpoint conditions by clicking the watchpoint in the BREAKPOINTS tab and entering a condition in the CONDITION textbox. Conditions work just like the IF statements described in the flow control section. The watchpoint will check your condition every time that the watchpoint variable changes. If your condition is true, it will pause the program; otherwise, it will continue. You can see the condition being set as `d_result = 20` for the watchpoint displayed in Figure 2.46.

Figure 2.46 Watchpoint with Condition in the Breakpoints Tab

Test the wachpoint using the condition d_result = 20 using 10 plus 10 in the selection screen. Then test it with d_result = 25 using 10 plus 10 in the selection screen again. You should see it only pause the program when d_result = 20.

Watchpoints in SAP GUI

Watch points are created after you're already in a debugging session, as noted previously, so open the debugging program and set a breakpoint on the line of code that checks whether the user is dividing by zero. Next, run the program and set the selection to add 10 and 10. After executing the program, you will enter the debugger, and you should see the CREATE WATCHPOINT button shown in Figure 2.47.

Figure 2.47 Create Watchpoint Button

Click the button, enter "d_result" in the VARIABLE textbox, and click the checkmark as shown in Figure 2.48.

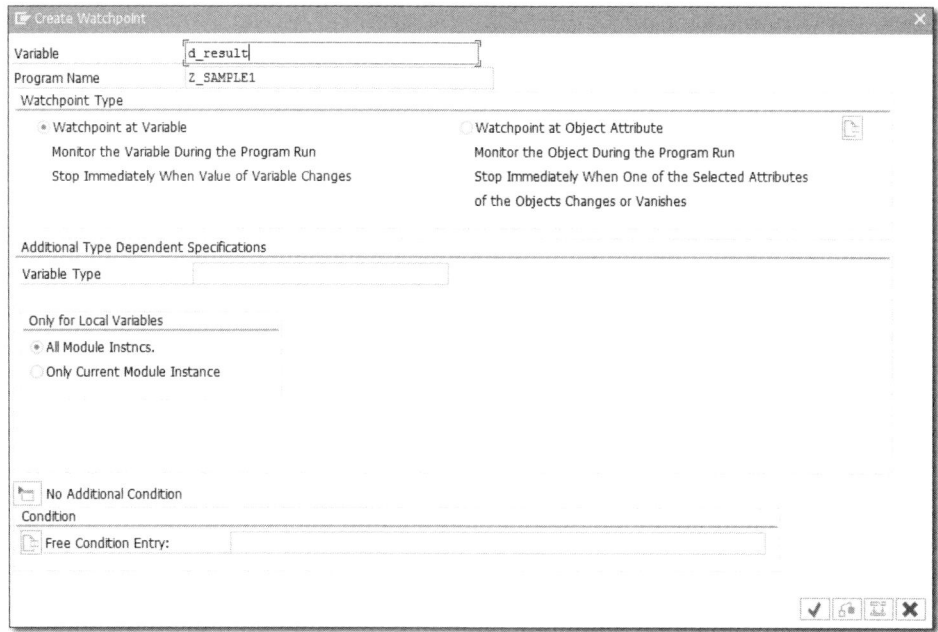

Figure 2.48 The Create Watchpoint Popup

Next, click CONTINUE or press [F8] to continue executing your code. Now, the debugger will stop on the line after the result variable has changed (Figure 2.49), and you will see a WATCHPOINT REACHED message shown in Figure 2.50.

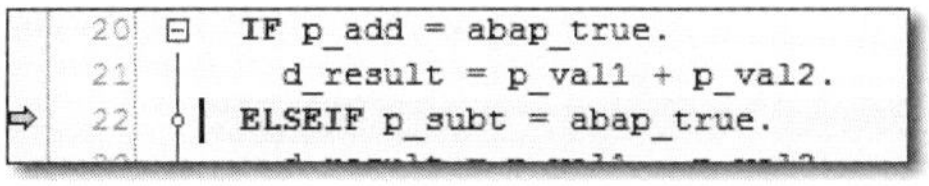

```
20  □   IF p_add = abap_true.
21          d_result = p_val1 + p_val2.
22  ◊|  ELSEIF p_subt = abap_true.
```

Figure 2.49 Watchpoint Stops Code Execution After Changing the Value of d_result

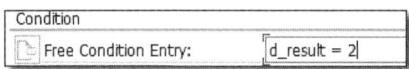

Figure 2.50 Watchpoint Reached Message

Watchpoint condition

If you want the watchpoint to only pause the program when the value of the variable you're watching is equal to a certain value, you can do that by entering a condition in the bottom of the CREATE WATCHPOINT screen as shown in Figure 2.51.

```
Condition
   Free Condition Entry:    d_result = 2
```

Figure 2.51 Free Condition Entry Inside the Create Watchpoint Popup

The condition that you enter works just like the IF statements you wrote earlier in the program. For example, you can run the program with 1 plus 1, create a watchpoint for d_result, and add the condition d_result = 2. When you continue the program, it will pause after d_result has changed only if the value of d_result is equal to 2. The debugger actually pauses when d_result changes and then evaluates the condition to decide whether or not to pause for you.

Tying It All Together

So far in this chapter, you've learned how to create a new ABAP program, create variables, process data inside of variables, use selection screens to gather input from a user, and debug to find out why your program isn't working correctly. Now, you'll apply what you've learned so far to create a basic report with a classic selection screen.

You won't use any standard SAP tables or functionality to do this, so don't worry if you're using a trial system.

The Problem

Create a program for calculating the total cost of an item when ordering it. The program should be called "Z_PROBLEM1", with the description "Problem 1". There should be three parameters on the selection screen: item name, item cost, and item quantity. The cost should be stored in a data type that only allows for two decimal places, and the quantity should be stored in only whole numbers.

The parameters should be within a frame with selection text that says Enter Selections Below. The completed selection screen should look like the image shown in Figure 2.52.

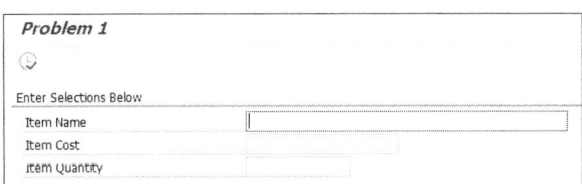

Figure 2.52 Problem 1 Selection Screen

You'll need to validate the data being entered by limiting the quantity to 999. If the user enters a quantity of more than 999, an error should be shown with the message Please enter quantity less than 999 (Figure 2.53).

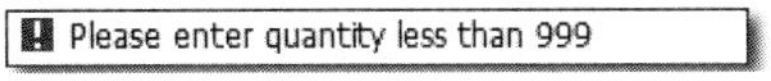

Figure 2.53 Error Message If Quantity Greater than 999 Entered

If there are no validation issues, the program should calculate the total cost and then output the following text (Figure 2.54):

The cost of <quanitity> <item>(s) is <total cost>.

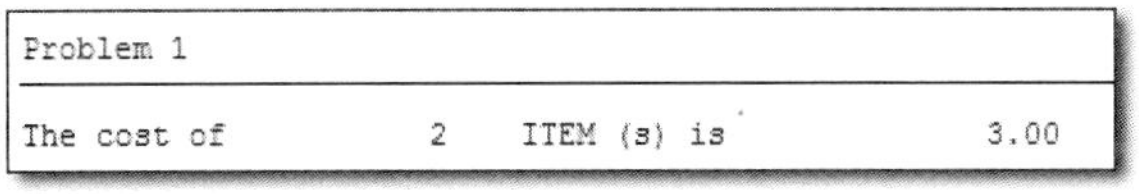

Figure 2.54 Example of Successful Output

The next section will provide a solution to this problem. Try to solve the problem without looking at the solution and then compare your code with what is provided in the solution.

The Solution

In Listing 2.17 we've provided a solution to the problem described in the previous section. Compare the code that you wrote with the code displayed here. If you were unable to solve the problem, try writing this code and debugging it to better understand how it works.

```
REPORT z_problem1.

SELECTION-SCREEN BEGIN OF BLOCK selection
  WITH FRAME TITLE text-001.
PARAMETER: p_item TYPE string,
           p_cost TYPE p DECIMALS 2,
           p_quan TYPE i.
SELECTION-SCREEN END OF BLOCK selection.

AT SELECTION-SCREEN.
  IF p_quan > 999.
    MESSAGE e000(38) WITH 'Please enter quantity less than
      999'.
  ENDIF.

START-OF-SELECTION.

  DATA: d_total TYPE p DECIMALS 2.

  d_total = p_cost * p_quan.

  WRITE: 'The cost of ', p_quan, ' ', p_item, '(s) is ',
    d_total.
```
Listing 2.17 Solution for Problem 1 Program

The selection screen uses a frame title pointing to text-001, a text element created in GOTO • TEXT ELEMENTS • TEXT SYMBOLS from the SAP GUI editor.

The item name is a string, so any description can be used; the cost is a packed number with a two-decimal limit, so prices will make sense; and quantity is an integer, so you can only have whole numbers.

The `AT-SELECTION-SCREEN` event is where you can define data validations. Here, the `MESSAGE` command throws an error if the user entered a quantity of over 999, determined with an `IF` statement checking the `QUANTITY` parameter.

In the `START-OF-SELECTION` event, declare `d_total` to store the total cost. The variable is another packed decimal, because you want the total to be limited to two decimal places. Then, calculate the total by multiplying the cost and quantity. Finally, write the result to the screen, and use chained statements to keep the output to a single line.

Summary

In this chapter, you learned the basic building blocks for any ABAP application. You learned how to create ABAP programs, variables, and the various data types that are available, and how to process the data contained in your variables using various arithmetic and math functions. You also added some binary logic through `IF` statements and loops. The chapter also covered how to interface with the user with classic ABAP selection screens and finally covered some debugging basics in both Eclipse and SAP GUI.

With these skills, you can now create and maintain ABAP programs that do not interface with a database!

Creating Data Dictionary Objects

The ABAP Data Dictionary builds on the basic data types covered in Chapter 2 to encompass domains, data elements, and transparent tables. These objects become tables in your database system. As a developer, you can create tables and query them without worrying about the type of database that is being used, because the data dictionary is able to work with many different database types.

This chapter starts with some database basics and covers how to design a database using an entity relationship diagram (ERD) and database normalization. Then we will go over the different types of data dictionary objects used in the SAP flights example tables, and you'll create your own custom data dictionary objects.

What Is a Data Dictionary?

A *data dictionary* is where database objects are created and maintained. You don't create any database objects directly in your database system; you create them only in the data dictionary.

Some of the terminology around an SAP system may be slightly different than what you may have learned when studying database systems, and if you're new to the idea of database systems, then all of this is also new. This is an introductory book, so we'll cover this topic (starting with the basic building blocks of a database system) in the following subsections.

Terminology

What Is a Database?

Before understanding what a data dictionary is, you must understand what a database is.

3 Creating Data Dictionary Objects

Excel workbook example

The simplest example of a database is an Excel workbook. A workbook contains multiple sheets of data, which can be connected in some way. For example, think of one sheet as a list of customers with basic contact information and another sheet as a list of customer purchases as shown in Figure 3.1. The customer probably has a unique name or ID to tie the two sheets together.

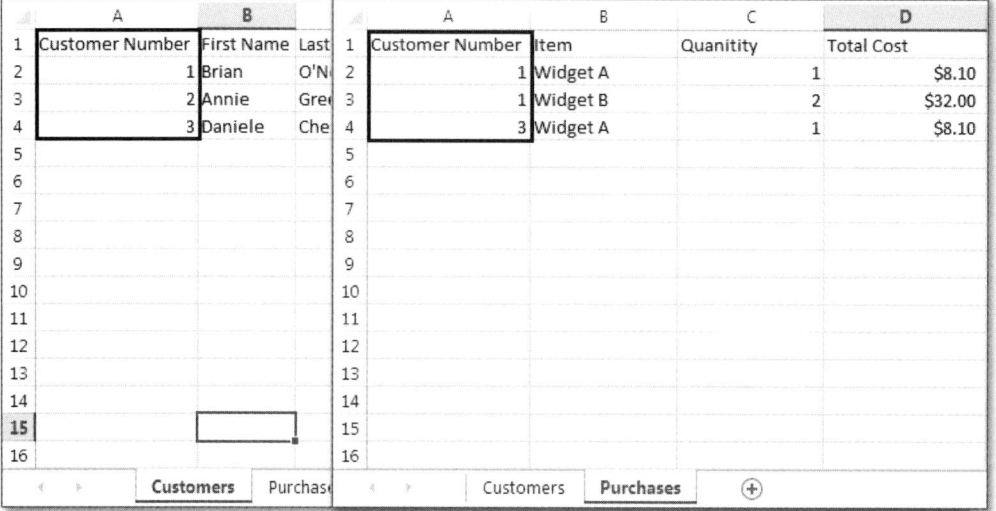

Figure 3.1 An Excel Workbook with Two Sheets: a List of Customers and a List of Customer Purchases

Tables

A database works the same way; just change the name "sheet" to "table." A *database* is a collection of tables that can have relationships. Databases can have thousands of tables with millions of rows, making them much more powerful than that Excel workbook we were talking about. A database is usually drawn as a long cylinder as shown in Figure 3.2 with an image depicting tables that would be stored within that database. The SAP term for a table is *transparent table*. A transparent table is defined in the data dictionary and stored in your database system.

What Is a Data Dictionary? 3

Figure 3.2 Conceptual Drawing of a Database

There are many database systems available, such as Microsoft SQL Server, Oracle, MaxDB, IBM DB2, and SAP HANA. All of those systems are supported by SAP NetWeaver, and because the data dictionary is what actually creates tables, you don't need to worry about which system is being used. As we mentioned in Chapter 1, the new S/4 HANA systems only run on SAP HANA databases.

Database systems

Data Elements

Now that you understand what a database is, it's time to get into data dictionary objects. When creating a typical Excel sheet, what's the first thing you do? You probably create a header row that explains what the data in each row means. The data dictionary takes on the role of that header data using *data elements*, which describe a column on the transparent table. The header in Figure 3.3 would correspond to data elements within a transparent table.

Customer Number	First Name	Last Name	Address	City	Region	Country
1	Brian	O'Neill	555 Lookout Rd	Reno	NV	USA
2	Annie	Greenhalgh	321 Clock Way	Portland	OR	USA
3	Daniele	Chessa	223 Via Bidone	Torino	PI	Italy

Figure 3.3 Example of a Table with the Header Highlighted

The data element does more than just give a description for table columns, though. In Excel, you can give something a name and enter any kind of data, but in the data dictionary you can define a *domain* to go

Domains

99

with that description, which describes the type of data that can be used with the data types discussed in Chapter 2. The domain restricts values to a given data type. This means, for example, that a domain of type i can't hold a decimal value. The domain definition will also be carried on to the table created in the backend database. The relationship between a table, domain and data type is illustrated in Figure 3.4.

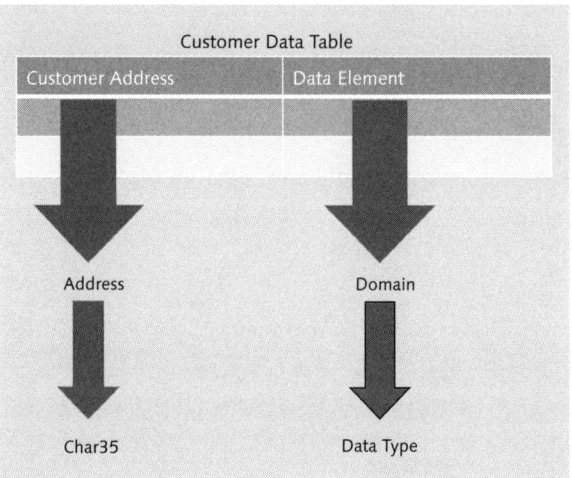

Figure 3.4 Data Element, Domain, and Data Type Relationship

Entity Relationship Diagrams

ERD Before we go further into the data dictionary, we need to cover *entity relationship diagrams*. ERDs form a universally recognized data modeling technique for any relational database management system.

 What Is a Relational Database Management System?

A *relational database management system* (RDBMS) is a database system built on the relational database model. A relational database is built on tables with rows and columns and a unique key for each row. Whenever you read about databases or tables in this book, you're reading about relational databases within an RDBMS.

There are nonrelational database systems, including NoSQL systems such as MongoDB, which has become more popular in recent years. These types of systems are far outside the scope of this book.

Entity Relationship Diagrams 3

An ERD is made of a collection of *entities*, and an entity represents a transparent table. The data inside the entity is a list of the different columns within the table. Entities also contain keys. A *primary key* is one or more columns that uniquely identifies a row, indicated by PK in the leftmost column. Figure 3.5 shows a table of flights, with Airline, FlightID, and FlightDate making up the primary key and other data elements listed to describe that flight.

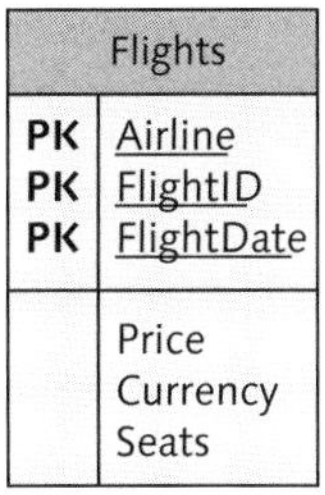

Entities

	Flights
PK	Airline
PK	FlightID
PK	FlightDate
	Price
	Currency
	Seats

Figure 3.5 Example Flights Entity

Because each item in the Flights entity corresponds to a column in a table, you can easily visualize this data as a table, such as in Table 3.1.

Airline	Flight ID	FlightDate	Price	Currency	Seats
American Airlines	1024	1/1/2016	100	USD	50
American Airlines	1025	1/1/2016	150	USD	50

Table 3.1 Records in Flights Table

Database Normalization

In this section, we will cover database normalization. Some of the rules around database normalization may not apply when working with SAP HANA based databases as a result of its column oriented architecture.

Assuming that the Flights table is the only table that you have, there are a few issues with it. First, we'll cover what those issues are, then we'll examine how to fix those issues using database normalization.

Looking at Table 3.1 what would happen if American Airlines had a merger and changed its name? You would have to update every row that lists American Airlines. This is called an *update anomaly*.

Update, deletion and insert anomalies

Creating Data Dictionary Objects

Because you only have the Flights table, if an airline had no flights, it would no longer exist in the system. However, maybe the airline has flights, but you just don't have any listed. This is known as a *deletion anomaly*.

The flight example didn't include the bookings for that flight. If it did, then a BookingID primary key would need to be added, and you'd need to create a new row every time a booking was created. This would result in a lot of redundant data being stored, as shown in Figure 3.6. This is called an *insert anomaly*.

Airline	FlightID	FlightDate	BookingID	Booking Name	Price	Currency	Seats
American Airlines	1024	1/1/2016	1	Brian ONeill	100	USD	50
American Airlines	1024	1/1/2016	2	Howard Hughs	100	USD	50
American Airlines	1024	1/1/2016	3	John Smith	100	USD	50
American Airlines	1024	1/1/2016	4	Annie Greenhalgh	100	USD	50
American Airlines	1025	1/1/2016	1	Daniel Jackson	150	USD	50
American Airlines	1025	1/1/2016	2	George Hill	150	USD	50

Figure 3.6 Tracking the BookingID and Booking Name in a Single Table

Database normalization — You can use the process of *database normalization* to move redundant data elements out of your table and into their own tables. Proper normalization, known as third normal form, will remove the anomalies noted previously. When your database is normalized, you need show the relationships among the different tables in your ERD. Take a look at Figure 3.7 for an example.

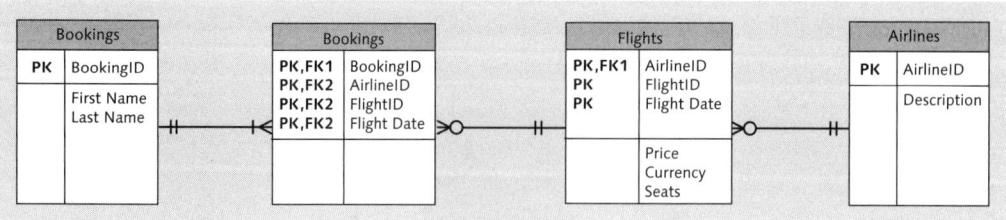

Figure 3.7 Normalized ERD with Separate Tables for Bookings and Airlines

In a third normal form table, all of the non-key attributes are dependent on a table key. In the example, the airline was moved to an airline table, so you only store the airline key in your flight table. Now, if you change the description of an airline in the airline table, it affects the description every time the airline is referenced. This also means that you have a record for an airline whether or not that airline has any existing flights. In addition, bookings are stored in their own table that references the Flights table. That means that any flight or booking changes can occur completely independent of each other.

Third normal form table

Relationships in ERDs

After creating additional tables, we can indicate how they're related using crow's foot notation. The *foreign key* (FK) attribute indicates attributes that are used to find related records in another table. Using the foreign key for AirlineID (i.e., AA) in the Flights table, you can find the airline description (i.e., American Airlines) for any airlines referenced.

Foreign keys

In the Figure 3.7 ERD, we used crow's foot notation (see Figure 3.8) to indicate some information about the relationships between the different tables.

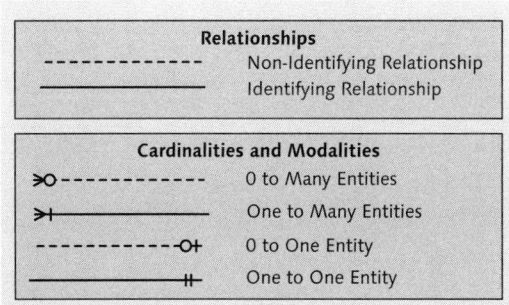

Figure 3.8 List of Crow's Foot Notations

The solid line between two entities indicates an *identifying relationship*, meaning that the relationship is created using the primary key of the other table. The relationship between the Flights table and Airline table in Figure 3.7 is an identifying relationship because AirlineID is part of the primary keys of both tables.

Types of relationships

A dotted line between two entities indicates a *nonidentifying relationship*, meaning that the relationship is not based on the primary key of the other table. There are no nonidentifying relationships in Figure 3.7.

Cardinalities and modalities

Cardinalities refers to the maximum number of times that an entity can be used in a relationship and *modalities* to the minimum number of times that an entity can be used in a relationship. Cardinalities are indicated by the first symbol on the relationship line and the modalities by the second symbol.

In the *zero-to-many relationship*, the modality is zero, indicated by the zero next to the three lines indicating the many cardinality. This means that the entity that the symbols are connecting to may have between zero and any number of entities in the relationship. This type of relationship exists between the Flights table and the Airport table in Figure 3.7 because an airport could have between zero and any number of flights.

In the *one-to many-relationship*, the modality is one, indicated by the straight line next to the three lines representing the many cardinality. This means that the entity that the symbols are connecting to must have between one and any number of entities in the relationship. This type of relationship exists between the Bookings and Bookings_flights tables in Figure 3.7, because a booking is required to have between at least one and any number of flights.

In the *zero-to-one relationship*, the modality is zero, indicated by the zero next to the single straight line representing the one cardinality. This means that the entity that the symbols are connecting to may have from zero to one entity in the relationship. This type of relationship does not exist in Figure 3.7 because we require at least one airline for each flight.

In the *one-to-one relationship*, the modality is one, indicated by the straight line next to a second straight line indicating a cardinality of one. This means that the entity that the symbols are connecting to must have one and only one entity in the relationship. An example of this relationship exists for the airline table in Figure 3.7: Each flight must have a single airline.

The Flight Data Model

What about a Many-to-Many Relationship?

When looking at Figure 3.7, you'll notice that every time there is a relationship with "to many" on one side, there is a "to one" relationship on the other side.

Because a booking can have many flights and flights can have many bookings, can we have a relationship with "to many" on both sides? No, we can't!

This is why we use the *junction table* called Bookings_flights in the middle, which has a relationship between bookings and flights as shown in Figure 3.7. The junction table facilitates the *many-to-many relationship* between the two tables because it has a one-to-many relationship with the Bookings table and a zero-to-many relationship with the Flights table.

It's much easier to design a normalized database using an ERD than to design it as you create it in the data dictionary screens. An ERD is at a high enough level that it can be used to validate your design with a user before you start creating the tables or writing code.

Why use an ERD?

The Flight Data Model

The last section used the example of bookings and flights because there is already a flight data model in every ABAP system. These flight tables are used in the ABAP documentation and training provided by SAP. The flights data model contains many more tables than the ones covered in the ERD diagram. For our purposes, we'll focus on using these tables from the perspective of someone trying to book a flight.

In the ERD diagram shown in Figure 3.7, a junction table allows bookings to have multiple flights. However, the SAP bookings table only allows for one flight to be booked! You're going to learn to create your own tables by adding tables that allow for bookings that have multiple flights.

Flight Example ERD

In the ERD shown in Figure 3.9, you can see how the flight data tables are set up as provided by SAP. This text won't cover every table or every field, but you can open the SAPBC_DATAMODEL package in Transaction SE80 and find all of the flight-related tables. Also, MANDT is not listed as a field, but it exists in every table and is always part of the primary key and a foreign key to table T000, which contains records for all of the clients for any system. MANDT is required for tables even in systems that use only one client.

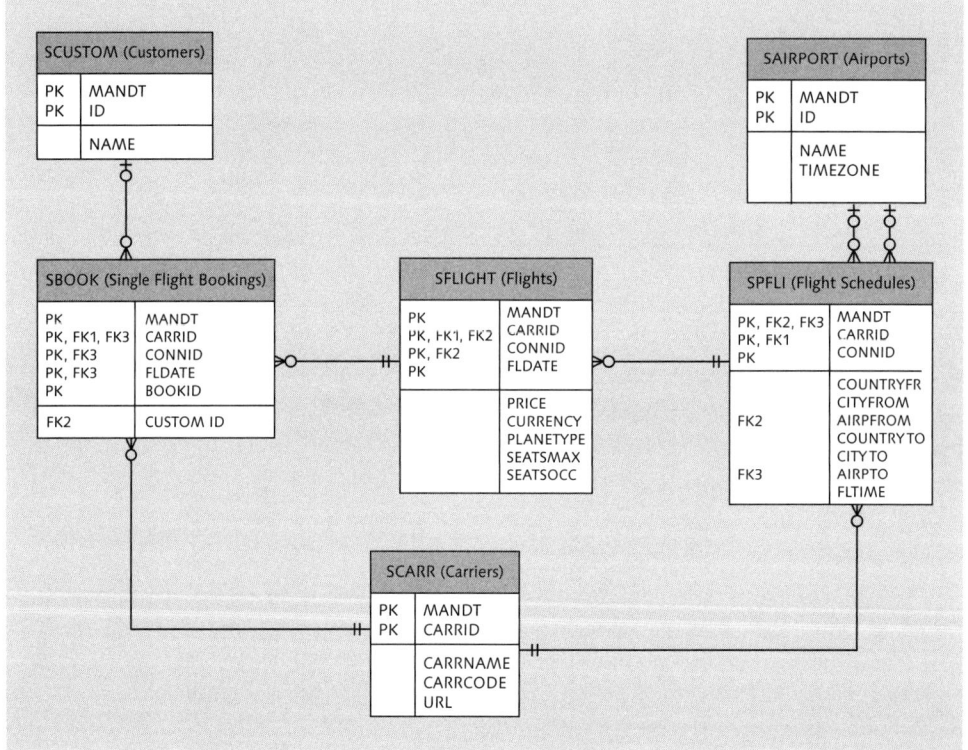

Figure 3.9 ERD Showing Standard SAP Tables

The standard tables shown in Figure 3.9 can be described as follows:

> SCUSTOM
> This table stores information about your customers.

> SAIRPORT
> This table stores all of your airport IDs and information about airports.

> SCARR
This table stores all of your carriers (airlines).

> SPFLI
This table stores the flight schedules for each airline—for example, flight 17 for American Airlines flies to San Francisco from New York and leaves at 11 a.m.

> SFLIGHT
This table stores the actual flights for a flight schedule—for example, flight 17 for American Airlines will fly January 12 and will cost $500.

> SBOOK
This table stores bookings for single flights; this means that a booking can only contain one flight.

You can see that the tables are normalized, because the master data tables (such as airports and customers) are all separated out of the tables in which they are referenced multiple times. This means that changes to customer information will take place in table SCUSTOM and not affect the bookings in table SBOOK.

Normalized tables

Because the tables provided by SAP do not include the ability to book multiple flight bookings, we are going to create two new tables, which are displayed in the ERD shown in Figure 3.10. We will explain how to create those tables in the next section.

Create new tables

The new tables are as follows:

> ZBOOK
Add your own table to handle the bookings, because the SAP standard table uses the CONNID (flight ID) and CARRID (carrier ID) fields as part of the table's primary key. You'll use those keys in your junction table instead, allowing one booking to have multiple flights, which may have multiple carriers.

> ZSBOOK_SFLIGHT
This is the junction table that will allow you to create a single booking that contains multiple flights, which can come from multiple carriers.

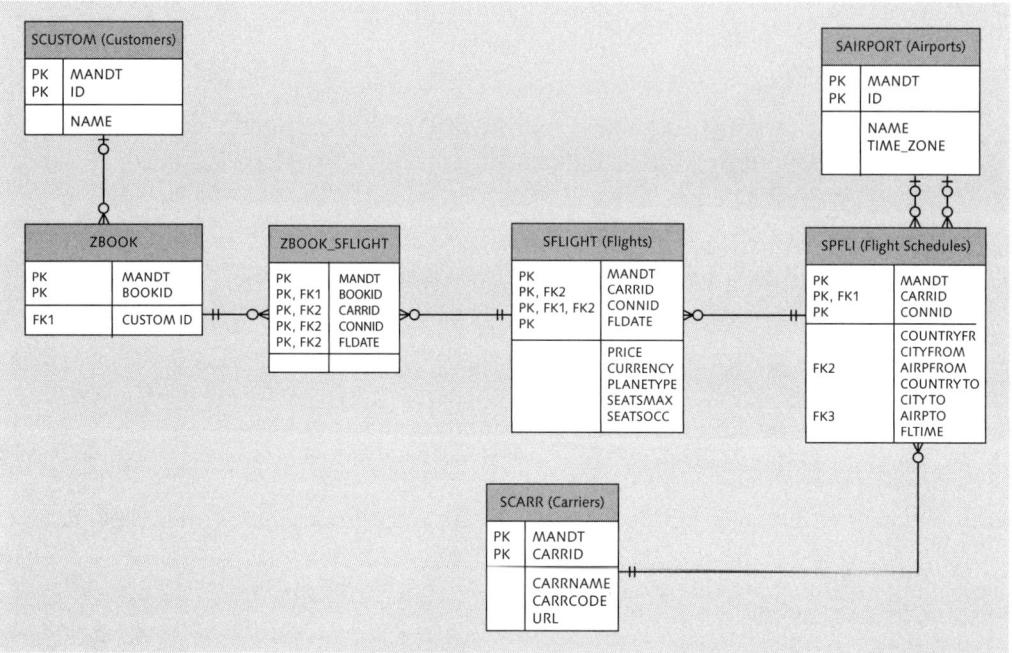

Figure 3.10 ERD of Flight Tables with Custom Tables Added

Creating and Editing Tables

The following sections will cover how to create transparent tables inside ABAP. Transparent tables represent a single table in a database. You will never have to create or edit the tables directly in the database system, and these instructions will work for any type of database system connected to your ABAP system.

Other table types — Transparent tables are not the only type of table in ABAP. *Pooled tables* and *clustered tables* are special types that store multiple tables within a single table in the database system. You may have to read data from those types of tables from legacy applications, but you should never create new pooled or clustered tables. These types of tables also no longer exist in SAP HANA systems.

Viewing the Flight Table Configuration

Before you start creating our own tables, let's take a look at the existing flights table. Run Transaction SE11 and enter "SFLIGHT" in the DATABASE TABLE textbox. Then, click DISPLAY as shown in Figure 3.11. Transaction SE11 is a single place where you can edit all types of data dictionary objects.

SE11

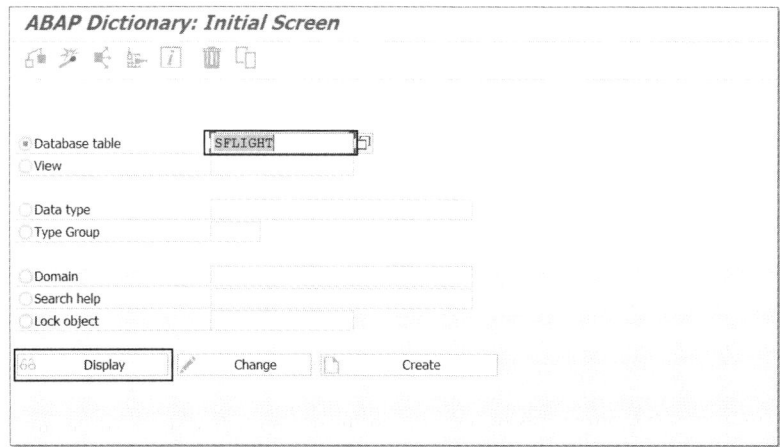

Figure 3.11 Displaying Table SFLIGHT in Transaction SE11

On the ATTRIBUTES tab, you'll see some basic technical information about the table SFLIGHT (Figure 3.12): who last changed the table, when the table was last changed, the package, and the original language. The last changed and package information can help when trying to investigate a table bug.

Attributes

 Searching for More in the Package

Expert Tip

> Especially when working with standard SAP-provided tables and programs, you may not be sure about the name of the program or data you're looking for. By getting the package of a table or program, you can then look up everything contained in that package. Sometimes, this can be a good investigative tool for solving what seems to be an unsolvable problem.

3 Creating Data Dictionary Objects

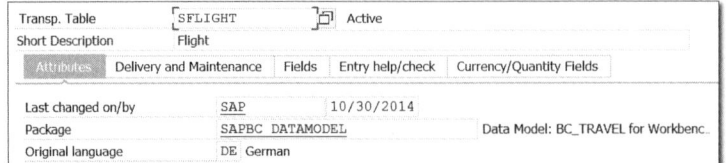

Figure 3.12 The Attributes Tab Displaying a Table

Delivery and maintenance

The DELIVERY AND MAINTENANCE tab shown in Figure 3.13 allows you to set the delivery class and the table view maintenance options. There are many delivery class options, but the ones we are going to cover are the application table and the customizing table class, which will be the only ones you should use in your custom applications.

Delivery class types

An application table (A) will contain master data, such as a list of airports, or transaction data, such as a list of bookings. Table SFLIGHT is set as an application table.

A customizing table (C) will contain records that customize how your application operates. For example, you may have a customizing table that switches whether or not bookings can have multiple flights. This customizing table can change the way a program works without changing any code.

The DATA BROWSER/TABLE VIEW MAINT. dropdown allows you to choose whether the data can be maintained (meaning data being added, updated or deleted) using a standard table maintenance program. There are three options for this drop down: DISPLAY/MAINTENANCE ALLOWED WITH RESTRICTIONS, DISPLAY/MAINTENANCE ALLOWED and DISPLAY/MAINTENANCE NOT ALLOWED.

Both of the DISPLAY/MAINTENANCE ALLOWED options allow users to view the records in the table with standard transactions such as se16n and sm30. The option WITH RESTRICTIONS means that the user would have to search for the specific records to change before changing the table, which may be required for larger tables to ensure that the user is changing the correct items. Without restrictions, means that the user can choose to edit the table with all records open to be edited. And lastly, the DISPLAY/MAINTENANCE NOT ALLOWED option prevents users from viewing or changing the table without using a program which directly calls the table using sql queries.

Creating and Editing Tables   3

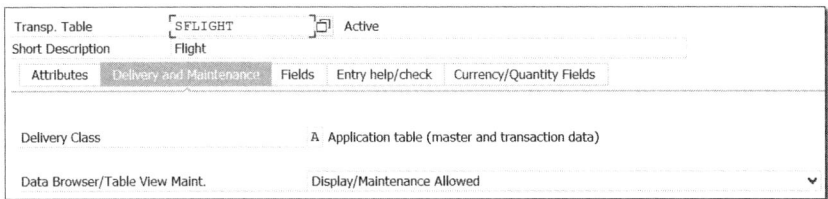

Figure 3.13 The Delivery and Maintenance Tab Displaying a Table

By default, the display table screen opens with the FIELDS tab selected as shown in Figure 3.14. *Field* is another word for a table's column. Each field describes a column in the database table. Fields can only contain letters, numbers, and the underscore and will always be in all uppercase. When looking at SAP standard tables, sometimes the naming of fields may not make sense. That's usually because many tables were initially created in German, so the field name may represent an abbreviated German word; however, the short description is translatable and will show the description for your selected language.

Fields

The first field listed in the left-hand column for table SFLIGHT is MANDT, which is added to most tables to indicate the client for which the data is relevant. It should always be part of a primary key and listed as the first field when used in a table. Customers have different clients for many reasons, and you should always add a MANDT field to your tables, even if your system only uses one client. The only time MANDT is not used is for cross-client customization tables, which configure system-wide settings regardless of client.

MANDT

The second column in the FIELDS tab contains the KEY checkbox, which indicates which fields make up the primary key for the table. For table SFLIGHT, the primary key is made of MANDT, CARRID, CONNID, and FLDATE or client, airline code, flight connection number, and flight date, respectively.

Keys

The next column is titled INITIAL VALUES and indicates whether an initial value will always be required in the database when updating a table. This is the same as setting the NOT NULL flag directly in a database. All key fields must have the INITIAL VALUES checkbox selected. An example of an initial value is 0 for an int data type.

Initial values

111

Data element   The next column shows the DATA ELEMENT for each field. The data element provides technical details about a given field. Following that are the DATA TYPE, LENGTH, and DECIMAL columns, which are populated based on information in the data element. These columns describe the basic data type that is being stored in the database and thus should correspond to a basic data type, like the ones covered in Chapter 2. For example, the `CARRID` field is a character (c) type of length 3.

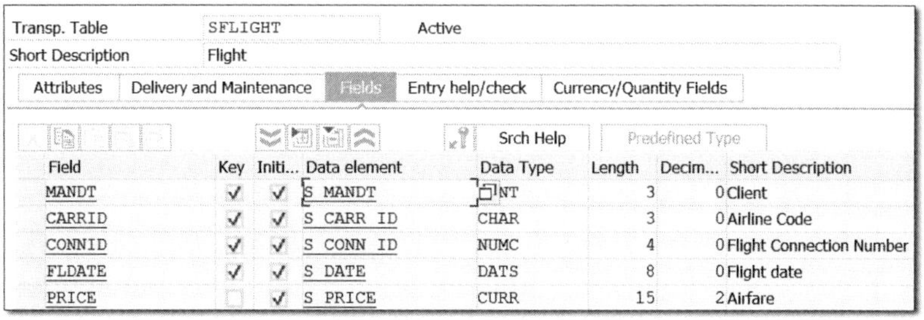

Field	Key	Initi...	Data element	Data Type	Length	Decim...	Short Description
MANDT	✓	✓	S_MANDT	INT	3	0	Client
CARRID	✓	✓	S_CARR_ID	CHAR	3	0	Airline Code
CONNID	✓	✓	S_CONN_ID	NUMC	4	0	Flight Connection Number
FLDATE	✓	✓	S_DATE	DATS	8	0	Flight date
PRICE		✓	S_PRICE	CURR	15	2	Airfare

Figure 3.14 The Fields Tab Displaying a Table

Entry Help/Check   In previous sections, we discussed foreign keys. You can see the foreign keys by selecting the ENTRY HELP/CHECK tab shown in Figure 3.16. The foreign keys here are used to tell classic screens possible options for the user to select as well as to require that whatever is entered exists in the table that the foreign key is connected to.

The field, data element, and data type fields are the same that we saw in the FIELDS tab, but are followed by the FOREIGN KEY column, which contains a checkbox for each field designated as a foreign key.

The *check table's* primary key contains the foreign key for the table you're currently looking at. You can open the display view for any of the check tables by double-clicking its name.

The next column, ORIGIN OF THE INPUT HELP, indicates the method to be used when creating input help for programs using this field. An example of input help is shown in Figure 3.15 for a program requiring the selection of an airport. That input help worked with a basic select option on airports without having to write any code outside of declaring the select option as we saw in Chapter 2.

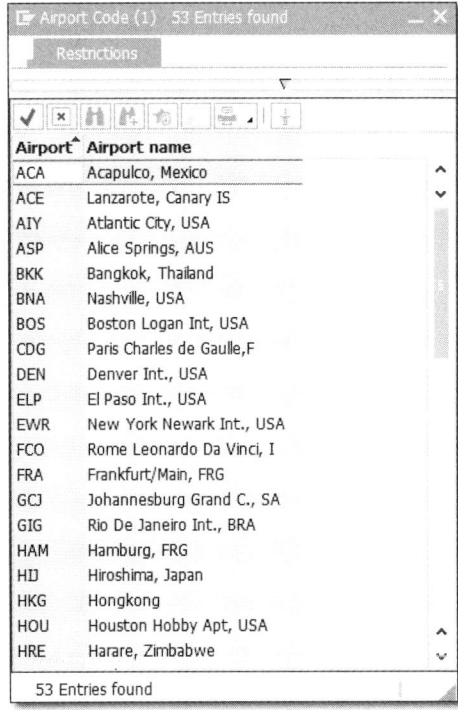

Figure 3.15 Input Help for Selecting an Airport

The search help (SRCH HELP) column shows search help for the given field. Search help can be defined here in the field, in the data element, or in the check table.

The last column under the ENTRY HELP/CHECK tab is DOMAIN (Figure 3.16), which we'll return to later in the chapter.

Field	Data element	Data Type	Foreign K...	Check table	Origin of the input help	Srch Help	D...	Domain
MANDT	S_MANDT	CLNT	✓	T000	Input help implemented with ch	H T000		MANDT
CARRID	S_CARR_ID	CHAR	✓	SCARR	Input help implemented with ch	H SCARR		S CARR ID
CONNID	S_CONN_ID	NUMC	✓	SPFLI	Input help implemented with ch	H SPFLI		S CONN ID
FLDATE	S_DATE	DATS			Input help based on data type			S DATE
PRICE	S_PRICE	CURR						S PRICE

Figure 3.16 The Entry Help/Check Tab Displaying a Table

Creating Data Dictionary Objects

Currency/
Quantity fields

The last tab when displaying a table is the CURRENCY/QUANTITY FIELDS tab, shown below in Figure 3.17. You'll learn more about currencies and quantities in more detail in Chapter 9, but for now it's important to know that fields can be assigned a currency or quantity in the table definition here.

In table SFLIGHT, the PRICE field is assigned a currency via the CURRENCY field. This allows you to know if the price is in US dollars or Euros. A QUANTITY field could indicate, for example, that the quantity of something is recorded in inches.

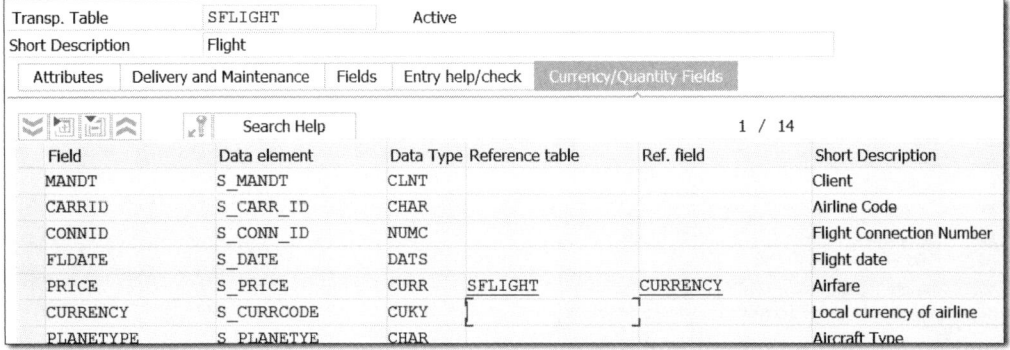

Figure 3.17 The Currency/Quantity Fields Tab Displaying a Table

Technical settings

You can click the TECHNICAL SETTINGS button pictured in Figure 3.18 to view the technical settings of the table (see the result for table SFLIGHT in Figure 3.19).

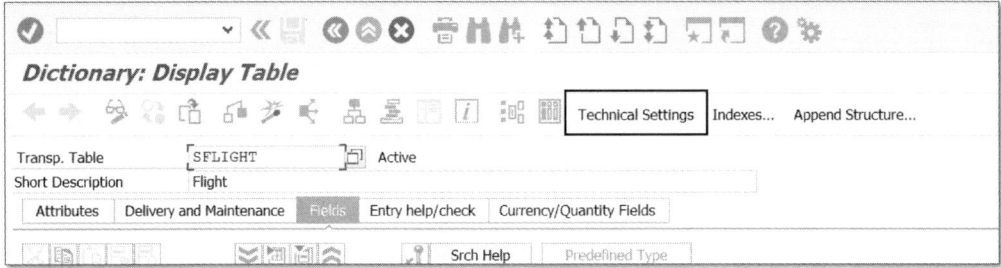

Figure 3.18 The Technical Settings Button

Creating and Editing Tables 3

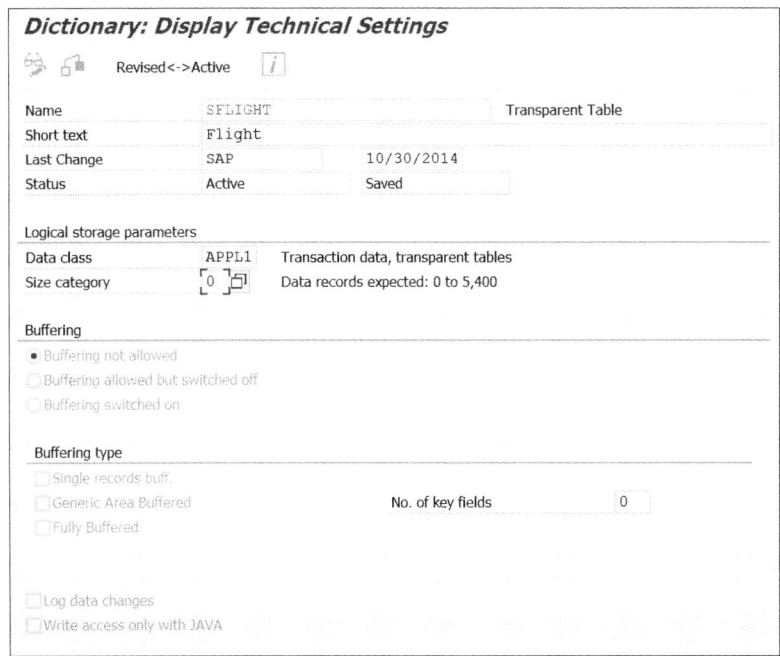

Figure 3.19 Table SFLIGHT Technical Settings

The first section in the technical settings (Figure 3.19) is LOGICAL STORAGE PARAMETERS, in which you can store a data class and size category. This information is used with Oracle and Informix database systems to determine where the database tables are physically stored. If you're not using one of those database types, you should still fill out these fields as accurately as possible. Table 3.2 describes the different data classes.

Logical storage parameters

Data Class	Description
APPL0: Master Data	Master data is frequently read and rarely updated. For example, in Figure 3.19 customer and airport data rarely changes.
APPL1: Transaction Data	Transaction data is frequently updated. An example of transaction data is bookings for flights.

Table 3.2 Types of Data Classes

Data Class	Description
APPL2: Organizational and Customizing Data	Organizational and customizing data typically only change when the system is first configured. An example of this is the configuration tables that configure how your SAP system works. This type of table could also be used to configure a custom application.

Table 3.2 Types of Data Classes (Cont.)

The second option under LOCAL STORAGE PARAMETERS shown in Figure 3.19 is SIZE CATEGORY, which is meant to determine how much space will be required for your table in the database; the amount of space can be increased in the future.

We'll come back to the BUFFERING options shown in Figure 3.19 in Chapter 4 when we discuss accessing the database. For now, just remember that this is where the buffering options are located.

The LOG DATA CHANGES checkbox at the bottom of Figure 3.19 will turn on logging for your table, meaning that every time an update occurs in the table, an entry will be added to the log table. This should only be used when there is a real need for table logging; it will slow down updates to your table.

The WRITE ACCESS ONLY WITH JAVA checkbox at the bottom of Figure 3.19 marks the table as only changeable from within a Java program. This is an ABAP book, so leave that unchecked.

Viewing the Flight Data

Now that you understand more about the design of table `SFLIGHT`, let's take a look at the data. Click on the CONTENTS button pictured in Figure 3.20 to open the data browser. The data browser can also be accessed using Transaction SE16 or with more options in Transaction SE16N.

Figure 3.20 Table Contents Button in Transaction SE11

The data browser provides various selection options that you can enter to limit the results; you can add or remove any selection option in SETTINGS • FIELDS FOR SELECTION.

Data browser

> **Tip**
>
> Before continuing, check your user parameters by clicking on SETTINGS • USER PARAMETERS... and ensuring that ALV GRID display is selected. This setting will present the table results in the most modern and user-friendly ALV grid. You can also choose to have the field name or field label displayed in the user parameters. The field name will be the technical name for the field that you saw in SE11, such as FLDATE, and the field label will be a user-friendly description for that field, such as Flight Date.

You also have the option to change the total number of records to be displayed using the MAXIMUM NO. OF HITS text box shown at the bottom of the screen in Figure 3.21. Leave the options set to their defaults (blank) and click the EXECUTE button, highlighted in Figure 3.21 or press [F8].

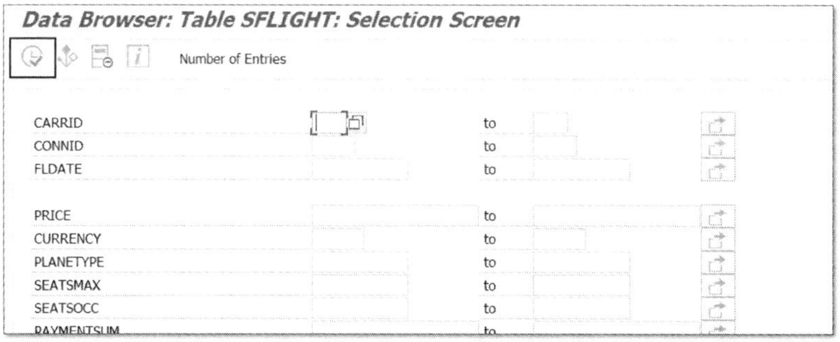

Figure 3.21 The Data Browser Screen

Because you left everything as default, you'll see up to 200 records from the top of table SFLIGHT in a view that should remind you of an Excel spreadsheet. Because table SFLIGHT does not contain 200 or more records, you can see the total number of records selected (108) in the header of the page as shown in Figure 3.22.

117

Creating Data Dictionary Objects

MAND	CARRI	CONNID	FLDATE	PRICE	CURREN	PLANETYPE	SEATSM	SEATSOC	PAYMENTSU	SEATSMAX_B	SEATSOCC_B
300	AA	17	04/23/2014	422.94	USD	747-400	385	374	192,522.43	31	28
300	AA	17	07/02/2014	422.94	USD	747-400	385	371	193,063.84	31	30
300	AA	17	09/10/2014	422.94	USD	747-400	385	371	191,904.96	31	31
300	AA	17	11/19/2014	422.94	USD	747-400	385	371	192,298.20	31	30
300	AA	17	01/28/2015	422.94	USD	747-400	385	54	28,747.25	31	5
300	AA	17	04/08/2015	422.94	USD	747-400	385	66	34,516.18	31	5
300	AA	17	06/17/2015	422.94	USD	747-400	385	2	845.88	31	0
300	AZ	555	04/23/2014	185.00	EUR	A310-300	280	271	58,454.45	22	22

Figure 3.22 Data Browser Results Showing Table SFLIGHT Records

Setting Up the Flights Example

Transaction SE38

If your flight table does not have any data, you may need to load data into the provided flight model tables. To do this, run the SAPBC_DATA_GENERATOR program by entering Transaction SE38 in SAP GUI. Enter "SAPBC_DATA_GENERATOR" in the program textbox and press F8 or click the EXECUTE button as shown in Figure 3.23.

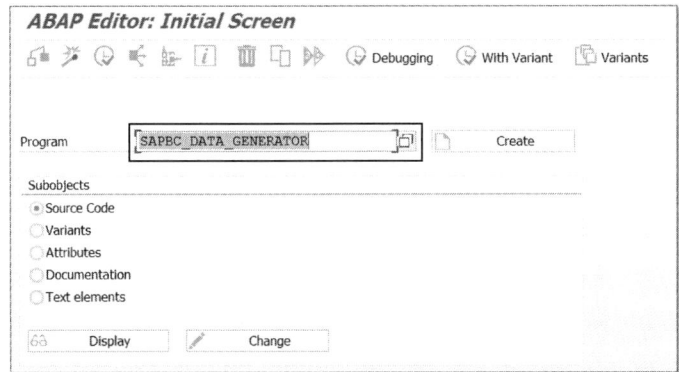

Figure 3.23 Running a Program from Transaction SE38

Once inside the program, select the STANDARD DATA RECORD radio button and click EXECUTE (Figure 3.24). This will create 26 flight schedules and 400 flights for you to use.

Creating and Editing Tables   3

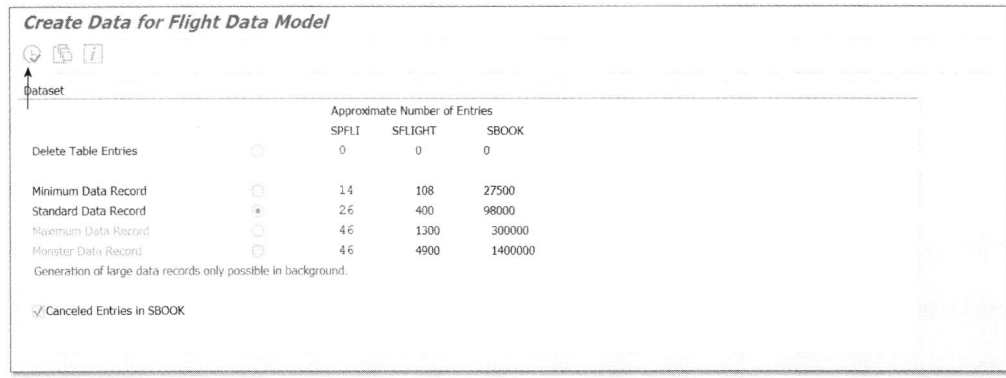

Figure 3.24 Create Flight Data

Creating an Append Structure

Back on the main display table screen, you can also see the APPEND STRUCTURE... button, which allows you to add additional columns to an existing SAP table. This can be useful when enhancing standard SAP functionality.

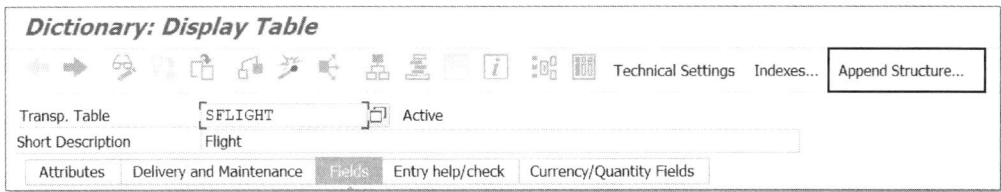

Figure 3.25 The Append Structure Button

Append the SFLIGHT structure to try this functionality out. First, click the APPEND STRUCTURE... button pictured in Figure 3.25. Then, set the append name to ZAWESOME and click the checkmark (Figure 3.26).

Create append structure

 Note

Append structures must be prefixed with a Z to indicate that they're custom objects and not standard SAP objects.

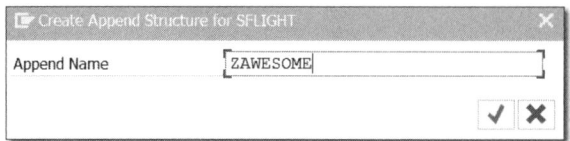

Figure 3.26 Creating a New Append Structure

You will notice that the CREATE APPEND STRUCTURE screen has the same tabs as in the VIEW TABLE screen. That means you have all of the same options for your new structure that are available when creating tables—but fields are called components here.

In the COMPONENTS tab, add a component named ZZIS_AWESOME, set TYPING METHOD to TYPES and COMPONENT TYPE to BOOLEAN, and press ⏎ Enter. You must always prefix your appending components with ZZ so that it doesn't conflict with future SAP field names. Yes, that's right: two Zs, not just one like in append structure ID and program names.

You'll see that the grayed-out information, such as data type and short description, is automatically filled in as shown in Figure 3.27. This information comes from the component type, which I'll cover in more detail later in the chapter.

You can also click the SHOW APPENDING OBJECT button located in the middle of Figure 3.27 to see what the table will look like with the new fields appended on the end.

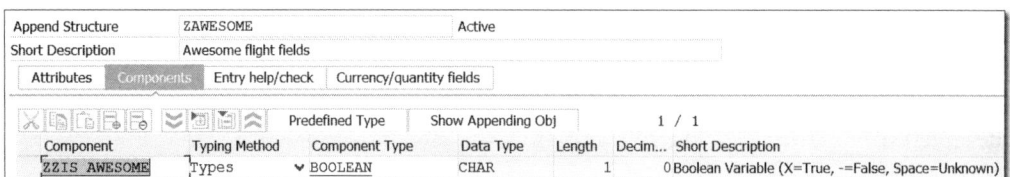

Figure 3.27 Adding Details to a New Append Structure

Next, click EXTRAS • ENHANCEMENT CATEGORY, select the checkmark for the informational message, and then select the CANNOT BE ENHANCED radio button (Figure 3.28), and click the COPY button. You don't want your custom tables and append structures to be enhanced; they should be directly changed, because they're not standard SAP objects.

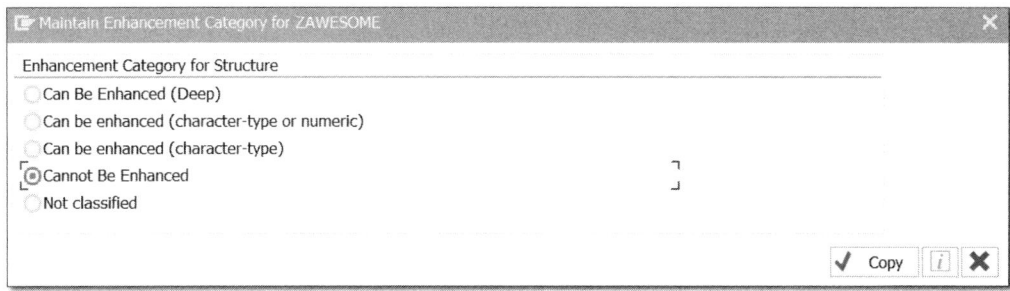

Figure 3.28 Enhancement Categories

Just as you had to activate your ABAP code, you'll need to activate your appending structure, via the same ACTIVATE button shown below in Figure 3.29.

Activate structure

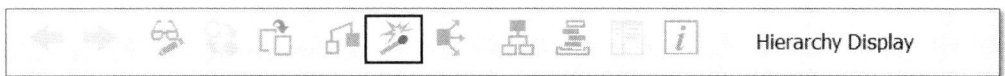

Figure 3.29 The Activate Button

Now that you have created the append structure, click SAVE and set the package to "$TMP" (or click the LOCAL OBJECT button) on the CREATE OBJECT DIRECTORY ENTRY popup.

After activating, you'll see the popup shown below in Figure 3.30 letting you know that warnings occurred during the activation. Don't worry about this; they're just warnings, not errors. Click YES to display the activation log (Figure 3.31).

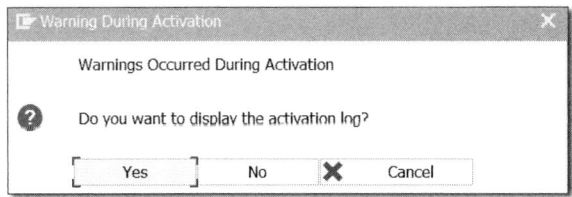

Figure 3.30 Warning during Activation Popup

The *activation log* can be displayed when activating various data dictionary objects and will show you any success, warning or error

Activation log

messages that occurred during the activation process as shown in Figure 3.31. When looking at the activation log, you'll notice that most of the records are actually success messages about objects that aren't SFLIGHT or your append structure. These other objects are structures, table types, and views that reference the table that you added your append structure to. Many of these structures are used in standard programs, meaning that values for your field will now be displayed in those standard programs.

Activation log warnings

The warnings in the activation log are indicated with a highlight and exclamation mark as shown in Figure 3.31. These are actually about standard tables such as SFLIGHT, which you can't adjust, so you can ignore these warnings.

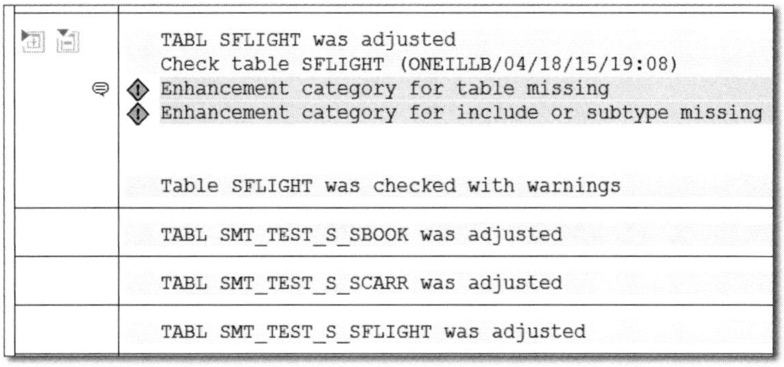

```
TABL SFLIGHT was adjusted
Check table SFLIGHT (ONEILLB/04/18/15/19:08)
⚠ Enhancement category for table missing
⚠ Enhancement category for include or subtype missing

Table SFLIGHT was checked with warnings

TABL SMT_TEST_S_SBOOK was adjusted

TABL SMT_TEST_S_SCARR was adjusted

TABL SMT_TEST_S_SFLIGHT was adjusted
```

Figure 3.31 The Activation Log from the Append Structure

Creating a Custom Transparent Table

Now that you've analyzed table SFLIGHTS to understand how tables are set up in ABAP, you're going to create some new tables for custom, multiflight bookings. Refer to Figure 3.10 to see the ERD of the required changes.

Create ZBOOK table

There are two custom tables that you need to create. First, create table ZBOOK. To do so, enter Transaction SE11, enter "ZBOOK" in the DATABASE TABLE textbox, and click the CREATE button highlighted in Figure 3.32.

You'll now be brought to the CHANGE TABLE screen with the DELIVERY AND MAINTENANCE tab selected. Enter a description for the table in

the SHORT DESCRIPTION textbox, such as "Custom Bookings Table". Set
DELIVERY CLASS to A and DATA BROWSER/TABLE VIEW MAINT. to DISPLAY/MAINTENANCE ALLOWED, as shown in Figure 3.33.

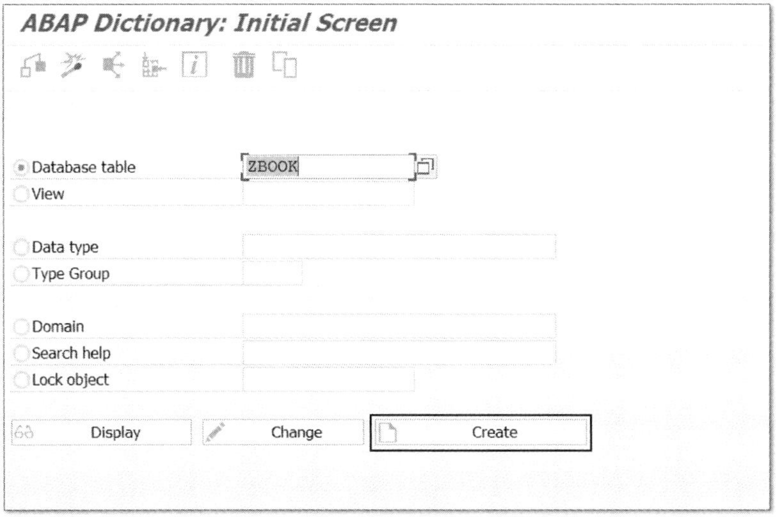

Figure 3.32 Creating Table ZBOOK in Transaction SE11

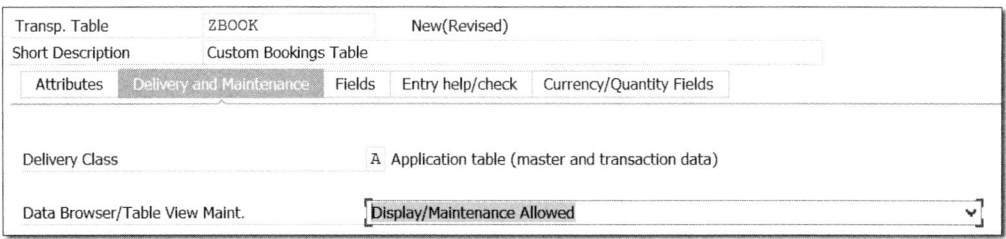

Figure 3.33 Delievery and Maintenance Settings for ZBOOK

Next, select the FIELDS tab. According to the ERD, there are three fields. MANDT should have the KEY and INITIAL VALUE checkboxes checked and a data element of MANDT. BOOKID should also have the KEY and INITIAL VALUE checkboxes checked and S_BOOK_ID as the data element. Finally, CUSTOMID should have only the INITIAL VALUES checkbox checked and S_CUSTOMER as the data element. The end result should match what is shown in Figure 3.34.

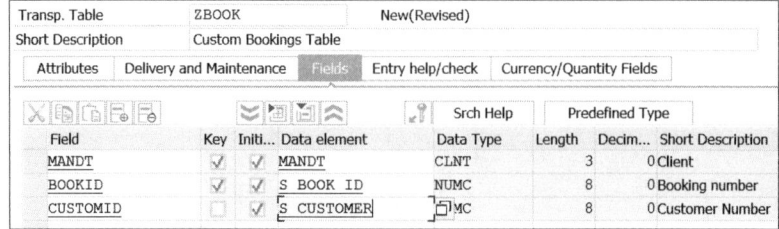

Figure 3.34 Fields for ZBOOK

Now, you need to set up the foreign keys. There are two foreign keys in this table: MANDT and CUSTOMID. To set the foreign keys, select the ENTRY HELP/CHECK tab, select the row for the MANDT field, and click the FOREIGN KEY button pictured in Figure 3.35.

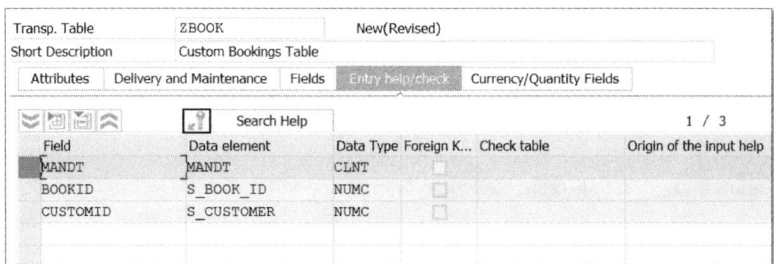

Figure 3.35 The Entry Help/Check Tab when Editing Table ZBOOK

You'll be prompted by the system asking if you want to create a proposal with values table T000 as check table as shown in Figure 3.36. This means that the system was able to detect an identifying primary key based on the data element for a given key. In this case, click YES, because T000 is the correct foreign key table for MANDT.

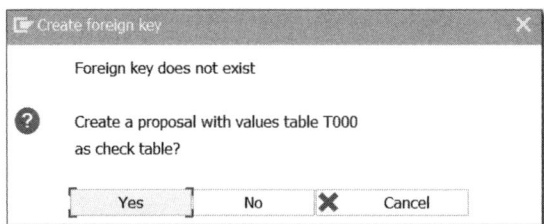

Figure 3.36 Popup when Creating a Foreign Key with a Detected Check Table

Next, you'll see the CREATE FOREIGN KEY popup. The SHORT TEXT textbox is an optional description field that you can use to store descriptions of your foreign key. A description is really not necessary, because MANDT is required for every client-dependent table. The check table T000 is already filled, because the system was able to determine the correct check table based on the data element.

The checkbox for CHECK REQUIRED in the SCREEN CHECK section indicates whether a screen using this field will be required to have a value that exists in the foreign key table. The ERROR MESSAGE selections allow you to select a custom error message if the required screen check fails. These should be left set to the default options for now, which are CHECK REQUIRED checked and ERROR MESSAGE options blank.

Next is the SEMANTIC ATTRIBUTES section. Select the radio button for KEY FIELDS/CANDIDATE, because this is an identifying relationship with table T000. Table 3.3 provides a description of all of the foreign key field type options.

Foreign key semantic attributes

Foreign Key Field Type	Description
Not specified	
Non-key-fields/candidates	This is a nonidentifying relationship, meaning that the foreign key field is not part of the primary key in the foreign key table. The ERD indicated this type of relationship with a dotted line.
Key fields/candidates	This is an identifying relationship, meaning that the foreign key field is a primary key in the foreign key table. The ERD indicated this type of relationship with a solid line.
Key fields of a text table	This is the same as the key fields/candidates option, except that an additional key not in our table is used to indicate the user's language.

Table 3.3 Foreign Key Field Types

Next is the CARDINALITY section. This is the same cardinality that we talked about when describing entity relationship diagrams. For the

Cardinality

MANDT foreign key, enter "1" and "CN" (Figure 3.37) for a one-to-many relationship. All of the cardinality options are described in Table 3.4.

Option	Description
1	One and only one record
C	Zero to one records
N	One to many records
CN	Zero to many records

Table 3.4 SAP Cardinality Options

Completed foreign key

Your completed MANDT foreign key should look like the screen shown in Figure 3.37.

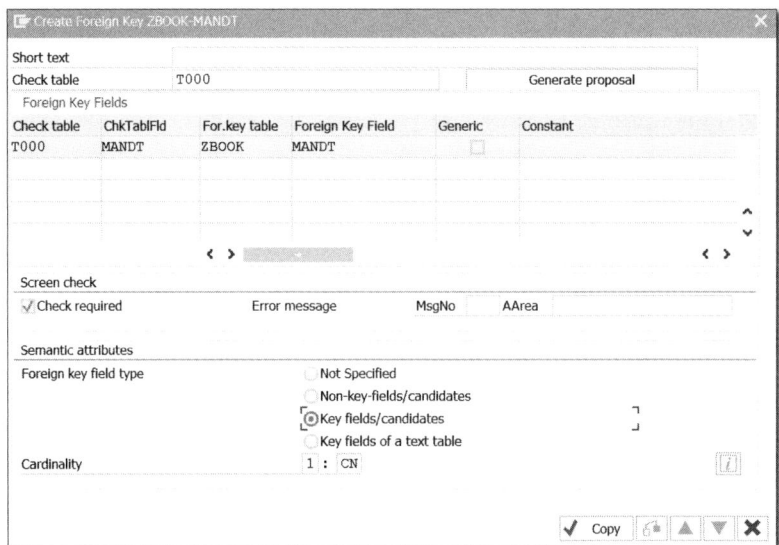

Figure 3.37 Creating the MANDT Foreign Key

Next, add a foreign key for CUSTOMID; click on the CUSTOMID field and click the FOREIGN KEY button. If the system does not suggest SCUSTOM as the check table, enter "SCUSTOM", click GENERATE PROPOSAL, and the correct fields will be populated. Next, click the screen check CHECK REQUIRED checkbox and set the FOREIGN KEY FIELD TYPE to KEY FIELDS/CANDIDATES and the CARDINALITY to `1:CN` as shown in Figure 3.38.

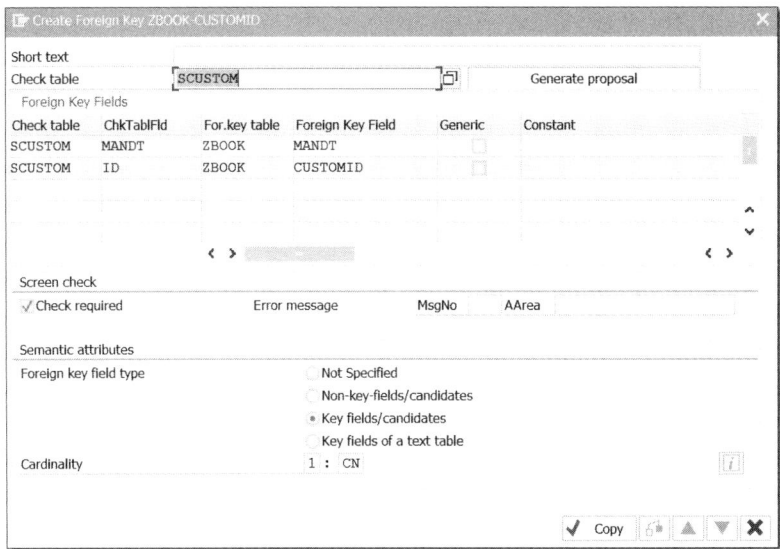

Figure 3.38 Creating the CUSTOMID Foreign Key

The ENTRY HELP/CHECK tab should now look like what we see in Figure 3.39 with the FOREIGN KEY checkbox checked and a check table listed for the `MANDT` and `CUSTOMID` fields.

Entry help/Check

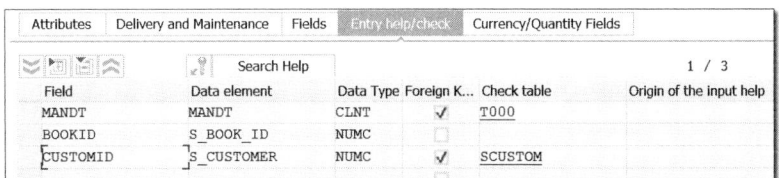

Figure 3.39 The Completed Entry Help/Check Tab

Next, click EXTRAS • ENHANCEMENT CATEGORY, click the checkmark for the informational message, and then select the CANNOT BE ENHANCED radio button, and click the COPY button.

Next, click the TECHNICAL SETTINGS button and set DATA CLASS to APPL1 and SIZE CATEGORY to 0. BUFFERING should remain set at

Technical settings

Buffering not allowed. Your technical settings should match what is shown in Figure 3.40. Click the Save button and click Back to return to the table.

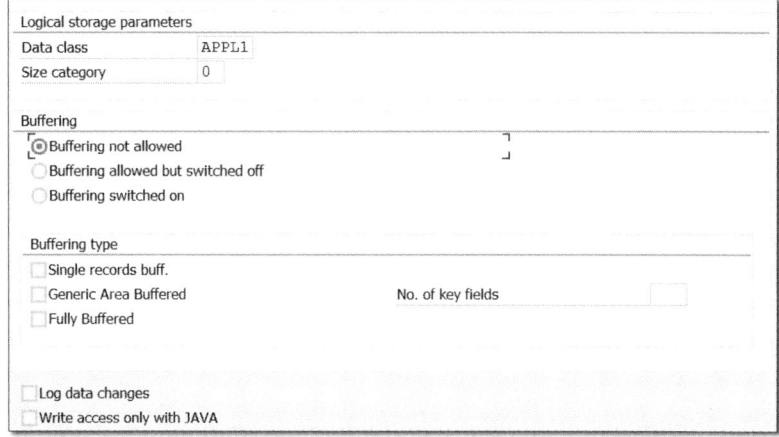

Figure 3.40 The Completed Technical Settings

Finally, click the Activate button to activate the table. Congratulations, you have created your first custom transparent table!

ZBOOK_SFLIGHT table

Next, create table ZBOOK_SFLIGHT following the same process we used to create the ZBOOK table. Go back to Transaction SE11 and enter the table name "ZBOOK_SFLIGHT" into the Database table textbox and click Create.

Next, change the Delivery and Maintenance tab to have a Delivery Class of A and to have the Data Browser/Table View Maint. Set to Allowed with Restrictions as shown below in Figure 3.41.

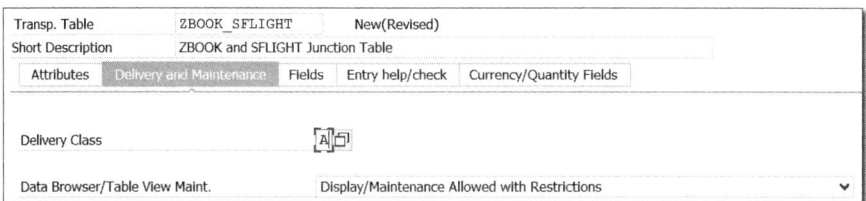

Figure 3.41 Delivery and Maintenance for Table ZBOOK_SFLIGHT

Next select the FIELDS tab and add the following fields:

- MANDT with the data element MANDT
- BOOKID with the data element S_BOOK_ID
- CARRID with the data element S_CARR_ID
- CONNID with the data element S_CONNID
- FLDATE with the data element S_DATE

Next select the KEY and INITIAL VALUES checkboxes for all of the fields. The final result should match what see below in Figure 3.42.

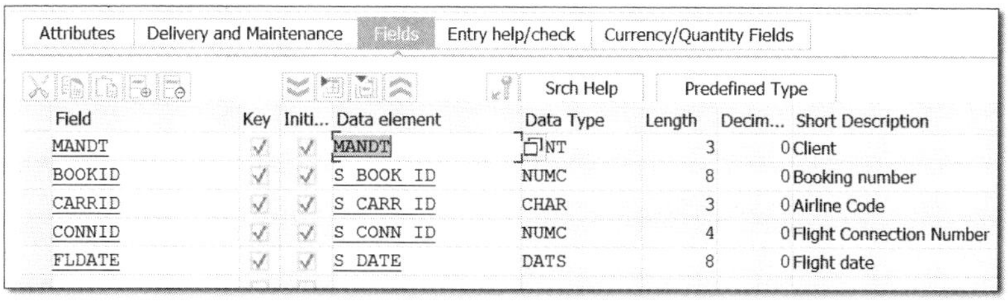

Field	Key	Initi...	Data element	Data Type	Length	Decim...	Short Description
MANDT	✓	✓	MANDT	INT	3	0	Client
BOOKID	✓	✓	S_BOOK_ID	NUMC	8	0	Booking number
CARRID	✓	✓	S_CARR_ID	CHAR	3	0	Airline Code
CONNID	✓	✓	S_CONN_ID	NUMC	4	0	Flight Connection Number
FLDATE	✓	✓	S_DATE	DATS	8	0	Flight date

Figure 3.42 Fields for ZBOOK_SFLIGHT

Next, we need to create foreign keys for all of our fields. To do this, first select the field MANDT and click on the foreign key button and you will see the same popup we saw earlier in Figure 3.36. Click YES to accept the proposal. Next, click the screen check CHECK REQUIRED checkbox and set the FOREIGN KEY FIELD TYPE to KEY FIELDS/CANDIDATES and the CARDINALITY to 1:CN.

Select the field BOOKID and click on the foreign key button. Then enter check table "ZBOOK" and press Enter. Click YES to accept the proposal. Click the screen check CHECK REQUIRED checkbox and set the FOREIGN KEY FIELD TYPE to KEY FIELDS/CANDIDATES and the CARDINALITY to 1:CN.

Now, select the fields CARRID, CONNID and FLDATE and click the foreign key button. The system will propose to use the SFLIGHT check table since these fields all make up the key to that table, click yes to use that proposal. Click the screen check CHECK REQUIRED checkbox and set the FOREIGN KEY FIELD TYPE to KEY FIELDS/CANDIDATES and the

CARDINALITY to 1:CN. Now that all of the foreign keys have been set, the Entry help/check tab should match what is shown in Figure 3.43.

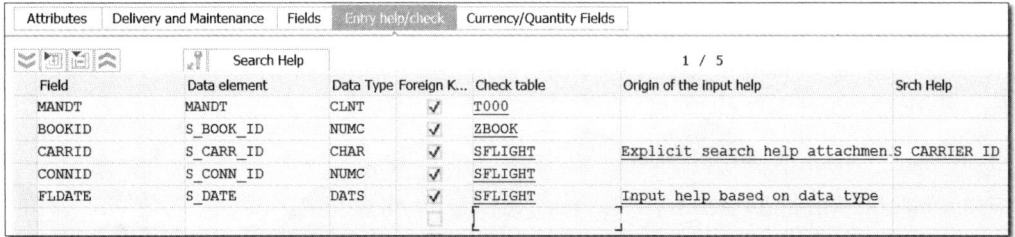

Figure 3.43 Entry Help/Check for ZBOOK_SFLIGHT

Data Elements

Data elements describe the different fields in a transparent table. So far, you've been able to reuse existing data elements, such as S_CARR_ID and S_CONNID. Sometimes you will need to create your own data elements as well, which we will cover in this section.

Viewing the S_BOOK_ID Data Element

When viewing table ZBOOK from Transaction SE11, double-click the data element S_BOOK_ID to view it as shown in Figure 3.44.

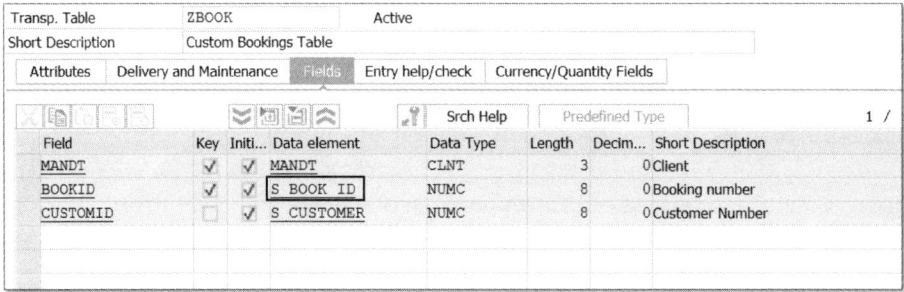

Figure 3.44 Viewing Table Data Elements

You can also view data elements by selecting the DATA TYPE radio button and entering the data element name in the corresponding text field in Transaction SE11.

A data element contains a short description, such as "Booking number" for S_BOOK_ID. The short description is used by technical users such as developers when trying to search for a usable data element.

When viewing data elements, there are four tabs of information. The first tab, ATTRIBUTES, shows the package containing the data element, who last changed it, when it was last changed, and the original language as shown below in Figure 3.45.

Attributes

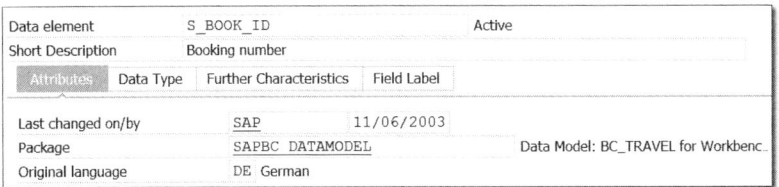

Figure 3.45 Displaying a Data Element

The next tab is DATA TYPE, where a domain is attached to the data element. In the S_BOOK_ID example shown below in Figure 3.46, there is a domain with the same name, S_BOOK_ID, and you can see that the domain has a DATA TYPE of NUMC with a LENGTH of 8. We will cover domains in more detail in the next section.

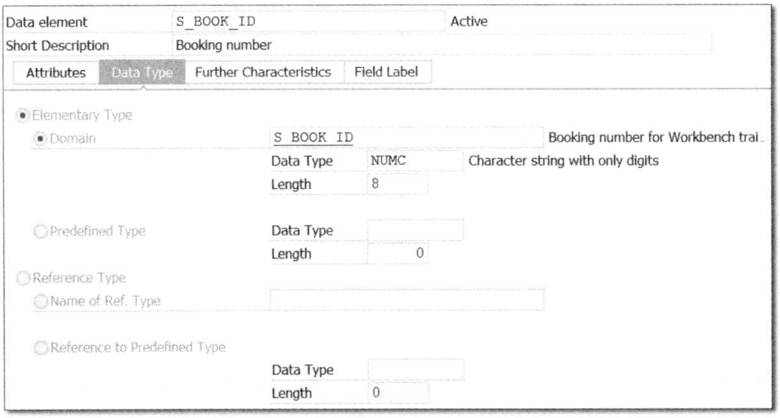

Figure 3.46 The Data Element Data Type Tab

The data element can also be assigned a predefined type instead of a domain. A predefined type will have fewer options than a domain.

Predefined data element

Reference types are out of scope for this section and should be avoided when creating transparent tables.

Further Characteristics The FURTHER CHARACTERISTICS tab shown below in Figure 3.47 allows you to set a search help for the data element. You also have the option to set a PARAMETER ID, which will allow ABAP programs to "remember" the last used value or to use a default from a user's parameter settings (SYSTEM • USER PROFILE • OWN DATA • PARAMETERS).

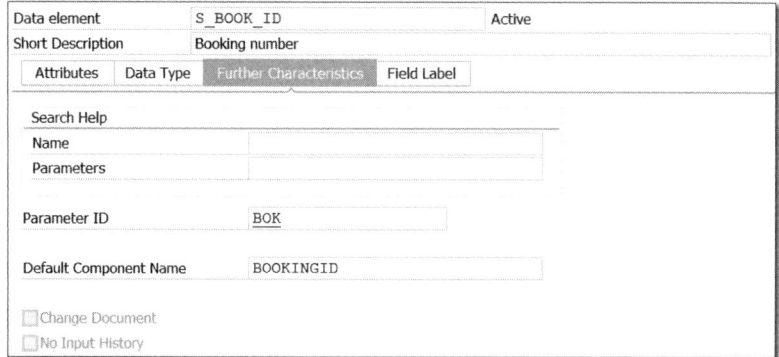

Figure 3.47 The Data Element Further Characteristics Tab

DEFAULT COMPONENT NAME is used in standard SAP data elements for defining BAPI components.

The CHANGE DOCUMENTS checkbox will mark the data element as relevant for change tracking, and the NO INPUT HISTORY checkbox is used to prevent the input history from being displayed. NO INPUT HISTORY is typically used for sensitive data when you do not want users to see values that they previously entered.

Field label Finally, the FIELD LABEL tab (Figure 3.48) allows you to enter a field label to be used when this data element is being displayed in a table within an ABAP program. A short, medium, or long label is used depending on the size of the column displaying the label. The LENGTH text boxes contain the maximum length of the field label text.

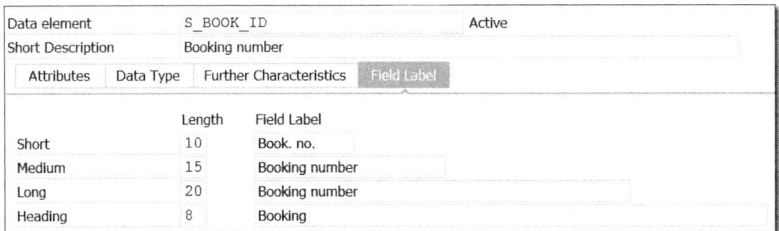

Figure 3.48 The Data Element Field Label Tab

Creating a New Data Element

Now that you've reviewed an existing data element, let's create a new one to track discounts on bookings. Because a discount will apply to the entire booking, it will be used in table ZBOOK. However, because a data element can be reused, you can apply the same data element to table ZBOOK_SFLIGHT to create a discount based on each flight.

Data elements can be created by using the new data element name in a field in a transparent table. To do this, go back to the ZBOOK transparent table and add a new field called DISCOUNT using the data element Z_DISCOUNT as shown below in Figure 3.49.

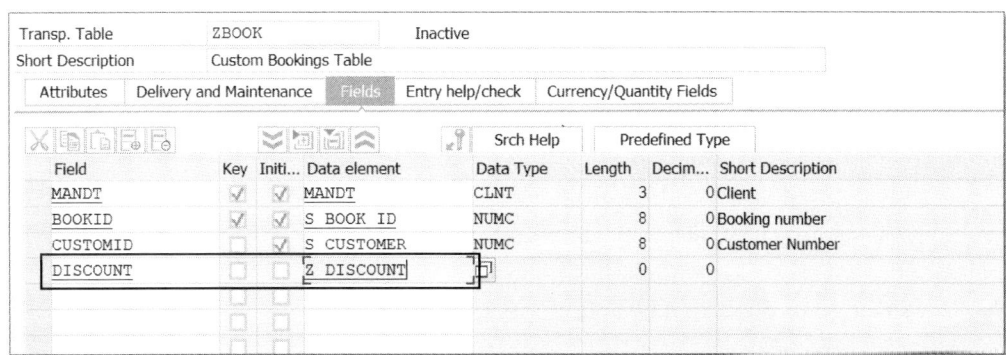

Figure 3.49 Adding the DISCOUNT Field with a New Data Element

Next, click SAVE and double-click the Z_DISCOUNT data element. You will be prompted with the popup shown in Figure 3.50. Click YES to enter the CREATE DATA ELEMENT screen.

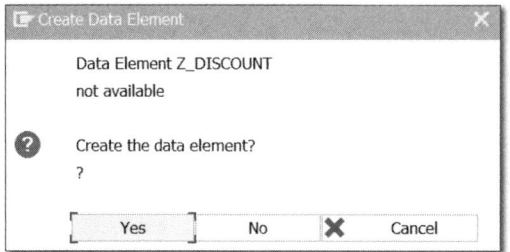

Figure 3.50 Popup to Create the Data Element

In your new data element, add a short description, such as "Discount Percentage". You'll create a domain in the next section; for now, select the predefined type DEC with a length of 2 and 2 decimal places, as shown in Figure 3.51. This will allow you to have values such as .15 for a 15% discount.

Figure 3.51 Creating a New Data Element

Next, select the FIELD LABEL tab and add the field label "Discount" for every field, as shown in Figure 3.52. The LENGTH field will be updated to the max default for each field type.

Click SAVE and activate both the data element Z_DISCOUNT and the table ZBOOK. Now, if you look back at table ZBOOK, you'll see the data type and description data populated for your DISCOUNT field based on the data element you created as shown in Figure 3.53.

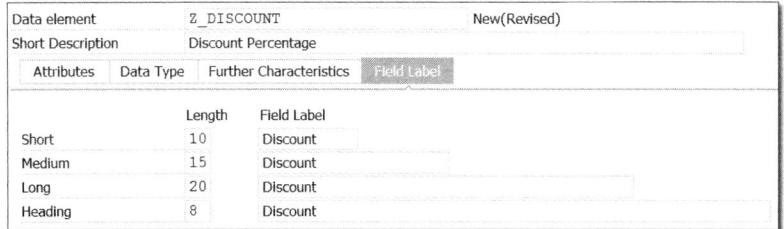

Figure 3.52 Adding Field Labels to a New Data Element

Transp. Table	ZBOOK			Active			
Short Description	Custom Bookings Table						

Field	Key	Initi...	Data element	Data Type	Length	Decim...	Short Description
MANDT	✓	✓	MANDT	CLNT	3	0	Client
BOOKID	✓	✓	S_BOOK_ID	NUMC	8	0	Booking number
CUSTOMID		✓	S_CUSTOMER	NUMC	8	0	Customer Number
DISCOUNT			Z_DISCOUNT	DEC	2	2	Discount Percentage

Figure 3.53 The New Field in ZBOOK with the Data Type and Description from a Newly Created Data Element

Domains

Now that you've looked at a data element in detail, let's take a look at the domains. Just as a data element can be used in multiple transparent tables, a domain can be used in multiple data elements. As you saw in the previous section, you can create data elements without specifying a specific domain. However, domains do have some technical attributes that cannot be set within a data element.

If you're unsure whether you need to create a domain or not, check with a senior developer; your company may have standards for this procedure. If you're still unsure, it would be best to create the domain: It doesn't take very long, the domain can be reused, and the technical settings discussed in this section can be updated in the future, which would update every data element using that domain.

When to create a domain

Viewing the BOOLEAN Domain

Before we create a new domain, let's take a look at the standard domain BOOLEAN. Open Transaction SE11, enter "BOOLEAN" in the DOMAIN text field, select the DOMAIN radio button, and click DISPLAY, as shown in Figure 3.54.

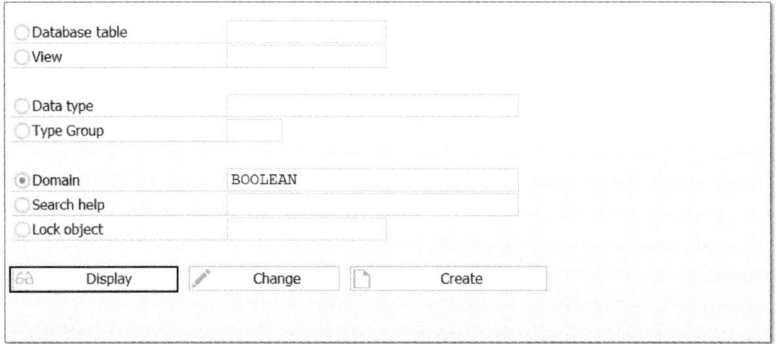

Figure 3.54 Opening the BOOLEAN Domain from Transaction SE11

Properties — Like the other data dictionary objects that you've looked at, a PROPERTIES tab contains the package and last changed information about the domain.

Definition — Within the DEFINITION tab, you can see the same data type options that were shown for the data element. The BOOLEAN domain pictured in Figure 3.55 has a CHAR data type with a length of 1.

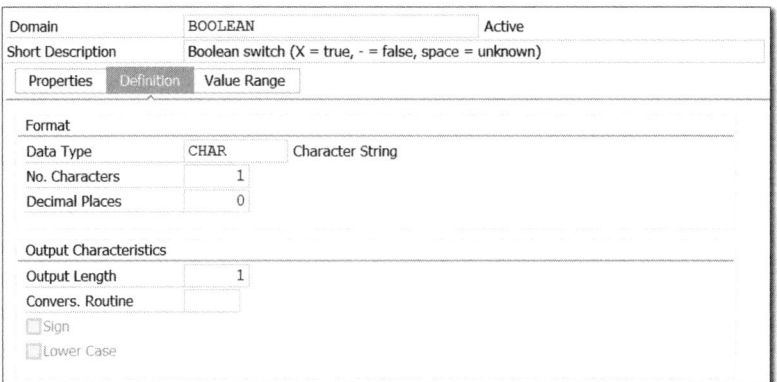

Figure 3.55 The Description Tab of the Standard BOOLEAN Domain

What's new here is the OUTPUT CHARACTERISTICS section, where you can define OUTPUT LENGTH and conversion routine (CONVERS. ROUTINE). The output length can be set so that what's displayed to the user is a different length than what's stored in the database table. A conversion routine is typically used for domains that contain an ID using leading zeros so that when the domain is displayed, the leading zeros are not. Selecting the SIGN checkbox will add a plus/minus sign to indicate the sign of the value, and selecting the LOWER CASE checkbox will let the UI know that values entered will be both uppercase and lowercase.

The VALUE RANGE tab allows you to restrict values for a given domain to a specific range. The `BOOLEAN` domain is a good example of this, because even though the data type is CHAR 1, the only values that can be entered are X, -, and a space character, as shown in Figure 3.56. In the VALUE RANGE tab, intervals can be defined to limit the possible values to a given interval or a value table to limit possible values to values existing on another table. Setting the VALUE TABLE field will let the system know to always suggest the entered table as a foreign key when using this domain.

Value range

Figure 3.56 The Value Range Tab for the BOOLEAN Domain

Creating a New Domain

Now that you've reviewed the different settings within a domain, let's create a domain for your discount. First, open the data element Z_DISCOUNT you created earlier in the chapter using Transaction SE11, and click the EDIT button to enter edit mode. Now, change the ELEMENTARY TYPE section radio button to DOMAIN, enter "Z_DISCOUNT" for the domain name, and click SAVE as shown in Figure 3.57.

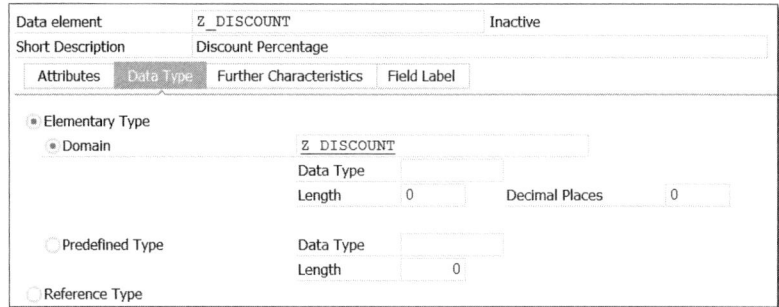

Figure 3.57 Adding a New Domain to the Data Element

Next, double-click the new domain Z_DISCOUNT; you will be asked if you want to create this domain, because it does not exist as shown in Figure 3.58. Click YES to continue, and create the domain Z_DISCOUNT.

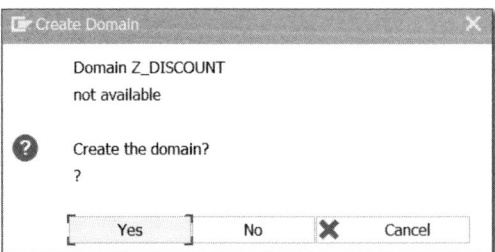

Figure 3.58 Popup to Create the New Domain

In your new domain, enter "Discount" for the short description and add the data type DEC with 2 characters and 2 decimal places from within the DEFINITION tab. Leave the rest of the options set to their defaults, as shown in Figure 3.59.

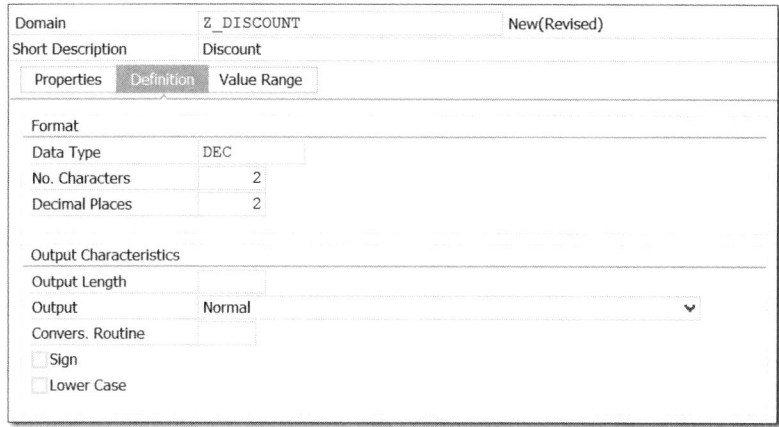

Figure 3.59 The Definition Tab of the New Domain

Next, click the VALUE RANGE tab and enter a value range of 0 (LOWER LIMIT) to 1 (UpperLimit), as shown in Figure 3.60. This will prevent anyone from providing a discount of over 100%, which would be a problem for your fictional company's bottom line.

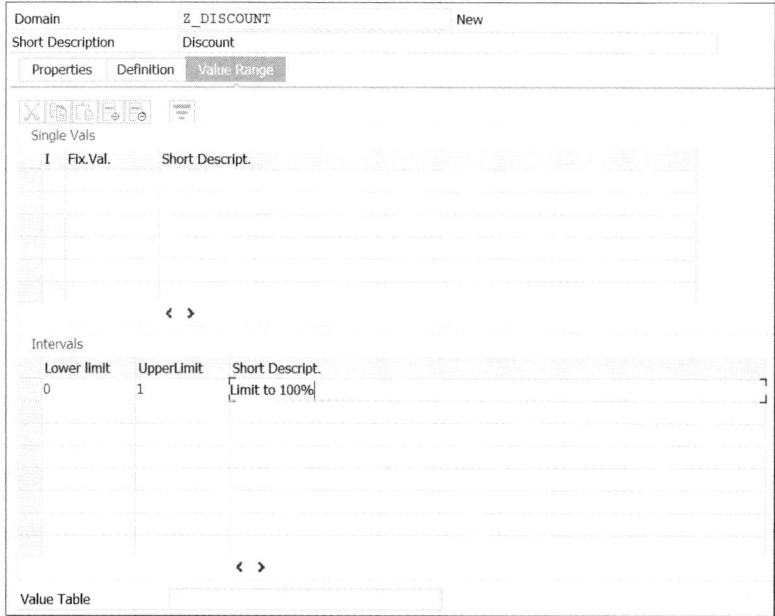

Figure 3.60 Adding a Value Range to the Newly Created Domain

Click SAVE and activate all of your inactive objects, which should include the domain, data type, and table. You will now see the settings from your domain displayed in the data element where the domain is used as shown in Figure 3.61.

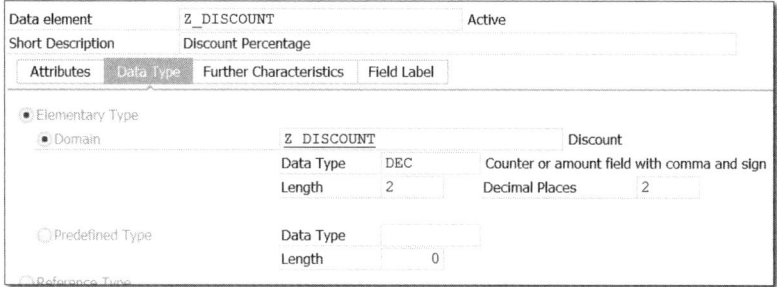

Figure 3.61 The Data Element Showing Details about the Newly Created Domain

Documentation

All of the data dictionary objects that you've worked with in this chapter have documentation attached to them. You should always attach documentation to any new data dictionary objects that you create so that, many years down the road, someone can figure out why you created the object without having to rely on you being there and remembering.

Displaying documentation

Take a look at the documentation for table SBOOK by opening the table in Transaction SE11 and selecting GOTO • DOCUMENTATION • DISPLAY; you'll see the documentation pictured in Figure 3.62. Documentation should be concise and meaningful and should not include information that someone can easily gather by looking at the table details, such as a list of field names.

Changing documentation

Next, open the new table that you created, ZBOOK, in SE11 so that you can add your own documentation. Select GOTO • DOCUMENTATION • CHANGE, and then you can enter your own documentation in the text editor, as shown in Figure 3.63.

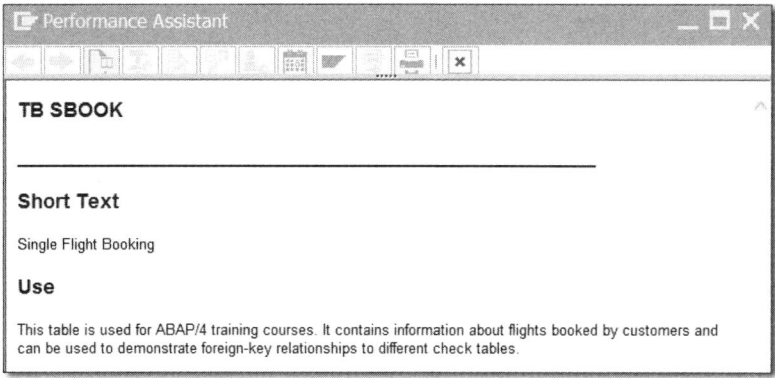

Figure 3.62 Table Documentation for SBOOK

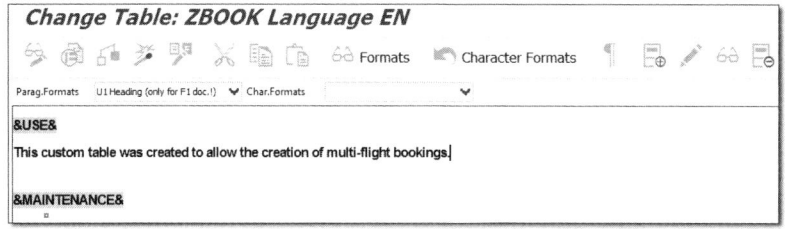

Figure 3.63 Creating Documentation for Custom Table ZBOOK

Maintenance Dialogs

Maintenance Dialogs are system generated programs that allow you to add, change and delete records in your table using transaction SM30.

To create a maintenance dialog, open your table for changes using Transaction SE11. Next, select UTILITIES • TABLE MAINTENANCE GENERATOR. You will see the screen pictured below in Figure 3.64. The authorization group selection can be used to limit who has authority to use the generated program. See your company's standards to determine what you should select for the AUTHORIZATION GROUP or choose &NC& to avoid having an authorization group. The FUNCTION GROUP textbox should contain a name that relates to your table and begins with ZFG, such as ZFG_BOOKINGS.

Create maintenance dialogs

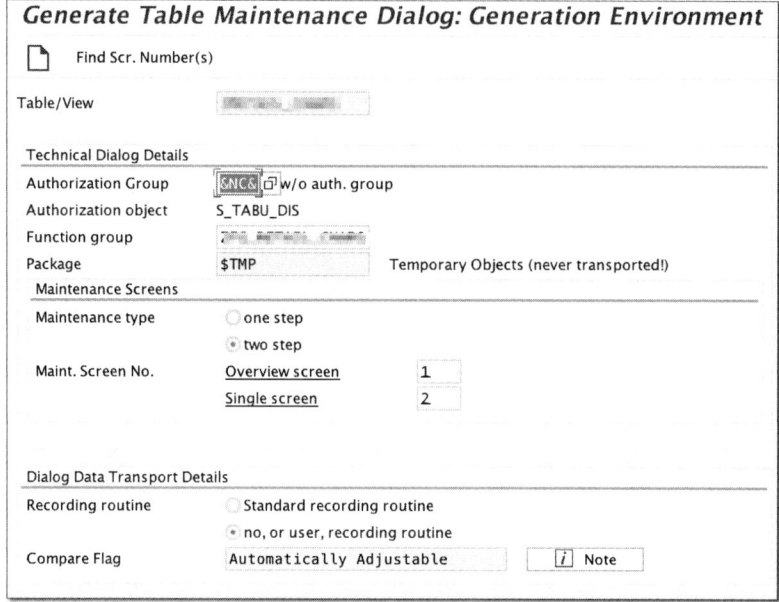

Figure 3.64 Generate Table Maintenance Dialog

Select the FIND SCR. NUMBER(S) button located at the top of the screen pictured in Figure 3.64 to fill the OVERVIEW SCREEN and SINGLE SCREEN options. After clicking that button, you will see the popup pictured below in Figure 3.65. Select the PROPOSE SCREEN NUMBER(S) radio button so that the system can choose the screen numbers to use.

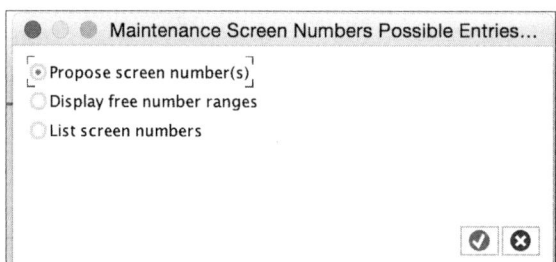

Figure 3.65 Propose Screen Number(s) popup

Finally, click the CREATE button to generate the maintenance dialog. You can test the maintenance dialog by entering Transaction

SM30 pictured below in Figure 3.66. All you need to do is enter your table in the TABLE/VIEW textbox and click the MAINTAIN button and you will be brought to a screen where you can create, change and delete records in the table.

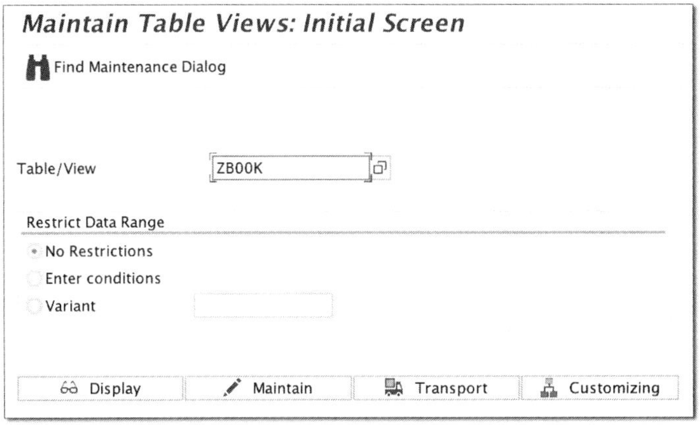

Figure 3.66 Maintain Table Views Screen

Structures and Table Types

Earlier in this chapter we covered how to create transparent tables that become tables stored in the database. It is also possible to create definitions of tables to be used as variables in our program and not stored in the database. We can do this by creating *structures*, which is a data variable that has only one line of data, but multiple fields. Additionally, we can create *table types*, which are create tables for a structure. The table that gets created will only exist within our ABAP code and not in the database.

Creating Structures

To create a structure, enter Transaction SE11 and select the DATA TYPE radio button. Next enter the structure name such as ZFLIGHT and then click the CREATE button as shown below in Figure 3.67.

Next, you will see the popup shown below in Figure 3.68. Select the STRUCTURE radio button and click the checkmark.

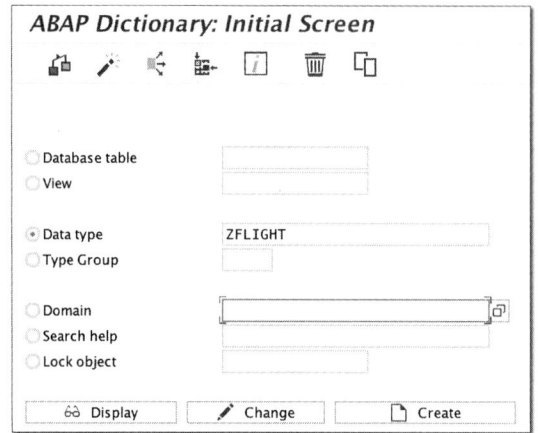

Figure 3.67 Creating a New Structure

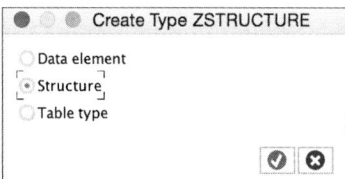

Figure 3.68 Choosing a Type of Data Type

In the change structure view, you will notice it looks just like the change transparent table view. Add the components FLIGHT_DATE with COMPONENT TYPE S_DATE and CARRID with COMPONENT TYPE S_CARR_ID and CONNID with COMPONENT TYPE S_CONN_ID as shown below in Figure 3.69.

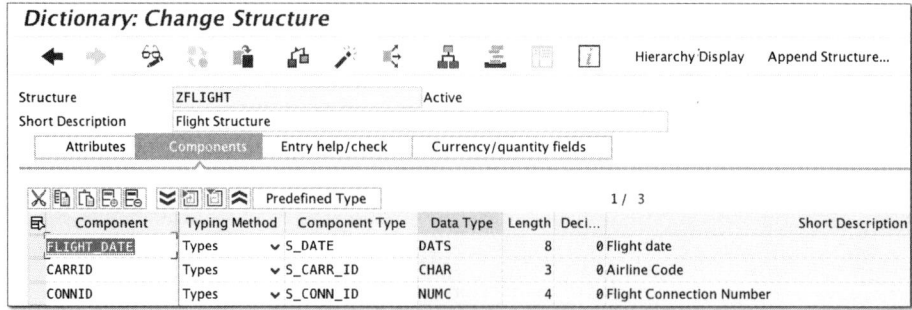

Figure 3.69 Creating a Structure

Just like a table, we can set an enhancement category. Select EXTRAS • ENHANCEMENT CATEGORY to set the category to CANNOT BE ENHANCED. Finally, activate the structure so it is available for your ABAP programs to use.

Structure enhancement category

Creating Table Types

Table types are also created using Transaction SE11. Select the radio button DATA TYPE and enter ZFLIGHTS in the text box to create a table type called ZFLIGHTS as shown in Figure 3.70.

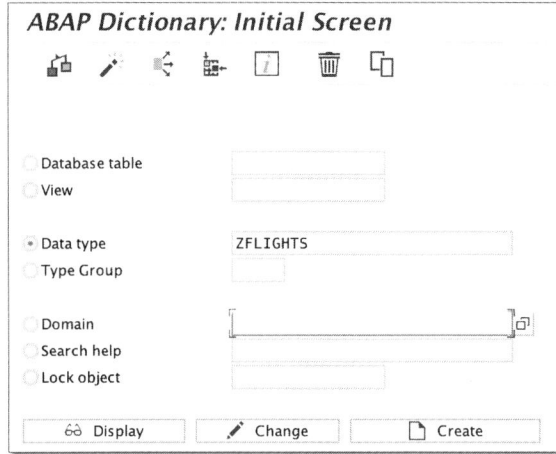

Figure 3.70 Creating a New Table Type

You will then be prompted to select a type of Data Type. Choose the TABLE TYPE radio button as shown in Figure 3.71.

Figure 3.71 Selecting the Table Type Data Type

In the CHANGE TABLE TYPE view, enter ZFLIGHT in the LINE TYPE textbox as shown in Figure 3.72. Then click the SAVE and ACTIVATE buttons.

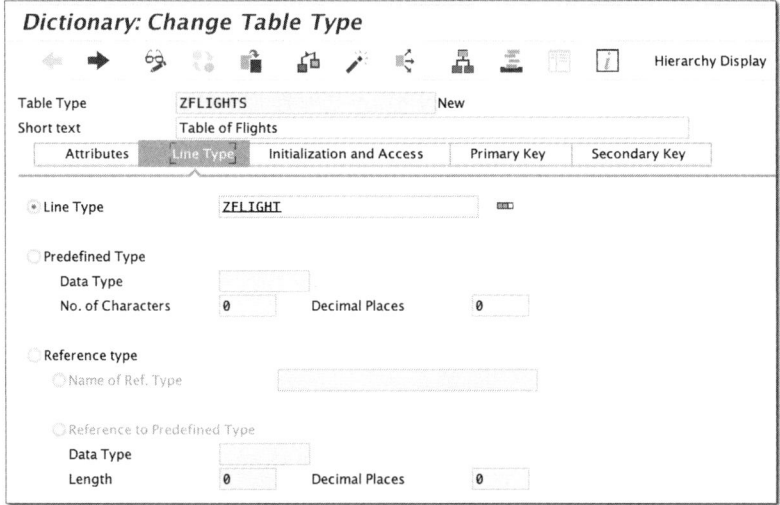

Figure 3.72 Setting a Table Type Line Type

Your table type is now available to be called from an ABAP program. It will be a table of the ZFLIGHT structure.

Summary

This chapter introduced the concepts of a database and data dictionary. It also covered how to properly design a relational database using ERDs and database normalization. Those skills can be reused for any relational database system, whether or not it's being used with an SAP ABAP system.

Next, we introduced the flight data model that exists in all SAP ABAP systems for training and learning the ABAP language. Then, you looked at a transparent table, data element, and domain created by SAP and created your own transparent table, data element, and domain.

Then the chapter covered documentation within the data dictionary and explained how to create your own documentation.

We also covered how to create maintenance dialogs so that you can create, change and delete records in your table without using an ABAP program.

Lastly, we covered structures and table types that allow you to have tables and structures within your ABAP program that are not necessarily tied to a table in the database.

Data dictionary objects are the core of most ABAP programs, and you will probably refer back to this chapter as you create new applications in your own SAP system. In the next chapter, you'll learn how to access the transparent tables that you've looked at and created.

Accessing the Database

So far, this book has introduced the ABAP language and covered how to create ABAP Data Dictionary objects. Now, we'll tie the previous two chapters together and cover how to use ABAP to access the ABAP Data Dictionary objects that you looked at in the last chapter. Using Open SQL we will be able to pull the data out of the database and into our program so that we can use it.

If you are familiar with SQL (Structured Query Language), then you should find that SAP's Open SQL is very similar to what you've used before. Open SQL will be the same no matter what database is used to run your SAP system. It's possible to execute native SQL in your ABAP code, but that's out of scope for this book and should be avoided unless absolutely necessary. Using Open SQL, your code is unaffected if the database system is later changed; using native SQL, your code may stop working after changing to a new database.

Open SQL

In ABAP 7.4 many changes were released to Open SQL, resulting in two ways of writing Open SQL statements, the new way and the old way. In this section we will cover both new Open SQL and old Open SQL. Even if your system is not currently on ABAP 7.4, you should be familiar with both the new and old versions. The old Open SQL will still execute in an ABAP 7.4 system. Throughout the chapter we will show examples in both the new Open SQL and the old Open SQL to highlight their differences.

New Open SQL

SQL Console in Eclipse

If you are currently working on an ABAP 7.4 SP8 system, you can use the SQL console built in to Eclipse. This is a way to write and test

Required version

Accessing the Database

Open SQL statements outside of an ABAP program. You can use it to test the Open SQL code in this chapter or you can test the code in this chapter from within an ABAP program.

Launching the SQL console

To launch the SQL console, right click on your ABAP project in Eclipse. The project will be the top level folder in your project explorer with the name of your ABAP system on it. Then select the option for SQL Console, which is highlighted in Figure 4.1 below.

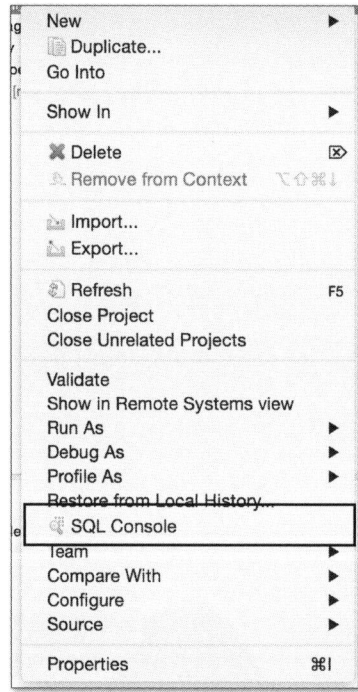

Figure 4.1 Opening the SQL Console in Eclipse

The SQL console has two sections. On the left is a console where an SQL query can be entered. Raw data is on the right, where the results of a query are displayed. An example of the SQL console after a query has been executed is shown below in Figure 4.2.

SELECT Statements

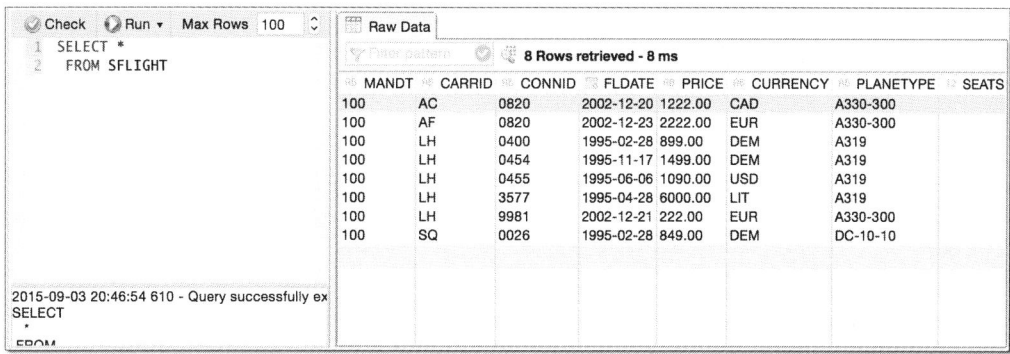

Figure 4.2 The Eclipse SQL Console

There are two buttons in the SQL Console toolbar shown below in Figure 4.3. The first, CHECK button, will verify if your Open SQL code is syntactically correct and the second RUN button, will run your query and return the results in the RAW DATA section on the right. Additionally, there is a MAX ROWS textbox where you can enter the maximum number of rows to be returned form the query.

Console toolbar

Figure 4.3 SQL Console toolbar

SELECT Statements

The most basic Open SQL command is the SELECT statement. SELECT statements are used to capture data from the database and put the results in memory accessible by your ABAP program. The results can be stored in either an internal table when there is a table of results or variables when there is only a single result. When testing the provided code, you can open the data variables in debug mode (see Chapter 2) to view the results or you can test the select statements in the eclipse SQL console when using systems that are ABAP version 7.4 SP8 or higher.

Capturing data

Basic SELECT Statements

A basic SELECT statement requires three basic keywords. SELECT, INTO TABLE and FROM. After SELECT, we list the fields we are selecting or a * to represent all fields. After INTO TABLE, we have the internal table where the results will be stored and lastly, is FROM, which is followed by the database table where we are pulling our data from.

 Internal Tables

We will cover internal tables in more detail in the next chapter; for now just think of them as another variable used to store a table of results.

In Listing 4.1, we are using old Open SQL to get all of the fields (indicated with the *) in the SFLIGHT table and save them in the internal table called t_results. If you are using the SQL console, *do not* include the first line.

```
DATA: t_results TYPE STANDARD TABLE OF sflight
SELECT *
INTO TABLE t_results
FROM SFLIGHT.
```
Listing 4.1 Example SELECT statement

The example SELECT statement from Listing 4.1 will select all of the flight data from table SFLIGHT and store them in a table called RESULTS. An example of some of the data that would be returned is displayed in Figure 4.4.

MANDT	CARRID	CONNID	FLDATE	PRICE	CURRENCY	PLANETYPE	SEATSMAX	SEATSOCC	PAYMENT
100	AC	0820	2002-12-20	1222.00	CAD	A330-300	320	12	0.00
100	AF	0820	2002-12-23	2222.00	EUR	A330-300	320	2	0.00
100	LH	0400	1995-02-28	899.00	DEM	A319	350	3	2639.00
100	LH	0454	1995-11-17	1499.00	DEM	A319	350	2	2949.00
100	LH	0455	1995-06-06	1090.00	USD	A319	220	1	1499.00
100	LH	3577	1995-04-28	6000.00	LIT	A319	220	1	600.00
100	LH	9981	2002-12-21	222.00	EUR	A330-300	320	12	0.00
100	SQ	0026	1995-02-28	849.00	DEM	DC-10-10	380	2	1684.00

Figure 4.4 Results from SELECT statement

 What If My Table Changes?

By using SELECT * in your query, any changes to tables (such as new fields) will automatically be incorporated into your results. If that's not the result that you want, it may be best to specify which columns you want.

SELECT Statements

In Listing 4.1, we selected all of the columns in the database, but we are also able to select only the columns we need, as shown in Listing 4.2. Notice that we used the table type defined in Chapter 3 to store only the fields that we were interested in. Notice that the fields are separated by a space.

```
DATA: t_results TYPE zflights.
SELECT fldate carrid connid
INTO TABLE zflights
FROM sflight.
```
Listing 4.2 Example SELECT Statements

We introduced inline data declarations in Chapter 2, where we were able to create data variables using the @DATA keyword. Using the new Open SQL, we can also use inline data declarations in our select statements. This way, the table structure being used is created based on your selection and you will not need to create a structure or table type first. This feature is only available on ABAP 7.4 SP8 systems or higher.

Inline data declarations

In the example in Listing 4.3, we do not define a table to store the results and instead use the inline data declaration with the @Data command with the table name in between the parenthesis. The inline data declaration requires the new Open SQL and as a result the fields need to be separated by a comma instead of a space. This is more like the SQL ANSI standard. Also, you will notice that anytime we use an ABAP variable, it must be prefaced with an @ symbol.

```
SELECT fldate, price
INTO TABLE @DATA(t_results)
FROM sflight.
```
Listing 4.3 Example SELECT Using Inline Data Declarations

SELECT SINGLE

Sometimes, you only want to see one row from a given table. You can accomplish that task with the SELECT SINGLE statement. Since you only select one row, you no longer use the INTO TABLE command. You instead use INTO followed by a variable, structure or inline data declaration to store the result as shown in Listing 4.4.

```
DATA: ld_date type s_date.
SELECT SINGLE fldate
```

```
INTO ld_date
FROM sflight.

SELECT SINGLE fldate
INTO @data(ld_inline_date)
FROM SFLIGHT.
```
Listing 4.4 SELECT SINGLE Example

Multiple Columns — If you are selecting multiple columns of data, you can store the results in multiple data variables. When using inline data declarations, the INTO must be on the last line.

```
DATA: ld_date   TYPE d,
      ld_carrid TYPE s_carr_id,
      ld_connid TYPE s_conn_id.
"old Open SQL
SELECT SINGLE fldate carrid connid
INTO (ld_date, ld_carrid, ld_connid)
FROM sflight.
"new Open SQL
SELECT SINGLE fldate, carrid, connid
FROM SFLIGHT
INTO (@DATA(ld_in_date), @DATA(ld_in_carrid), @DATA(ld_in_connid)).
```
Listing 4.5 Selecting Multiple Columns into Different Variables

You can also select multiple columns of data and store them in a structure, like the structure ZFLIGHT which we created in Chapter 3.

```
DATA:ls_flight TYPE zflight.
"old Open SQL
SELECT SINGLE fldate carrid connid
INTO ls_flight
FROM sflight.
"new Open SQL
SELECT SINGLE fldate, carrid, connid
INTO @DATA(ls_in_flight)
FROM SFLIGHT.
```
Listing 4.6 Selecting Multiple Columns into Individual Variables

Just as with the other SELECT statements, you can use SELECT SINGLE * to select every field from a single row.

SELECT…UP TO n ROWS

So far, you've learned how to select all of the rows in a table and how to select one row from a table, but maybe you just want five rows, for example; that's where the addition of UP TO n ROWS comes in. This command sets a maximum number of rows to be selected, meaning you won't have an issue if you use UP TO 5 ROWS and only two rows exist. In that scenario, the result would just include the two rows.

The UP TO n ROWS command can be used to limit the amount of data that is returned so that the system does not get stuck loading too many rows. An example using the UP TO n ROWS command is shown below in Listing 4.7.

Limiting Returned Data

```
DATA: t_results TYPE STANDARD TABLE OF SFLIGHT.
"old Open SQL
SELECT *
INTO TABLE t_results
FROM SFLIGHT
UP TO 5 ROWS.
"new Open SQL
SELECT *
INTO TABLE @DATA(t_in_results)
FROM SFLIGHT
UP TO 5 ROWS.
```
Listing 4.7 SELECT…UP TO n ROWS Example

SELECT…WHERE

So far, you've limited the SELECT results to one row or to a specified number of rows, but most likely you'll also want to limit your results based on some values in the database. This is where the WHERE clause comes in. A WHERE clause allows you to limit the results to only those that contain specified values.

WHERE clauses

The WHERE clause uses a condition, just like IF statements, which we covered in Chapter 2. Also like IF statements, multiple conditions can be combined in a single WHERE clause using the AND and OR keywords, as shown in Listing 4.8.

```
DATA: lt_flights TYPE zflights.
"old Open SQL
SELECT fldate carrid connid
INTO TABLE lt_flights
```

```
FROM sflight.
WHERE carrid = 'AA'
AND planetype = '747-400'.
"new Open SQL
SELECT fldate, carrid, connid
INTO TABLE @DATA(lt_in_flights)
FROM SFLIGHT
WHERE carrid = 'AA'
AND planetype = 747-400.
```
Listing 4.8 Example SELECT...WHERE Using the AND Keyword

NULL conditions

One difference between `IF` statements and the `WHERE` clause is that the test for `IS INITIAL` or `IS NOT INITIAL` cannot be used in a `WHERE` clause. Instead, database records with no value for a field can be `NULL`, so use the condition `IS NULL` or `IS NOT NULL` in this situation.

 Null vs. Initial Values

Variables declared within your ABAP program are given an initial value. For example, a variable of type `i` would have the initial value of 0, such as the one defined below:

`DATA: d_variable TYPE i.`

If you wanted to find every row with a value of 0 for a specified field in your database, you'd use `WHERE field = 0`. Zero is not considered null.

If you wanted to find every row that had no value entered, you'd use `WHERE field IS NULL`.

The null condition can only be met for fields that did not have the INITIAL VALUES checkbox selected when created in Transaction SE11.

INSERT

The `INSERT` command can be used to insert new records in the database. You can use this command to insert a single record in the database or a table of records.

When inserting records into the database, you will need to store your data in a structure of the table by using the transparent table name as the data type for your variable. You can then fill it with the values that you want to insert in the database, as shown in Listing 4.9. The structure or table being used with INSERT must have the same number of fields as the transparent table. It's always best to use structures or tables of the transparent table type for inserts so that you know that the data types within the structure or table match the table you are inserting into.

```
DATA: d_booking TYPE zbook.
d_booking-bookid = 1.
d_booking-customid = 2.
"old Open SQL
INSERT zbook FROM d_booking.
"new Open SQL
INSERT zbook FROM @d_booking.
```
Listing 4.9 INSERT Example Using a Structure

 Defining MANDT

> You should notice that in the insert in Listing 4.9 we do not define the MANDT key value. The system will actually take care of that for us. The system will always use our logged in client for any SELECTS, UPDATES, etc. on the database.

Inserting rows from an internal table works just like inserting data from a structure, as shown in Listing 4.10. Chapter 5 will cover internal tables in more detail.

```
DATA: d_booking TYPE zbook,
 t_booking TYPE STANDARD TABLE OF zbook.

d_booking-bookid = 2.
d_booking-customid = 2.
APPEND d_booking TO t_booking.

d_booking-bookid = 3.
d_booking-customid = 2.
APPEND d_booking TO t_booking.
"old Open SQL
INSERT zbook FROM t_booking.
"new Open SQL
INSERT zbook FROM @t_booking.
```
Listing 4.10 INSERT Example Using a Table

MODIFY/UPDATE

Updating database records

When you want to update a record in the database, use the `MODIFY` command. The `MODIFY` command can also be used instead of `INSERT`, because it will insert the specified record if it does not exist and update the record if it does. However, unlike `INSERT`, you can only specify one record in a structure with `MODIFY`. The `MODIFY` command will find the record that you want to change using the key in the structure and will update all of the corresponding fields (Listing 4.11).

```
DATA: s_booking TYPE zbook.
s_booking-bookid = 1.
s_booking-customid = 3.
"old Open SQL
MODIFY zbook FROM s_booking.
"new Open SQL
MODIFY zbook FROM @s_booking.
```
Listing 4.11 MODIFY Example

Differences between MODIFY and UPDATE

The `UPDATE` command works just like the `MODIFY` command, except that it will not insert the record if it doesn't exist. Also, `UPDATE` can use a structure or internal table when updating the database. The example in Listing 4.12 uses a structure to update a record in the `sflight` database table.

```
DATA: s_booking TYPE zbook,
      t_bookings TYPE STANDARD TABLE OF zbook.
"using a structure
s_booking-bookid = 1.
s_booking-customid = 4.
"old Open SQL
UPDATE zbooking FROM s_booking.
"new Open SQL
UPDATE zbooking FROM @s_booking.

"using a table
APPEND s_booking TO t_bookings.
"old Open SQL
UPDATE zbooking FROM t_bookings.
"new Open SQL
UPDATE zbooking FROM @t_bookings.
```
Listing 4.12 Example Using Update with a Structure and Table

You can also use the UPDATE command with SET and WHERE to update fields for a selection of records. Multiple columns can be defined in the SET expression, as shown in Listing 4.13, where the seatsmax field and planetype field will be updated for every record with a planetype of '747-400'.

Updating selection of records

```
"old Open SQL
UPDATE sflight
SET seatsmax = 400 planetype = '747'
WHERE planetype = '747-400'.
"new Open SQL
UPDATE sflight
SET seatsmax = 400, planetype = '747'
WHERE planetype = '747-400'.
```
Listing 4.13 UPDATE...SET Example with Multiple Columns

DELETE

The DELETE command is used for deleting records from the database using a structure or internal table with keys to identify the records to be deleted. Because the DELETE command only uses a key, you don't need to identify the entire row to be deleted in the table or structure being used as shown in Listing 4.14.

```
DATA: s_booking TYPE zbook.
s_booking-bookid = 1.
"old Open SQL
DELETE zbook FROM d_booking.
"new Open SQL
DELETE zbook FROM @d_booking.
```
Listing 4.14 DELETE...FROM Example

An example using a WHERE condition in a DELETE FROM command is shown below in Listing 4.15.

Deleting records with WHERE clause

```
"old/new Open SQL
DELETE FROM sflight
WHERE planetype = '747'.
```
Listing 4.15 Example of DELETE FROM Using a WHERE Clause

INNER JOIN

Joining multiple tables together

Chapter 3 covered database design and relationships between multiple tables. When selecting data from the database, you may want to see data from a combination of tables that have a relationship. You can accomplish this by using an INNER JOIN. The syntax for an INNER JOIN is a SELECT statement with the addition of INNER JOIN followed by the table that you want to join and ON with the keys that you want to use to join the tables. The keys are specified using the table name ~ key field name. Any field can be used in the INNER JOIN, but it must match with a field in the original table. An example INNER JOIN is shown below in Listing 4.16.

```
DATA: d_date TYPE s_date,
      d_time TYPE s_dep_time.
"old Open SQL
SELECT SINGLE fldate deptime
INTO (d_date, d_time)
FROM SFLIGHT
INNER JOIN SPFLI
ON sflight~carrid = spfli~carrid
AND sflight~connid = spfli~connid.
"new Open SQL
SELECT SINGLE fldate, deptime
INTO (@d_date, @d_time)
FROM SFLIGHT
INNER JOIN SPFLI
ON sflight~carrid = spfli~carrid
AND sflight~connid = spfli~connid.
```
Listing 4.16 INNER JOIN Example

The INNER JOIN matches the rows of each table based on the keys listed in the ON command to create a new table (which is the two tables joined together), and then the fields selected are returned, as shown in Figure 4.5. When using an INNER JOIN, a corresponding record must be found in all tables involved in the join, or no record will be displayed.

If the field selected exists in both tables, such as the CARRID field in the preceding example, then the table that you want to select the field from must be indicated by prefixing the field with the table name and a tilde. Refer to Listing 4.17 for an example.

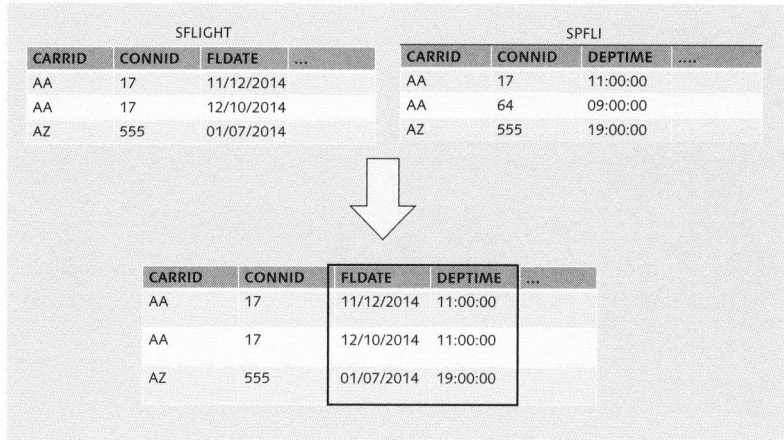

Figure 4.5 INNER JOIN Example Diagram

```
DATA: d_carrid TYPE s_carr_id,
      d_date   TYPE s_date,
      d_time   TYPE s_dep_time.
"old Open SQL
SELECT sflight~carrid fldate deptime
INTO ( d_carrid, d_date, d_time )
FROM sflight
INNER JOIN spfli
ON sflight~carrid = spfli~carrid
AND sflight~connid = spfli~connid.

"new Open SQL
SELECT sflight~carrid, fldate, deptime
INTO ( @d_carrid, @d_date, @d_time )
FROM sflight
INNER JOIN spfli
ON sflight~carrid = spfli~carrid
AND sflight~connid = spfli~connid.
```
Listing 4.17 INNER JOIN Example Showing the Table Indicator for Field Selections

Indicating the table name is not too difficult in this simple example, but it can get very wordy, especially when there are multiple tables being joined together. Luckily, you can use aliases to shorten the table name. Listing 4.18 renames `sflight` to `f` (flight) and `spfli` to `s` (schedule) using the `AS` command.

Table aliases

```
DATA: d_carrid TYPE s_carr_id,
      d_date   TYPE s_date,
```

4 Accessing the Database

```
         d_time   TYPE s_dep_time.
"old Open SQL
SELECT f~carrid fldate deptime
INTO ( d_carrid, d_date, d_time )
FROM sflight AS f
INNER JOIN spfli AS s
ON f~carrid = s~carrid
AND f~connid = s~connid.

"new Open SQL
SELECT f~carrid, fldate, deptime
INTO ( @d_carrid, @d_date, @d_time )
FROM sflight AS f
INNER JOIN spfli AS s
ON f~carrid = s~carrid
AND f~connid = s~connid.
```
Listing 4.18 INNER JOIN Example Using Table Aliases

When using table aliases, it's best to use a shortened name that makes sense so that you don't become confused. Listing 4.18 shorted the table names to one letter, but that one letter corresponded to the purpose of the table (f for flight and s for schedule). You can use a, b, c, and so on, but it will get confusing quickly.

INNER JOIN with WHERE clause

You can add a WHERE clause, which can limit the results by values in either table. As with SELECT fields, you are only required to specify the table containing the field you want to limit with your WHERE clause when the field exists in both tables, as shown in Listing 4.19.

```
DATA: d_carrid TYPE s_carr_id,
      d_date   TYPE s_date,
      d_time   TYPE s_dep_time.

"old Open SQL
SELECT f~carrid fldate deptime
INTO ( d_carrid, d_date, d_time )
FROM sflight AS f
INNER JOIN spfli AS s
ON f~carrid = s~carrid
AND f~connid = s~connid
WHERE airpfrom = 'JFK'
AND planetype = '747-400'.

"new Open SQL
SELECT f~carrid, fldate, deptime
INTO ( @d_carrid, @d_date, @d_time )
```

```
FROM sflight AS f
INNER JOIN spfli AS s
ON f~carrid = s~carrid
AND f~connid = s~connid
WHERE airpfrom = 'JFK'
AND planetype = '747-400'.
```
Listing 4.19 INNER JOIN Example with Where Clause

With `INNER JOIN`s, you can join multiple tables, but too many tables joined can begin to affect performance. In order to avoid performance issues, always try to join tables on their primary keys. Sometimes, you may need to perform multiple `SELECT`s instead of combining as much as you can into a single `SELECT`.

INNER JOIN performance issues

Listing 4.20 joins four tables together so that you can see all of the bookings for customer 3264 along with fields from all of the different tables. This is much better than doing individual `SELECT`s on each of the tables. We are only showing the new Open SQL example for this, so that we can use inline data declaration instead of defining a table to hold the results.

```
SELECT bookid, carrname, b~connid, b~fldate, deptime
INTO TABLE @data(t_results)
FROM SBOOK AS b
INNER JOIN SFLIGHT AS f
ON b~carrid = f~carrid
AND b~connid = f~connid
AND b~fldate = f~fldate
INNER JOIN spfli AS s
ON b~carrid = s~carrid
AND b~connid = s~connid
INNER JOIN scarr as c
ON b~carrid = c~carrid
WHERE custom_id = 3264.
```
Listing 4.20 INNER JOIN Example with Multiple Table Join

LEFT OUTER JOIN

In an `INNER JOIN`, a record must exist in all tables included in the join, but with a `LEFT OUTER JOIN`, the record will still be displayed even if the table you're joining doesn't have a corresponding record. The syntax for a `LEFT OUTER JOIN` is the same as the `INNER JOIN`; only the keyword name has changed as shown in the example in Listing 4.21.

```
DATA: d_date    TYPE s_date,
      d_time    TYPE s_dep_time.
"old Open SQL
SELECT SINGLE fldate deptime
INTO ( d_date, d_time )
FROM sflight
LEFT OUTER JOIN spfli
ON sflight~carrid = spfli~carrid
AND sflight~connid = spfli~connid.

"new Open SQL
SELECT SINGLE fldate, deptime
INTO ( @d_date, @d_time )
FROM sflight
LEFT OUTER JOIN spfli
ON sflight~carrid = spfli~carrid
AND sflight~connid = spfli~connid.
```
Listing 4.21 LEFT OUTER JOIN Example

In Figure 4.6, we removed flight AA-17 from table SPFLI. If you ran an INNER JOIN, your results would not include any details for flight AA-17, but because we ran a LEFT OUTER JOIN, DEPTIME is null/initial.

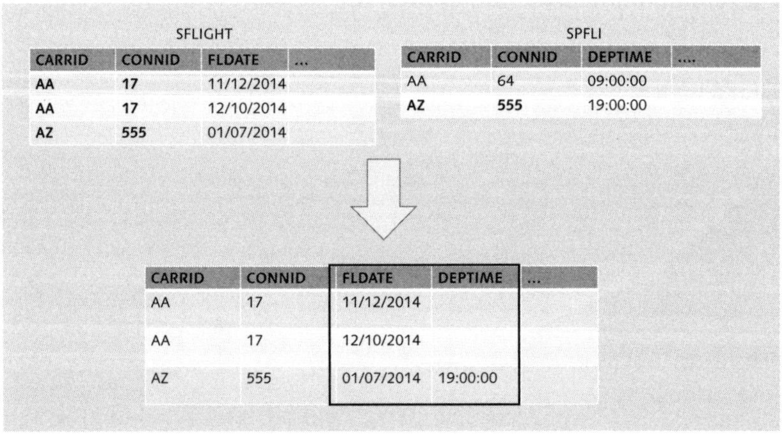

SFLIGHT					SPFLI			
CARRID	CONNID	FLDATE	...		CARRID	CONNID	DEPTIME	....
AA	17	11/12/2014			AA	64	09:00:00	
AA	17	12/10/2014			AZ	555	19:00:00	
AZ	555	01/07/2014						

CARRID	CONNID	FLDATE	DEPTIME	...
AA	17	11/12/2014		
AA	17	12/10/2014		
AZ	555	01/07/2014	19:00:00	

Figure 4.6 LEFT OUTER JOIN Example Diagram

With old Open SQL You cannot use a WHERE clause or an additional INNER JOIN using fields in a table that is included in a LEFT OUTER JOIN, but you can include these fields in a select using the new Open SQL. With this added functionality, we can use WHERE IS NULL to find only the records that did not match as shown in Listing 4.22 below.

Combining LEFT OUTER JOIN with other statements

```
SELECT fldate, deptime
INTO TABLE @DATA(t_flights)
FROM sflight
LEFT OUTER JOIN spfli
ON sflight~carrid = spfli~carrid
AND sflight~connid = spfli~connid
WHERE spfli~deptime IS NULL.
```
Listing 4.22 Left Outer Join Example Using WHERE...IS NULL

A single SELECT statement can include a combination of INNER JOINs and LEFT OUTER JOINs, but make sure you keep an eye on the SELECT performance when creating your SELECT statements.

FOR ALL ENTRIES IN

The INNER JOIN and OUTER JOIN operations are database table to database table, but what if you want to join between a database table and an internal table? This is where the Open SQL command FOR ALL ENTRIES IN can be used.

The FOR ALL ENTRIES IN command works just like an INNER JOIN, using an internal table from your program as the joining table except

Joining against internal tables

instead of using ON to declare the fields to match on, we use WHERE and the internal table uses a – instead of a ~ as shown in Listing 4.23 where we use the results from a select on the table zbook to find records in the scustom table.

```
DATA: t_book TYPE STANDARD TABLE OF zbook,
      t_custom TYPE STANDARD TABLE OF scustom.
"old Open SQL
SELECT *
INTO TABLE t_book
FROM zbook.

SELECT *
INTO TABLE t_custom
```

```
FROM scustom
FOR ALL ENTRIES IN t_book
WHERE scustom~customid = t_book-customid.

"new Open SQL
SELECT *
INTO TABLE @t_book
FROM zbook.

SELECT *
INTO TABLE @t_custom
FROM scustom
FOR ALL ENTRIES IN @t_book
WHERE scustom~customid = @t_book-customid.
```
Listing 4.23 FOR ALL ENTRIES IN Example

Even though conceptually FOR ALL ENTRIES IN works like an INNER JOIN, when the open SQL is translated in to native SQL, it's actually transformed into a long list of WHERE statements, as seen in Figure 4.7.

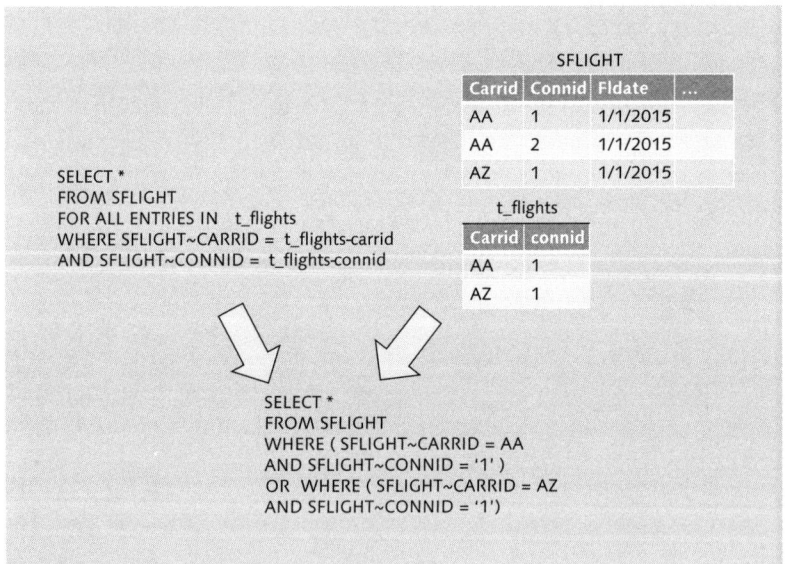

Figure 4.7 FOR ALL ENTRIES IN Example

Using FOR ALL ENTRIES IN in Internal Tables

Because the FOR ALL ENTRIES IN command is translated into many WHERE commands, it's important that you check whether your table has the condition IS INITIAL before using it in a FOR ALL ENTRIES IN SELECT statement.

If your internal table has no data inside it, your selection will be translated into native SQL with no WHERE statements, meaning that you could be selecting the entire table!

In order to prevent this situation, every time you use FOR ALL ENTRIES IN, first check if your internal table has any rows inside of it using one of the following IF statements, and then make sure that your SELECT statement is within that IF statement block:

IF t_table IS NOT INITIAL.
IF lines(t_table) > 0.

With SELECT Options

When you were creating your classic selection screens with select-options, there were many different options for selecting data, such as selecting single values and single ranges or excluding single values and ranges, as shown in Figure 4.8.

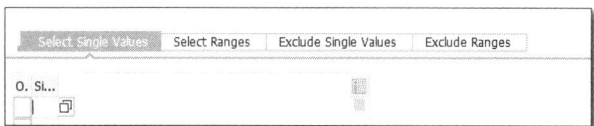

Figure 4.8 SELECT Options Tabs

You can easily use selection options in a WHERE statement for a given field, using the WHERE..IN command with the IN keyword instead of an = as shown in Listing 4.24

```
DATA: d_carrid TYPE s_carr_id,
 t_sflight TYPE STANDARD TABLE OF sflight.
SELECTION-SCREEN BEGIN OF BLOCK selection.
    SELECT-OPTIONS: so_carr for d_carrid.
SELECTION-SCREEN END OF BLOCK selection.
```

```
"old Open SQL
SELECT *
INTO TABLE t_sflight
FROM sflight
WHERE carrid IN so_carr.

"new Open SQL
SELECT *
INTO TABLE @t_sflight
FROM sflight
WHERE carrid IN @so_carr.
```
Listing 4.24 WHERE...IN SELECT Example

Selection Option structure

The selection options are actually an internal table of ranges. A range is a structure with the four components described in Table 4.1.

Sign	The sign can be either I or E: ▶ I: Inclusive (contains this value or range) ▶ E: Exclusive (does not contain this value or range)
Option	The option declares the type of comparison to be used with the low/high fields: ▶ EQ: Equal to (=) ▶ NE: Not equal to (<>) ▶ GE: Greater than or equal to (>=) ▶ GT: Greater than (>) ▶ LE: Less than or equal to (<=) ▶ LT: Less than (<) ▶ CP: Contains pattern ▶ NP: Does not contain pattern ▶ BT: Between low and high ▶ NB: Not between low and high
Low	The low value for a between/not between comparison, or the comparison value when not using a between comparison.
High	The high value for a between/not between comparison.

Table 4.1 Selection Structure

Remember that if the sign is set to exclusive, it will return values that did not meet the sign test. That means that if the sign is E, the option is NE, and the low is 5, the value selected would be 5. That would be the same as a sign of I, option of EQ, and low of 5.

Just like when using FOR ALL ENTRIES IN, using a selection table in your SELECT will be translated into a long WHERE clause when it runs as native SQL on the database.

New Open SQL

Now that we have reviewed the different types of commands that we can use in Open SQL statements, this section will review some of the changes with new Open SQL that you have probably noticed as well as some that have not yet been displayed.

You probably noticed that when using the new Open SQL syntax, we separated columns with a comma and prefixed any ABAP variables with a @ symbol. Additionally, we can specify all of the columns of a particular table in a join using the table~* syntax as shown below in Listing 4.25.

New Open SQL syntax

```
SELECT sflight~*, spfli~deptime
FROM sflight
INNER JOIN spfli
ON sflight~carrid = spfli~carrid
AND sflight~connid = spfli~connid
INTO TABLE @DATA(t_flights).
```
Listing 4.25 Example Selecting All Columns from an INNER JOIN TABLE

When using inline data declarations, we can set the name of the different structure components using the AS command when selecting the database columns. If we do not use this command, the names will match the name of the column which we are selecting. An example demonstrating this is shown below in Listing 4.26 where we renamed the fldate column to flight_date.

```
SELECT SINGLE fldate AS flight_date, carrid
FROM sflight
INTO @DATA(s_flight).

DATA(d_date) = s_flight-flight_date.
```
Listing 4.26 Example Showing a Named Column

Prior to new Open SQL, the `INTO` or `INTO TABLE` command always had to be either after the `SELECT` or after the `FROM`. With new Open SQL, it can now be located after a WHERE clause at the end of a statement. This makes the SQL query much more readable and is demonstrated below in Listing 4.27. Note that `UP TO n ROWS` must still be placed after the `INTO TABLE` command.

```
SELECT *
FROM sflight
WHERE carrid = 'AA'
INTO TABLE @DATA(t_flights).
```
Listing 4.27 Example Showing INTO TABLE After a WHERE clause

Table Locks

Deadlocks Anytime you update a database using Open SQL, the risk for a deadlock exists. A *deadlock* occurs when two updates to a database occur at the same time. Luckily, you can address this situation by locking database records. It's important that you lock the table every time you have an update.

Locks are not restricted to locking a single table; they can be used to lock all tables that are impacted by the changes that you are making. Also, if you have multiple application servers in your environment, the lock will be enforced across all the systems.

It's possible to check for a lock before locking a table, but not necessary, because you will get an error when setting the lock if a lock is already set. In the split second between checking if a lock is set and setting a lock, someone else could have already set a lock.

Lock concept Figure 4.9 illustrates an overview of the lock concept. In the deadlock scenario, two users are updating the same record in the database at the same time. In the lock scenario, two users are trying to set a lock at the same time, but only the first one gets to do so. The first user then updates the table while the second user is still trying to set the lock, and then the first user releases the lock, enabling the second user to set his or her lock.

Table Locks 4

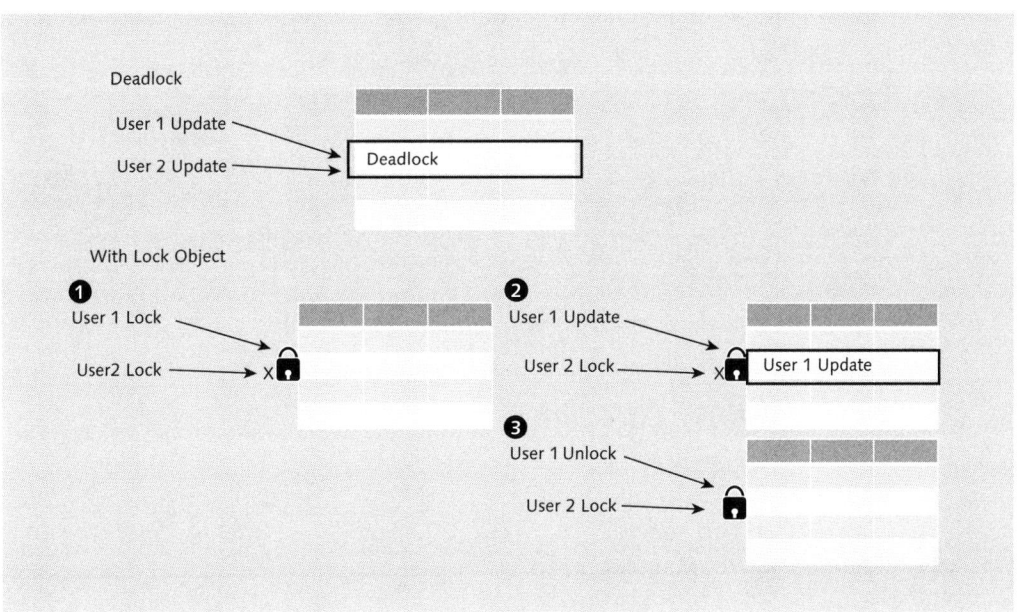

Figure 4.9 Lock Concept Overview

There are different types of locks; use the one that makes sense for your situation (Table 4.2).

Type of Lock	Description
Exclusive lock (E)	Locked data can be displayed and edited only the user who set the lock.
Shared lock (S)	Multiple users can read the data, and multiple shared locks from different users can be set. Exclusive locks are rejected.
Optimistic lock (O)	Behaves like a shared lock, but can be converted to an exclusive lock.
Promote optimistic lock (R)	Converts an optimistic lock into an exclusive lock.

Lock types

Table 4.2 Types of Database Locks

Locks also can have one of three different scopes (Table 4.3).

Lock scopes

Scope Value	Affect
1	Can be released with a DEQUEUE function module call or by reaching the end of a program.
2	A COMMIT WORK or ROLLBACK WORK command will release the lock. This type of lock can continue past the end of a program.
3	Both of the scope 1 and 2 conditions must be met before the lock is released.

Table 4.3 Scope Value for Database Locks

Viewing Table Locks

Now that you know how locks work, let's take a look at an existing one. Locks should already exist for any standard SAP tables or business objects in your system. You should only need to create new ones for your custom tables.

Table locks, like the other ABAP Data Dictionary objects, can only be accessed using Transaction SE11 in SAP GUI. From there, select the LOCK OBJECT radio button, enter "ENQ_SFLIGHT" in the textbox, and click DISPLAY.

Lock attributes The ATTRIBUTES tab displayed in Figure 4.10 shows some basic information about the lock parameter and also contains a checkbox indicating whether the lock can be set from a Remote Function Call (RFC). A table may be locked through an RFC from another system calling a transaction to update the table or business object.

Lock tables The TABLES tab displayed in Figure 4.11 will list all of the tables that are affected by this lock and the type of lock that you're using. Because no additional tables are listed in the secondary table area, you know that this lock will only lock records in table SFLIGHT.

The LOCK MODE field shows WRITE LOCK, meaning that this is an exclusive lock that will prevent other users from writing to the locked records by default. You will see later in this section that you can also determine the mode when you set the lock in your code.

Table Locks

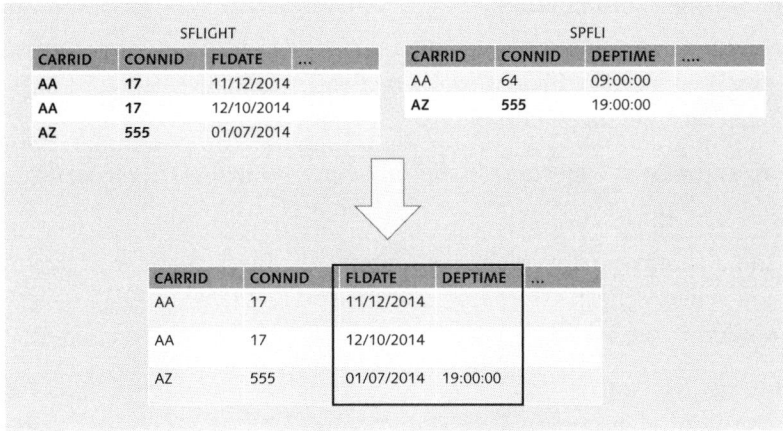

Figure 4.10 The Attributes Tab of the Lock Object Display

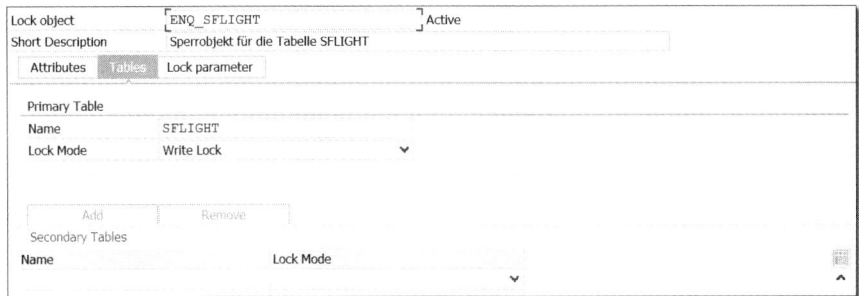

Figure 4.11 The Tables Tab of the Lock Object Display

The LOCK PARAMETER tab (Figure 4.12) will indicate which parameters are used to lock the records in the table. If an entire primary key is listed, only one record will be locked. If a partial primary key is listed, all of the records found using the provided parameters will be locked.

Lock parameters

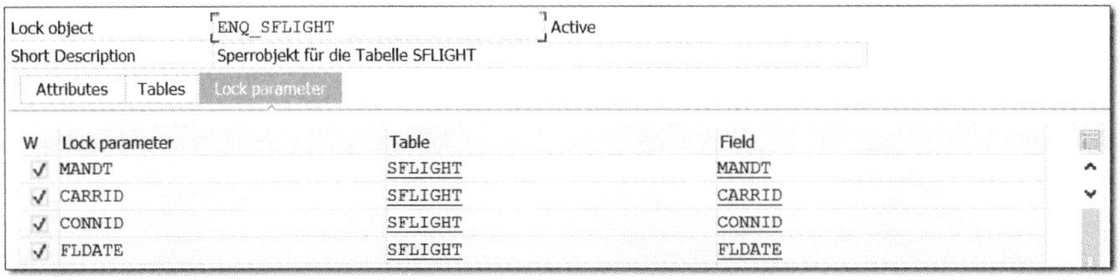

Figure 4.12 The Lock Parameter Tab of the Lock Object Display

Creating Table Locks

Now that you've reviewed a standard lock provided by SAP, create your own lock for the new tables that you created in Chapter 3. First, enter Transaction SE11 in SAP GUI.

Select the LOCK OBJECTS radio button, enter "EZBOOK" in the textbox, and click the CREATE button. All lock objects must begin with an "E."

Add a short description for your new lock object. A simple description such as "Lock Object for ZBOOK and ZBOOK_SFLIGHT tables" would be fine.

Lock attributes   In the ATTRIBUTES tab, select the checkbox for ALLOW RFC, as shown in Figure 4.13. This checkbox will allow other ABAP systems to set the lock through an RFC connection. This is very useful if you ever have two systems sending data to each other through an RFC connection.

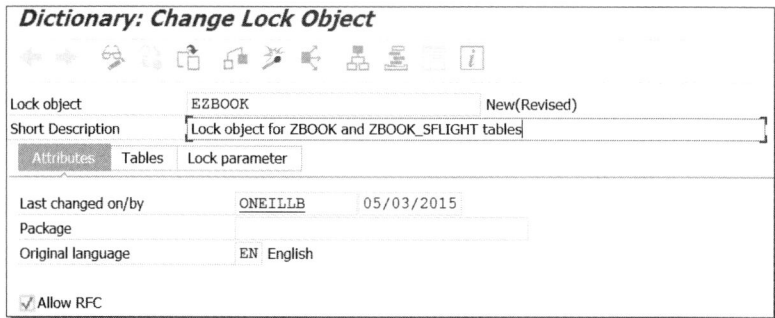

Figure 4.13 The Attributes Tab for the New Lock Object

Lock tables   In the TABLES tab, add "ZBOOK" as the primary table. Then, click ADD, and select the ZBOOK_SFLIGHT table. Both the primary table and the secondary table should have WRITE LOCK selected as the lock mode, meaning that the lock will prevent others from writing to the table, but not prevent others from reading the table. The end result should match the screen shown in Figure 4.14.

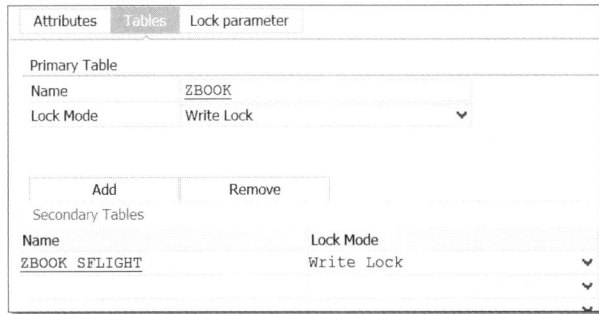

Figure 4.14 The Tables Tab When Creating a New Lock Object

Next, select the LOCK PARAMETER tab. You will see that all of the fields used as primary keys for our tables are shown. Deselect the checkboxes for `CARRID`, `CONNID`, and `FLDATE`, as indicated in Figure 4.15. This way, when you lock the tables, you also will lock all related records for a supplied `BOOKID`.

Lock parameter

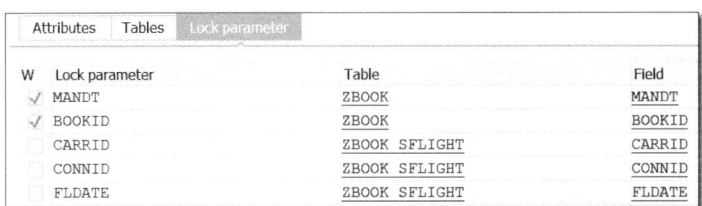

Figure 4.15 The Lock Parameter Tab When Creating a New Lock Object

Click SAVE and activate the lock object. It should be saved as a local object (`$TMP` package).

Setting Table Locks

Now that you've viewed an existing lock in the ABAP Data Dictionary and created a new one, it's time to cover how to set the locks from within your ABAP code.

Every ABAP Data Dictionary lock object creates two function modules: one to create the lock and one to release the lock. The function module to create the lock is `ENQUEUE _<lock name>` and the one to release the lock is `DEQUEUE _<lock name>`. We'll cover function modules in more detail in Chapter 6; for now, just know that a function module calls another block of code.

Lock function module

Now, create a new ABAP program called Z_LOCK_TEST. If you're using Transaction SE80, go to EDIT • PATTERN, select the CALL FUNCTION radio button (Figure 4.16), enter "ENQUEUE_EZBOOK" in the textbox, and click the green checkmark.

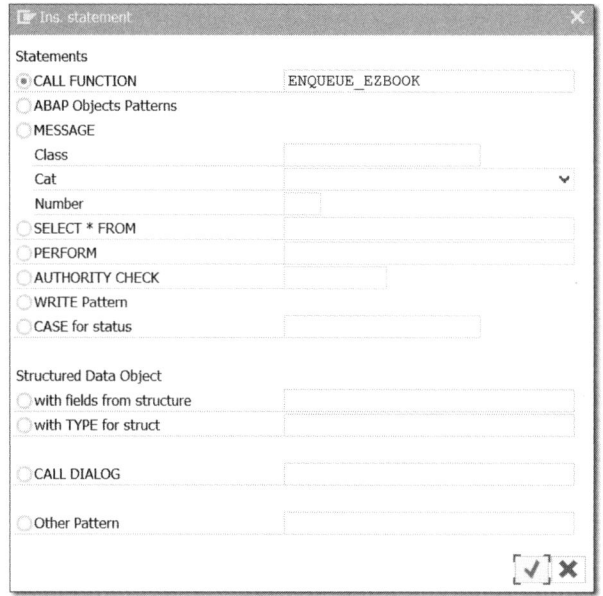

Figure 4.16 The Pattern Selection Popup

If you're using ABAP in Eclipse, enter CALL FUNCTION ' and start typing "ENQUEUE_ZBOOK", but select the complete term from the autocomplete options. If you don't see the list of autocomplete options, press [Ctrl]+[Space] to get the autocomplete options to appear. When you see the correct function module, highlight it and click [Shift]+[Enter].

As a result, the system will create a call to the function module with all of the optional parameters commented out. Uncomment all of the lines by removing the asterisk (*) when present at the beginning of a line, and change the values to match the ones shown in Listing 4.28.

```
CALL FUNCTION 'ENQUEUE_EZBOOK'
 EXPORTING
    MODE_ZBOOK         = 'E'
    MODE_ZBOOK_SFLIGHT = 'E'
    MANDT              = SY-MANDT
    BOOKID             = 1
    X_BOOKID           = abap_false
    _SCOPE             = '1'
    _WAIT              = abap_true
    _COLLECT           = abap_false
 EXCEPTIONS
    FOREIGN_LOCK       = 1
    SYSTEM_FAILURE     = 2
    OTHERS             = 3.
IF sy-subrc <> 0.
 MESSAGE ID sy-msgid TYPE sy-msgty NUMBER sy-msgno
          WITH sy-msgv1 sy-msgv2 sy-msgv3 sy-msvg4.
ENDIF.
```
Listing 4.28 Setting Up the Locking Function Module

The MODE parameter sets the mode to use a key to indicate one of the values listed in Table 4.2. In Listing 4.28, it's set to 'E', meaning that it will be an exclusive lock on both table ZBOOK and table ZBOOK_SFLIGHT. The MANDT and BOOKID parameters are used to indicate the key for which you'll be locking records. In this example, it's currently set to lock the records for BOOKID 1 and the system that you're currently logged in to (sy-mandt). The X_BOOKID parameter indicates whether the second argument (BOOKID) should be populated with an initial value.

Lock parameters

The _SCOPE parameter sets the scope to one of the values described in Table 4.2. Select a scope of 1, because you'll also be using the DEQUEUE function module to release the lock. The _WAIT parameter indicates whether or not the lock should wait and try again if it detects that the lock is already set. The _COLLECT parameter determines whether the lock request should be placed in a local lock container or sent directly to the lock server. If you choose to use the local lock container, then you need to call the function module FLUSH_ENQUEUE to move all of your lock requests to the lock server at the same time. You don't need to use this functionality now, because you're only setting one lock and don't need to worry about collecting multiple locks together.

The exceptions indicate why a lock did not get set correctly. You'll learn more about exceptions in Chapter 6 when you'll examine function modules in more detail. You may notice Listing 4.28 replaced the default space character with `abap_false`. There is no difference between `abap_false` and a space character; you can use either interchangeably.

Now, add the code in Listing 4.29 to the top of your ABAP program. This code will set up the data to be used to update the database.

```
DATA: d_zbook TYPE zbook.
d_zbook-bookid = 1.
d_zbook-customid = 1.
```
Listing 4.29 Data to Be Used When Updating Database

Unlocking the table

Next, add the code in Listing 4.30 to the bottom of your ABAP program to update the database and remove the database lock. Remove ENDIF at end of the code from Listing 4.28 before adding the new code, which will ensure that the MODIFY code only runs if the lock is successfully set.

```
ELSE.
 MODIFY zbook FROM d_zbook.
ENDIF.

CALL FUNCTION 'DEQUEUE_EXBOOK'
    EXPORTING
        mode_zbook        = 'E'
        mode_zbook_sflight = 'E'
        mandt             = SY-MANDT
        bookid            = 1
        x_bookid          = abap_false
        _scope            = '1'
        _synchron         = abap_false
        _collect          = abap_false
        .
```
Listing 4.30 Code to Update Database and Remove Database Lock

Specify the same parameters in the DEQUEUE function module to indicate that you're removing the same lock. The only new parameter is _synchron, which indicates whether the lock removal should be completed synchronously or asynchronously. If you may be creating more locks affecting the same records you're locking, then you should make it synchronous so that you don't start processing the next change until the lock is removed; otherwise, passing `abap_false` to allow it to run asynchronously should be fine.

Performance Topics

You want to limit the communication to and from the database as much as possible, because every time a call to the database is made, the application server has to open a connection, submit your query, and then close the connection and transfer the data over the network. Therefore, its good practice to use joins to get the data you need with a limited number of SELECT statements.

However, using too many joins can cause even worse performance. Make sure you balance your queries in a way that makes sense. There's no rule about this; you just need to test and experience and use full primary keys when possible. Also if you have an SAP HANA database, you will want to learn about some of the nuances of an SAP HANA database to ensure that you are utilizing the database in the most efficient way possible.

Balancing queries

Also, always avoid having a SELECT statement inside a loop. Try to gather everything you need in a single call, and process the results in a loop in local memory.

You can also lower the number of calls to the database by buffering your tables. Buffering saves table records in the application server's buffer memory, which allows data to be returned much more quickly; however, be cautious not to store tables that are too large in the buffer, or you'll soon overload your system's memory. Refer to Table 4.4 for an explanation of the different types of buffering.

Buffering

Buffering Type	Affect
Single records buffered	If SELECT SINGLE is used, the record will be read from the buffer or added to the buffer. This option should be used for large tables with records that are regularly accessed using SELECT SINGLE.

Table 4.4 Buffering Types

Buffering Type	Affect
Generic area buffered	This option buffers an area based on a given number of fields. For example, if the key is made of five fields, up to four of them could be used to define the buffer area. When records from the buffer area are selected, the area is buffered in the memory. This type of buffer should be used when a certain area in tables is regularly queried, and the table is too large to be fully buffered.
Fully buffered	This type of buffer will load the entire table into the application server's memory. This will improve performance for all queries to the table, but should only be used for small tables that are continually queried, because it will use the most memory.

Table 4.4 Buffering Types (Cont.)

The table buffer can be set in Transaction SE11 by maintaining a table's technical details. You will need to select the BUFFERING SWITCHED ON radio button in the BUFFERING section, and select the appropriate BUFFERING TYPE checkbox shown below in Figure 4.17.

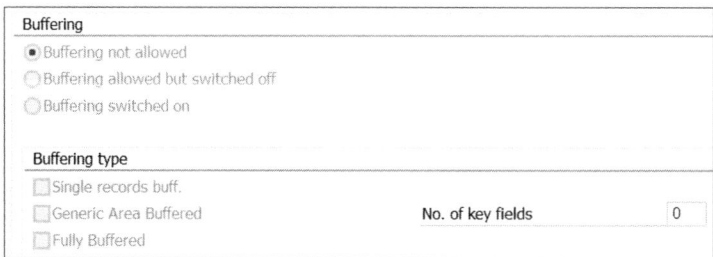

Figure 4.17 Buffering Options

Obsolete Database Access Keywords

There are a few ways to access the database that should be avoided if possible. Many ABAP systems are old, and because ABAP is always backward compatible, you may run in to these types of statements. However, try to avoid adding them to the new code base.

SELECT...ENDSELECT

The `SELECT...ENDSELECT` statements are not officially obsolete, but they can make your code much more difficult to understand. The code between the `SELECT` and `ENDSELECT` statements will be looped through for every record in a table. You'll learn about better ways to loop through your results in Chapter 5.

In the example shown in Listing 4.31 the commented pseudocode "`Do something` will be executed for every record resulting from the `SELECT` statement.

```
SELECT * FROM ZBOOK
INTO @DATA(result).
   "Do something
ENDSELECT.
```
Listing 4.31 SELECT...ENDSELECT Example

Short Form Open SQL

The short form `SELECT` has been an obsolete ABAP statement for a long time. If you see this in an ABAP program, you should take the time to replace it with updated code, because it can be hard to understand and troubleshoot—especially for new ABAP developers.

Short form Open SQL statements work by first declaring the tables using the `TABLES` keyword. Then, the `SELECT` is written without using the `INTO` keyword. The data selected is accessed using the table name instead of a declared variable. Listing 4.32 shows an example.

```
TABLES: zbook.
SELECT * FROM zbook.
   WRITE: zbook-bookid.
ENDSELECT.
```
Listing 4.32 Short Form Open SQL Example

Summary

This chapter covered how to work with the database connected to your ABAP system using Open SQL commands with both old Open SQL and new Open SQL. You should now be able to read data from the database, update the database, and select data based on select options from the user.

You also learned how to create and set table locks used when you update the database to ensure that you avoid deadlock, which occurs when two people update the same record in a database at the same time.

Then, the chapter covered some database performance topics to keep in mind when working with databases, including how to improve performance using table buffering.

The next chapter will cover how to store the results from your table access in working memory and process those results.

Storing Data in Working Memory

5

So far, you've learned how to perform some basic data processing using ABAP, how to create ABAP Data Dictionary objects using SAP GUI, and how to read data from the transparent tables in the database using open SQL.

In this chapter, you'll explore different ways to take the data from the database and store it in a working memory table (also known as an *internal table*) to process it. You'll discover different ways to process the data and learn about some outdated methods you shouldn't use to process the data.

Using ABAP Data Dictionary Data Types

Chapter 2 introduced how to create variables with basic data types (i, d, t, c, etc.); you then used those data types to create domains and data elements in Chapter 3. Just like you created variables with the basic data types, you can also create variables with ABAP Data Dictionary objects. This is the preferred method to create variables in ABAP programs that work with the database (which should be all ABAP programs), because any changes to the ABAP Data Dictionary objects will affect the related programs automatically.

Data Types

You can create data types that refer to a domain, data element, or table field. An example of each is shown in Listing 5.1.

Creating data types

```
DATA: d_plane        TYPE S_PLANE,   "Domain
      d_plane_type   TYPE S_PLANETYE, "Data Element
      d_plane_type2  TYPE sflight-planetype. "Table Field
```
Listing 5.1 Variables Created from ABAP Data Dictionary Objects

183

5 Storing Data in Working Memory

All of the examples in Listing 5.1 result in the same type of variable being created. However, if you know the table and field that you're working with, using that information is the safest choice, because the data element for the field potentially could be changed.

You also can choose to create a variable based on a transparent table. This will create a structure of the table, which is the equivalent of a single row from the table. The structure in Listing 5.2 is based on the table sflight.

```
DATA: s_flight TYPE sflight.
```
Listing 5.2 Creating a Structure Based on a Transparent Table

Structure components

You can then access any of the components from the sflight structure using a dash (–) followed by the field name. Listing 5.3 adds values to the different fields of the structure; you can then modify the database table using the structure from your program.

```
s_flight-carrid = 'AA'.
s_flight-connid = 17.
s_flgiht-fldate = 20150101.
MODIFY sflight FROM s_flight.
```
Listing 5.3 Adding Values to a Table Structure and Then Modifying the Database With That Structure

Using like

Just as it is possible to create variables that use a structure or table type from the ABAP Data Dictionary or a type that we defined in our program, we can also create a variable that is based on the type of another variable. An example of this is shown in Listing 5.4 where we use the LIKE keyword to indicate what variable our variable should be based on. Both s_flight and s_flight2 in Listing 5.4 will have the same structure.

```
DATA: s_flight TYPE sflight,
      s_flight2 LIKE s_flight.
```
Listing 5.4 Example Using LIKE Instead of TYPE

We can also use LIKE LINE OF to create a variable that contains the structure of a table variable. In Listing 5.5 below, s_flight will contain the structure from the table t_flights which is based on the table type we created in chapter 3. To demonstrate that `s_flight` is a structure, we all change one of its components.

```
DATA: t_flights TYPE zflights,
 s_flight LIKE LINE OF t_flights.
      s_flight-carrid = 'AA'.
```
Listing 5.5 Example Using LIKE LINE OF

Creating Your Own Structures

The last section covered how to create structures based on transparent tables defined in the ABAP Data Dictionary. Sometimes, you may want to define your own structures in your code to be used for processing data, or if you aren't selecting all of the fields in a table and aren't on an ABAP 7.4 SP8 or higher system, you'll need to define your own structures, because you can't use inline data declarations yet in your system. The structures that are created are just like the ABAP Data Dictionary structures that we introduced in Chapter 3, except that these structures are only usable from within the program where they are being defined, unlike the ABAP Data Dictionary structures which can be used in any ABAP program.

You can create your own structures within your ABAP code using the TYPES keyword instead of the DATA keyword that we used for defining variables. The fields of a structure are defined in between the BEGIN OF <name> and END OF <name> keywords. Each field is defined with a type, which works just like defining any other variable type, so you can use a basic data type or an ABAP Data Dictionary-based data type. An example of creating your own structure data type is shown below in Listing 5.6, where we prefixed the name with y_ indicating that it is a structure defined in our code.

Defining your own structures

```
TYPES: BEGIN OF y_my_type,
  carrid TYPE sflight-carrid,
       connid TYPE sflight-connid,
       END OF y_my_type.
```
Listing 5.6 New Structure Data Type Made of Two Fields

After defining the type, you can create a variable of that type as shown in Listing 5.7. We cannot use the type by itself, it must be used as part of a variable. The naming used in the below example starts with `s_` indicating that the type is a structure.

```
DATA: s_my_type TYPE y_my_type.
```
Listing 5.7 New Variable Using Custom Structure Data Type

A common use for your own structure data types is to save the results of a `SELECT` statement that doesn't use all of the fields in the table (when we cannot use inline data declarations), as shown in Listing 5.8.

```
SELECT SINGLE carrid connid
INTO s_my_type
FROM sflight.
```
Listing 5.8 Using Custom Structure Data Type with SELECT Statement That Does Not Select All Fields

In Chapter 3 we created both a structure and a table type of that structure. From within our code we can also create a table from our own structure or from a structure defined in the ABAP Data Dictionary. An example of this is shown below in Listing 5.9 where we add a table type definition of our structure defined in code. Table types are defined similar to how we define variables, but with the `TYPES` keyword. We define the table type name followed by `TYPE STANDARD TABLE OF` and the structure name. In Listing 5.9 we named our table type with the prefix `yt_` meaning table type.

```
TYPES: BEGIN OF y_my_type,
       carrid TYPE sflight-carrid,
              connid TYPE sflight-connid,
       END of y_my_type,
              yt_my_type TYPE STANDARD TABLE OF y_my_type.
```
Listing 5.9 Creating a Table Type from within Our Code

Field Symbols

Access data in working memory

When dealing with working memory, you'll typically make use of *field symbols*, which allow you to access data in working memory without making a copy of that data. This is similar to pointers used in other programming languages. A pointer is very descriptive, because the field symbol points to areas of memory instead of actually being loaded with the data itself. This allows them to run faster than variables that have to have data copied into them. Additionally, changing a field symbol will change the data that it is pointing to, which could be a record in an internal table for example. We will be using field symbols throughout this chapter.

Field symbols are declared just like other variables, but use the keyword `FIELD-SYMBOLS:` instead of `DATA:` and wrap the variable name with angle brackets (`<>`), as shown in Listing 5.10.

Declare field symbols

```
FIELD-SYMBOLS: <s_sflight> TYPE sflight.
```
Listing 5.10 Defining a New Field Symbol

You can assign a value to a field symbol using the `ASSIGN` keyword. This will make the field symbol point to the same location in memory as the assigned variable. In Listing 5.11, changes to `s_flight` or `<s_flight>` both have the same effect on `s_flight`.

Assigning value to field symbols

```
DATA: s_flight TYPE sflight.
FIELD-SYMBOLS: <s_flight> TYPE sflight.
ASSIGN s_flight TO <s_flight>.
s_flight-carrid = 'AA'.
<s_flight>-carrid = ''.
```
Listing 5.11 Using Field Symbols with the ASSIGN Keyword

GETWA_NOT_ASSIGNED Exception

After creating a field symbol, it must be assigned a value before you can access it. If you try to access it before you assign a value to it, you will see a `GETWA_NOT_ASSIGNED` exception. This is the same as a null pointer error in other programming languages.

You can check if a field symbol is assigned a value in memory via `IF <field symbol> IS ASSIGNED`.

Beginning in ABAP 7.4, we can declare field symbols using inline data declaration. This can save a lot of time and lines of a program since we are defining the field symbol at the same time that we are assigning it as shown in Listing 5.12 using the command `FIELD-SYMBOL` followed by the field symbol name within parenthesis.

Inline data declaration

5 Storing Data in Working Memory

```
DATA: s_flight TYPE sflight.
ASSIGN s_flight to FIELD-SYMBOL(<s_flight>).
s_flight-carrid = 'AA'.
<s_flight>-carrid = ''.
```
Listing 5.12 Inline Data Declaration with Field Symbol

Now that we have covered how to create our own structures, table types, and field symbols, we will cover the different types of tables that can be used to store data within our program. Each table type has its own advantages and disadvantages. Using the correct data type for your situation can greatly impact the performance of your ABAP program.

Standard Table

Standard tables are the most basic table type. A standard table is much like a database's transparent table or a worksheet in Excel. Typically, data is selected from a database and stored in a standard table so that you can analyze the results or perform some action based on the results.

Defining Standard Tables

Inline data declarations

Anytime you store data from a SELECT statement in a table created using inline data declarations, you store the data in a standard table. An example creating a standard table using inline data declarations is shown in Listing 5.13.

```
SELECT *
INTO TABLE @DATA(results)
FROM sflight.
```
Listing 5.13 Creating a Standard Table Using Inline Data Declarations

Creating a standard table

You can also create standard tables when creating a new variable using the TYPE STANDARD TABLE OF keyword followed by a structure type or transparent table. An example of this is shown in Listing 5.14 where we create a standard table containing the same structure of the sflight table.

```
DATA: t_sflight TYPE STANDARD TABLE OF sflight.
```
Listing 5.14 Creating a New Standard Table Variable

Standard Table

When using a structure based on a transparent table, that table is not created with any keys defined. Defining a key is optional, but a key is required to complete some of the commands that we will explore later in this section. You will need to decide whether or not to add a key based on how you access the table. We recommend that you start with no keys and then add keys as needed.

Defining keys

A standard table can have a nonunique primary key added. You will learn about table types later in the chapter that require unique keys. The nonunique nature of a primary key means that you will not get an exception if you insert two rows that have the same key.

A key is defined by adding the KEY keyword followed by the fields that make up the key. An example of this is shown in Listing 5.15 using table sflight. You will notice that the example matched the key of the database's transparent table, except that it does not include MANDT. When you select data from the database, the ABAP system will always select the client based on the client that you're currently logged in to, so you don't need to worry about identifying records based on MANDT.

```
DATA: t_flight TYPE STANDARD TABLE OF sflight
    WITH KEY carrid connid fldate.
```
Listing 5.15 Standard Table with a Primary Key Defined

 Limitation of the LIKE keyword

If you created a table using the LIKE keyword, you will not be able to define keys for that table. However, any keys defined in the variable being copied, would also exist in the variable defined using LIKE as shown below:

```
DATA: t_flight TYPE STANDARD TABLE OF sflight
    WITH KEY carrid connid fldate,
t_flight_copy LIKE t_flight.
```

You can also create tables of your own data structures without the use of a table type using TYPE STANDARD TABLE OF. You can then use that table to store the results from a SELECT statement as shown in Listing 5.16.

```
TYPES: BEGIN OF y_my_type,
        carrid TYPE sflight-carrid,
        connid TYPE sflight-connid,
       END OF y_my_type.

DATA: t_my_type TYPE STANDARD TABLE OF y_my_type.

SELECT carrid connid
INTO TABLE t_my_type
FROM sflight.
```
Listing 5.16 Creating a Standard Table From a Custom Structure Data Type

READ TABLE

You can read a single record from a standard table using the READ TABLE keyword. You also need to define either an INDEX or a TABLE KEY to indicate the record that is being selected. When you read a table, you can read either INTO a variable or ASSIGNING a field symbol. An example using both INTO and ASSIGNING is shown in Listing 5.17 where we read the record in the table with an INDEX of 1, meaning it is the first record in the table.

```
DATA: t_flights TYPE STANDARD TABLE OF sflight,
      s_flight TYPE sflight.
FIELD SYMBOLS: <s_flight> TYPE sflight.

SELECT *
FROM sflight
INTO TABLE t_flights.

READ TABLE t_flights INTO s_flight INDEX 1.
READ TABLE t_flights ASSIGNING <s_flight> INDEX 1.
```
Listing 5.17 Example Using the READ TABLE Keyword

Inline data declarations We can also use inline data declarations here to define the variables we are reading INTO or ASSIGNING as part of the READ TABLE command instead of defining our variables at the top of our program. The example in Listing 5.18 demonstrates using inline data declarations.

```
SELECT *
FROM sflight
INTO TABLE @DATA(t_flights).

READ TABLE t_flights INTO DATA(s_flight) INDEX 1.
```

```
READ TABLE t_flights ASSIGNED FIELD-SYMBOL (<s_flight>)
INDEX 1.
```
Listing 5.18 Example Using READ TABLE with Inline Data Declarations

 Index 0

Unlike arrays in other programming languages, when reading a specific table INDEX, the first record's index is 1, not 0.

When you use the INTO keyword with a variable, a copy of the record is made and stored in the variable. This means that changes to that variable will not affect the corresponding row in the table, as shown in Figure 5.1. The INTO keyword should only be used when you need to create a copy of the data in the table; otherwise, we recommend that you use a field symbol with the ASSIGNING keyword.

INTO vs ASSIGNING

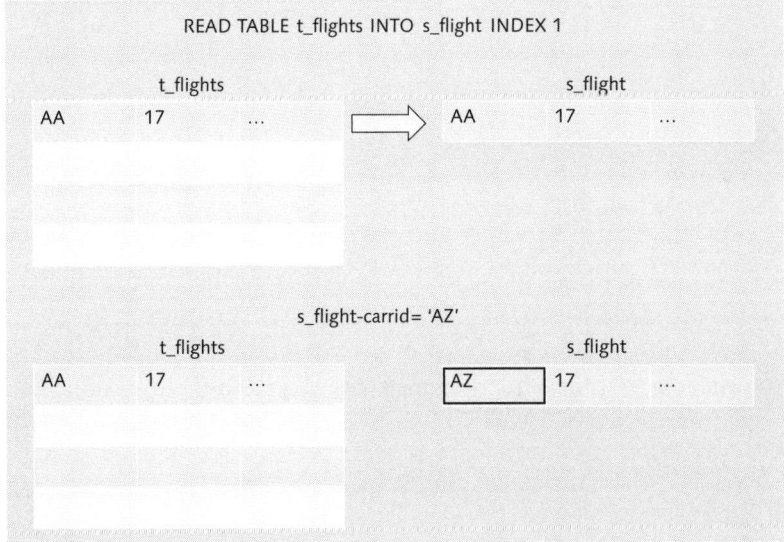

Figure 5.1 Using READ TABLE...INTO

When using a field symbol with the ASSIGNING keyword, you only create a pointer to the data in the table. Because you aren't copying any data into memory, using the field symbol will lead to better

Assigning

performance. When you make changes to the field symbol, it will directly change the data inside your table, as shown in Figure 5.2.

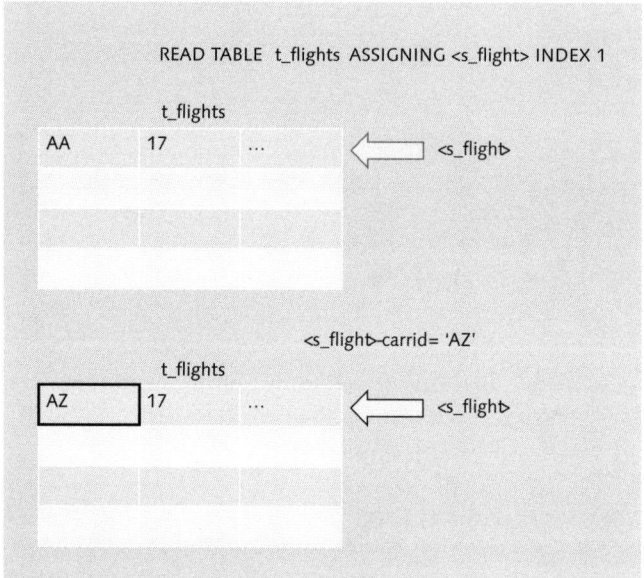

Figure 5.2 Using READ TABLE...ASSIGNING

WITH TABLE KEY   Most likely, you don't know the index of the record you're looking for, but you can use WITH TABLE KEY instead of INDEX to find the record you need. All you need to do is enter the field name, the equals sign, and the value you're looking for. You can use from one to any number of fields as part of the key separated by a space. The example in Listing 5.19 demonstrates this ability, continuing the code from Listing 5.17.

```
READ TABLE t_flights ASSIGNING <s_flight>
  WITH TABLE KEY carrid = 'AA' connid = 17
  fldate = 20150107
```
Listing 5.19 READ TABLE...WITH TABLE KEY Example

This code will return the first record found that meets the key requirements. You aren't restricted to any sort of key from the database, but keep in mind if you aren't using a unique key, you may not get the record you are seeking, because the first record found will be returned.

When READ TABLE returns a value, it will set the system variable sy-tabix to the index of the current record in the table that you're reading.

sy-tabix

 Using sy-subrc

sy-subrc is a system variable that the ABAP system will update after each READ TABLE call. The value will always be set to 0 when the read is successful.

You can ensure that a record is found by using an IF statement to check whether sy-subrc is equal to 0. You should always perform this check before working with the results of READ TABLE. The following example enhances the earlier code examples with a sy-subrc check:

```
READ TABLE t_flights ASSIGNING <sflight> INDEX 1.
IF sy-subrc = 0.
    <sflight>-carrid = 'AZ'
ENDIF.
```

LOOP AT

Just as you used READ TABLE to look at a single record from within a standard table, you can use LOOP AT to cycle through all of the records within a standard table and insert them into a variable or field symbol using the INTO or ASSIGNING keyword like we used with READ TABLE.

If you don't declare any additional options, LOOP AT will go through every record and execute any code between LOOP AT and ENDLOOP for each record. Listing 5.20 demonstrates the LOOP AT syntax. The field symbol example will change every row of the standard table to have a carrid of AZ.

```
DATA: t_flights TYPE STANDARD TABLE OF sflight,
      s_flight TYPE sflight.
FIELD SYMBOLS: <s_flight> TYPE sflight.

SELECT *
FROM sflight
INTO TABLE t_flights.
```

```
LOOP AT t_flights INTO s_flight.
    s_flight-carrid = 'AZ'.
ENDLOOP.
LOOP AT t_flights ASSIGNING <s_flight>.
    <s_flight>-carrid = 'AZ'
ENDLOOP.
```
Listing 5.20 Using LOOP AT...ENDLOOP

Inline data declarations

Just like we saw with READ TABLE, we have the option to use inline data declaration when using LOOP AT. An example using inline data declarations is shown below in Listing 5.21.

```
SELECT *
FROM sflight
INTO TABLE @DATA(t_flights).

LOOP AT t_flights INTO DATA(s_flight).
    s_flight-carrid = 'AZ'.
ENDLOOP.
LOOP AT t_flights ASSIGNING FIELD-SYMBOL(<s_flight>).
    <s_flight>-carrid = 'AZ'.
ENDLOOP.
```
Listing 5.21 LOOP AT...ENDLOOP Example With Inline Data Declarations

Using WHERE

You can also limit the rows that will be looped with the WHERE keyword, which limits the results in the same way as WITH TABLE KEY, which we used in the READ TABLE example. Unlike the READ TABLE example we now have all of the comparative operators covered in Chapter 2. For example, you can limit the rows to flights that occurred after a specified date, as shown in Listing 5.22.

```
LOOP AT t_flights ASSIGNING <s_flight>
WHERE fldate > '20150101'.
    <s_flight>-carrid = 'AZ'.
ENDLOOP.
```
Listing 5.22 LOOP AT...WHERE Example

 SY-TABIX

Every time you loop through the table, the value of system variable sy-tabix will be updated with the index of the current record in the table that you're looping through.

Inserting Rows in a Standard Table

There are multiple options for updating standard tables, just as we saw the many options for transparent tables in the database in Chapter 4.

You can use the INSERT keyword to add a new row to the bottom of the table, as shown in Listing 5.23. We must use a structure of the same type as the table by using INSERT followed by the structure name and then INTO TABLE followed by the standard table name.

```
DATA: s_flight_row TYPE sflight,
      t_flights TYPE STANDARD TABLE OF sflight.

s_flight_row-carrid = 'AA'.
s_flight_row-connid = '017'.
INSERT s_flight_row INTO TABLE t_flights.
```
Listing 5.23 INSERT Keyword with a Standard Table

You can also insert the row of data in a specified index by adding an INDEX option, which will set the index of the row currently at the specified index and all of the subsequent rows one lower, as shown in Listing 5.24, which is a continuation of Listing 5.23. Listing 5.24 inserts the new record in the first index position, moving the old record to the second index position.

Using an index

```
d_flight-carrid = 'AZ'.
INSERT d_flight INTO TABLE t_flights INDEX 1.
```
Listing 5.24 INSERT Keyword with the Addition of INDEX

If there are two tables of the same structure, there's a quick way to combine them without having to iterate through each record. The syntax for this is INSERT LINES FROM followed by the table name that you want to load the records from, and INTO TABLE followed by the table name that you want to load the records to, as shown in Listing 5.25. This method can work up to 20 times faster than looping through the records of a table and inserting them one by one.

Combining two like-structured tables

In Listing 5.25 we create two tables and a structure and then fill the structure with some basic data and insert it into table t_flights1. Then, we change one of the values in the structure and insert it into t_flights2. At this point, t_flights1 has two records, whereas t_flights2 has zero records. Then, we use INSERT LINES FROM to copy both records from table t_flights1 into table t_flights2.

```
DATA: t_flights1 TYPE STANDARD TABLE OF sflight,
      t_flights2 TYPE STANDARD TABLE OF sflight,
      d_flight   TYPE sflight.
d_flight-carrid = 'AA'.
d_flight-conned = '017'.
INSERT d_flight INTO TABLE t_flights1.
d_flight-carrid = 'AZ'.
INSERT d_flight INTO TABLE t_flights1.

INSERT LINES FROM t_flights1 INTO TABLE t_flights2.
```
Listing 5.25 INSERT LINES FROM

Changing Rows of a Standard Table

You can also use the MODIFY TABLE keyword to change a specific row of a standard table based on a provided structure. This keyword relies on matching table indexes to determine which record to change. The syntax is MODIFY TABLE followed by the standard table name, then FROM and the structure with the updated record as shown in Listing 5.26.

```
DATA: t_flights TYPE STANDARD TABLE OF sflight,
      s_flight  TYPE sflight.
s_flight-carrid = 'AA'.
s_flight-connid = '017'.
s_flight-fldate = 20150101.
INSERT s_flight INTO TABLE t_flights.
S_flight-price = 500.
MODIFY TABLE t_flights FROM s_flight.
```
Listing 5.26 Using MODIFY to Change a Standard Table

Changing multiple rows

You can also change multiple rows of a standard table with the MODIFY keyword by adding the TRANSPORTING and WHERE commands. Enter MODIFY instead of MODIFY TABLE, list the table's fields that you want to modify after TRANSPORTING, and the rows that will be affected will be determined by the WHERE clause at the end. This is useful when you have a requirement to complete a mass change on many rows of a standard table, as shown in Listing 5.27.

```
DATA: t_flights TYPE STANDARD TABLE OF sflight,
      s_flight  TYPE sflight.
```

Standard Table 5

```
SELECT *
INTO TABLE t_flights
FROM sflight.
s_flight-price = 500.
MODIFY t_flights FROM s_flight
  TRANSPORTING price WHERE carrid = 'AA'.
```
Listing 5.27 Using MODIFY to Change Multiple Rows of an Internal Table

As when using the UPDATE...SET...WHERE Open SQL command, you should always be careful when making these kinds of changes; you could change more records than you intend to.

You can also change a specified index of the table by using INDEX followed by the index number instead of using the WHERE clause. The TRANSPORTING option, which allows you to select specific fields to update, is optional when specifying the INDEX and must come after specifying the INDEX, as shown in Listing 5.28 where we change the value of price on the 5th record in the table.

Change specified index

```
DATA: t_flights TYPE STANDARD TABLE OF sflight,
      s_flight  TYPE sflight.
SELECT *
INTO TABLE t_flights
FROM sflight.
s_flight-price = 500.
MODIFY t_flights FROM s_flight INDEX 5 TRANSPORTING price.
```
Listing 5.28 Using MODIFY to Change a Standard Table with INDEX

Deleting Rows of a Standard Table

There are various options for deleting rows from a standard table. As with the methods for inserting or changing lines in a table, use the option that makes the most sense for what you're trying to do.

If you already have the row that you're using in a local data structure, you can use that structure to indicate the row that needs to be deleted. The DELETE TABLE command uses the primary key of the structure to find and delete the corresponding row from the standard table. If no primary key is defined when the standard table is defined, then the key is made up of the entire row, meaning the structure must match an entire row of the table. An example of the DELETE TABLE functionality using an entire row of data is shown in Listing 5.29, where we

Delete table functionality

SELECT data from a database, store the second record in a field symbol structure and then use that structure to delete a record using DELETE TABLE.

```
DATA: t_flights TYPE STANDARD TABLE OF sflight.
FIELD-SYMBOLS: <s_flight> TYPE sflight.
SELECT *
INTO TABLE t_flights
FROM sflight.
READ TABLE t_flights ASSIGNING <s_flight> INDEX 2.
DELETE TABLE t_flights FROM <s_flight>.
```
Listing 5.29 DELETE TABLE...FROM Example

Delete with keys

When you have a key defined in the table, you can use a structure that only has the key defined to delete the corresponding record from the standard table, as shown in Listing 5.30.

```
DATA: t_flights TYPE STANDARD TABLE OF sflight
   WITH KEY carrid connid fldate,
      s_flight TYPE sflight.
SELECT *
INTO TABLE t_flights
FROM sflight.
s_flight-carrid = 'AA'.
s_flight-connid = 17.
s_flight-fldate = '20150107'
DELETE TABLE t_flights FROM <s_flight>.
```
Listing 5.30 DELETE TABLE...FROM Example Using Key Fields Only

You can also specify the key in the DELETE command itself by replacing FROM with WITH TABLE KEY followed by the keys that define the record that you want to delete, as shown in Listing 5.31.

```
DATA: t_flights TYPE STANDARD TABLE OF sflight
   WITH KEY carrid connid fldate.
SELECT *
INTO TABLE t_flights
FROM sflight.
DELETE TABLE t_flights
   WITH TABLE KEY carrid = 'AA' connid = 17
   fldate = '20150107'.
```
Listing 5.31 Using DELETE TABLE...WITH TABLE KEY

Sorted Table

You can also delete rows in a standard table based on a WHERE clause. This is similar to the OPEN SQL DELETE FROM...WHERE that you saw in Chapter 4. The example in Listing 5.32 will delete every row with the AA carrier and flight 17 using the DELETE keyword, followed by the table name, and then WHERE followed by the select conditions.

Delete with WHERE

```
DATA: t_flights TYPE STANDARD TABLE OF sflight
  WITH KEY carrid connid fldate.
SELECT *
INTO TABLE t_flights
FROM sflight.
DELETE t_flights WHERE carrid = 'AA' AND connid = 17.
```
Listing 5.32 DELETE...WHERE Example

Sorted Table

A sorted table can be searched through at a quicker rate than a standard table, but will be slightly slower when inserting records than a standard table, caused when the system ensures that the sorted key is maintained.

Defining Sorted Tables

You can create a sorted table by defining the new table as a sorted table when creating it, or you can take advantage of the benefits of a sorted table by using the SORT keyword with an existing standard table.

When creating a sorted table, you need to create a variable of TYPE SORTED TABLE with a key that will be used to sort the table. The key can be either UNIQUE or NON-UNIQUE, as shown in Listing 5.33. Using a unique key is will cause an exception to occur if a record is inserted with that uses an existing key.

Defining key to sort table

```
DATA: t_sorted_flights TYPE SORTED TABLE OF sflight
    WITH UNIQUE KEY carrid connid fldate,
    t_sorted_flights2 TYPE SORTED TABLE OF sflight
    WITH NON-UNIQUE KEY carrid connid.
```
Listing 5.33 Creating Sorted Tables

Sorted Selects

When these tables are used in a SELECT statement, the results will be sorted while inserting them in to the sorted table.

Sorting standard tables

We can also sort standard tables using the SORT keyword followed by the table name, then BY and the fields that you want to sort by, and optionally whether the field should be ASCENDING or DESCENDING. The fields will be sorted in an ascending order if an order is not specified. The example in Listing 5.34 will sort the carrid field in ascending order because that's the default, the connid field in ascending order because ASCENDING was added, and the fldate field in descending order because DESCENDING was added. Remember that the sort order is set for each field individually, not for all fields together that you want to sort.

```
DATA: t_flights TYPE STANDARD TABLE OF sflight.

SELECT *
FROM sflight
INTO TABLE t_flights.

SORT t_flights BY carrid connid ASCENDING fldate DESCENDING.
```
Listing 5.34 Sorting a Standard Table

You can't sort a table of the sorted type; you'll see a syntax error if you try to do it.

ITAB_ILLEGAL_SORT_ORDER Exception

If a table of the sorted table type is changed to not be sorted by its key, an ITAB_ILLEGAL_SORT_ORDER exception will occur.

This can happen as a result of inserting a row that changes the sort order of the table.

Inserting, Changing, and Deleting Sorted Rows

Now that we have covered how to define sorted tables, in this section we will cover how to change the sorted table through inserting, changing and deleting rows in sorted tables. We will focus on the areas that are different from what we saw with standard tables.

You are allowed to insert rows into a sorted table using the `INSERT` keyword with either an index or a key, but you run the risk of throwing an illegal sort order exception if you use an index. An example of an insert using a key and index is shown in Listing 5.35.

Sorted INSERT

```
DATA: t_flights TYPE SORTED TABLE OF sflight
    WITH NON-UNIQUE KEY carrid connid fldate,
    s_flight TYPE sflight.
SELECT *
FROM sflight
INTO TABLE t_flights.

s_flight-carrid = 'AA'.
s_flight-connid = 17.
s_flgiht-fldate = '20150101'.

INSERT s_flight INTO TABLE t_flights.
"Could cause sort order exception
INSERT s_flight INTO t_flights INDEX 2.
```
Listing 5.35 Using INSERT with Sorted Tables

The same rule also applies to changing rows in a sorted table. Changing rows using the sorted table's primary key will always work with no issues. Specifying an index or mass change may be syntactically correct, but it can cause an illegal sort order if the change affects the key values, as shown in Listing 5.36. The mass change `MODIFY` is acceptable as long as the field being changed is not part of the sorted table's key.

```
DATA: t_flights TYPE SORTED TABLE OF sflight
    WITH NON-UNIQUE KEY carrid connid fldate,
    s_flight TYPE sflight.
SELECT *
FROM sflight
INTO TABLE t_flights.

s_flight-carrid = 'AA'.
s_flight-connid = 17.
s_flgiht-fldate = '20150101'.

MODIFY TABLE t_flight FROM s_flight.
"Could cause illegal sort order exception
```

```
MODIFY t_flight FROM s_flight INDEX 2.
MODIFY t_flight FROM s_flight
  TRANSPORTING connid WHERE carrid = 'AA'.
```
Listing 5.36 Good and Bad Ways to Change Records in a Sorted Table

There are no additional rules for deleting rows in a sorted table, because deleting rows will preserve the sorted order.

BINARY SEARCH

The `READ TABLE` and `LOOP AT` commands work the same as they do with standard tables, except that you can speed up search times significantly by using `BINARY SEARCH` when searching through the table. A binary search can only be used with tables that are sorted.

READ TABLE performance

When you used `READ TABLE WITH KEY` or `LOOP AT WHERE` earlier in the chapter, the system started at the first row and checked each record until it found a match, as illustrated in Figure 5.3.

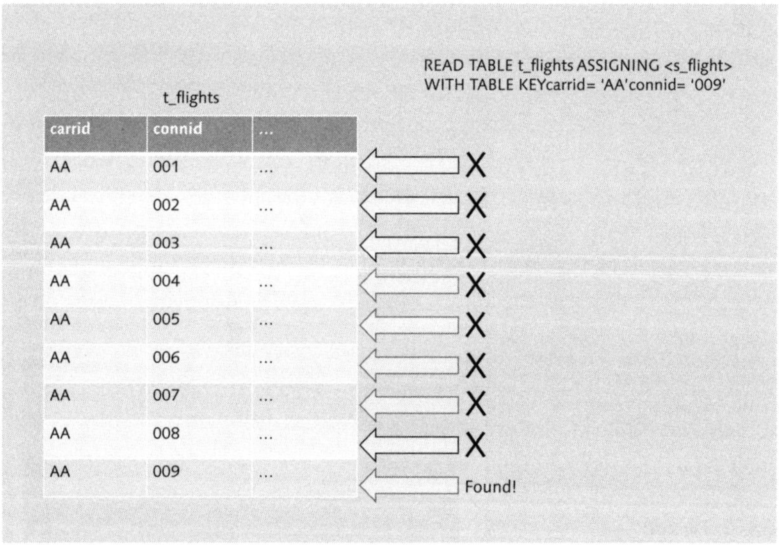

Figure 5.3 How the READ TABLE Search Works

BINARY SEARCH performance

Using the `READ TABLE` method like this is fine for smaller tables, but it can really drag down the performance of your program when working with tables of more than 100 rows. You can greatly improve the search when using sorted tables by adding the BINARY SEARCH keyword to your READ TABLE WITH TABLE KEY or LOOP AT WHERE statement. BINARY SEARCH will look at the record in the middle of the table, test whether the value you're looking for is higher or lower, and then check the record in the middle of the higher or lower half of the table. The search will continue to do this until it finds the record matching the provided key, as illustrated in Figure 5.4. In Figure 5.4, the system only had to test three different values before it found the correct one, compared with the illustration in Figure 5.3, which tested eight records before the same value was found.

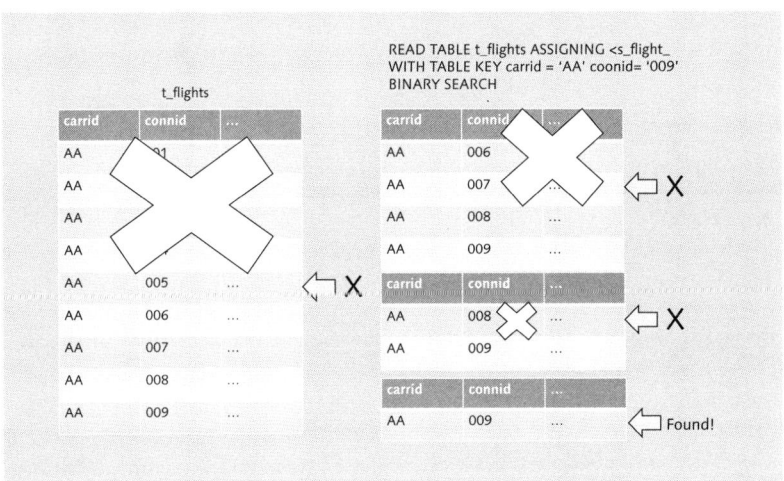

Figure 5.4 BINARY SEARCH Addition

An example using BINARY SEARCH in ABAP is shown in Listing 5.37. Even though this example uses a table defined as a sorted table, it could have also been completed with a standard table that was sorted.

BINARY SEARCH in ABAP

```
DATA: t_flights TYPE SORTED TABLE OF sflight
   WITH UNIQUE KEY carrid connid fldate.
FIELD SYMBOLS: <s_flight> TYPE sflight.

SELECT *
INTO TABLE t_flights
FROM sflight.

READ TABLE t_flights ASSIGNING <s_flight>
WITH KEY carrid = 'AA' connid='0017' fldate=20140423
```

```
BINARY SEARCH.
IF sy-subrc = 0.
    WRITE:'Record Found'.
ENDIF.
```
Listing 5.37 Binary Search Example

DELETE ADJACENT DUPLICATES FROM

The powerful DELETE ADJACENT DUPLICATES FROM command has the ability to delete duplicate records from the table when working with sorted tables. This command will delete records with the same primary key value that are adjacent to each other. It will also work with standard tables that have been sorted, but remember that if no key is defined, the key will be the entire record. The example in Listing 5.38 inserts two identical rows into table t_flights and then removes one of the rows so that only one remains.

```
DATA: t_flights TYPE SORTED TABLE OF sflight
    WITH UNIQUE KEY carrid connid fldate,
      s_flight TYPE sflight.
s_flight-carrid = 'AA'.
s_flight-connid = 17.
s_flight-fldate = '20150101'.
INSERT s_flight INTO TABLE s_flight.
INSERT s_flight INTO TABLE s_flight.
DELETE ADJACENT DUPLICATES FROM t_flights.
```
Listing 5.38 DELETE ADJACENT DUPLICATES FROM Example

COMPARING non-keys — You may not want to use the table's key to look for duplicates, in which case you can use the COMPARING command to define the specific fields that you want to use to find duplicates, or COMPARING ALL FIELDS to delete only records that completely match.

 Adjacent Duplicates

Remember that the DELETE ADJACENT DUPLICATES FROM command only deletes adjacent duplicates, so if you define specific fields to be compared, the table should be sorted by those fields.

An example using COMPARING with certain fields and COMPARING ALL FIELDS is shown in Listing 5.39, which first removes an exact duplicate and then removes a duplicate that only matches on two of the three key fields.

```
DATA: t_flights TYPE SORTED TABLE OF sflight
   WITH UNIQUE KEY carrid connid fldate,
      s_flight TYPE sflight.
s_flight-carrid = 'AA'.
s_flight-connid = 17.
s_flight-fldate = '20150101'.
INSERT s_flight INTO TABLE s_flight.
INSERT s_flight INTO TABLE s_flight.
DELETE ADJACENT DUPLICATES FROM t_
flights COMPARING ALL FIELDS.
s_flight-carrid = 'AZ'
DELETE ADJACENT DUPLICATES FROM t_flights
   COMPARING connid fldate.
```

Listing 5.39 DELETE ADJACENT DUPLICATES FROM Example with COMPARING Options Shown

Hashed Table

So far, you've learned about standard tables, which require no keys, and sorted tables, which require either unique or non-unique keys. Next, we'll explore hashed tables, which always requires unique keys.

Defining Hashed Tables

The hashed table is defined using TYPE HASHED TABLE OF and must always be defined including WITH UNIQUE KEY, as shown below in Listing 5.40.

```
DATA: t_flights TYPE HASHED TABLE OF sflight
   WITH UNIQUE KEY carrid connid fldate.
```

Listing 5.40 Defining a Hashed Table

A hashed table works differently than the other tables you've seen. The actual table contents are stored unsorted in memory, and a hash board is created that contains the unique keys for the data. This means that you find the row of data with the table key, without having to search through the table at all. The hash table and hash board are illustrated in Figure 5.5.

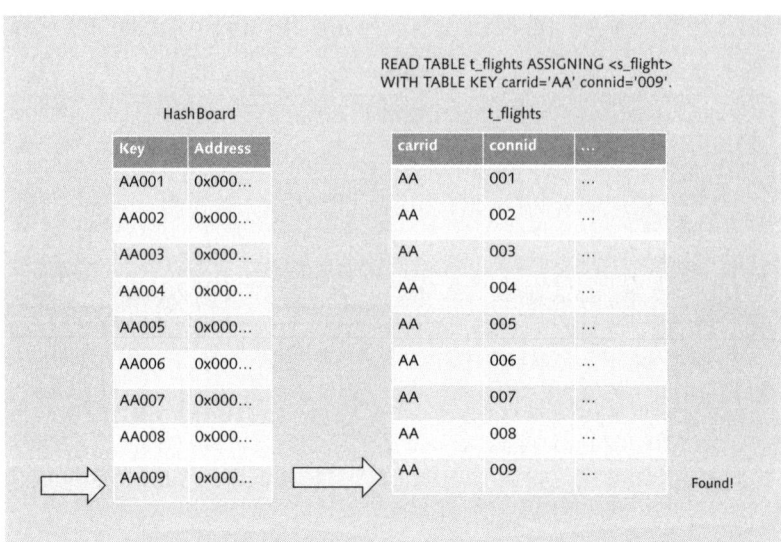

Figure 5.5 Retrieving a Record from a Hash Table

Sorting hashed tables

As a result of the hash board being separate from the table itself, the table can be sorted in any order without violating the hash board and unique key, as shown in Listing 5.41.

```
DATA: t_flights TYPE HASHED TABLE OF sflight
  WITH UNIQUE KEY carrid connid fldate.
SELECT *
INTO TABLE t_flights
FROM sflight.
SORT t_flights BY price.
```
Listing 5.41 Sorting of a Hashed Table

Reading Hashed Tables

Hashed tables can be read at a rate much faster than standard or sorted tables, because the program can instantly look up the key from the hash board and use it to instantly find the row in the working memory.

When using the READ TABLE command to read records from the hashed table, you will get a syntax error if you try to use the INDEX command, because no index is used with the hash board.

To take advantage of the better read performance provided by hashed tables, you will need to use the entire key when using READ TABLE, as shown in Listing 5.42.

```
DATA: t_flights TYPE HASHED TABLE OF sflight
   WITH UNIQUE KEY carrid connid fldate.
FIELD-SYMBOLS: <s_flight> TYPE sflight.

SELECT *
INTO TABLE t_flights
FROM sflight.

READ TABLE t_flights ASSIGNING <s_flight>
WITH TABLE KEY carrid = 'AA' connid = '0017'
   fldate = '20140423'.
```
Listing 5.42 Creating and Accessing a Hashed Table

We can also use READ TABLE…WITH KEY instead of WITH TABLE KEY to avoid using the full primary key, but this read would ignore the hash table as if the table was a standard table.

Non-primary key read

Reading a hashed table using the LOOP AT keyword will ignore the hash board and read the data in the order stored in the table. This means that WHERE with LOOP AT will not use the hashed table, even if WHERE utilizes the table's unique key.

Inserting, Changing, and Deleting Hashed Table Rows

Although hashed tables will let you use an index when inserting or changing rows, you'll get a syntax error anytime you try to define a specific index to insert or change a row. The only way to INSERT or MODIFY a row is by utilizing the table key, as shown in Listing 5.43.

```
DATA: t_flights TYPE HASHED TABLE OF sflight
   WITH UNIQUE KEY carrid connid fldate,
      s_flight TYPE sflight.
s_flight-carrid = 'AA'.
s_flight-connid = 17.
s_flight-fldate = '20150101'.
INSERT s_flight INTO TABLE t_flights.
s_flight-fldate = '20150102'.
INSERT s_flight INTO TABLE t_flights.
s_flight-price = 200.
MODIFY TABLE t_flights FROM s_flight.
```
Listing 5.43 Inserting and Changing Rows of a Hashed Table

Trying to insert a record that uses an existing key will not cause an exception, but the command will set the value of `sy-subrc` to 4.

Deleting rows   Deleting rows of a hashed table works just like as in standard and sorted tables, as described in previous sections. The only difference is that trying to delete a record by using a specific index will throw a syntax error, because there is no index for hashed tables.

Which Table Should Be Used?

The table type that you should use depends on the design of your specific program. There is no one-size-fits-all answer. You should base your decision on the number of records that will be in the table, how records are inserted in your table, and how records are read from your table. Figure 5.6 illustrates how a different table type can affect the performance of searching based on the table size relative to the amount of records in a table.

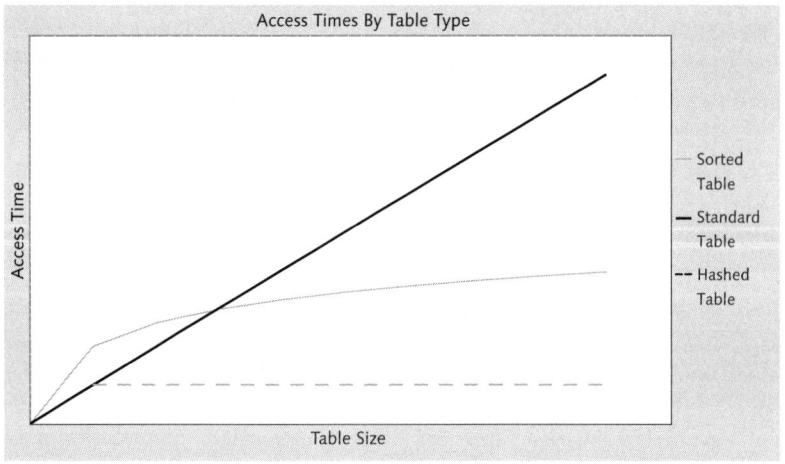

Figure 5.6 Relationships between Table Size, Table Type, and Access Time

Table search performance   The standard table search in a big O notation is O(n), meaning that the maximum amount of time will grow for each new record added to the table. The binary search of a sorted table is represented by O(log n), meaning that it will actually be slower than a standard table search for small tables; as the table gets larger, the maximum amount of time needed to search that table grows only slightly. Finally, the hashed table is represented by O(1), meaning that the time to search on a hashed table will stay the same no matter how many records are present.

Remember that using READ TABLE without the unique key of the hashed table or using LOOP AT WHERE with a hashed table will ignore the hash, changing the access time performance from O(1) to O(n), which is the same as the standard table performance. Also, searching a sorted table without indicating BINARY SEARCH will cause that table to be accessed like a standard table, changing your performance from O(log n) to O(n).

 What Is Big O Notation?

Big O notation is used to describe the relative representations of complexity in an algorithm.

In Figure 5.6 it shows how the different table types relate to each other. Big O notation works for comparing the different table accesses because they are all doing the same thing: accessing a table.

If we were to include the big O notation for an algorithm that adds two numbers together, the result would be O(n), the same result we have for finding records in a standard table. The actual performance of that process is actually much faster than accessing a table, so it's important to only use this notation when comparing algorithms that accomplish the same thing.

Also, because this notation measures relative complexity, it doesn't mean that having 1,000 records will necessarily be slower than 100 records when searching a standard table. It's still possible that the first record read in a table read will be the one you're looking for, but that becomes less and less likely as the table grows.

Relative complexity

Performance when reading data is not the only thing affected by changing the table type; performance when inserting data into that table is also affected. When inserting data, the standard table is the

Insert performance

fastest, followed by the sorted table, and the hashed table is the slowest. This makes sense, because there are no requirements for a standard table, whereas the hashed table requires that you create a record in your table and the hash board.

The best way to know when to use what table type is to continue to experiment when writing ABAP programs. See how changing the type affects the program performance, and adjust as necessary. Do what makes sense for your program. Table 5.1 summarizes the performance differences among the different table types.

Table Type	Standard	Sorted	Hash
INSERT	Fastest	Middle	Slowest
READ	Slowest	Middle (with binary search)	Fastest (using table key)
UPDATE	Same	Same	Same
DELETE	Same	Same	Same

Table 5.1 Performance Differences between Types

Updating ABAP Data Dictionary Table Type

In Chapter 3 we created a table type called ZFLIGHTS, but did not choose the type of table it would be or what kind of key it would have. As a result, the table type was created as a standard table. Now that we understand more about tables in our ABAP program, we will cover some of the additional options for table types in the ABAP Data Dictionary.

To change our existing table type, enter Transaction SE11, select the DATA TYPE radio button, enter ZFLIGHTS in the corresponding textbox, and press the CHANGE button as shown in Figure 5.7.

Initialization and access

From the change table type screen, select the INITIALIZATION AND ACCESS tab as shown in Figure 5.8. From this tab we can choose between the standard, sorted and hashed tables using the appropriate radio button. You will also notice a textbox for INITIAL LINE NUMBER, entering a value here will indicate the ABAP program to reserve space in memory for a table with that many rows when creating a variable which uses this table type.

Updating ABAP Data Dictionary Table Type 5

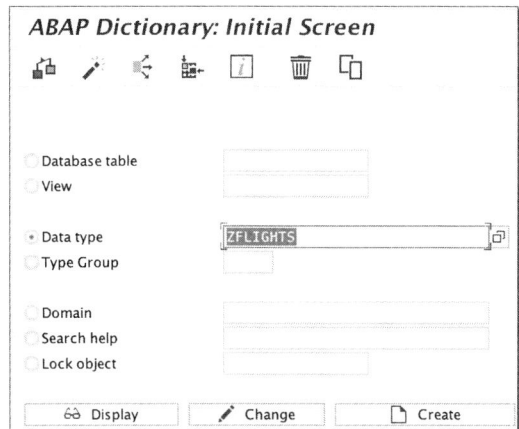

Figure 5.7 Changing the ZFLIGHTS Table Type from Transaction SE11

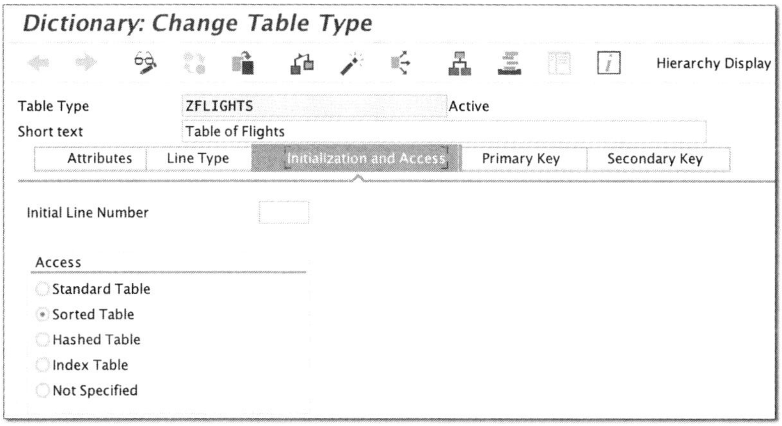

Figure 5.8 Table Type Initialization and Access Tab

In the PRIMARY KEY tab shown below in Figure 5.9, we can set a primary key for our table type as well by selecting the KEY COMPONENTS radio button and either the UNIQUE or NON-UNIQUE radio button for the Key category. This will allow you to click the CHOOSE COMPONENTS button to choose which components will be used in the key. In Figure 5.9 we have a non-unique key using the components FLIGHT_DATE and CARRID.

Primary key

211

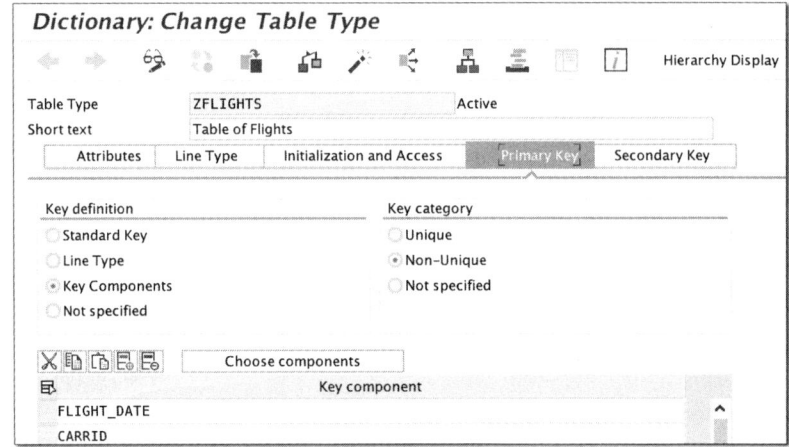

Figure 5.9 Table Type Primary Key Tab

Copying Table Data

There are multiple ways that you can copy table data from one table to another. You can use the equals sign, the same way that you assign values to variables, as shown in Listing 5.44.

```
DATA: t_table1 TYPE sflght,
      t_table2 TYPE sflight.
SELECT *
INTO TABLE t_table1
FROM sflight.

Table_2 = table1.
```
Listing 5.44 Using the Equals Sign to Copy Data to One Table from Another Table

However, sometimes you may need to copy data from one table to another, but you don't have all of the same fields in the table you're copying to. In such a case, you can use MOVE-CORRESPONDING to copy the fields from one table to another, as long as the fields have the same name in both tables. For example, Listing 5.45 copies all of the records in table t_sflight into table t_flight_price, even though table t_flight_price contains only a subset of the fields in t_sflight.

```
TYPES: BEGIN OF y_flight_price,
         carrid TYPE sflight-carrid,
         connid TYPE sflight-connid,
         price  TYPE sflight-price,
       END OF y_flight_price.
DATA: t_sflight TYPE STANDARD TABLE OF sflight,
      t_flight_price TYPE STANDARD TABLE OF y_flight_price.

SELECT *
INTO TABLE t_sflight
FROM SFLIGHT.

MOVE-CORRESPONDING t_sflight TO t_flight_price.
```
Listing 5.45 Using MOVE-CORRESPONDING

Displaying Data from Working Memory

A common ABAP program is a report that will pull a selection of data from the database and display the results to the user. We can display the results to the user using an ALV grid. *ALV* stands for **S**AP **L**ist **V**iewer and is an easy way to display data stored inside of an internal table. An example ALV grid is shown below in Figure 5.10.

Figure 5.10 An ALV Grid Filled with Flight Data

5 Storing Data in Working Memory

ALV features
Some features built in to the basic ALV grid is the ability to resize columns and change the order by dragging them around. More advanced ALV grids include the ability to sort by columns, create and save layouts and export to an excel spreadsheet. You can find sample ALV programs in the package `SALV_OM_OBJECTS`.

Basic ALV grid
We can easily create the above ALV grid with the code displayed in Listing 5.46. ALV grids use object oriented technology, with the `cl_salv_table` class. We will cover object oriented syntax in Chapter 6. For now, just note that we can use the bolded code below to display any table to the use, by replacing `t_flights` with the table that you want to display.

```
DATA: t_flights TYPE STANDARD TABLE OF sflight,
      gr_alv TYPE REF TO cl_salv_table.

SELECT *
FROM sflight
INTO TABLE t_flights.
cl_salv_table=>factory( importing r_salv_table = gr_alv
                        changing t_table = t_flights ).
gr_alv->display( ).
```
Listing 5.46 Basic ALV Grid Example

We can also improve the above example by using inline data declarations as shown in Listing 5.47.

```
SELECT *
FROM sflight
INTO TABLE @DATA(t_flights).
cl_salv_table=>factory( importing r_salv_table = DATA(gr_alv)
                        changing t_table = t_flights ).
gr_alv->display( ).
```
Listing 5.47 Basic ALV Grid Example Using Inline Data Declaration

Obsolete Working Memory Syntax

The obsolete working memory syntax is used for short form table access. Short form table access is a slower way to access data in a table when compared to using field symbols and make it less clear when you are working with a table or a structure. Just as with short form

SQL access, we recommend taking the time to remove and rewrite this code.

WITH HEADER LINE

Some developers add the `WITH HEADER LINE` to their table definitions because a syntax error told them to do so. Any time you see a syntax error suggesting that you need to add `WITH HEADER LINE` to your table definition, it typically means that you're using an outdated ABAP keyword and should use something different and more modern.

The header line is typically used so that the short form table access has visibility to the different fields within the table. An example definition of a standard table with a header line is shown here:

```
DATA: t_flights TYPE sflight WITH HEADER LINE.
```

OCCURS

An alternative to specifying a structure as a new table is to use the keyword `OCCURS` followed by a number. This specifies the size of the internal table that is created. Note that this is completely unnecessary for modern ABAP programs since we can use the `TYPE STANDARD TABLE` keyword instead. An example using the `OCCURS` keyword is shown here:

```
DATA: t_flights TYPE sflight OCCURS 10.
```

Square Brackets ([])

Using square brackets when accessing a table is completely unnecessary as long as you are avoiding the dreaded short form ABAP. The square brackets are meant to indicate that you're trying to access the table data and not the table header. However, because you shouldn't be using the `WITH HEADER LINE` keyword, this is completely unnecessary.

Short Form Table Access

Short form access is used with the `READ TABLE` and `LOOP AT` commands to read or loop at the table in to a structure of the same name instead of saving the data in another structure or field symbol. This can make the code very hard to read, because there is no difference between the table name and structure. Using `ASSIGNING` to put the data in a field symbol will lead to better performance than using the short form. Short form access requires that a header line be defined in the table being accessed this way as shown in Listing 5.48 where we read the `t_flights` table and loop through the `t_flights` table to change the price to 100.

```
DATA: t_flights TYPE sflight WITH HEADER LINE.
SELECT *
INTO TABLE t_flights
FROM sflight.
READ TABLE t_flgihts.
t_flights-price = 100.
LOOP AT t_flgihts.
t_flights-price = 100.
ENDLOOP.
```
Listing 5.48 Reading a Table Using Short Form Table Acccess

Summary

So far, you've explored how to process data in ABAP, how to read from a database, and how to use working memory to store the data from a database and display it to the user. You now have all of the basic building blocks for writing ABAP programs.

It's important that you use the right table type for each situation when writing ABAP programs. Choosing the right type will usually depend on the design of the ABAP program and the type of data you're working with. Experience and experimenting with the different table types is the best way to gain familiarity and know when to use each type. The worst thing that you can do is to only use the standard tables, which can slow down performance when working with a lot of data.

You also learned about some obsolete table syntax that should be avoided. This syntax is included in the book to help if you need to fix an old program, but sometimes it may be easier to just rewrite an old program than try to make constant small changes to it.

In the next chapter, you'll learn how to organize all of the things covered so far to write clean and easy-to-understand programs.

Making Programs Modular

So far, this book has covered a number of technical methods that allow you to do specific things using ABAP programs. You discovered different ways to process data, read data from a database, and work with data in working memory. In this chapter, we will discuss how to organize, or *modularize*, your program using object-oriented programming to complete all of these tasks. We will cover modularization using classes, global classes, function modules and subroutines.

Modularization involves placing specific sequences of ABAP statements in a module, instead of placing all the statements in a single main program. There are two very important reasons that you need to modularize your program instead of having just one long program that executes from the beginning to the end. First, you want to write programs that are easy for other programmers to read and understand. Second, you want to be able to reuse common functions multiple times in a single program or across multiple programs and avoid redundancy.

What is modularization?

In addition, modularization has the added benefit of making ABAP programs easier to support and enhance after they have been written.

Separation of Concerns

Separation of concerns is a principal used to separate a program into different layers, each with its own function. Imagine an ABAP program that was created to report on some data from the database. You could break that program into three different parts, one part to read the data from the database, another part to process the data, and a third part to display the results, as shown conceptually in Figure 6.1.

6   Making Programs Modular

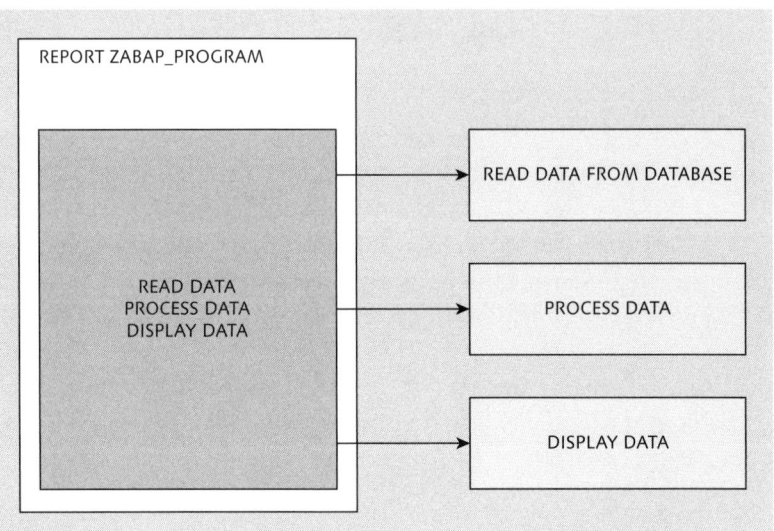

Figure 6.1 Using Seperation of Concerns to Break a Program into Single-Function Units

When you break your program into these three different sections, you then have one place to make changes to any of those functions.

Procedural programs

Back in the ancient days of computing, people would write long programs using punch cards that had to be executed from the beginning to the end and probably scheduled to run at a certain time. Today, applications are used by people in real time, which means that you need to change your application to meet the user's sometimes crazy expectations. Programs designed to run from the beginning to end are called *procedural programs*.

In a typical ABAP journey, it's normal to see an old program written in a procedural format—and then you'll hear from a user that the program is supposed to process data in some way that isn't working. You'll have to go through the long process of reading the program and debugging to figure out where the data is changed, only to find that the data is read and changed all over the place.

Separation of Concerns 6

In order to avoid writing procedural nightmare programs, use the separation of concerns principal to keep each unit focused on performing only one function, and name each unit based on the function that it performs. This makes it much easier to understand the program, fix it, and enhance it. Remember that you may write the program once, but someone else may have to fix or change it, possibly years later! Therefore, after using the plan in Figure 6.1, if users returned to you and said that they wanted additional data from the database, you would know exactly what unit to change, and if they wanted the ability to refresh the data, you would know that you can add the ability to call the read data from the database after displaying the data. If you had just one long program, it would be harder to find out exactly where you need to make changes, and you definitely would not be able to reuse any particular unit; the program would all be one long unit.

Why use separation of concerns?

Of course, each person's interpretation of a unit focused on performing only one function might be different. That's where this concept can become more of an art than a science. If the units are made too small, it can be confusing because there are so many; if they are made too large, it can be confusing because there's so much code in a single unit. Remember that you're both writing a program and trying to make it easy for the next person to fix and enhance.

Figure 6.2 expands on the original conceptual drawing in Figure 6.1 to demonstrate breaking up and naming units for each function that they perform. This example demonstrates a program that gets a list of possible flights based on a search, calculates the price of the flight options, and displays the results to the user. Each unit completes one function, and each unit has a descriptive name. If a person said that there was an issue with the price being calculated, you would know exactly what unit of code he or she was talking about.

Naming different units

6 Making Programs Modular

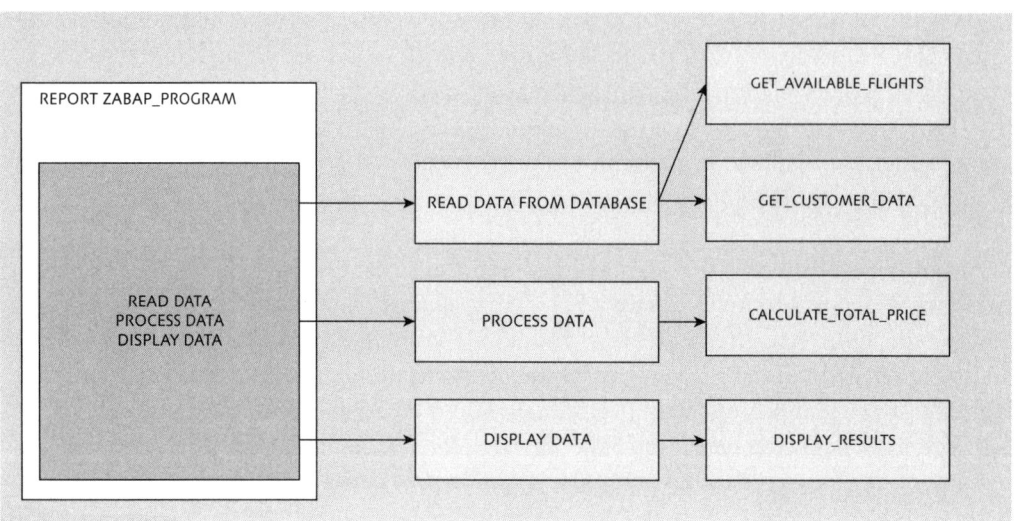

Figure 6.2 Seperation of Concerns with Named Code Units

Changing units of code

Just because you created certain units of code when the application was created doesn't mean that you can't add more. It's common to have to add additional functionality in a single unit of code, in which case you should determine if the additional functionality might need to be in its own functional unit of code. If each unit is expected to perform one function, ask yourself if the new code is really completing that same function or if it's its own unit. Also, anytime the new code is something that could be reused, then it should be in its own unit. Once your code is completed and working, it is always good practice to go back and see what kind of improvements you can make to your code and find any code that is repeated and could be modularized.

Now that you understand the concept of Separation of Concerns, we will cover how to utilize it using object-oriented programming.

Introduction to Object-Oriented Programming

OOP

The recommended method for modularizing ABAP programs is to use object-oriented programming. There are some people in the ABAP community who are unsure about object-oriented programming and have even posed the idea that there is ABAP and OO-ABAP (object-oriented ABAP). The fact is that there is no ABAP versus OO-ABAP: just ABAP with good developers and bad developers.

If you have written object-oriented programs in other languages, you will find that there are a few ABAP quirks, but all of the concepts that you have seen in other languages will apply in ABAP as well.

What Is an Object?

A programming *object* is designed around the idea of objects in the real world. A good introductory conceptual example is that of a car. A car has attributes that describe its current state, such as fuel level and current speed, and attributes that describe the object, such as manufacturer and model. There are also a few methods that describe how we interact with the car, such as accelerate, decelerate, and refuel. Figure 6.3 shows a conceptual drawing of this car object.

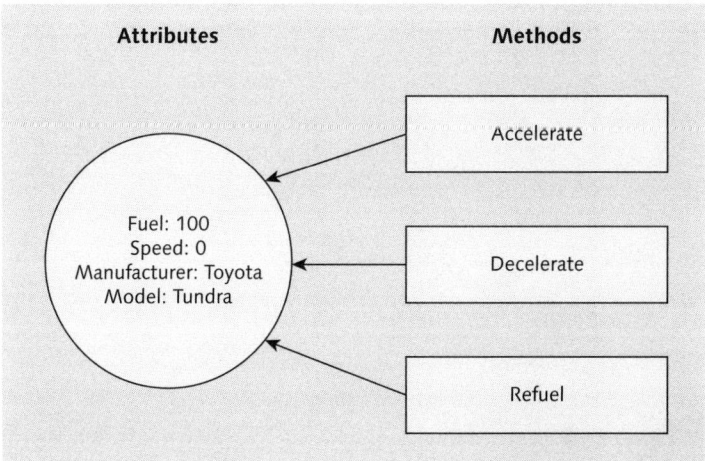

Figure 6.3 The Car Object

Each of the object's methods is a functional unit designed to complete one task. Each attribute of the object is a variable that all of the methods have access to. The pseudocode in Listing 6.1 shows what the code in the accelerate method could look like.

```
METHOD ACCELERATE.
    SPEED = SPEED + 5.
ENDMETHOD.
```
Listing 6.1 Pseudocode of Accelerate Method

Classes

Now, say that the example in Figure 6.3 specifically refers to a Toyota Tundra, but you want to create additional objects for different types of cars. This is where classes come in. Each object is actually an instantiation of a *class*, and you can have multiple objects of the same class. Again think back to the real-life example of a car; the Toyota Tundra is a type of car, and all cars can accelerate, decelerate, and refuel, but this particular car is going at a certain speed and has a certain fuel level. When creating objects, all of the code is stored in the class, but you can create multiple objects that use that code, and each will have its own set of attributes to describe it, as shown conceptually in Figure 6.4. You can think of the class in this example as a mold, whereas the objects are those items created from that mold.

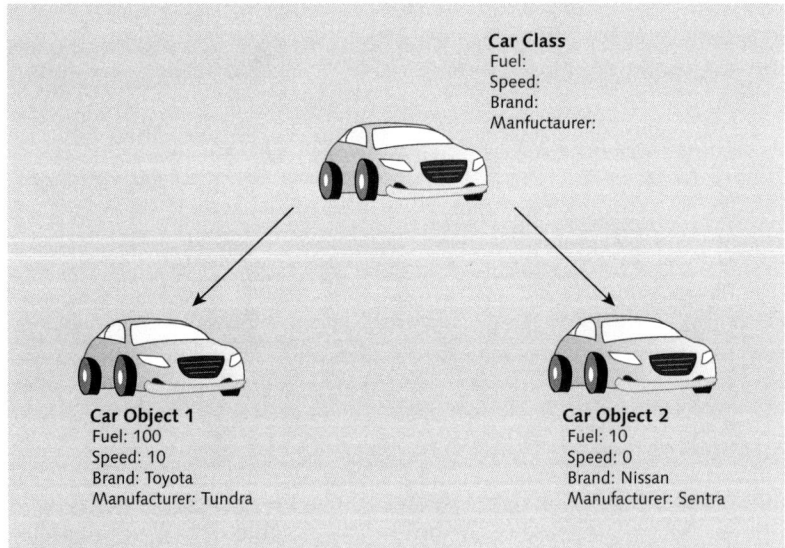

Figure 6.4 Relationship between Class and Object

Modularizing with Object-Oriented Programming

Just because you are using object-oriented programming doesn't mean you have to use it to build multiple objects. You could also have one object that holds all of the logic for your program. Each method will represent a single function, as discussed in the section on the separation of concerns principle. Looking back at Figure 6.2, each different unit could be represented as a method in a flight finder class, as shown in Figure 6.5.

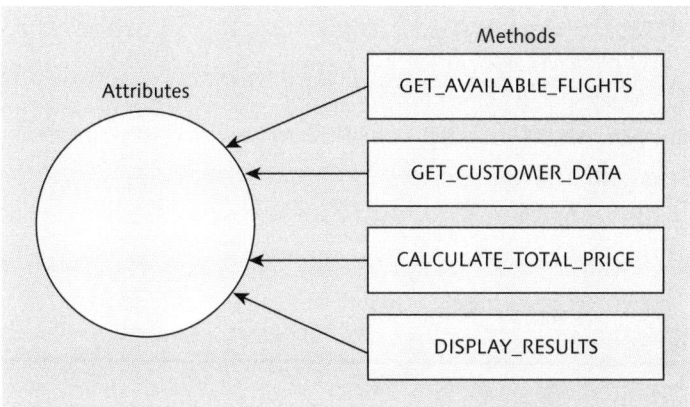

Figure 6.5 Flight Finder Class Concept

Each class method can be created with the ability to take and return data. For example, when creating the method for calculating the total price in Figure 6.5, you could pass a value containing the results from the get available flights method.

Passing data to methods

Structuring Classes

Now that you understand some of the concepts of object-oriented programming, you can begin to learn how to create classes and objects in ABAP. If the object-oriented concepts do not make sense yet, perhaps seeing the actual code in action will help. We'll first cover how to create a local class within a program and then how to create a global class that can be used across multiple programs.

Implementation vs. Definition

In ABAP, every class requires a definition and an implementation. The definition lists the different attributes and methods of a class, whereas the implementation contains the actual code for all of the methods. The definition must come before the implementation and must also come before an object is created from the class. The class is defined by using the CLASS keyword, followed by the name of the class and then either DEFINITION or IMPLEMENTATION depending on what you are declaring. The example in Listing 6.2 contains the definition of a class with no attributes or methods. Prefix the class name with lcl to indicate that it's a local class, meaning that it's being created inside of an ABAP Program. Since we are demonstrating local classes, you can insert the code in this section into any ABAP program for testing. Since both the definition and implementation are contained within a CLASS and ENDCLASS keyword, they do not need to be next to each other when being defined.

```
CLASS lcl_car DEFINITION.
ENDCLASS.
CLASS lcl_car IMPLEMENTATION.
ENDCLASS.
```
Listing 6.2 Definition and Implementation of a Class

Creating Objects

Now that you've created a basic class, you can create objects of that class. Remember that a class is like a design, and you can build multiple objects using that design.

Object variables — There are two parts to creating an object. The first part is to define the object variable. This is just like creating variables, which we introduced in Chapter 2, except that you will use TYPE REF TO instead of just TYPE to indicate the class to be used when creating the object. The example in Listing 6.3 uses the prefix o_ to indicate an object.

For objects, you then use the command CREATE OBJECT followed by the object variable to instantiate the object, as shown in Listing 6.3 Just like creating your own data types using the TYPES command, the class definition must come before creating an object using that class.

```
CLASS lcl_car DEFINITION.
ENDCLASS.

DATA: o_car TYPE REF TO lcl_car.
CREATE OBJECT o_car.
```

```
CLASS lcl_car IMPLEMENTATION.
ENDCLASS.
```
Listing 6.3 Creating an Object from a Class

Public and Private Sections

Before adding attributes and methods to the class definition, you will need to decide whether those attributes and methods should be public, private, or protected.

Public attributes and methods can be used within the class or outside of the class, from the main program, or even from another class.

Private attributes and methods can only be used from within the class itself, meaning that another class or the main program is unable to read the attributes or call the methods that are listed as private.

Protected attributes and methods can only be used from within the class itself, just like the private attributes and methods. The difference with protected attributes and methods is that they can be inherited from a subclass, unlike a private attribute or class. We will revisit protected attributes and methods when we cover inheritance later in the chapter.

The public and private sections are defined in the class implementation using the PUBLIC SECTION and PRIVATE SECTION keywords. Listing 6.4 adds those sections to the class definition.

```
CLASS lcl_car DEFINITION.
PUBLIC SECTION.
PRIVATE SECTION.
ENDCLASS.
ClASS lcl_car IMPLEMENTATION.
ENDCLASS.
```
Listing 6.4 Adding the Public and Private Sections to the Class Definition

Next, you can add attributes to public or private sections, by creating variables, just like the ones discussed in Chapter 2. The variables must be defined after a section to determine whether they're public or private.

These attributes will be available globally to all of your methods; if they're public, they'll also be available globally outside of your methods. Listing 6.5 adds public attributes for fuel, speed, brand, and manufacturer and a private attribute for the current gear.

Read Only attributes Public attributes can also be given a READ-ONLY property, which will make them readable outside of the class and changeable only from within the class. In Listing 6.5, the attribute d_manufacturer is set to be read-only.

```
CLASS lcl_car DEFINITION.
PUBLIC SECTION.
    DATA: d_fuel TYPE i,
          d_speed TYPE i,
          d_brand TYPE string,
          d_manufacturer TYPE string READ-ONLY.
PRIVATE SECTION.
    DATA: d_gear TYPE i.
ENDCLASS.
CLASS lcl_car IMPLEMENTATION.
ENDCLASS.
```
Listing 6.5 Adding Public and Private Attributes to the Car Class

Class Methods

Definition Methods are the place to store all of your code, in single units of work designed to complete one function. Each method should have a name describing the action that it will complete. First, you have to define the method using the keyword METHODS in the class definition, and then write the method's code in the class implementation in between the words METHOD and ENDMETHOD. Listing 6.6 expands on the car example to add the definition and an empty implementation for the accelerate, decelerate, and refuel methods. When adding methods, you will get a syntax error if the method is not defined in both the definition and implementation of the class.

```
CLASS lcl_car DEFINITION.
PUBLIC SECTION.
    DATA: d_fuel TYPE i,
          d_speed TYPE i,
          d_brand TYPE string,
          d_manufacturer TYPE string.
    METHODS: accelerate,
             decelerate,
             refuel.
PRIVATE SECTION.
    DATA: d_gear TYPE i.
```

```
ENDCLASS.
CLASS lcl_car IMPLEMENTATION.
    METHOD accelerate.
    ENDMETHOD.
    METHOD decelerate.
    ENDMETHOD.
    METHOD refuel.
    ENDMETHOD.
ENDCLASS.
```
Listing 6.6 Adding Public Classes to the Car Class

Now, you can add code to the methods. The code will go in the class implementation section, and each method will share all of the attributes declared in the definition. Listing 6.7 adds some programming logic to each of the methods, and you can see that they are all able to access the class attributes.

Implementation

You can also declare variables within methods, such as ld_max in the REFUEL method shown in Figure 6.11. These variables are considered local variables since they will not be visible or usable outside of the methods in which they're declared. For that reason, they are prefixed with a ld_ meaning local data variable, instead of d_, meaning global data variable.

Local variables

```
CLASS lcl_car DEFINITION.
PUBLIC SECTION.
    DATA: d_fuel TYPE i,
          d_speed TYPE i,
          d_brand TYPE string,
          d_manufacturer TYPE string.
    METHODS: accelerate,
             decelerate,
             refuel.
PRIVATE SECTION.
    DATA: d_gear TYPE i.
ENDCLASS.
CLASS lcl_car IMPLEMENTATION.
    METHOD accelerate.
        d_speed = d_speed + 5.
        d_fuel = d_fuel - 5.
    ENDMETHOD.
    METHOD decelerate.
        d_speed = d_speed - 5.
        d_fuel = d_fuel - 2.
    ENDMETHOD.
    METHOD refuel.
```

6 Making Programs Modular

```
            DATA: ld_max TYPE I VALUE 100.
            d_fuel = ld_max.
        ENDMETHOD.
ENDCLASS.
```
Listing 6.7 Adding Logic to Methods in the Car Class

Calling methods

Now that you've defined some methods which contain some code, you can define an object, create it, and call the methods contained in the object. To call an object's method, you enter the object name followed by an arrow (->), then the method name, and then the open and close parentheses (()), with any parameters in between the parentheses. Table 6.1 shows how a method is called via an example using the car object created earlier in this section.

| Object->method_name(parameters) | o_car->accelerate() |

Table 6.1 How to Call a Method

The code for calling methods has to be included after the object has been defined and created, but it can come before the definition of the object, as shown in Listing 6.8.

```
CLASS lcl_car DEFINITION.
PUBLIC SECTION.
    DATA: d_fuel TYPE i,
          d_speed TYPE i,
          d_brand TYPE string,
          d_manufacturer TYPE string.
    METHODS: accelerate,
             decelerate,
             refuel.
PRIVATE SECTION.
    DATA: d_gear TYPE i.
ENDCLASS.
DATA: o_car TYPE REF TO lcl_car.
CREATE OBJECT o_car.
o_car->accelerate( ).
ClASS lcl_car IMPLEMENTATION.
    METHOD accelerate.
        d_speed = d_speed + 5.
        d_fuel = d_fuel - 5.
    ENDMETHOD.
    METHOD decelerate.
        d_speed = d_speed - 5.
        d_fuel = d_fuel - 2.
```

```
        ENDMETHOD.
        METHOD refuel.
            DATA: d_max TYPE i VALUE 100.
            d_fuel = 100.
        ENDMETHOD.
ENDCLASS.
```
Listing 6.8 How to Call a Method in an Object

Now you can set a breakpoint within the method and execute the program and you will see the execution stack will show where the method was called from. If you are using Eclipse, the stack should look like what we see in Figure 6.6. The `accelerate` method is listed and before that is START-OF-SELECTION, which is the ABAP event that starts executing our code.

Methods in the execution stack

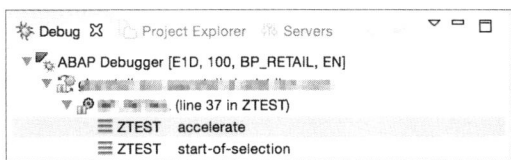

Figure 6.6 Execution Stack in Eclipse

Now, we can select the `start-of-selection` item in the stack to see the line of code where the `accelerate` method was called as shown in Figure 6.7.

```
 31    o_car->accelerate( ).
```

Figure 6.7 Eclipse Showing Where the Start-Of-Selection Stack

We can do the same thing from the SAP GUI debugger, when your breakpoint inside of the `accelerate` method is hit, you will notice the ABAP AND SCREEN STACK section will appear as shown in Figure 6.8.

St...	Stac...	...	Event Type	Event	Program	Na...		
→	4		METHOD	ACCELERATE	ZTEST		ZTEST	
	3		EVENT	START-OF-SELECTION	ZTEST		ZTEST	
	2		PAI MODULE	SYST-ABRUN				
	1		PAI SCREEN	1000	SAPMSSY0			

Figure 6.8 ABAP and Screen Stack in SAP GUI

6 Making Programs Modular

We can then click the START-OF-SELECTION item and the debugger will bring up the section of code that called our accelerate method as shown in Figure 6.9.

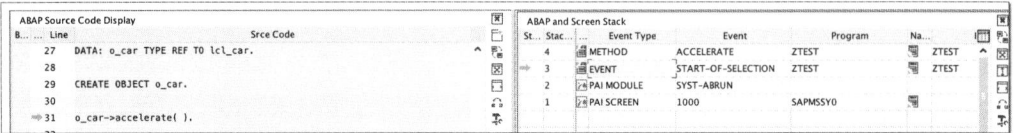

Figure 6.9 SAP GUI Debugger Execution Stack

Importing, Returning, Exporting, and Changing

When using your car class, users do not want to accelerate at a rate of 5; they want to specify the amount of acceleration to occur, which makes sense. There are a few ways to pass data to and from methods, as described in Table 6.2.

Importing	A copy of one or more variables is passed to the method.
Returning	The actual variable is returned by the method. Returning can only be used to return one variable.
Exporting	A copy of one or more variables are returned from the method.
Changing	The actual variable is passed to the method, and any changes to that variable will change the original. (Also known as passing by reference.)

Table 6.2 Ways to Pass Data to and from a Method

Importing

You can change the accelerate method to import a variable to indicate the amount of speed that you want to increase by. This is handled in Listing 6.9 by adding the IMPORTING command followed by a variable definition for the variable that will be copied in to the method and used to set the rate of acceleration for the car object. After adding the IMPORTING variable in the definition, that variable can now be accessed in the method implementation. The prefix ip here indicates an IMPORTING parameter.

Now that you've defined the IMPORTING parameter, you also can pass the value for that parameter within the parentheses when calling the method, as shown in Listing 6.9.

```
CLASS lcl_car DEFINITION.
PUBLIC SECTION.
    DATA: d_fuel TYPE i,
          d_speed TYPE i,
          d_brand TYPE string,
          d_manufacturer TYPE string.
    METHODS: accelerate IMPORTING ip_accel_rate TYPE i,
             decelerate,
             refuel.
PRIVATE SECTION.
    DATA: d_gear TYPE i.
ENDCLASS.
DATA: o_car TYPE REF TO lcl_car.
CREATE OBJECT o_car.
o_car->accelerate( 5 ).
CLASS lcl_car IMPLEMENTATION.
    METHOD accelerate.
        d_speed = d_speed + ip_accel_rate.
        d_fuel = d_fuel - 5.
    ENDMETHOD.
    METHOD decelerate.
        d_speed = d_speed - 5.
        d_fuel = d_fuel - 2.
    ENDMETHOD.
    METHOD refuel.
        d_fuel = 100.
    ENDMETHOD.
ENDCLASS.
```

Listing 6.9 Adding the Ability to Import Variables in Methods

Next, you can change the method to check if the fuel is at zero; if it is, then the car will not accelerate. When you call the method, you want to know if it worked or not, so return a Boolean parameter that will be true if the method worked and false if it did not. The Boolean parameter is defined in the class definition using the RETURNING keyword followed by VALUE and the variable name within parentheses, as shown in Listing 6.10, with the prefix rp indicating a returning parameter.

Returning

Because the returning parameter is a Boolean, also create the Boolean variable d_is_success in the main program and set it to the result of the method call in Listing 6.10, meaning that d_is_success will be set to the value of rp_is_success after calling the accelerate method.

Making Programs Modular

```abap
CLASS lcl_car DEFINITION.
PUBLIC SECTION.
    DATA: d_fuel TYPE i,
          d_speed TYPE i,
          d_brand TYPE string,
          d_manufacturer TYPE string.
    METHODS: accelerate IMPORTING ip_accel_rate TYPE i
             RETURNING VALUE(rp_is_success)
                TYPE bool,
             decelerate,
             refuel.
PRIVATE SECTION.
    DATA: d_gear TYPE i.
ENDCLASS.
DATA: o_car TYPE REF TO lcl_car,
      d_is_success TYPE bool.
CREATE OBJECT o_car.
d_is_succcess = o_car->accelerate(5).
ClASS lcl_car IMPLEMENTATION.
    METHOD accelerate.
        IF d_fuel - 5 > 0.
            d_speed = d_speed + ip_accel_rate.
            d_fuel = d_fuel - 5.
            rp_is_success = abap_true.
        ELSE.
            rp_is_success = abap_false.
        ENDIF.
    ENDMETHOD.
    METHOD decelerate.
        d_speed = d_speed - 5.
        d_fuel = d_fuel - 2.
    ENDMETHOD.
    METHOD refuel.
        d_fuel = 100.
    ENDMETHOD.
ENDCLASS.
```

Listing 6.10 Class Including Returning Parameter

Method chaining

The returned variable can also be used in line with other ABAP keywords using *method chaining*, which was added to the ABAP language in ABAP 7.02. For example, you can call the `accelerate` method from Listing 6.10 from within an `IF` statement and use the returning parameter as part of the `IF` statement, as shown in Listing 6.11.

```abap
...
DATA: o_car TYPE REF TO lcl_car,
      d_is_success TYPE bool.
```

232

```
CREATE OBJECT o_car.
IF o_car->accelerate(5) = abap_true.
    WRITE: 'It worked!'.
ENDIF.
...
```
Listing 6.11 Using the Returning Parameter as Part of an IF Statement

If you want to import multiple parameters, you can do so by including the additional parameters after the IMPORTING command in the class definition. When you list multiple variables, you will also need to specify which variable you are passing within the parentheses, as shown in Listing 6.12.

Import multiple parameters

```
CLASS lcl_car DEFINITION.
PUBLIC SECTION.
    DATA: d_fuel TYPE i,
          d_speed TYPE I,
          d_brand TYPE string,
          d_manufacturer TYPE string.
    METHODS: accelerate IMPORTING ip_accel_rate TYPE i
                                  ip_other_param TYPE i
              RETURNING VALUE(rp_is_success)
                 TYPE bool,
              decelerate,
              refuel.
PRIVATE SECTION.
    DATA: d_gear TYPE i.
ENDCLASS.
DATA: o_car TYPE REF TO lcl_car,
      d_is_success TYPE bool.
CREATE OBJECT o_car.
d_is_succcess = o_car->accelerate( ip_accel_rate = 5
  ip_other_param = 1 ).
ClASS lcl_car IMPLEMENTATION.
..
ENDCLASS.
```
Listing 6.12 Adding Multiple IMPORTING Parameters

You can also mark parameters as optional by adding OPTIONAL after the parameter's definition, which means that the parameter will have an initial value when the method runs if a value is not entered for that parameter. If there are multiple importing parameters but only one is not marked as optional, you can pass only the required parameter without identifying the parameter names, as shown in Listing 6.13.

Optional parameters

Making Programs Modular

```
CLASS lcl_car DEFINITION.
PUBLIC SECTION.
    DATA: d_fuel TYPE i,
          d_speed TYPE i,
          d_brand TYPE string,
          d_manufacturer TYPE string.
      METHODS: accelerate IMPORTING ip_accel_rate TYPE i
                                    ip_other_param TYPE i OPTIONAL
                RETURNING VALUE(rp_is_success)
                   TYPE bool,
                decelerate,
                refuel.
PRIVATE SECTION.
    DATA: d_gear TYPE i.
ENDCLASS.
DATA: o_car TYPE REF TO lcl_car,
      d_is_success TYPE bool.
CREATE OBJECT o_car.
d_is_succcess = o_car->accelerate( 5 ).
ClASS lcl_car IMPLEMENTATION.
..
ENDCLASS.
```
Listing 6.13 Optional Importing Parameters

Returning multiple parameters
The RETURNING parameter only allows you to return one parameter, but if you need to return multiple parameters, you can use EXPORTING parameters. EXPORTING parameters are defined just like IMPORTING parameters, but using both requires identifying which parameters are IMPORTING and which are EXPORTING when calling the corresponding method, as shown in Listing 6.14.

Exporting
The parameters that are EXPORTING from the method will be IMPORTING into the main program; note how the naming changes in Listing 6.14. You cannot use both EXPORTING and RETURNING in the same method definition. EXPORTING parameters are always optional.

```
CLASS lcl_car DEFINITION.
PUBLIC SECTION.
    DATA: d_fuel TYPE i,
          d_speed TYPE I,
          d_brand TYPE string,
          d_manufacturer TYPE string.
      METHODS: accelerate IMPORTING ip_accel_rate TYPE i
                           EXPORTING ep_is_success TYPE bool,
                decelerate,
                refuel.
```

```
PRIVATE SECTION.
    DATA: d_gear TYPE i.
ENDCLASS.
DATA: o_car TYPE REF TO lcl_car,
      d_is_success TYPE bool.
CREATE OBJECT o_car.
o_car->accelerate( EXPORTING ip_accel_rate = 5
                   IMPORTING ep_is_success = d_is_success ).
ClASS lcl_car IMPLEMENTATION.
..
ENDCLASS.
```
Listing 6.14 EXPORTING Parameters

The last option for passing variables to or from methods is CHANGING. CHANGING parameters are passed into a method like IMPORTING parameters but can also be changed and returned like EXPORTING parameters. Unlike with an IMPORTING parameter, when calling a method and using a CHANGING parameter, you will always have to specify that it is a CHANGING parameter. Just as with EXPORTING parameters, you can't have both a CHANGING and a RETURNING parameter. The car object example has been updated to use a CHANGING parameter in Listing 6.15.

Changing

```
CLASS lcl_car DEFINITION.
PUBLIC SECTION.
    DATA: d_fuel TYPE i,
          d_speed TYPE I,
          d_brand TYPE string,
          d_manufacturer TYPE string.
    METHODS: accelerate IMPORTING ip_accel_rate TYPE i
                        CHANGING cp_is_success TYPE bool,
             decelerate,
             refuel.
PRIVATE SECTION.
    DATA: d_gear TYPE i.
ENDCLASS.
DATA: o_car TYPE REF TO lcl_car,
      d_is_success TYPE bool.
CREATE OBJECT o_car.
o_car->accelerate( EXPORTING ip_accel_rate = 5
                   CHANGING  cp_is_success = d_is_success ).
ClASS lcl_car IMPLEMENTATION.
..
ENDCLASS.
```
Listing 6.15 CHANGING Parameters

Returning vs. Exporting/Changing

When possible, use RETURNING parameters to help write more concise, easier-to-read code. RETURNING parameters will also make your ABAP code look more similar to other object-oriented languages, allowing someone who learned other languages first to more easily understand your program. The real power of RETURNING parameters is the ability to use method chaining with other ABAP keywords, as shown in Listing 6.11.

Constructors

Constructors are special methods used to set the state of an object before you start calling its methods. For example, you can set the manufacturer and model of the car object when you first create it using a constructor.

Creating a constructor

A constructor is created by creating a method called constructor. This method will be called by the CREATE OBJECT keyword, and any required parameters must be passed when using CREATE OBJECT. The example in Listing 6.16 specifies the model and manufacturer in the constructor, and those parameters are used to update the class attributes.

```
CLASS lcl_car DEFINITION.
PUBLIC SECTION.
    DATA: d_fuel TYPE i,
          d_speed TYPE i,
          d_model TYPE string,
          d_manufacturer TYPE string.
    METHODS: accelerate IMPORTING ip_accel_rate TYPE i
        RETURNING VALUE(rp_is_success)
          TYPE bool,
        decelerate,
        refuel,
        constructor
        IMPORTING ip_manufacturer TYPE string
                  ip_model        TYPE string.
PRIVATE SECTION.
    DATA: d_gear TYPE i.
ENDCLASS.
DATA: o_car TYPE REF TO lcl_car,
      d_is_success TYPE bool.
```

```
CREATE OBJECT o_car EXPORTING ip_manufacturer = 'Toyota'
                              ip_model        = 'Tundra'.
d_is_success = o_car->accelerate( 5 ).
CIass lcl_car IMPLEMENTATION.
METHOD constructor.
    d_manufacturer = ip_manufacturer.
    d_model        = ip_model.
ENDMETHOD.
..
ENDCLASS.
```
Listing 6.16 Car Object with a Constructor

The constructor is typically used to set variables that determine the state of the object, but it can be used to initialize the object in any way. For example, the constructor can read data from a database table to fill some private or public variables. Remember that the constructor will only be run once when creating the object.

Recursion

When using separation of concerns, you can use *recursion* to reuse a unit of work thanks to method chaining, which we introduced in Listing 6.11. Recursion works by calling a method from inside the same method, which can make your code much more compact and understandable than following a procedural approach, which may just result in one long program with the same code repeated over and over. Because you call a method from inside the same method using the results of the earlier call, recursion only works when you use a RETURNING parameter in your method.

To demonstrate recursion, let's write a method to calculate a given number of the Fibonacci sequence. The Fibonacci sequence is an infinite sequence starting with 0 and 1 and then adding the current number to the last number to get the next number in the sequence. For example: 0, 1, 1, 2, 3, 5, 8, and 13. If you are familiar with agile scrum planning, you may have used Fibonacci numbers to estimate work.

Fibonacci sequence

In Listing 6.17, to calculate the Fibonacci number you recursively call the calculate method, meaning that we call it from within the calculate method and set the returning value to its result. During this call, call with a value of one less than the current importing parameter and add the result of that to the result of calling the method with a value of two less than the current importing parameter. You don't want the recursive call to run forever, of course, so if the method is called with a value of one or less, it will return the value of the parameter that was called. Try running the code in Listing 6.17 in debug mode and step through the program to see the recursion in action.

```
CLASS lcl_fibonacci DEFINITION.
PUBLIC SECTION.
     METHODS: calculate IMPORTING ip_place TYPE i
                        RETURNING VALUE(rp_value) TYPE i.
ENDCLASS.
DATA: o_fib TYPE REF TO lcl_fibonacci,
      d_result TYPE i.
CREATE OBJECT o_fib.
d_result = o_fib->calculate( 4 ).
CLASS lcl_fibonacci IMPLEMENTATION.
METHOD calculate.
    IF ip_place <= 1.
         rp_value = ip_place.
    ELSE.
         rp_value = calculate( ip_place -
 1 ) + calculate( ip_place - 2 ).
    ENDIF.
ENDMETHOD.
ENDCLASS.
```

Listing 6.17 Calculating a Fibonacci Number with Recursion

Figure 6.10 provides a conceptual image of what is happening during the recursive call in Listing 6.17 when trying to find the fourth number of the Fibonacci sequence. Because the code only returns the importing parameter value when it is 1 or less, the numbers added up are always 1 or 0.

A need for a recursive method will not exist in every ABAP program that you write, but when it can be used, it's very useful and can make your program much more understandable.

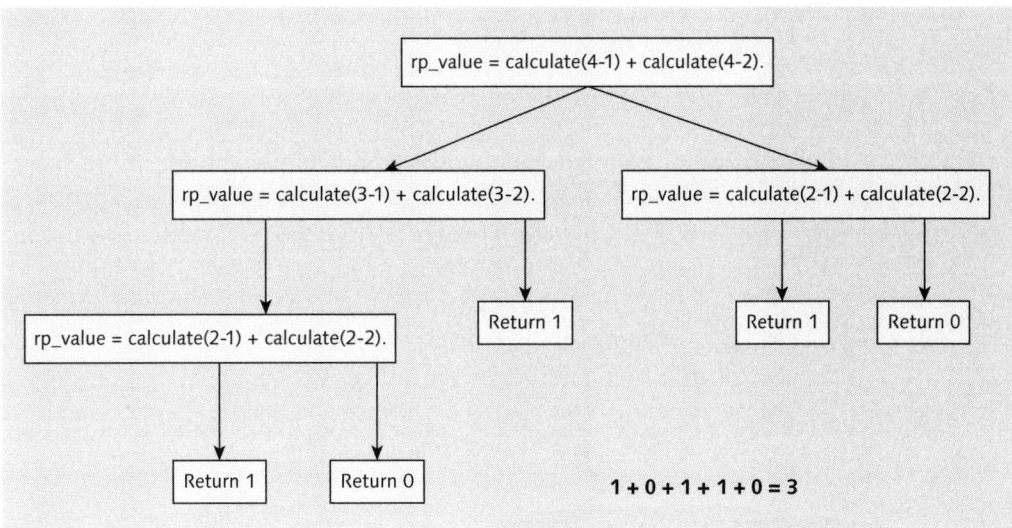

Figure 6.10 Fibonacci Recursive Call

Inheritance

When using object oriented programming, we have the ability to take on attributes and methods from another class through the use of *inheritance*. The class that we are inheriting from is called a *superclass* and the class that is inheriting is called a *subclass*.

Inheritance, like recursion, is a powerful benefit of object-oriented programming that we do not necessarily use with every program that we write.

In Listing 6.18, we added a new class, called lcl_truck which inherits from the car class by using the INHERITING FROM keyword as part of the class definition. Since lcl_truck inheriting from lcl_car, we can call all of the same methods that are in lcl_car and it will execute the code in the lcl_car implementation. This class can be defined below the code that we have already covered.

INHERITING FROM

```
...
CLASS lcl_truck DEFINITION
INHERITING FROM lcl_car.
ENDCLASS.

DATA: o_truck TYPE REF TO lcl_truck.
```

Making Programs Modular

```
CREATE OBJECT o_truck.
o_truck->accelerate(5).

CLASS lcl_truck IMPLEMENTATION.
ENDCLASS.
```
Listing 6.18 Demonstrating Class Inheritance

Redefining methods

We also have the option of redefining a method so that we use the code inside the `lcl_truck` implementation instead of the `lcl_car` implementation. To do that, we need to declare the method in the subclass without any parameters and include the REDEFINITION keyword as shown in Listing 6.19. Notice that we still have access to the same public variables and the returning parameter that we were able to use in the superclass method.

```
...
CLASS lcl_truck DEFINITION
INHERITING FROM lcl_car.
 PUBLIC SECTION.
      METHODS: accelerate REDEFINITION.
ENDCLASS.

DATA: o_truck TYPE REF TO lcl_truck.
CREATE OBJECT o_truck.

o_truck->accelerate(5).

CLASS lcl_truck IMPLEMENTATION.
    METHOD accelerate.
        d_speed = 1.
        rp_is_success = abap_true.
    ENDMETHOD.
ENDCLASS.
```
Listing 6.19 Demonstrating Redefining a Method in a Subclass

Protected section

Unlike methods in the superclass, methods in the subclass are unable to access the private methods or attributes of the superclass. If you want to create attributes or methods that are private but can also be accessed from inside of a subclass, then you must define them in the protected section. In Listing 6.20 we demonstrate this by adding a protected variable to the `lcl_car` definition which we can then call from within the `lcl_truck` class.

```
CLASS lcl_car DEFINITION.
PUBLIC SECTION.
    DATA: d_fuel TYPE i,
          d_speed TYPE i,
          d_model TYPE string,
          d_manufacturer TYPE string.
     METHODS: …
PRIVATE SECTION.
    DATA: d_gear TYPE i.
PROTECTED SECTION.
    DATA: d_protected TYPE i.
ENDCLASS.
…
CLASS lcl_truck DEFINITION
INHERITING FROM lcl_car.
 PUBLIC SECTION.
        METHODS: accelerate REDEFINITION.
ENDCLASS.
…
CLASS lcl_truck IMPLEMENTATION.
    METHOD accelerate.
        d_speed = 1.
        rp_is_success = abap_true.
        d_protected = 1.
    ENDMETHOD.
ENDCLASS.
```
Listing 6.20 Class Demonstrating a Protected Attribute

Global Classes

So far, you've learned about local classes, which are created and run inside of a local program. However, there are many use cases in which you'll want to use classes across multiple programs. A common use of global classes is to create interfaces with custom tables that you have written. This allows for a couple of things: First, you can handle locking of tables within the methods of your class, instead of having to lock and unlock tables in the programs that access the table. Second, you can write methods that allow you to access the data in your custom table(s) without having to write your own `SELECT` statements. How you use global classes really depends on the design of your tables and applications and the problem that you're trying to solve.

Multiple views The code for creating and changing the classes is mostly the same as what you saw for local classes. When using SAP GUI to create the class, there are two views: a source code view and a forms view. The resulting code will be the same, but the forms view allows the ABAP system to write some of the code itself.

Source control One thing that is different about using global classes is the way that they're broken up into different pieces. Each piece has its own source control history and must be activated on its own. The breakup of a class into different pieces makes it possible for multiple developers to work on the same class simultaneously.

The different pieces of a global class are the public, private, and protected sections and each method implementation. This allows you to treat each method as an individual program in terms of source control and activation. The public, private, and protected sections are a bit of a special case, however. These sections are automatically generated when using the forms view in SAP GUI, so any comments entered in these areas will be overwritten. You can still create and edit these sections with your own code, which will be kept, but any comments will be lost.

How to Create Global Classes in Eclipse

Using Eclipse to create classes is the preferred method and we'll look at that first, but we will also cover how to create them using Transaction SE80 later in the section.

To begin, select FILE • NEW • ABAP CLASS; you'll see the NEW ABAP CLASS wizard appear. Select the package $TMP to save the new class as a local object, enter "ZCL_GLOBAL_CLASS" as the class name, and enter "Global Class" as the description, as shown in Figure 6.11. Just as with ABAP programs, your class needs to be prefixed with a Z. You can use the prefix ZCL to indicate that the class you're creating is a custom global class.

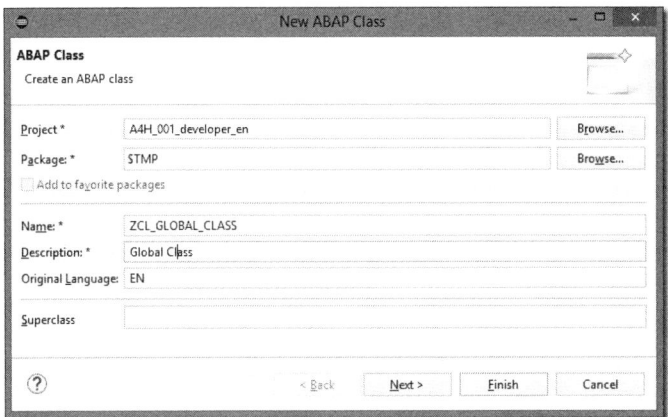

Figure 6.11 Creating a New Global Class in Eclipse

You'll see your new class with the basic structure for a class laid out for you, as shown in Figure 6.12. This should look familiar; it's the same structure that you saw with the local classes. The only change is the addition of the PUBLIC keyword, indicating a global class. Additionally, FINAL keyword is optional and indicates that the class cannot be inherited from and the CREATE PUBLIC keyword, allows an object to be created from the class anywhere where the class is visible.

Global class keywords

```
▶ ⓒ ZCL_GLOBAL_CLASS ▶
 1  CLASS zcl_global_class DEFINITION
 2    PUBLIC
 3    FINAL
 4    CREATE PUBLIC .
 5
 6    PUBLIC SECTION.
 7    PROTECTED SECTION.
 8    PRIVATE SECTION.
 9  ENDCLASS.
10
11
12
13  CLASS zcl_global_class IMPLEMENTATION.
14  ENDCLASS.
```

Figure 6.12 New Class Created in Eclipse

How to Create Global Classes in Transaction SE80

If you're using Transaction SE80 as your ABAP IDE, select CLASS/ INTERFACE from the dropdown in the center of left side of the screen, type "ZCL_GLOBAL_CLASS" in the textbox below the dropdown in the center left of the screen, and press [Enter].

You will be prompted with a popup asking if you want to create ZCL_GLOBAL_CLASS because it doesn't exist as shown in Figure 6.13. Click the YES button.

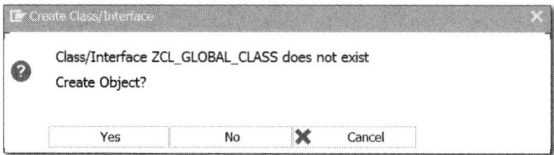

Figure 6.13 Create Class/Interface Popup

In the next popup, enter "Global Class" in the DESCRIPTION field and leave the rest of the options set to their defaults, as shown in Figure 6.14. The FINAL checkbox indicates that other classes cannot inherit from this class. Select the SAVE button to continue.

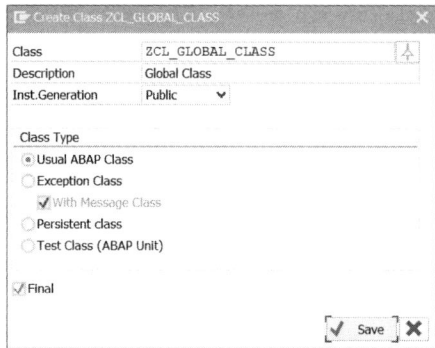

Figure 6.14 Create Class Popup

In the CREATE OBJECT DIRECTORY ENTRY popup, click the LOCAL OBJECT button or enter "$TMP" for the package name, and click the SAVE button. For production objects, you should use a package created for your project.

Forms view   After creating the class, the editor will show the class in the default forms view. The forms view can be used to change the structure of the class and add attributes and methods, and it will generate the class definition code automatically. You can also click the SOURCE CODE-BASED button (Figure 6.15) to view the entire class as code.

Global Classes 6

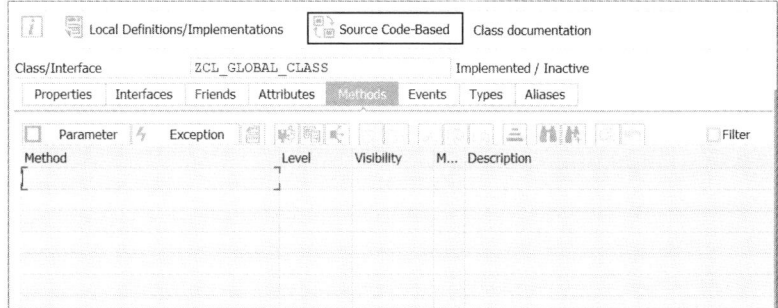

Figure 6.15 Forms View of a Class, with Source Code-Based Button Highlighted

The source code view shown in Figure 6.16 should look similar to what you saw when working with local classes. Whichever method you choose to use should be based on personal preference, but the source code view is recommended if you are going to use Transaction SE80 as your primary IDE.

Source code view

```
Class Source                    Inactive
 1  class ZCL_BOOKINGS definition
 2      public
 3      final
 4      create public .
 5
 6    public section.
 7    protected section.
 8    private section.
 9  ENDCLASS.
10
11
12
13  CLASS ZCL_BOOKINGS IMPLEMENTATION.
14  ENDCLASS.
```

Figure 6.16 New Class in the Source Code View

Using the Form-Based View in Transaction SE80

You can now return to the form-based view by clicking the FORM-BASED button, if you are still looking at the source code view. The form-based view will generate the code for the class definition and add the method definitions to the class implementation. Everything in the form-based view can be done manually in the source code view; which you use is a matter of personal preference.

There are many things that you can do with classes that I haven't covered yet and things that are out of scope for this book, so don't feel overwhelmed by all of the tabs and options in the form-based view. In this section, you will learn how to use the form-based view to add methods and attributes to a class.

Creating a method

First, create a new method. To do so, select the METHODS tab and enter "METHOD1" in the first row of the METHOD column; this will name your new method METHOD1. Next, under LEVEL, select INSTANCE METHOD. When you worked with local classes earlier in the chapter, those were instance methods; static methods are out of scope for this book and should be avoided if possible.

Next, select PUBLIC under VISIBILITY; this will set the method as public by defining it in the public section of the class definition. You can also add a description in the last column, which will only be visible from the form-based view. The name of your method should typically be descriptive enough on its own. The end result should look as shown in Figure 6.17.

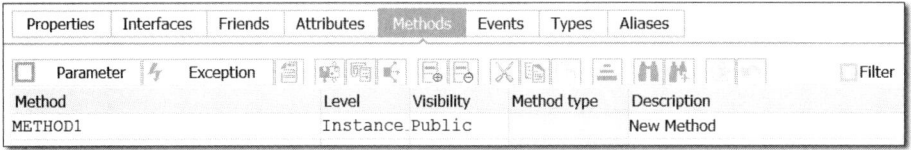

Figure 6.17 Adding a Method Using the Form-Based View

Parameters

Next, select the method and click the PARAMETER button. From here, you can add parameters for your method. The parameter name goes in the first column; enter "ip_parameter". The next column, TYPE, indicates whether the parameter is importing, exporting, returning, or changing. Select IMPORTING for this parameter.

Next, there are two checkboxes, one for PASS VALUE and one for OPTIONAL. You're required to pass a value for returning parameters, but can pass a value for any importing parameters as well. Passing a value for a parameter means that any changes to the parameter in the method will change the parameter that was passed into the method instead of changing a copy of that parameter. The OPTIONAL checkbox will make that parameter optional.

The next column, TYPING METHOD, indicates whether the data type should be created using the keyword TYPE, TYPE REF TO, or LIKE. Select the typing method TYPE. Next, the ASSOCIATED TYPE column indicates the data type to be used for the parameter; enter "I" to indicate an integer data type. You can also add a default value and description; as with the method description, this description is only visible to other developers using the form-based view.

Next, add a second parameter named "rp_value". This parameter should be of type returning with a typing method of TYPE and an associated type of i for integer. Both parameters are shown in Figure 6.18.

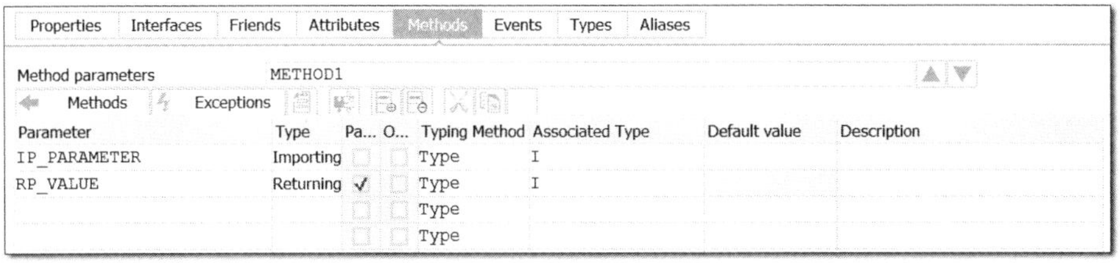

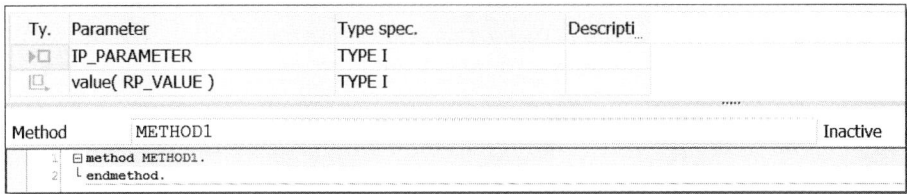

Figure 6.18 Adding Parameters Using the Form-Based View

Now, click the METHODS button to return to the methods list, and double-click your method to enter the method implementation, where you can write your code. You will notice that the editor restricts you to only the method you selected. From here, you can also click the SIGNATURE button to toggle the signature display that will show the parameters you defined for the method as shown in Figure 6.19.

Method implementation

Figure 6.19 Editng a Method Using the Form-Based View

Next, click BACK to return to the form-based view and click on the ATTRIBUTES tab to add some attributes to your new class. Enter "D_I"

Attributes

in the first row of the ATTRIBUTE column to indicate that the attribute name will be D_I. Next, select INSTANCE ATTRIBUTE under the LEVEL column. Static attributes are out of scope for this book and should be avoided if possible.

Next, set VISIBILITY to PUBLIC to indicate that this attribute will be defined in the public section. The READ-ONLY checkbox will make the attribute read-only from outside of the class, but the attribute can still be changed within your methods. Next, set TYPING to TYPE and ASSOCIATED TYPE to I for integer.

The button to the right of the ASSOCIATED TYPE column is used to create complex types (Figure 6.20). Clicking that button will take you to the public, private, or protected section so that you can add your own custom attributes that aren't defined in the ABAP Data Dictionary.

Attribute	Level	Visibility	Read-Only	Typing	Associated Type	Description	Initial value
D_I	Instance Attribute	Public	☐	Type	I		
			☐	Type			
			☐	Type			
			☐	Type			

Figure 6.20 Adding Attributes Using the Form-Based View

Now that you've added a method and some variables using the form-based view, save your changes and click the SOURCE CODE-BASED VIEW button to see the automatically generated code (Figure 6.21). You will notice that the generated code still closely resembles what you saw with the local classes. The only differences are some added comments before the method and an added exclamation point (!) before the method parameters. The exclamation point is an escape symbol that allows you to use an ABAP keyword such as `RETURNING` as the name of a variable.

Any additional class examples in this book will only include the actual code, not the form-based view configuration. You should be familiar enough with classes by this point to use either the form-based view or the source code view interchangeably. We recommend using Eclipse or the source code view exclusively.

```
Class Source              Inactive
 1  class ZCL_GLOBAL_CLASS definition
 2    public
 3    final
 4    create public .
 5
 6  public section.
 7
 8    data D_I type I .
 9
10    methods METHOD1
11      importing
12        !IP_PARAMETER type I
13      returning
14        value(RP_VALUE) type I .
15  protected section.
16  private section.
17  ENDCLASS.
18
19
20
21  CLASS ZCL_GLOBAL_CLASS IMPLEMENTATION.
22
23
24  * <SIGNATURE>---------------------------------------------------
25  * | Instance Public Method ZCL_GLOBAL_CLASS->METHOD1
26  * +-------------------------------------------------------------
27  * | [--->] IP_PARAMETER             TYPE        I
28  * | [<-()] RP_VALUE                 TYPE        I
29  * +--------------------------------------------------</SIGNATURE>
30    method METHOD1.
31    endmethod.
32  ENDCLASS.
```

Figure 6.21 Viewing the Code Generated by the Form-Based View

Obsolete Modularization

Now that you are familiar with modularizing your code using the modern object oriented approach, we will also cover some of the obsolete modularization techniques. You will need to be familiar with these techniques when working with old code or may need to use them for technical reasons.

Function Modules

Using function modules cannot be avoided in many ABAP programs, because some of SAP's standard functionality requires it in areas such as database table locks; however, you should never manually create new function modules. Any situation that calls for a function module to be created can use a global class instead. In fact, function modules were actually SAP's first attempt at making ABAP object oriented.

With that said, it's good to understand how function modules work, because they're prevalent in many customer systems and standard

6 Making Programs Modular

SAP code and may be required for technical reasons, such as creating a remote function call (RFC).

Function groups Similar to how methods are contained inside of a class, function modules are contained inside of a function group. The function group is created with two include files, one for global data (attributes in classes) and one that contains all of the function modules (methods in classes) in the group.

Any global data or function group attributes will hold the same value until the end of the program, but variables defined in the function module itself will only hold the same value until the end of the function call.

In your code, you call the function module itself instead of the group, and there's only one instance of the function group. This is unlike class objects, which can have multiple instances, as was illustrated by the car example in Figure 6.4.

Creating Function Groups and Modules in Eclipse

In Eclipse, you can create a new function group by selecting FILE • NEW • OTHER...; then expand the ABAP folder and select the option for ABAP FUNCTION GROUP in the popup as highlighted in Figure 6.22, and click NEXT.

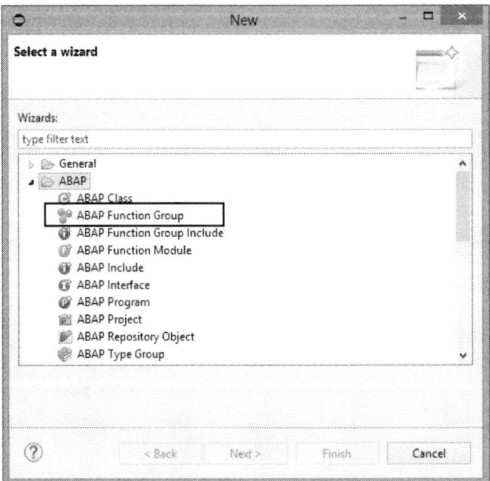

Figure 6.22 Creating a New ABAP Function Group

In the NEW ABAP FUNCTION GROUP wizard, enter the package "$TMP" to save it as a local object and enter "ZFG_FUNCTION_GROUP" for the function group name. The function group name will have to start with a Z as noted previously for programs and classes to indicate a custom function group. You can also prefix the name with "ZFG" to indicate that it is a function group. Remember that the function groups are like classes, so the name should indicate the type of object that the function group will be working with. Finally, enter a description, which may be used by other developers trying to find your function group. An example of the correct values is shown in Figure 6.23.

ABAP function group wizard

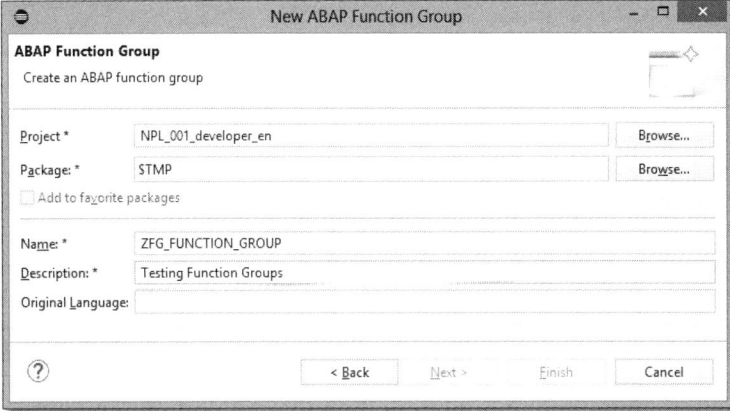

Figure 6.23 New ABAP Function Group Popup

The function group code displayed in Figure 6.24 shows the two include files that make up the function group. The `INCLUDE` file ending in "TOP" will contain any global data variables that will be accessible by any of the function modules in the function group just like attributes of a class are available for all of the class methods. The `INCLUDE` ending in UXX will contain `INCLUDE`s for all of the function modules created, which are just like class methods.

INCLUDE

To create the function module, select FILE • NEW • OTHER..., expand the ABAP folder, and select ABAP FUNCTION MODULE. You can also right-click the function group you just created from the Eclipse project explorer and select NEW • ABAP FUNCTION MODULE. This action will open the NEW ABAP FUNCTION MODULE popup (Figure 6.25).

Function module

251

Making Programs Modular

```
 [R6D] ZFG_FUNCTION_GROUP
  LZFG_FUNCTION_GROUPTOP
 1  ***********************************************************
 2  *   System-defined Include-files.                          *
 3  ***********************************************************
 4     INCLUDE LZFG_FUNCTION_GROUPTOP.      " Global Data
 5     INCLUDE LZFG_FUNCTION_GROUPUXX.      " Function Modules
 6
 7  ***********************************************************
 8  *   User-defined Include-files (if necessary).             *
 9  ***********************************************************
10  * INCLUDE LZFG_FUNCTION_GROUPF...       " Subroutines
11  * INCLUDE LZFG_FUNCTION_GROUPO...       " PBO-Modules
12  * INCLUDE LZFG_FUNCTION_GROUPI...       " PAI-Modules
13  * INCLUDE LZFG_FUNCTION_GROUPE...       " Events
14  * INCLUDE LZFG_FUNCTION_GROUPP...       " Local class implement
15  * INCLUDE LZFG_FUNCTION_GROUPT99.       " ABAP Unit tests
```

Figure 6.24 Code of a New Function Group

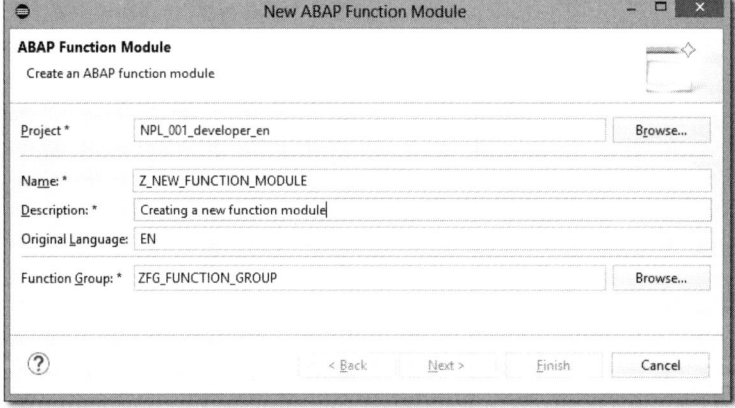

Figure 6.25 New ABAP Function Module Popup

From the popup, enter "Z_NEW_FUNCTION_MODULE" for the function module name. Because the code does not call the function group but instead calls the function module directly, the function module name is global, and each name can only be used once. A good practice is to prefix the function module name with something indicating the function group name after the required "Z_" prefix.

Next, enter a description that describes what the function module does to benefit other developers trying to find your function module. Finally, make sure that you enter the correct function group in which the new function module should be contained in the FUNCTION GROUP textbox, and click NEXT and then the FINISH button.

The new function module should open, and you can enter any code in between the `FUNCTION` and `ENDFUNCTION` keywords.

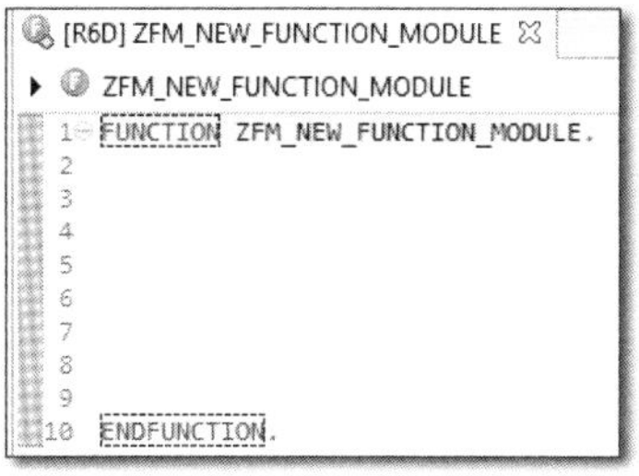

Figure 6.26 Newly Created Function Module in Eclipse

Just like class methods, function modules have `IMPORTING`, `EXPORTING`, and `CHANGING` parameters. These are defined in the function module by entering the type of parameter followed by a declaration of the data type, as shown in Listing 6.21.

Function module parameters

```
FUNCTION ZFM_NEW_FUNCTION_MODULE.
    IMPORTING
        ip_param TYPE i.
    EXPORTING
        ep_param TYPE i.
    CHANGING
        cp_param TYPE i.

ENDFUNCTION.
```
Listing 6.21 Adding Parameters to a Function Module

You can also pass table parameters using the `TABLES` keyword, but this is obsolete and unnecessary, because you can pass a parameter of a table type instead.

Creating Function Groups in Transaction SE80

If you are using Transaction SE80 as your ABAP IDE, select FUNCTION GROUP from the dropdown in the center of left side of the screen, type "ZFG_FUNCTION_GROUP" in the textbox below the dropdown in the center left side of the screen, and press ⏎Enter.

You will be prompted with a popup asking if you want to create ZFG_FUNCTION_GROUP because it doesn't exist (Figure 6.27). Click the YES Button.

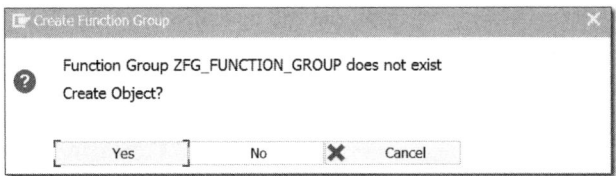

Figure 6.27 Create Function Group Popup

Creating a function group

You'll then be prompted with the CREATE FUNCTION GROUP popup pictured in Figure 6.28. Leave the function group name as ZFG_FUNCTION_GROUP, and enter "New function group" in the SHORT TEXT textbox. The SHORT TEXT and FUNCTION GROUP values are used by other developers trying to find your function group, so they should typically describe the type of data or objects that you're working with.

The PERSON RESPONSIBLE field will default to your username. You can leave this as is or change it, depending on your company's standards. Next, click the SAVE button to continue.

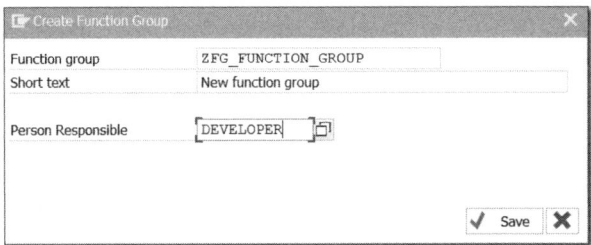

Figure 6.28 Create Function Group Popup

In the CREATE OBJECT DIRECTORY ENTRY popup, click the LOCAL OBJECT button or enter "$TMP" for the package name, and click the SAVE button. For production function groups, you should use a package created for your project.

Include files

Your function group has now been created containing two include files, which you should see listed on the left side of the screen (see

Figure 6.29). The INCLUDE files ending in TOP will contain any global data variables that will be accessible by any of the function modules in the function group. The INCLUDE ending in UXX will contain INCLUDEs for all of the function modules created.

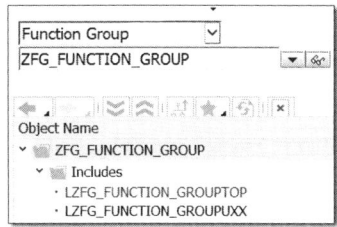

Figure 6.29 New Function Group Files in SE80

To create the function module, you can either select FUNCTION MODULE from the dropdown, type "ZFM_NEW_FUNCTIONMODULE" in the textbox, and press ⏎, or you can right-click the ZFG_FUNCTION_GROUP folder and select CREATE • FUNCTION GROUP.

Creating a function module

You will then see the CREATE FUNCTION MODULE popup pictured in Figure 6.30. From the popup, enter "Z_NEW_FUNCTION_MODULE" for the function module name; unlike a global class method, it must be prefixed with Z. Because the code doesn't call the function group but instead calls the function module directly, the function module name is global, and each name can only be used once. A good practice is to prefix the function module name with something indicating the function group name.

Next, ensure that FUNCTION GROUP is set to the correct value; it should be ZFG_FUNCTION_GROUP for this example. Finally, to benefit other developers trying to find your function module, enter a description of what the function module does in the SHORT TEXT field; for this example, enter "Creating a new function module". Then, click SAVE.

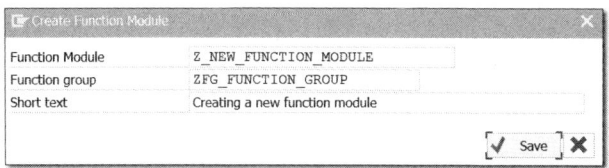

Figure 6.30 Create Function Module Popup

Function module parameters

You will now see a screen similar to the global class form-based view. Just like class methods, function modules have IMPORTING, EXPORTING, and CHANGING parameters. These are defined in the IMPORT, EXPORT, and CHANGING tabs. Function modules also have a TABLES tab used to define parameters that are passed as tables, which is obsolete and should be avoided. Instead of using the tables parameters, you should pass a table type in one of the other parameters.

To add the IMPORTING parameter, select the Import tab and enter "IP_PARAM" for the parameter name, "TYPE" for TYPING and "I" for Associated Type as shown in Figure 6.31. This will create an importing parameter of IP_PARAM.

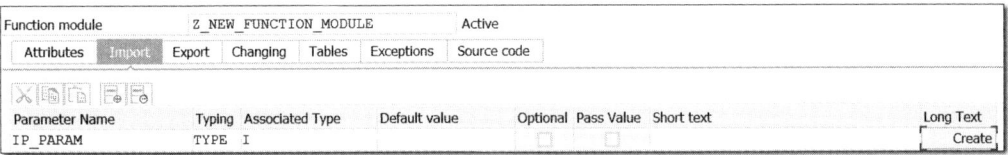

Figure 6.31 Adding an Import Parameter to a Function Module

Next, click on the EXPORT tab and enter parameter "EP_PARAM" with TYPING "TYPE" and ASSOCIATED TYPE "I" as shown in Figure 6.32.

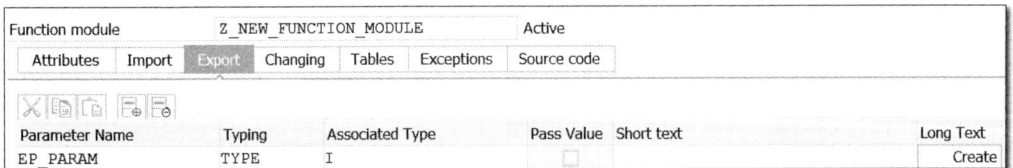

Figure 6.32 Adding an Export Parameter to a Function Module

Finally, select the CHANGING tab and enter parameter "CP_PARAM" with TYPING "TYPE" and ASSOCIATED TYPE "I".

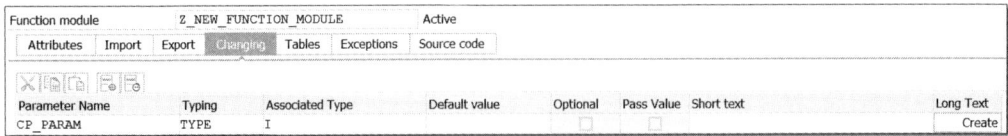

Figure 6.33 Adding a Changing Parameter to a Function Module

Now, you can select the Source Code tab, where you will be able to make changes to the function module, just as you made changes earlier to the method of a global class.

Calling Function Modules

You can call a function module using the `CALL FUNCTION` keyword followed by the function module name in single quotes ('). The parameters are passed by indicating the type of parameter and then the parameter name, equals sign, and the value that you want to pass to the parameter. Like we saw with class methods, a parameter importing into the function module is exporting from your code. The parameters importing into your program are always optional when calling a function module. An example calling `Z_NEW_FUNCTION_MODULE` is shown in Listing 6.22.

```
DATA: d_i TYPE i.
CALL FUNCTION 'Z_NEW_FUNCTION_MODULE'
    EXPORTING
        ip_param = 1
    IMPORTING
        ep_param = d_i
    CHANGING
        cp_param = d_i.
```
Listing 6.22 Calling a Function Module

Some function modules will return a parameter or table indicating the results of executing the function and any errors. Some function modules use exceptions to indicate whether or not the function call was successful. We will cover these types of exceptions in Chapter 10.

Form Subroutines

Form subroutines are probably the most commonly used way to modularize programs, even though they've been marked as obsolete in ABAP documentation.

Subroutines are easy to create. They use the `FORM` keyword followed by the subroutine name to define the beginning of the subroutine and `ENDFORM` to define the end of the subroutine. A subroutine can be called using the `PERFORM` keyword followed by the subroutine name and will execute any code within that subroutine, as shown in

Perform

Listing 6.23. No additional code can be entered after ENDFORM, just additional subroutines.

```
PERFORM my_subroutine.
FORM my_subroutine.
    WRITE: 'Hello World'.
ENDFORM.
```
Listing 6.23 Using a Subroutine

Declaring data in a subroutine

As with methods, local data can be declared within the subroutine and will only be accessible within that subroutine. Subroutines can also import parameters with the USING keyword and change parameters with the CHANGING parameter. These parameters work just like their function module and class-based counterparts. An example of a subroutine with parameters is shown in Listing 6.24.

```
DATA: d_i TYPE i.
PERFORM my_subroutine USING d_i
  CHANGING d_i.
  FORM my_subroutine
  USING up_param TYPE i
  CHANGING cp_param TYPE i.

ENDFORM.
```
Listing 6.24 Subroutine with USING and CHANGING Parameters

Summary

This chapter covered some modularization concepts, such as using separation of concerns to divide code into units that each complete only one function, and introduced object-oriented programming as a way to modularize code to meet the separation of concerns principle.

Remember that separation of concerns and object-oriented programming make your code easier to read and understand for the next developer who will have to look at it and fix any issues.

Next, you learned how to create classes and objects in ABAP. You discovered how methods can be used not only to modularize your code but also to make it compact through options such as recursive method calls.

We then covered global classes, which can be called by any program in the system, and how to create them both in Eclipse and using Transaction SE80 in SAP GUI.

The chapter concluded by looking at some obsolete code modularization techniques using function modules and subroutines. Even though you shouldn't be writing new subroutines and function modules, these are important to understand in order to maintain old ABAP systems.

In the next chapter, you will take everything you've learned so far in the book and apply it to create a new custom application that will run inside your ABAP system.

Creating a Shopping Cart Example

So far in the book, you have learned the basic building blocks of any ABAP program. In this chapter, you'll apply your new knowledge to create a new application that will run inside your ABAP system. Because you won't be using any functionality included in systems such as SAP ERP or SAP CRM, you can complete this with any ABAP system, including a developer edition.

A typical ABAP project will either enhance existing functionality or encompass entirely new functionality that didn't exist previously in the system. Although most of a company's processes may be handled through the standard ABAP system, there may be additional processes that give the company an edge over their competitors or processes that are unique for that company or industry. This is where custom applications are required.

Typical projects

In this chapter, we will create one such custom application: a shopping cart. If you were developing an ABAP program for a company, a requirement like this would probably integrate with the existing quote-to-order process within an SAP ERP system.

The chapter will present a business scenario and step through a solution to create an application for that scenario. You can also try to read the business scenario and complete the required tasks without looking at the solution and then refer back to the solution to compare what you did against what's shown in the chapter. As soon as you begin to create applications, the programming process becomes more of an art than a science, and there will be multiple correct ways to accomplish the task at hand. In the following chapters, we will update our solution we some additional data and features.

The Design

A company is launching an e-commerce site and wants to keep track of customers' shopping carts in its ABAP backend system. The shopping carts can be maintained from the website as well as by users of the ABAP system.

The customer data already exists in the transparent table SCUSTOM (provided with the flight example in Chapter 3), which has its definition shown below in Figure 7.1. Each customer will have a shopping cart for their customer ID, which can have zero to many products. We will need to create a new table for storing a list of products that are for sale on our site and another table for storing the items in each customer's shopping cart.

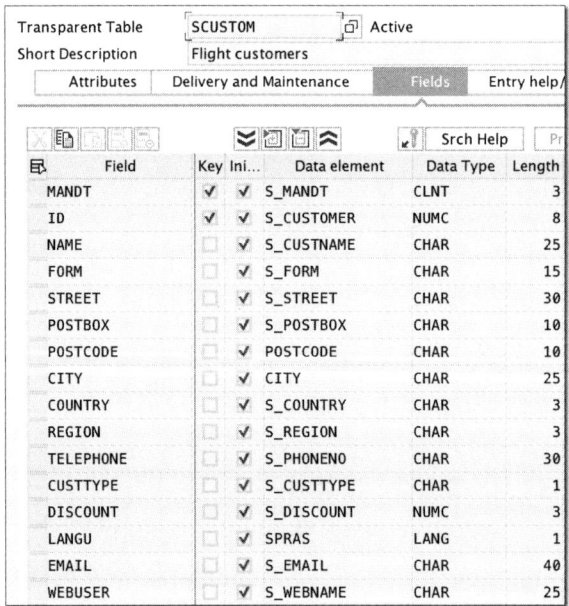

Figure 7.1 SCUSTOM Table Definition

We also need to create a single global class for updating and reading the shopping cart tables. With the global class, whether the cart table is updated from the ABAP programs that we will create or from a hypothetical program used to create an API for a website, the database will always be accessed from the same piece of code giving us a single place to update when new requirements arise.

The company will have some backend administrators who will need to be able to add products to the products table, update customer shopping carts and view the contents of a shopping cart.

The Database

We will use the existing table SCUSTOM as a list of all of the company's customers. If this table is empty, you can fill it by running the program SAPBC_DATA_GENERATOR.

We will create a new transparent table, ZPRODUCT, to store the products available for sale through the site. This table will have a primary key, which will be the product ID. The table will also have a description field to store a long description of the product.

We'll need to create an additional table, ZCART, to store a list of all of the products in customer shopping carts. The primary key for this table will include both the customer id and the product id.

Use the ERD in Figure 7.2 to guide your setup of the tables. We will also walkthrough the different steps to create the tables in the Database Solution section.

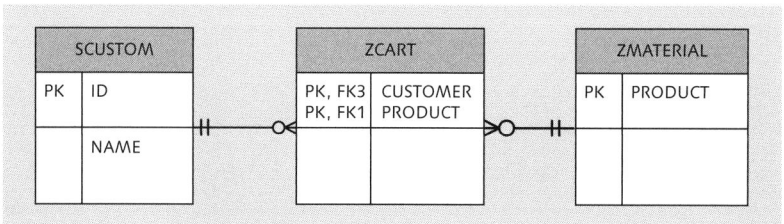

Figure 7.2 ERD Diagram of Database Solution

The Global Class

We will create a global class called ZCL_SHOPPING_CART that will handle interaction with the shopping cart table ZCART. Before we begin programming, we can design the class based on what kind of functions it will need to complete. You can draw the class design in a UML (Unified Modeling Language) diagram, as shown in Figure 7.3 where we have the name of the class in the top title area and any attributes in the first section and methods in the second section.

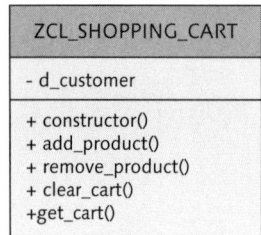

Figure 7.3 UML Diagram of the ZCL_SHOPPING_CART

UML

In Figure 7.3, you can see that the shopping cart class should have a `customer` attribute and methods to complete the actions of getting the cart, adding products to the cart, removing products from the cart and clearing the cart. The elements in the UML diagram should cover all of the functions that require access to the shopping cart database tables, but we should never feel like a design is carved from stone, since we could always go back and add methods.

When creating methods, they should typically be named in a format starting with the action to be completed followed by a description of the item we are completing the action with. For example with the `add_product` method, the action is add and the item is product.

The Access Programs

Backend users will need to be able to access ABAP programs to display or update customer shopping carts and another add or update products that are for sale. You should create two programs, one for the shopping carts and one for the products. Before writing any code we want to create wireframes to determine what the user interface will look like and what functionality will be included. *Wireframes* are a typical design technique, in which we draw up a design for a user interface without actually writing any code. Some common tools to create wireframe designs include a piece of paper and pen or PowerPoint slides. The below wireframe examples (Figure 7.4, Figure 7.5) were created using a tool called balsamiq, which creates designs that look like they were drawn on paper. We want wireframes that are simple and can be changed on the fly so that we can update them while showing them to future users.

The first program will be used to create and update the products that are available for sale using a screen like the wireframe in Figure 7.4. Because the products table does not have a global class, this program should handle updating the records, removing records and displaying the table.

Product maintenance

Figure 7.4 Product Maintenance Selection Screen

The next program displays and updates shopping carts. This program should allow users to add products, remove products, clear carts and display carts using a screen like the wireframe in Figure 7.5.

Cart maintenance

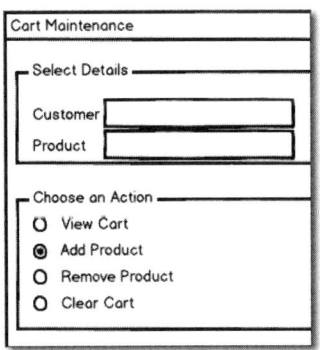

Figure 7.5 Cart Maintenance Selection Screen

> **➕ Using the Global Class**
>
> The shopping cart program should never call the tables directly; it should always use the shopping cart global class.

Database Solution

Now that we have designed our shopping cart solution we will create the necessary transparent tables within the ABAP Data Dictionary for saving and reading shopping cart and product data. We will use the steps introduced in Chapter 3 to complete this section.

Data Elements

Before we create the table, we will create any new data elements that would be used. When looking at the ERD diagram in Figure 7.2 above, it looks like we will need to create a new data element for the PRODUCT and DESCRIPTION fields, since the customer fields have already been created for the SCUSTOM table.

Product ID data element

First, we will create the product identifier data element. To do this, enter Transaction SE11, select the DATA TYPE radio button and enter "ZPRODUCTID" in the corresponding text box and click the CREATE button as shown below in Figure 7.6.

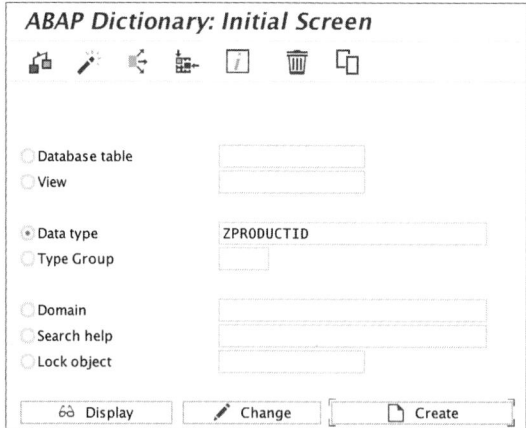

Figure 7.6 Creating a New Data Element from Transaction SE11

Select the DATA ELEMENT radio button from the popup pictured in Figure 7.7 below.

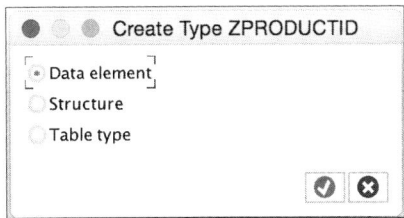

Figure 7.7 Create Type ZPRODUCTID Popup

Next, enter "ID for shopping cart products" in the SHORT DESCRIPTION textbox. Ensure that the ELEMENTARY TYPE and DOMAIN radio buttons are selected and enter "ZPRODUCTID" in the DOMAIN textbox as shown below in Figure 7.8.

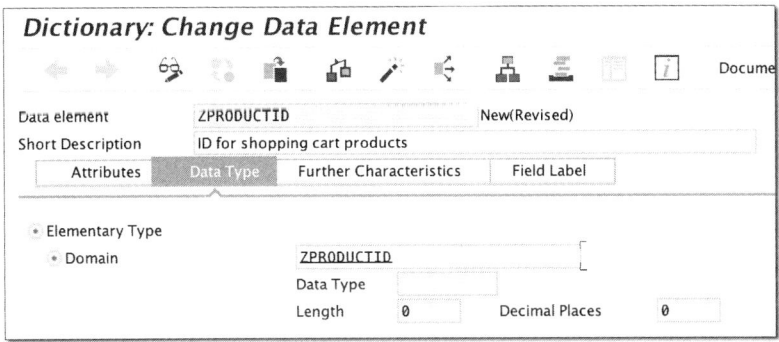

Figure 7.8 Data Type Settings for the ZPRODUCTID Data Element

Next, select the FIELD LABEL tab and enter the label "Product" for all of the different labels as shown below in Figure 7.9.

Now, click the SAVE button and save the data element to the $TMP package. Next, go back to the DATA TYPE tab and double click the DOMAIN ZPRODUCTID. You will see the popup in Figure 7.10 asking if you want to create this domain since it does not exist. Click the YES button to continue.

Product ID domain

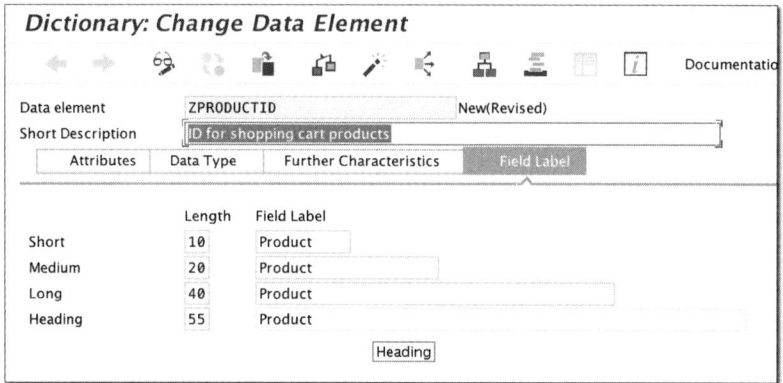

Figure 7.9 Field Label Options for the ZPRODUCTID Data Element

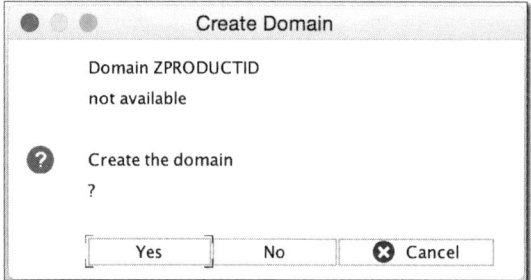

Figure 7.10 Domain ZPRODUCTID Creation Popup

The CHANGE DOMAIN screen will open with the DEFINITION tab selected. Enter "CHAR" in the DATA TYPE textbox and "18" in the NO. CHARACTERS textbox as shown in Figure 7.11 below. You can now save and activate the domain the data element. Make sure that you select $TMP for the local object package if prompted.

Product description data element

Next, we will create a data element to use for the definition field called ZPRODUCT_DESC. From Transaction SE11 select the DATA TYPE radio button and enter "ZPRODUCT_DESC" in the corresponding textbox and click the CREATE button as shown in Figure 7.12 below.

Database Solution

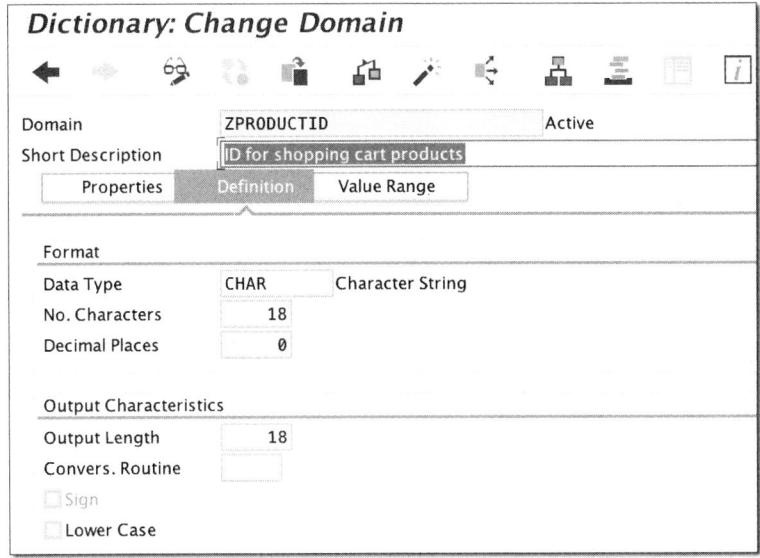

Figure 7.11 Domain ZPRODUCTID Definition Settings

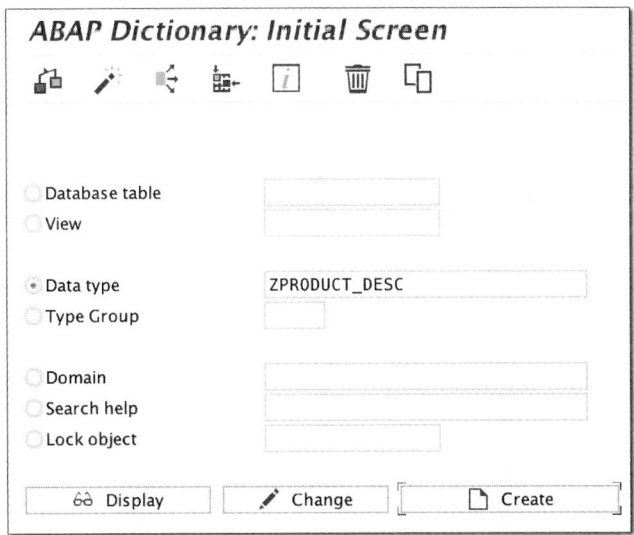

Figure 7.12 Creating Data Element ZPRODUCT_DESC from Transaction SE11

Select DATA ELEMENT from the create data type popup to continue. In the change data element screen, add "Description for shopping cart products" in the SHORT DESCRIPTION textbox. With the DATA TYPE tab selected, add "ZPRODUCT_DESC" in the DOMAIN textbox with the ELEMENTARY TYPE and DOMAIN radio buttons selected as shown in Figure 7.13 below.

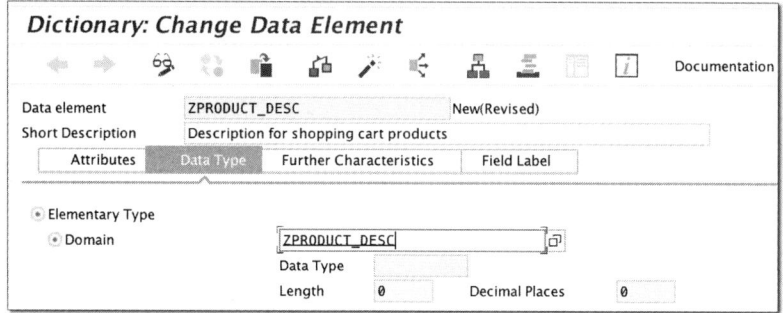

Figure 7.13 Data Type Settings for the ZPRODUCT_DESC Data Element

Next, select the FIELD LABEL tab and add "Desc" for the SHORT FIELD LABEL and "Description" for all other FIELD LABELS as shown in Figure 7.14 below.

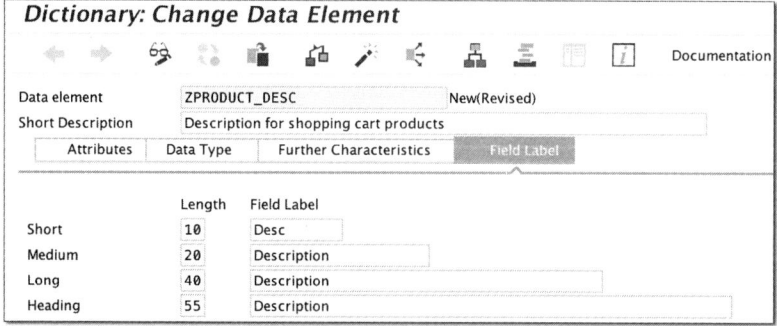

Figure 7.14 Field Label Settings for the ZPRODUCT_DESC Data Element.

Product description domain

Press the SAVE button and choose the package $TMP to save the data element as a local object. Then, select the Data Type tab and double click on the DOMAIN ZPRODUCT_DESC. When prompted if you want to create the domain, select the YES button.

Database Solution

Now, in the change domain screen add "Description for shopping cart products" in the SHORT DESCRIPTION textbox. With the DEFINITION tab selected, enter "CHAR" in the DATA TYPE textbox and "40" in the NO. CHARACTERS textbox. Also, check the checkbox for LOWER CASE in the bottom of the screen to allow descriptions in lower and upper case. Your DEFINITION tab should match what is shown in Figure 7.15 below. You can now press the SAVE button and choose to save the domain in the $TMP package and then press ACTIVATE to activate both the domain and the data element.

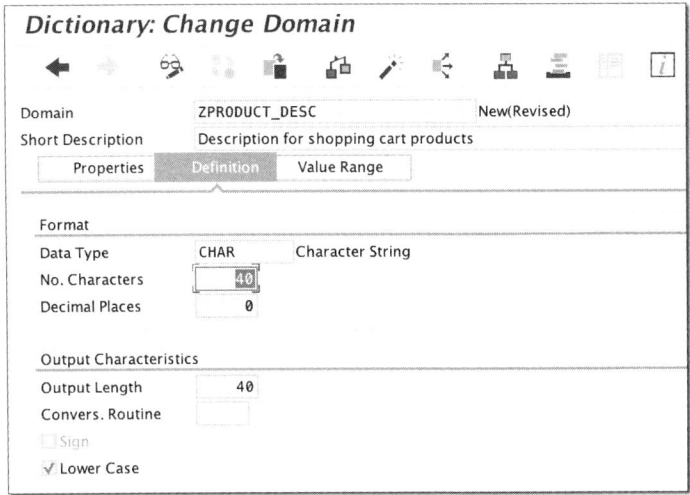

Figure 7.15 Definition Settings for the ZPRODUCT_DESC Domain

Now that the new data elements are created, we will add our new transparent tables in the next section.

Transparent Tables

First we will create the ZPRODUCT table. To create the transparent table enter Transaction SE11, select the DATABASE TABLE radio button and enter "ZPRODUCT" in the text box as shown in Figure 7.16. Next, click the CREATE button.

Zproduct table

7 Creating a Shopping Cart Example

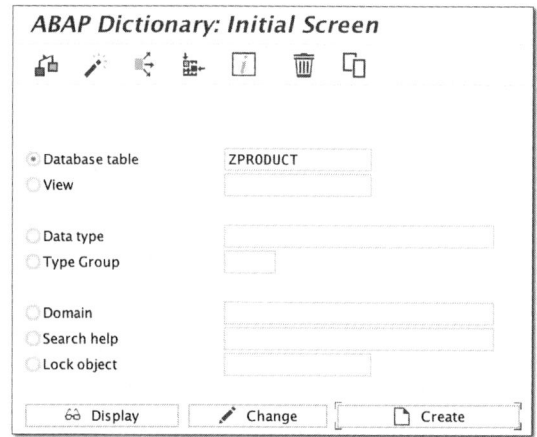

Figure 7.16 Creating the ZPRODUCT Table from Transaction SE11

Next, in the DELIVERY AND MAINTENANCE tab, set the SHORT DESCRIPTION to "Shopping Cart Products", the DELIVERY CLASS textbox to "A" for Application table (master and transaction data) and the DATA BROWSER / TABLE VIEW MAINT. selection to DISPLAY / MAINTENANCE ALLOWED as shown in Figure 7.17.

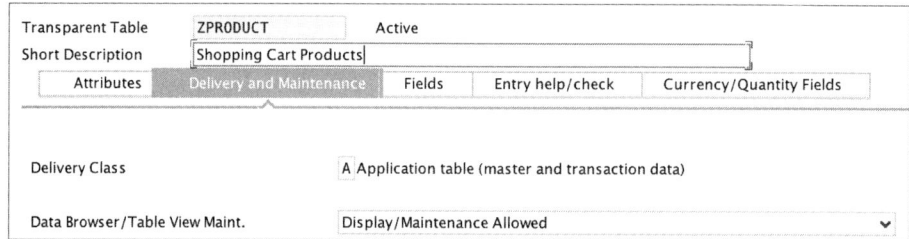

Figure 7.17 Delivery and Maintenance Settings for Table ZPRODUCT

Next, in the FIELDS tab we will add three fields: MANDT, PRODUCT and DESCRIPTION. We may not show the MANDT field when designing our table using an ERD diagram, but we should include it in every table. MANDT should use the DATA ELEMENT MANDT, PRODUCT should use our new DATA ELEMENT ZPRODUCTID and DESCRIPTION should use our new DATA ELEMENT ZPRODUCT_DESC. Additionally, fields MANDT and PRODUCT should have the KEY and INITIAL VALUE checkboxes checked as shown below in Figure 7.18.

272

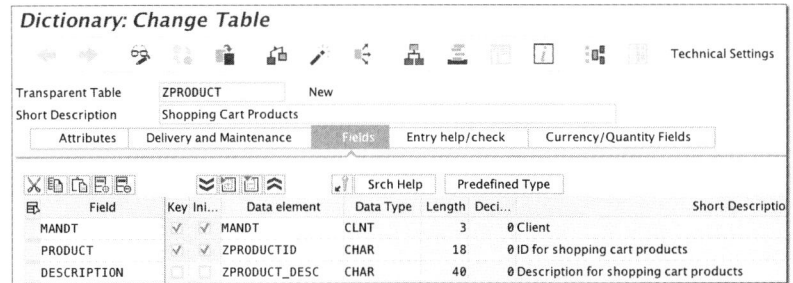

Figure 7.18 Transparent Table Field Tab Settings

Next, we need to set MANDT as a foreign key. To do this, highlight the MANDT field and press the FOREIGN KEY button. You will see a popup that asks if you to use table T000 as a check table, select the YES button to continue.

ZPRODUCT foreign keys

In the CREATE FOREIGN KEY popup, the CHECK TABLE textbox should be auto populated with table T000, if not set the value as T000. Next, select the KEY FIELDS/CANDIDATES radio button and set the cardinality as 1:CN as shown in Figure 7.19 and click the COPY button to create the key.

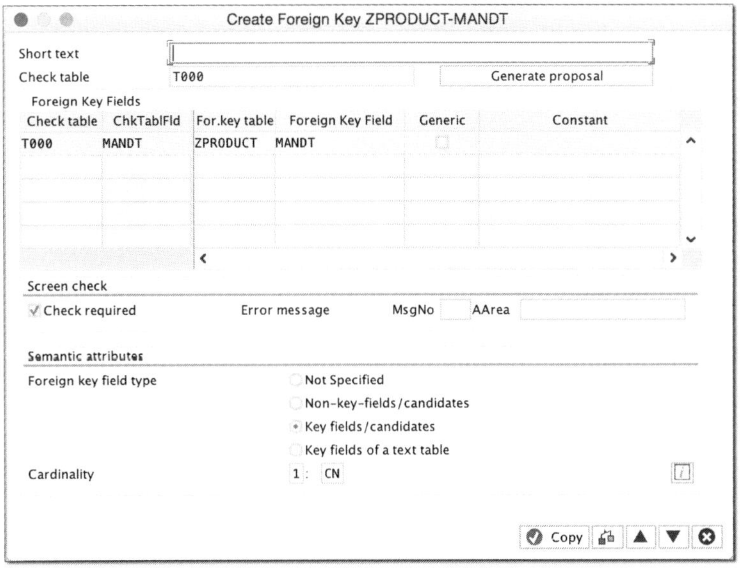

Figure 7.19 Create MANDT Foreign Key Settings

273

7 Creating a Shopping Cart Example

ZPRODUCT technical settings

Next, press the SAVE button to save the changes we have made so far. Next, click the TECHNICAL SETTINGS button and set the DATA CLASS to APPL0 indicating that the data stored in the table is master data, and SIZE CATEGORY 0, indicating that we are expecting 0 to 5,000 records in our table, as shown in Figure 7.20. Leave all other technical settings options as their default options. Press the SAVE button to save the technical settings and press the BACK button to return to the change table screen.

Figure 7.20 Technical Settings for the ZPRODUCT Table

Next, change the enhancement category by selecting EXTRAS • ENHANCEMENT CATEGORY and select the CANNOT BE ENHANCED radio button. Press the SAVE button to save the table and enter package "$TMP" to save the table as a local object and then press the ACTIVATE button to activate the table.

ZPRODUCTID value range

Now that we have created the ZPRODUCT table, we need to update the ZPRODUCTID domain to indicate that the ZPRODUCT table contains the possible values for ZPRODUCTID domain. To do this, go back to Transaction SE11 and select the DOMAIN radio button and enter "ZPRODUCTID" in the corresponding textbox as shown in Figure 7.21 and then click the CHANGE button.

Next, select the VALUE RANGE tab and enter "ZPRODUCT" in the VALUE TABLE textbox at the bottom of the screen as shown in Figure 7.22 below. Then press the SAVE button and ACTIVATE button to activate your changes.

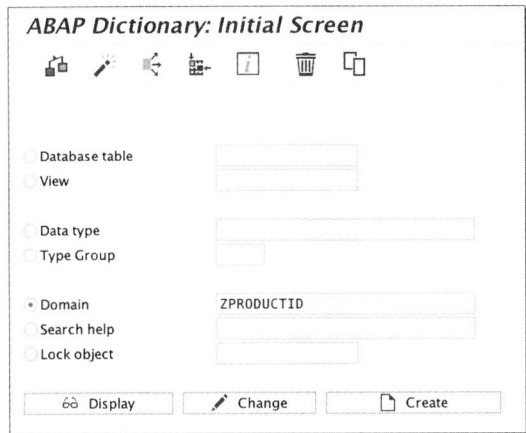

Figure 7.21 Selecting a Domain from Transaction SE11

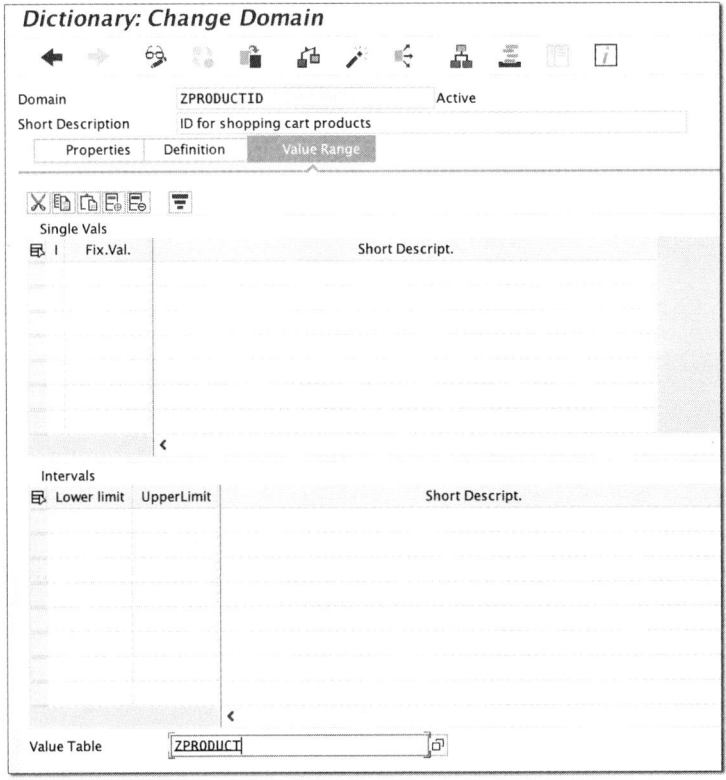

Figure 7.22 Updating the ZPRODUCTID Domain Settings

7 Creating a Shopping Cart Example

ZCART table Next we will create the ZCART table, used to store the products for customer's carts. To do this, go back to Transaction SE11 and select the DATABASE TABLE radio button and enter "ZCART" in the corresponding text box as shown in Figure 7.23 below. Then select the CREATE button.

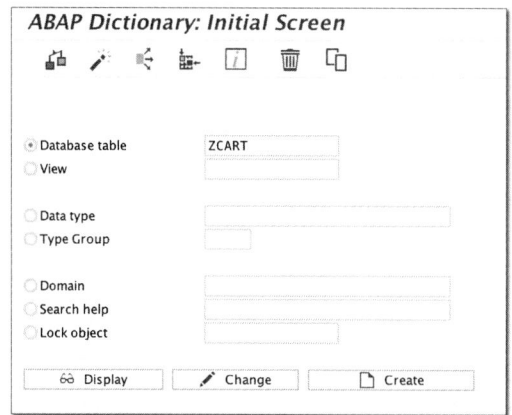

Figure 7.23 Creating Transparent Table ZCART from Transaction SE11

Now, from the DELIVERY AND MAINTENANCE tab, set the DELIVERY CLASS to "A" for master and transaction data and set the DATA BROWSER / TABLE VIEW MAINT. selection to DISPLAY/MAINTENANCE ALLOWED as shown in Figure 7.24.

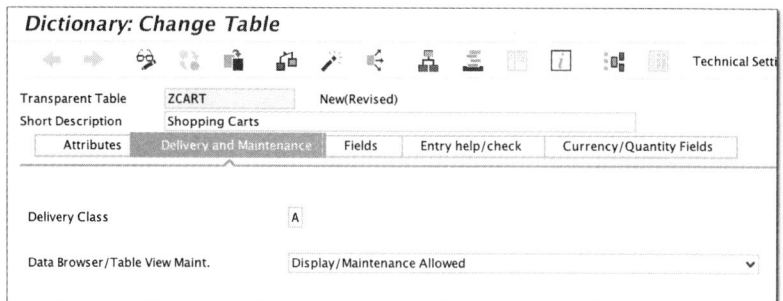

Figure 7.24 Delivery and Maintenance Settings for the ZCART Transparent Table

Next, select the FIELDS tab and add the FIELD "MANDT" with DATA ELEMENT "MANDT", FIELD "CUSTOMER" with DATA ELEMENT "S_CUSTOMER" and FIELD "PRODUCT" with DATA ELEMENT

276

"ZPRODUCTID". Then, select the KEY and INITIAL VALUES checkboxes for all of these fields as shown in Figure 7.25.

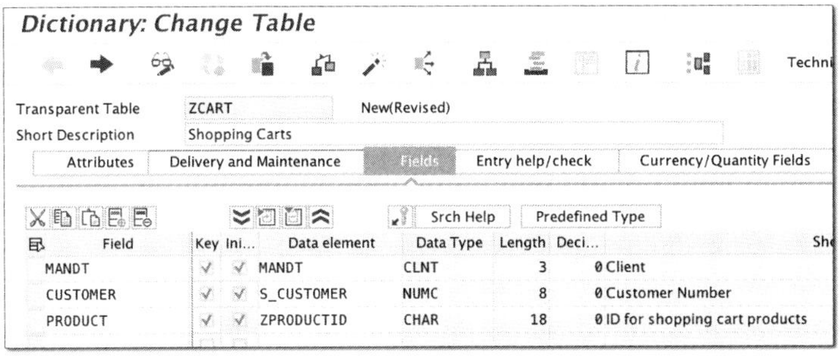

Figure 7.25 Fields Tab Setting for the ZCART Transparent Table

Now, select the MANDT field and click the FOREIGN KEY button. You will see a popup asking if you want to use a proposal for table T000, select the YES button. In the CREATE FOREIGN KEY popup, select the KEY FIELDS/CANDIDATES radio button for FOREIGN KEY FIELD TYPE and 1:CN for the CARDINALITY as shown in Figure 7.26. Then select the COPY button to create the foreign key.

ZCART foreign keys

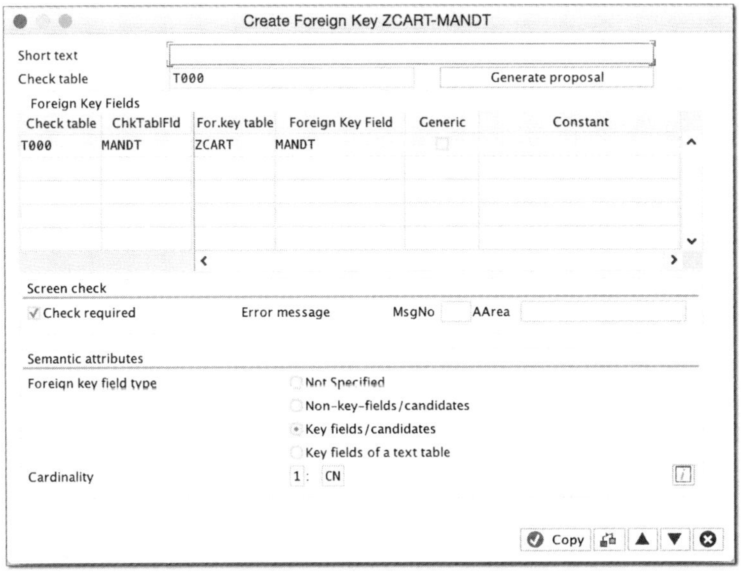

Figure 7.26 Create Foreign Key Settings for MANDT

Next, select CUSTOMER field and press the FOREIGN KEY button. You might see a popup asking if you want to use the proposed SBUSPART table, select the No button. Then, in the CREATE FOREIGN KEY popup, enter "SCUSTOM" as the check table and press enter. You will then be prompted asking if you want to use the proposed fields for this table. Press the YES button. Next, select the KEY FIELDS/CANDIDATES radio button for the FOREIGN KEY FIELD TYPE and 1:CN for the CARDINALITY as shown in below in Figure 7.27. Next, press the COPY button to save the foreign key.

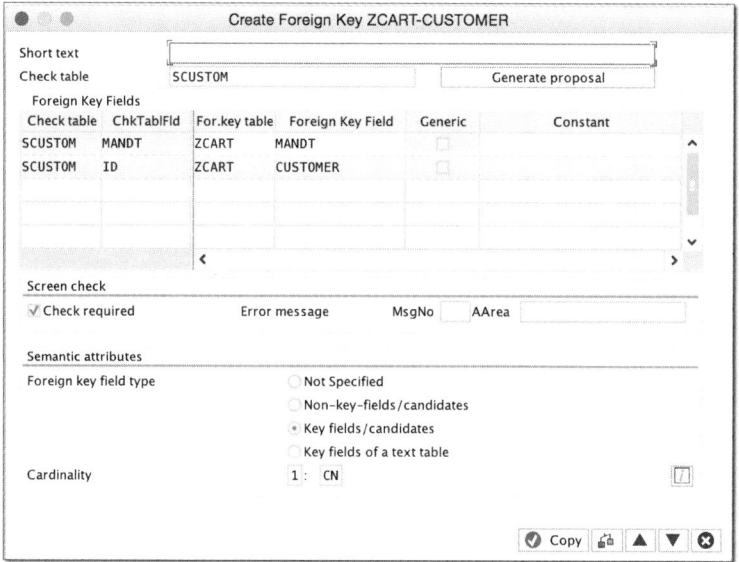

Figure 7.27 Customer Foreign Key Settings

Next, select the PRODUCT field and press the FOREIGN KEY button. You will see a popup asking if you want to use a proposal with the ZPRODUCT table. Select YES. Next, select the KEY FIELDS/CANDIDATES radio button for the FOREIGN KEY FIELD TYPE and 1:CN for the CARDINALITY as shown in below in Figure 7.28. Then, press the COPY button to save the foreign key.

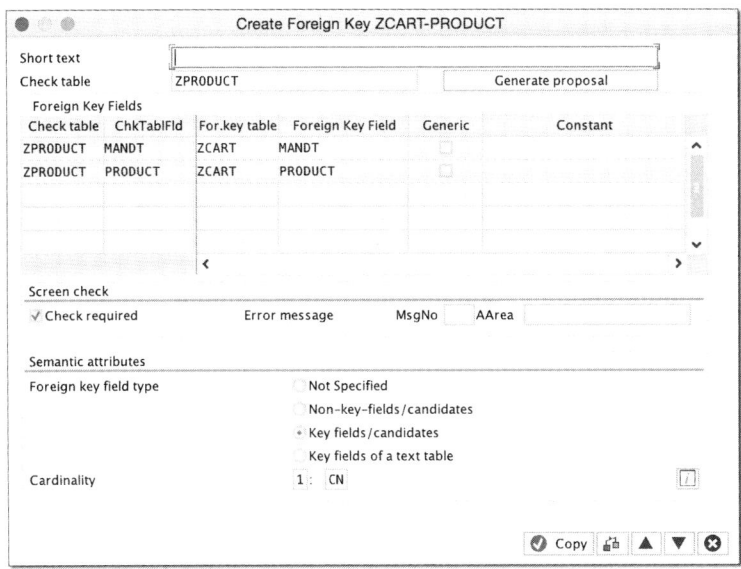

Figure 7.28 Foreign Key Settings for Product Foreign Key

Now, select the SAVE button and select package $TMP to save the table as a local object. Then press the TECHNICAL SETTINGS button and enter APPL1 for the DATA CLASS textbox indicating that this is a transaction table and 0 for the SIZE CATEGORY indicating that the table is expected to have 0 to 10,000 records as shown below in Figure 7.29. Then click the SAVE button to save the changes and the BACK button to return to the change table view.

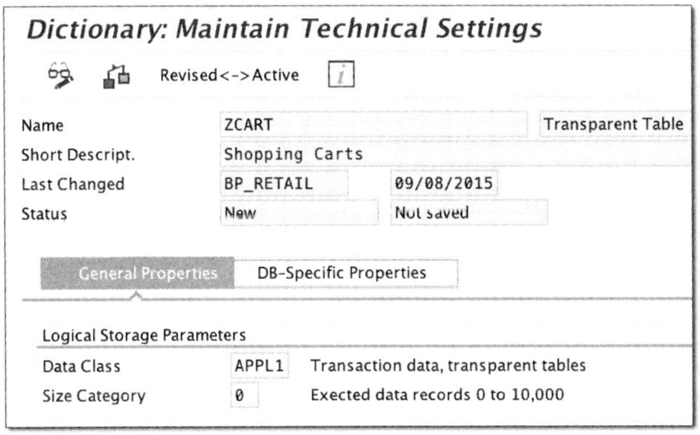

ZCART technical settings

Figure 7.29 Technical Settings for the ZCART Transparent Table

7 Creating a Shopping Cart Example

Next, select EXTRAS • ENHANCEMENT CATEGORY and select the radio button for CANNOT BE ENHANCED to set a value for the enhancement category. Then press the ACTIVATE button to activate the table.

We have now created the two required custom tables for our shopping cart solution. In the next section we will create the global class that will access our custom tables.

Accessing the Database Solution

In this section we will create the global class ZCL_SHOPPING_CART used to access and update the ZCART table. We will focus on the actual code for the class, so it is recommended that you use either the SOURCE-BASED VIEW in Transaction SE80 or the Eclipse IDE to follow. In the design section, we used UML to create a design for our global class. That design is shown below in Figure 7.30.

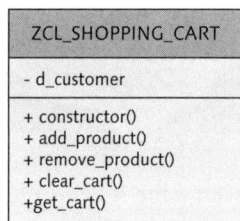

Figure 7.30 UML Diagram of ZCL_SHOPPING_CART

Class definition

From the UML diagram, we can create the class definition, as shown in Listing 7.1. This is the required parts of a class definition with the d_customer private attribute listed, which will be accessible by all of the methods we create, but not outside of the class.

```
CLASS zcl_shopping_cart DEFINITION
    PUBLIC
    FINAL
    CREATE PUBLIC.

PUBLIC SECTION.
PROTECTED SECTION.
PRIVATE SECTION.
    d_customer TYPE scustom-id.
ENDCLASS.
```
Listing 7.1 Shopping Cart Class Definition

Next we will add the definition of the `constructor` method shown in Listing 7.2. Notice that for the `constructor`, we set the importing parameter `ip_customer` as a type `scustom-id`, which represents a customer id. This way, when the class is created, we can set the customer to be used instead of using customer as a parameter for every method.

```
CLASS zcl_shopping_cart DEFINITION
    PUBLIC
    FINAL
    CREATE PUBLIC.

PUBLIC SECTION.
    METHODS:
    constructor IMPORTING ip_customer TYPE scustom-id.
PROTECTED SECTION.
PRIVATE SECTION.
    d_customer TYPE scustom-id.
ENDCLASS.
```

Listing 7.2 Adding the CONSTRUCTOR Method to the ZCL_SHOPPING_CART Definition

Next, we will add the definition for the `add_product` and `remove_product` methods. Both of these methods will have an importing parameter of `ip_product` of type `zproduct-product`, which represents the product id that we want to add or remove as shown in Listing 7.3.

```
CLASS zcl_shopping_cart DEFINITION
    PUBLIC
    FINAL
    CREATE PUBLIC.

PUBLIC SECTION.
    METHODS:
    constructor IMPORTING ip_customer TYPE scustom-id,
    add_product IMPORTING ip_product TYPE zproduct-product,
    remove_product IMPORTING ip_product
        TYPE zproduct-product.
PROTECTED SECTION.
PRIVATE SECTION.
    d_customer TYPE scustom-id.
ENDCLASS.
```

Listing 7.3 Adding the ADD_PRODUCT and REMOVE_PRODUCT Methods to the Class ZCL_SHOPPING_CART

Next, we will add the `clear_cart` method which will clear all of the items in the shopping cart. This method will not need any parameters as shown in Listing 7.4.

Creating a Shopping Cart Example

```
CLASS zcl_shopping_cart DEFINITION
    PUBLIC
    FINAL
    CREATE PUBLIC.

PUBLIC SECTION.
    METHODS:
   constructor IMPORTING ip_customer TYPE scustom-id,
   add_product IMPORTING ip_product TYPE zproduct-product,
   remove_product IMPORTING ip_product
     TYPE zproduct-product,
   clear_cart.
PROTECTED SECTION.
PRIVATE SECTION.
     d_customer TYPE scustom-id.
ENDCLASS.
```
Listing 7.4 Adding the CLEAR_CART Method

Table type attribute

The `get_cart` method will need to return all of the products in a customer's shopping cart as well as the description of those products, so we will need a new table type to use as the type of our returning parameter in the `get_cart` method. We can create that table type using either the ABAP Data Dictionary as discussed in Chapter 3 or by defining a new type and table type within the class public section as shown in Listing 7.5 below. Notice that we defined a primary key for the table type, this is a requirement when using table types as method's returning parameter.

```
CLASS zcl_shopping_cart DEFINITION
    PUBLIC
    FINAL
    CREATE PUBLIC.

PUBLIC SECTION.
    TYPES: BEGIN OF y_cart,
           product TYPE zproduct-product,
           description TYPE zproduct-description,
           END OF y_cart,

   yt_cart TYPE STANDARD TABLE OF y_cart WITH KEY product.
    METHODS:
   constructor IMPORTING ip_customer TYPE scustom-id,
   add_product IMPORTING ip_product TYPE zproduct-product,
   remove_product IMPORTING ip_product
     TYPF zproduct-product,
   clear_cart.
```

```
PROTECTED SECTION.
PRIVATE SECTION.
    d_customer TYPE scustom-id.
ENDCLASS.
```
Listing 7.5 Adding a Table Type to the Public Section of ZCL_SHOPPING_CART

Now, we can now add a method for `get_cart`, which will have a returning parameter of `rt_cart` which will use our new table type `yt_cart`. We do not need any importing parameters because we set the customer id with the constructor.

```
CLASS zcl_shopping_cart DEFINITION
    PUBLIC
    FINAL
    CREATE PUBLIC.

PUBLIC SECTION.
      TYPES: BEGIN OF y_cart,
             product TYPE zproduct-product,
             description TYPE zproduct-description,
             END OF y_cart,

   yt_cart TYPE STANDARD TABLE OF y_cart WITH KEY product.
      METHODS:
    constructor IMPORTING ip_customer TYPE scustom-id,
    add_product IMPORTING ip_product TYPE zproduct-product,
    remove_product IMPORTING ip_product
       TYPE zproduct-product,
    clear_cart,
    get_cart RETURNING VALUE(rt_cart) TYPE yt_cart.
PROTECTED SECTION.
PRIVATE SECTION.
    d_customer TYPE scustom-id.
ENDCLASS.
```
Listing 7.6 Adding the GET_CART Method to the ZCL_SHOPPING_CART Class

Now that our definition is complete, we are ready to start the class implementation. First, we will create all of the methods and use pseudo code to provide an overview of the code we will write. *Pseudocode* is a non-executable description of what you want your program to do and is written using comments. Next, you will add pseudocode to design your different methods. Pseudocode for the `zcl_shopping_cart` class implementation is shown in Listing 7.7.

Class implementation

7 Creating a Shopping Cart Example

```
CLASS zcl_shopping_cart IMPLEMENTATION.
METHOD constructor.
"save customerid
ENDMETHOD.
METHOD add_product.
"create structure
"MODIFY database with structure
ENDMETHOD.
METHOD remove_product.
"DELETE database using parameter
ENDMETHOD.
METHOD clear_cart.
"DELTE database using customer attribute
ENDMETHOD.
METHOD get_cart.
"SELECT databaseusing customer attribute
ENDMETHOD.
ENDCLASS.
```
Listing 7.7 Pseudocode for Methods in ZCL_SHOPPING_CART

Now, we are ready to start turning the pseudocode in to real code. Let's start with the `constructor` method shown in Listing 7.8. The `constructor` method will simply take the importing parameter and save it to the private attribute `d_customer` and we can complete that in one line of code.

```
METHOD constructor.
    d_customer = ip_customer.
ENDMETHOD.
```
Listing 7.8 The constructor ZCL_SHOPPING_CART Method

Next, we will create the `add_product` and `remove_product` methods. Both methods will declare a local structure `ls_cart` (`ls` prefix means local structure) of type `zcart` and insert the importing parameter and customer attribute into the local structure. The `add_product` will use the `MODIFY` Open SQL command to update the database with the structure and the `remove_product` will use the `DELETE` Open SQL command to delete the structure from the database as shown below in Listing 7.9.

```
METHOD add_product.
    DATA: ls_cart TYPE zcart.
    ls_cart-customer = d_customer.
```

```
    ls_cart-product = ip_product.

    INSERT zcart FROM ls_cart.
ENDMETHOD.
METHOD remove_product.
    DATA: ls_cart TYPE zcart.
    ls_cart-customer = d_customer.
    ls_cart-product = ip_product.

    DELETE zcart FROM ls_cart.
ENDMETHOD.
```
Listing 7.9 The ADD_PRODUCT and REMOVE_PRODUCT ZCL_SHOPPING_CART Methods

Next, the `clear_cart` method will remove all records from the zcart table for the customer id we have stored in our private attribute. We are able to do this with one line of code using the DELETE FROM...WHERE Open SQL command as shown below in Listing 7.10.

```
METHOD clear_cart.
    DELETE FROM zcart WHERE customer = d_customer.
ENDMETHOD.
```
Listing 7.10 The CLEAR_CART Method for ZCL_SHOPPING_CART

Lastly, the `get_cart` method will use an Open SQL SELECT statement to get all of the products for the customer's shopping cart products and their description using an INNER JOIN. In Listing 7.11, we show the SELECT in both old Open SQL and new Open SQL. Since the returning parameter is a table type, we can load the returning table with our SELECT.

```
METHOD get_cart.
    "new Open SQL
    SELECT zcart~product, description
    FROM zcart
    INNER JOIN zproduct
    ON zcart~product = zproduct~product
    WHERE zcart-customer = d_customer
    INTO TABLE @rt_cart.

    "old Open SQL
    SELECT zcart~product description
    INTO TABLE rt_cart
    FROM zcart
    INNER JOIN zproduct
```

```
      ON zcart~product = zproduct~product
    WHERE zcart-customer = d_customer.
ENDMETHOD.
```
Listing 7.11 The GET_CART Method for ZCL_SHOPPING_CART

Creating Classic Screens for the Solution

Now that you have the global class for accessing the shopping cart data, we need to create ABAP applications for maintaining our tables directly from the SAP system. In a typical ABAP project, these programs would probably use more advanced user interfaces such as ABAP Web Dynpro or SAPUI5.

As mentioned in the design section, we will create two ABAP programs. One for maintaining and displaying the products table and one for maintaining and displaying the customer shopping carts.

Product Maintenance Program

Product maintenance wireframe

The first program we will create is the product maintenance program. The selection screen wireframe from the design section is shown below in Figure 7.31 for reference.

Figure 7.31 Wireframe Design for the Product Maintenance Program

Now, create a new ABAP program with the name `zproduct_maint` and description `Product Maintenance` using your preferred development IDE.

Creating Classic Screens for the Solution

First we will create the selection screen using the code in Listing 7.12 which is based on the design in Figure 7.31 and creates the top part of our selection screen with a BLOCK...WITH FRAME TITLE and two parameters, one for product and one for description. Notice we added the LOWER CASE property to the description parameter to allow for a description in both upper and lower case.

Selection Screen

```
REPORT zproduct_maint.
SELECTION-SCREEN BEGIN OF BLOCK product
  WITH FRAME TITLE text-001.
    PARAMETERS: p_prod TYPE zproduct-product,
                P_desc TYPE zproduct-description LOWER CASE.
SELECTION-SCREEN END OF BLOCK product.
```
Listing 7.12 Product selection parameters in ZPRODUCT_MAINT

Next, we will add the second selection block from Figure 7.31, which will be a group of parameters using the RADIOBUTTON GROUP property so that they will be displayed as radio buttons using the code in Listing 7.3. Notice that they all have the same radio button group (act) indicating that only one can be selected.

```
SELECTION-SCREEN BEGIN OF BLOCK action
  WITH FRAME TITLE text-002.
    PARAMETERS: p_upd TYPE boolean RADIOBUTTON GROUP act,
                p_rem TYPE boolean RADIOBUTTON GROUP act,
    p_dis TYPE boolean RADIOBUTTON GROUP act.
SELECTION-SCREEN END OF BLOCK action.
```
Listing 7.13 Action Selection Parameters in ZPRODUCT_MAINT

Now, we can set the selection texts for our selection screen. If you are using Eclipse as your IDE, right click the program listed in your PROJECT EXPLORER and select OPEN WITH SAP GUI. Now using either Eclipse or Transaction SE80 in the GUI, select GOTO • TEXT ELEMENTS • SELECTION TEXTS. From the CHANGE SELECTION TEXTS screen, select the DICTIONARY REF. checkbox for p_desc and p_prod and enter Display Products for item p_dis, Remove Product for item p_rem and Add/Update Product for item p_upd as shown in Figure 7.32.

Selection Texts

Next, select the TEXT SYMBOLS tab and add symbol 001 with the text Select a Product and symbol 002 with the text Choose an Action as shown below in Figure 7.33.

287

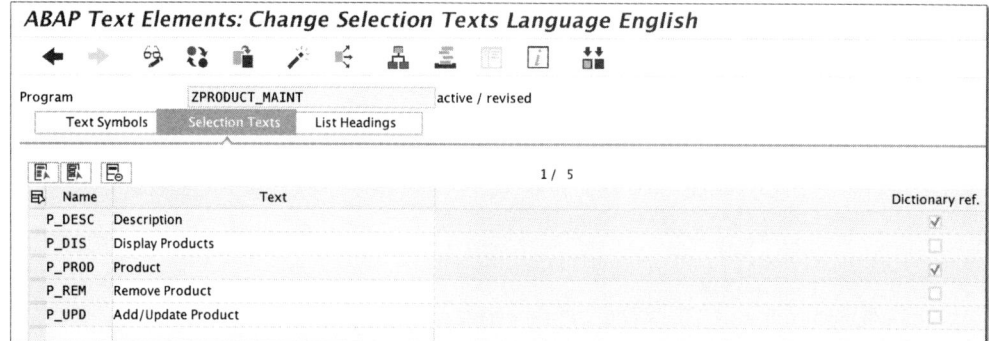

Figure 7.32 Selection Text Options for ZPRODUCT_MAINT

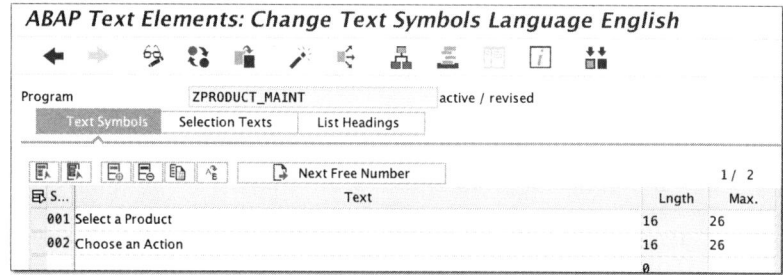

Figure 7.33 Text Symbol Options for ZPRODUCT_MAINT

Next, click the ACTIVATE button and activate both the program and the program text for ZPRODUCT_MAINT. We can now go back to our code and test our program by selecting the RUN button in Eclipse or the DIRECT PROCESSING button in Transaction SE80. We should see the selection screen pictured below in Figure 7.34 which closely resembles the wireframe design from the design section.

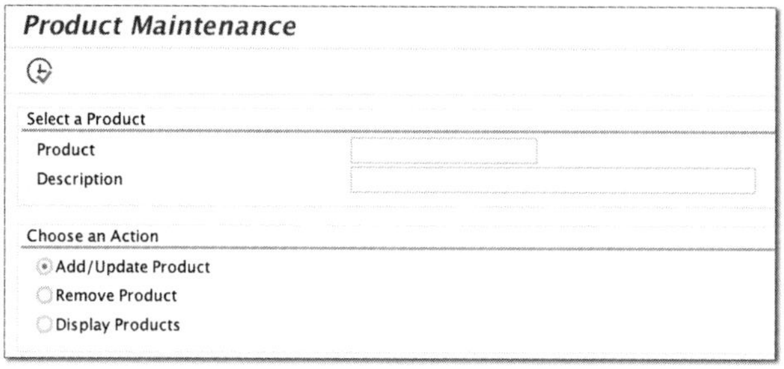

Figure 7.34 ZPRODUCT_MAINT Selection Screen

Now that the selection screen looks correct, we can start to add our code to the `zproduct_maint` program. This is a small program, so we will not create a local class for it at this time. The code in Listing 7.14 will directly follow the selection screen code and will store the product and description parameters in a structure of type `zproduct`. Then it will test whether the `p_upd` parameter or `p_rem` parameter was selected. If `p_upd` was selected, it will use the `MODIFY` Open SQL command and if `p_rem` was selected, it will use the `DELETE` Open SQL command to update the database using our populated structure. We will also write a success message to the screen after the database has been updated.

Main program

```
DATA: s_product TYPE zproduct.
s_product-product = p_prod.
s_product-description = p_desc.
IF p_upd = abap_true.
    MODIFY zproduct FROM s_product.
    WRITE: 'Update Completed'.
ELSEIF p_rem = abap_true.
    DELETE zproduct FROM s_product.
    WRITE: 'DELETE Completed'.
ENDIF.
```
Listing 7.14 Handling Updates and Deletes in ZPRODUCT_MAINT

Next we will add the code to handle when the `p_dis` radio button is selected. For this option, we will want to select a list of all products and their descriptions and output the results to an ALV grid, which we covered in Chapter 5. The code in Listing 7.15 uses new Open SQL and inline data declarations and so will require and ABAP 7.4 SP8 or higher system and would be placed before the `ENDIF` at the end of Listing 7.14.

```
….
ELSEIF p_dis = abap_true.
    SELECT product, description
    FROM zproduct
    INTO TABLE @DATA(t_products).

    CL_SALV_TABLE=>factory(
        IMPORTING r_salv_table = DATA(gr_alv)
        CHANGING t_table = t_products ).
Gr_alv->display( ).
ENDIF.
```
Listing 7.15 Handling the Display with New Open SQL and Inline Data Declarations

The code in Listing 7.16 can be used instead of Listing 7.15 for systems that are on a version before ABAP 7.4 SP8. Notice that we have to declare a data type to for our output table to display the product and description in a table. In Listing 7.16 the variable definitions would be at the top of the program, following the selection screen and the code following ELSEIF would be before the ENDIF at the bottom of Listing 7.14.

```abap
...
TYPES: BEGIN OF y_product,
       product TYPE zproduct-product,
       description TYPE zproduct-description,
       END OF y_product.

DATA: s_product TYPE zproduct,
      t_products TYPE STANDARD TABLE OF y_product,
      gr_alv TYPE REF TO cl_salv_table.
...
ELSEIF p_dis = abap_true.
    SELECT product description
      INTO TABLE t_products
      FROM zproduct.

    cl_salv_table=>factory( IMPORTING r_salv_table = gr_alv
             CHANGING t_table = t_products ).
    gr_alv->display( ).
ENDIF.
```
Listing 7.16 Handling the Display for Non-ABAP 7.4 SP8 Systems

Testing the program

The maintain products program is now complete. Select the ACTIVATE button to activate the program and then we can test our program by selecting the RUN ▶ button in Eclipse or the DIRECT PROCESSING ⚡ button in Transaction SE80.

Shopping Cart Maintenance Program

Cart maintenance wireframe

Next, we will create an ABAP program for displaying and maintaining the shopping cart table. This program will utilize the global class zcl_shopping_cart to handle the table updates. The wireframe from the design section is showed below in Figure 7.35.

Now, create a new ABAP program with the name "zcart_maint" and description "Cart Maintenance" using your preferred development IDE.

Creating Classic Screens for the Solution

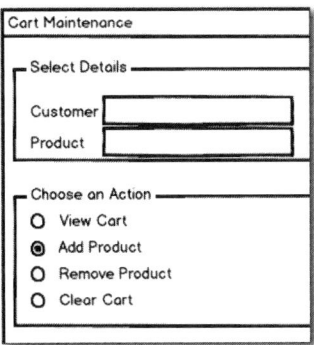

Figure 7.35 Wireframe Design for the Cart Maintenance Program

First, we will create the selection screen using the code in Listing 7.17 which is based on the design in Figure 7.35 and creates the top part of our selection screen with a BLOCK...WITH FRAME TITLE and two parameters, one for customer and one for product. Notice that we used the option OBLIGATORY to make the customer parameter required.

Selection screen

```
REPORT zcart_maint.
SELECTION-SCREEN BEGIN OF BLOCK cart
  WITH FRAME TITLE text-001.
PARAMETERS: p_cust TYPE zcart-customer OBLIGATORY,
            p_prod TYPE zcart-product.
SELECTION-SCREEN END OF BLOCK cart.
```
Listing 7.17 Top Selection Screen Block for ZCART_MAINT

Next we will add the second selection screen block, which uses the RADIOBUTTON GROUP to display a group of radio buttons used to determine what action the user wants to complete using the code below in Listing 7.18 which will be placed below the code from Listing 7.17.

```
SELECTION-SCREEN BEGIN OF BLOCK action
  WITH FRAME TITLE text-002.
PARAMETERS: p_view  TYPE boolean RADIOBUTTON GROUP act,
            p_add   TYPE boolean RADIOBUTTON GROUP act,
            p_rem   TYPE boolean RADIOBUTTON GROUP act,
            p_clear TYPE boolean RADIOBUTTON GROUP act.
SELECTION-SCREEN BEND OF BLOCK action.
```
Listing 7.18 Bottom Selection Screen Block for ZCART_MAINT

291

Selection texts

Now, we can set the selection texts for our selection screen. If you are using Eclipse as your IDE, right click the program listed in your PROJECT EXPLORER and select OPEN WITH SAP GUI. Now using either Eclipse or Transaction SE80 in the GUI, select GOTO • TEXT ELEMENTS • SELECTION TEXTS. From the CHANGE SELECTION TEXTS screen, select the DICTIONARY REF. checkbox for p_cust and p_prod and enter "View Cart" for item p_view, "Add Product" for item p_add and "Remove Product" for item p_rem and "Clear Cart" for p_clear as shown in Figure 7.36.

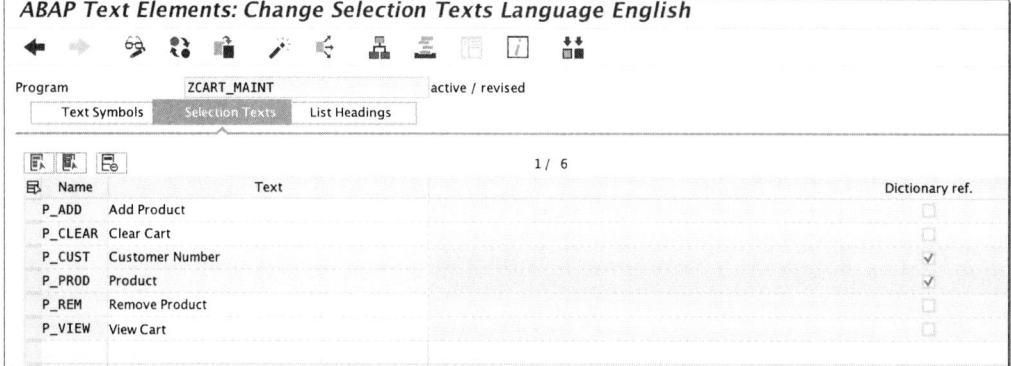

Figure 7.36 Selection Texts for ZCART_MAINT

Next, select the TEXT SYMBOLS tab and add symbol 001 with the text "Select Details" and symbol 002 with the text "Choose an Action" as shown below in Figure 7.37.

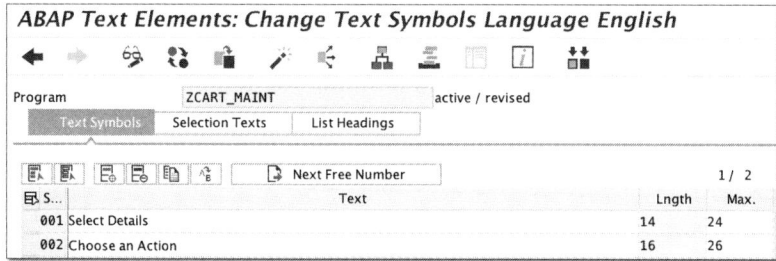

Figure 7.37 Text Symbols for ZCART_MAINT

Next, click the ACTIVATE button and activate both the program and the program text for ZCART_MAINT. We can now go back to our code and test our program by selecting the RUN ⏵ button in Eclipse or the DIRECT PROCESSING ⏵ button in Transaction SE80. We should see the selection screen pictured below in Figure 7.38, which closely resembles the wireframe design from the design section.

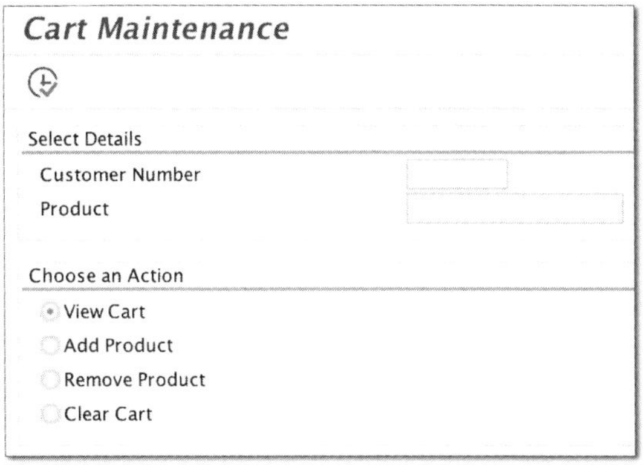

Figure 7.38 Selection Screen Output for ZCART_MAINT

Now that our selection screen is complete, we can add the code for our program. The program should be small and so will not require a local class to be created. First, we will need to declare the shopping cart class and create an object using the code below in Listing 7.19, which will come directly after the selection screen code.

Main program

```
DATA: o_cart TYPE REF TO zcl_shoppping_cart.
CREATE OBJECT o_cart EXPORTING ip_customer = p_cust.
```
Listing 7.19 Creating the shopping cart object in zcart_maint

Now that we have the shopping cart class, we can add code for the different action radio buttons, beginning with the VIEW CART radio button. The code in Listing 7.20 requires an ABAP 7.4 SP8 or higher system or higher because it uses inline data declarations to store the results from the get_cart method in a table and to create an ALV grid and display the results. The code in Listing 7.20 should be placed directly after the line beginning with CREATE OBJECT.

```
IF p_view = abap_true.
    DATA(t_cart) = o_cart->get_cart.
    Cl_salv_table=>factory(
      IMPORTING r_salv_table = DATA(gr_alv)
```

```
                                      CHANGING t_table = t_cart ).
      gr_alv->display( ).
ENDIF.
```
Listing 7.20 View Cart Code for CART_MAINT Using Inline Data Declarations

If your system is not ABAP 7.4 SP8 or higher, you can use the code in Listing 7.21, which will complete the same function as Listing 7.20, but will declare the different variables instead of using inline data declarations.

```
DATA: t_cart TYPE o_cart->yt_cart,
      gr_alv TYPE REF TO cl_salv_table.
IF p_view = abap_true.
    t_cart = o_cart->get_cart( ).
    cl_salv_table=>factory( IMPORTING r_salv_table = gr_alv
                            CHANGING t_table = t_cart ).
    gr_alv->display( ).
ENDIF.
```
Listing 7.21 View Cart Code for CART_MAINT without Inline Data Declarations

Next, we will add the code for removing products, adding products, and clearing carts using the code in Listing 7.22. Since all of the logic for these actions are in zcl_shopping_cart, we need to simply check which radio button is selected and call the corresponding method. After each update, we should write to the screen to let the user know that the operation completed. The code in Listing 7.22 should be entered before the line ENDIF at the end of our program.

```
ELSEIF p_add = abap_true.
    o_cart->add_product( p_prod ).
    WRITE:'Product Added'.
ELSEIF p_rem = abap_true.
    o_cart->remove_product( p_prod ).
    WRITE: 'Product Removed'.
ELSEIF p_clear = abap_true.
    o_cart->clear_cart( ).
    WRITE: 'Cart cleared'.
ENDIF.
```
Listing 7.22 Additional Action Code for ZCART_MAINT

Testing the program

The maintain cart program is now complete. Select the ACTIVATE button to activate the program and then we can test our program by selecting the RUN ⊙▾ button in Eclipse or the DIRECT PROCESSING ⮐ button in Transaction SE80.

Summary

So far, this book has covered how to write basic ABAP programs, how to create tables in the database, how to access tables in the database, and how to create local and global ABAP classes.

This chapter reviewed many of the concepts that we used so far in the book by creating a new shopping cart solution with custom tables, programs and classes. We will expand on this solution through the rest of this book to add some additional complexity and features.

If you're having trouble understanding anything up to this point, debugging the code in the shopping cart example and stepping through what happens in the different classes and can help you understand what is happening. Debugging is a great method for learning, especially when you're at the point at which you're creating fully functioning examples.

PART II
Finishing Touches

Working with Strings and Texts

In a typical ABAP program, there are different reasons that you may need to manipulate strings and texts. For example, you may need to translate your program to make it available in a different language, or you may need to manipulate some of the data coming out of the database before displaying it to the user.

You also may need to write a program that handles a data interface from another system or data that is imported from an Excel spreadsheet, and that data may need to be formatted before being saved to the database.

In this chapter, we will discuss manipulating strings and text and translating programs, then update the shopping cart example introduced in Chapter 7 to be available in another language.

String Manipulation

You can manipulate strings to format data for the user or even to format data from the user. There are many ways to work with strings and many functions that can be used to work with strings.

String Templates

String templates were added to the ABAP language with ABAP 7.02 and allow you to complete string manipulations with much less code than was possible in earlier ABAP releases.

We first used strings when you created text string literals, in the "Hello, World!" example in Chapter 2. A string literal uses the single quote character (') marks the beginning and end of a string, as shown in Listing 8.1.

String literals

8 Working with Strings and Texts

```
DATA: d_string TYPE string.
d_string = 'Hello World'.
```
Listing 8.1 Hello, World! Using String Literals

String template A string template is created by enclosing text in pipe characters (|), as shown in Listing 8.2.

```
d_string = |Hello World|.
```
Listing 8.2 Hello, World! Using String Templates

Listing 8.1 and Listing 8.2 both produce the same result, but string templates really come in handy when you need to combine data from other variables with your string, as shown in Listing 8.3.

```
DATA: d_number TYPE i VALUE 123.
d_string = |{ d_number } widgets ordered|.
```
Listing 8.3 Using String Templates to Combine Variables and String

This means that you can also call a method that returns a numeric or character-based value and that value will be displayed in the string, as shown in Listing 8.4.

```
d_string = |{ o_widgets->get_num() } widgets ordered|.
```
Listing 8.4 Using String Templates with a Method

You can also include calculation expressions in your string template, as shown in Listing 8.5.

```
d_string = |{ o_widgets->get_num() + 5 } widgets ordered|.
```
Listing 8.5 Adding a Calculation Expression inside the String Template

Special characters If you need to use special characters in your string, you will need to escape those characters using a backslash character (\). A special character in a string template is a backslash (\), a pipe (|), or curly brackets ({ }). The example in Listing 8.6 demonstrates using the backslash for all special characters. Notice that you escape a backslash with as \\.

```
...
d_string = |we can use \|, \{ and \} if prefixed with a \\|.
```
Listing 8.6 Using Backslash to Escape Special Characters

You can also chain string templates, meaning that you combine independent string templates using two ampersands (&&). A common use of chaining string templates is to help format text through multiple lines in your IDE.

Chaining strings

```
d_string = |some text| &&
           | some more text|.
```
Listing 8.7 Chaining String Templates

Some additional options when including other data types in your string template are called *embedded expressions*, which can be quite useful. The WIDTH, PAD, and ALIGN expressions can be used together to impact how a string of data is presented when entered into the string template. WIDTH will add spaces after the provided string data, PAD will replace those added spaces with a given character, and ALIGN will align the string data to the left, middle, or right (see Listing 8.8).

Embedded expressions

```
d_string |{'left' WIDTH = 10 ALIGN = LEFT PAD = '1'}|.
d_string |{'center' WIDTH = 10 ALIGN = CENTER PAD = '2'}|.
d_string |{'right' WIDTH = 10 ALIGN = RIGHT PAD = '3'}|.
```
Listing 8.8 WIDTH, ALIGN, and PAD Embedded Expressions

CASE is another embedded expression; it will change a given string's case to all uppercase or all lowercase (see Listing 8.9).

```
d_string = |{ 'aBc' CASE = UPPER }|.
d_string = |{ 'aBc' CASE = LOWER }|.
```
Listing 8.9 CASE Embedded Expression

The SIGN embedded expression will allow you to define the format of a plus or minus sign on a given number (see Listing 8.10). This embedded expression can be useful when working with forms generated in your ABAP environment.

```
d_string = |{ 123 SIGN - LEFTPLUS }|.
```
Listing 8.10 SIGN Embedded Expression

Table 8.1 lists all of the possible options to use with the SIGN embedded expression.

SIGN	Description	Example
LEFT	Minus sign displayed on the left	123, -123
LEFTPLUS	Minus sign and plus sign displayed on the left	+123, -123
LEFTSPACE	Minus sign or space displayed on the left	123, -123
RIGHT	Minus sign displayed on the right	123, -123
RIGHTPLUS	Minus sign and plus sign displayed on the right	+123, -123
RIGHTSPACE	Minus sign or space displayed on the right	123, -123

Table 8.1 SIGN Embedded Expression Options

The DECIMALS expression will allow you to define the number of decimal places to display in the string template. When dropping decimals, it will round the result as shown in Listing 8.11 below, which will set the value of d_string to 1.24.

```
DATA: d_decimal TYPE decfloat16 VALUE '1.236'.
d_string = |{ d_decimal DECIMALS = 2 }|.
```
Listing 8.11 DECIMALS Embedded Expression

String Functions

ABAP also has various string functions that you can use to manipulate an existing string or to get more information about that string. The format for using string functions is variable = function(value)., with some variations if the function requires you to specify the type of parameter that is being passed as a value. The following examples present a selection of useful string functions.

strlen function

Probably the most used function is strlen, which gets the length of a string as shown in Listing 8.12, which will set the value of d_string to 5.

```
DATA: d_string TYPE string VALUE 'Hello',
      d_length TYPE i.
d_length = strlen( d_string ).
```
Listing 8.12 strlen String Function

The `condense` function will remove the leading, trailing, and any extra (more than one) spaces within a given string. The string is passed using the parameter `val` as shown in Listing 8.13, which will set `d_string` to "blah blah". Make sure you set a space between `val` and `=`.

condense function

```
d_string = condense( val = '  blah   blah   ' ).
```
Listing 8.13 condense String Function

The `concat_lines_of` function allows you to concatenate lines of a table into a single string separated by a specified character or string. A line of a table includes every column in that table. You can see an example of this function in Listing 8.14.

concat_lines_of function

```
DATA: t_table TYPE STANDARD TABLE OF string.

APPEND 'value1' TO t_table.
APPEND 'value2' TO t_table.

d_string = concat_lines_of( table = t_table sep = ' ' ).
```
Listing 8.14 concat_lines_of String Function

There are a couple of different `substring` functions, which will return a new string from a piece of an existing string. The most basic `substring` function has three parameters: `val` for the value of the string; `off` for the offset, indicating where to start pulling out the new string; and `len` for the length of the string to be returned. When using `substring`, you can enter a value for `len`, `off`, or both. In the example in Listing 8.15, there is a value set for both `off` and `len` and the value of `d_string` will be 'the'.

substring function

```
d_string = substring( val = 'this is the whole string'
  off = 8 len = 3 ).
```
Listing 8.15 substring String Function

You can also use `substring_from`, `substring_before`, `substring_after`, or `substring_to` to determine the substring offset and length based on a substring inside of the given string. The substring that you're looking for is indicated using the `sub` parameter, and the string you're searching through is indicated using the `val` parameter. Table 8.2 provides descriptions of the different `substring` functions.

303

8 Working with Strings and Texts

Type	Description
substring_from	Specified substring and all following characters
substring_after	All characters after specified substring
substring_before	All characters before specified substring
substring_to	Specified substring and all characters before

Table 8.2 Substring Function Types

The example in Listing 8.16 shows how each of the different `substring` function types act differently, given the same substring and string value. The values for `d_string` will be "whole string", "string", "the", and "the whole".

```
d_string = substring_from( val = 'the whole string'
  sub = 'whole' )
d_string = substring_after( val = 'the whole string'
  sub = 'whole' )
d_string = substring_before( val = 'the whole string'
  sub = 'whole' )
d_string = substring_to( val = 'the whole string'
  sub = 'whole' )
```
Listing 8.16 Using Different Substring String Functions

Text Symbols

We briefly discussed text symbols in Chapter 2 when adding a title to a frame on the selection screen. This section will go into more detail about using text symbols and will cover how to translate them. Anytime you are defining text that will be displayed to the user, you should be using text symbols. The reason is that even if your application is currently only being used in one language, it could be expanded to other languages in the future. Text symbols make translating programs easy.

Creating Text Symbols

Using text elements

Text symbols can be created for an ABAP program or global class in the SAP GUI; currently, this functionality is not available when using the Eclipse IDE, so you will need to right click the program or class and select OPEN IN SAP GUI to access the text symbols when using eclipse. You can access the text elements by selecting GOTO • TEXT ELEMENTS • TEXT SYMBOLS when editing your program or class in Transaction SE80.

From there, you can enter an alphanumeric symbol identifier in the first column, followed by the text that you want included in your text symbol in the text column, and press ⌊Enter⌋. The LNGTH and MAX. columns will be automatically populated.

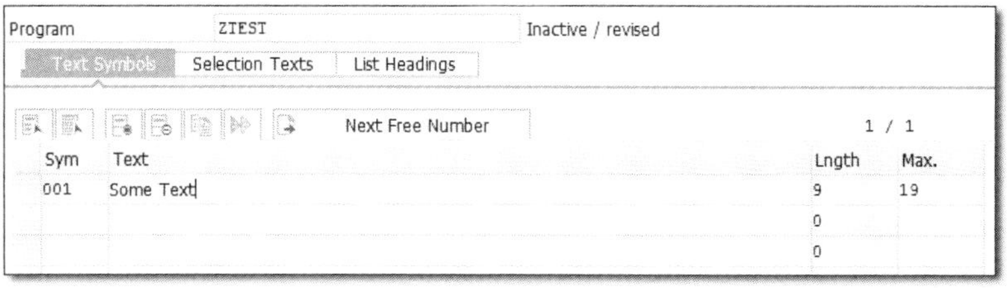

![Maintain Text Symbols Screen showing program ZTEST with Text Symbols tab, symbol 001 "Some Text" with Length 9 and Max 19]

Figure 8.1 Maintain Text Symbols Screen

You can then use the text symbol in your code by loading it into a string variable or using it as part of a string template, as shown in Listing 8.17.

```
DATA: d_string type string.
d_string = text-001.
d_string = |symbol: { text-001 }|.
```
Listing 8.17 Code Using a Text Symbol

Another way to create a text symbol is to declare a string literal using single quotes (') and follow it with parenthesis with the text symbol number inside the parenthesis, as shown in Listing 8.18. You cannot use string templates when creating text symbols with this method.

Using string literals

```
DATA: d_string TYPE string.
d_string = 'Some Text'(001).
```
Listing 8.18 Creating a Text Symbol in Line

When using this method to create text symbols, it's important that you run the text symbol comparison, which will resolve any conflicts if your text symbol is defined multiple times or is not listed as a text symbol, something that's required for translating applications.

Text symbol comparison

You can complete the symbol comparison by entering the text symbol screen from SAP GUI by selecting GOTO • TEXT ELEMENTS • TEXT SYMBOLS. Then, click the COMPARE TEXT SYMBOLS button pictured in Figure 8.2. The program source code and program texts will need to be activated before comparing text symbols, and you will need to be in edit mode if you want to resolve the issues discovered in the symbol comparison tool.

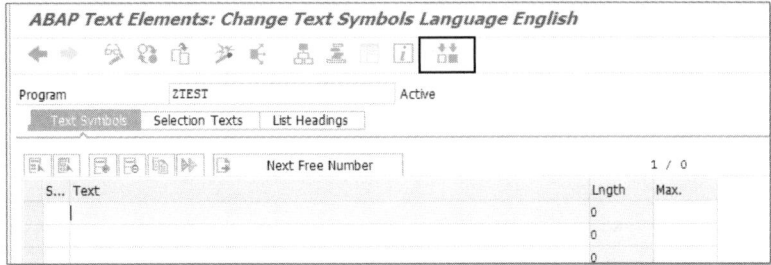

Figure 8.2 Compare Text Symbols Button

You will be brought to the ABAP TEXT SYMBOL ANALYSIS screen pictured in Figure 8.3. The analysis will indicate if there are unused text symbols that can be deleted, text symbols that were added inline and do not exist yet in the pool, or text symbols that are defined differently in the program or the pool. The *text pool* that is being referred to here is the screen shown in Figure 8.1. A checkmark to the right indicates that no issues were found in the analysis.

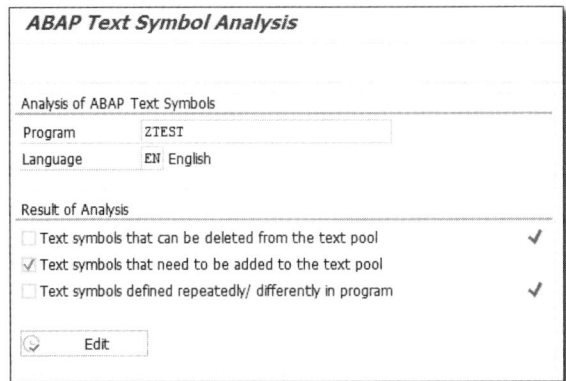

Figure 8.3 ABAP Text Symbol Analysis Screen

Figure 8.3 shows that the text symbol in Listing 8.18 was defined and that nothing currently exists in the text pool. If you click the EDIT button, you will see the screen shown in Figure 8.4.

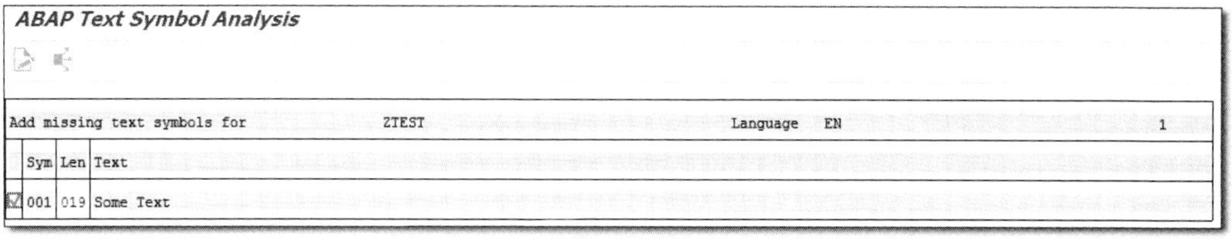

Figure 8.4 Editing Missing Text Symbols Using ABAP Text Symbol Analysis

The leftmost of the two buttons at the top of Figure 8.4 will add the selected text symbols to the text pool. The second button will show where the text symbol is currently used in the program code, as shown in Figure 8.5.

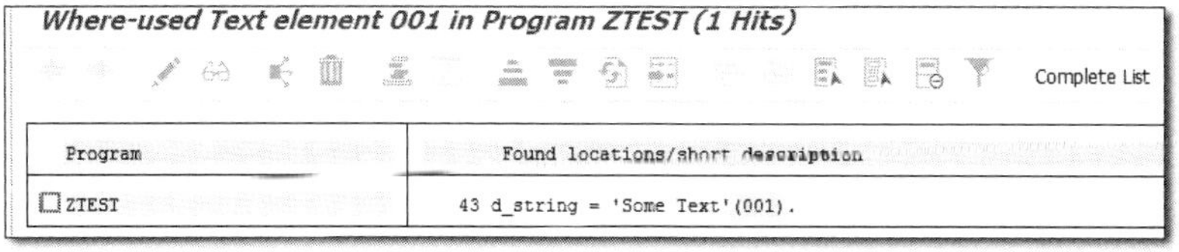

Figure 8.5 Result of Using the Where-Used Function

In Figure 8.5, you can see that the text symbol was declared once in program ZTEST on line 43. If you go back and click the first button that loads text into the text pool, you will then see Figure 8.6, which shows that the change was successful; all sections now show a checkmark, and below the results, text reads, TEXTPOOL HAS BEEN CHANGED AND CAN BE WRITTEN BACK.

To make the change effective, click the SAVE button.

If the text symbols have different values defined in the program or if the value in the program conflicts with the value in the text pool, you have the ability to select which one is the correct; make your selection, and click the leftmost button shown at the top of Figure 8.7 to continue.

8 Working with Strings and Texts

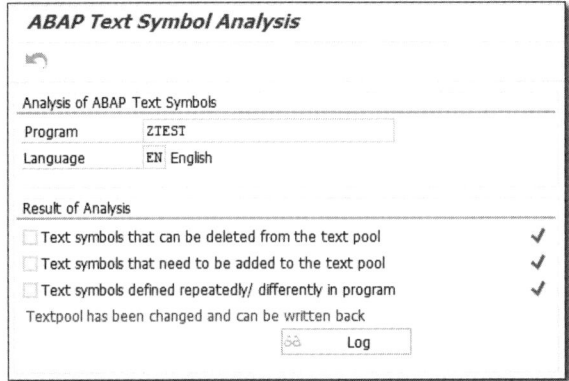

Figure 8.6 Result after Resolving Text Symbol Analysis Issue

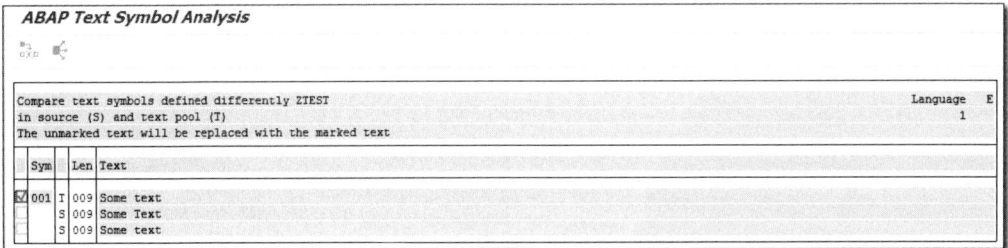

Figure 8.7 Resolving Multiple Text Symbol Definintions

When saving, you will be brought to a screen showing the additional definitions; here, they can be updated or changed to different text symbols, as shown in Figure 8.8. Clicking SAVE will save the results and update the source code accordingly.

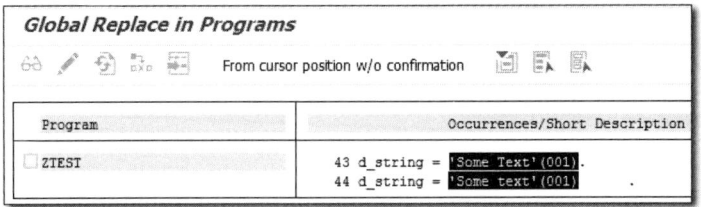

Figure 8.8 Editing Conflicting Text Symbol Definitions

Translating Text Symbols

Once your program is completed in the language of your choice, all of your text symbols are correctly created, and the comparison analysis has not found any issues, then you are ready to translate your application into a new language.

After opening your program in SAP GUI using SE80, select GOTO • TEXT ELEMENTS • TEXT SYMBOLS. From the DISPLAY TEXT SYMBOLS screen, select GOTO • TRANSLATION. You will see the popup shown in Figure 8.9, from which you can select a language to translate your application into; click the checkmark to continue.

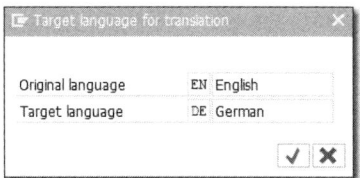

Figure 8.9 Target Language for Translation Popup

In the screen pictured in Figure 8.10, you can enter the translation below the original language text for both the title and your text symbol. However, you're restricted by the max length defined in the text pool, shown by the number in the parentheses on the right side of the screen. As you can see in Figure 8.10, you can't enter the full translation for SOME TEXT (*einge text*), because the max length is 9, which would leave us two characters short.

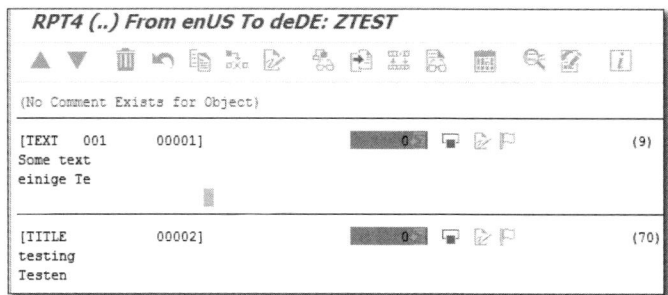

Figure 8.10 Translation Screen

Working with Strings and Texts

Updating the max length

The text symbol max lengths are used to ensure that a translated text is not so long that it causes issues when displaying the program. Assume that your program does not have this issue, so you can extend the max length in the text pool as shown in Figure 8.11 below to allow you to enter the full translation.

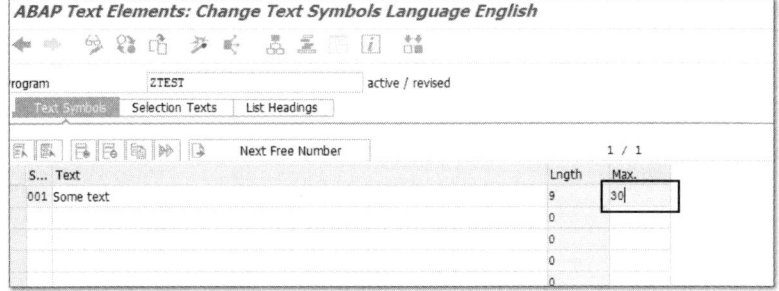

Figure 8.11 Extending Text Symbol Max Length

Then, go back to the translation screen by selecting GOTO • TRANSLATION and enter the full translation. Once the translation is entered, click the 🔲 button highlighted in Figure 8.12 to use the entered translation, and click SAVE.

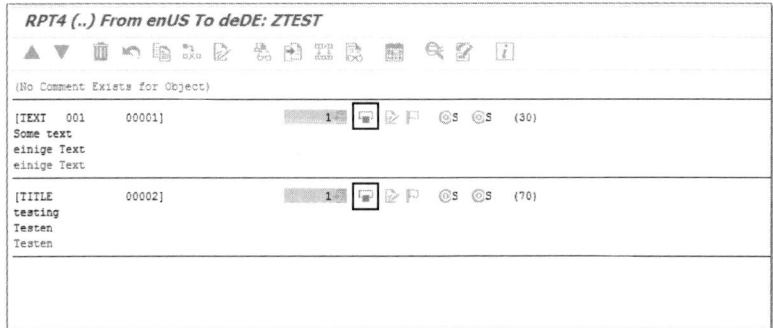

Figure 8.12 Saving the Translation

Test translation

You can now test your translation by logging on using the logon language that you translated to by entering that language from the initial logon screen in SAP GUI, as shown in Figure 8.13.

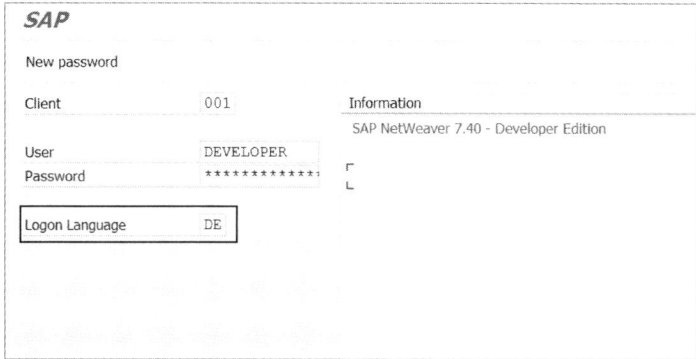

Figure 8.13 SAP GUI Logon Screen with Logon Language Highlighted

Now, when you run the program, anywhere the text symbol is displayed to the user, it will be shown in the translated language, as shown in Figure 8.14.

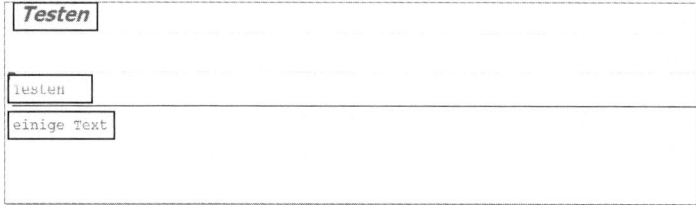

Figure 8.14 Translated Program Result

Translating Data in Tables

The last section introduced text symbols and covered how to translate the text symbols, but you typically will also have descriptive data stored in the database that will need to be translated. For example, you may have a product stored in your database that requires a locally translated description in various languages.

If you have access to a full SAP ERP system, you will notice that there are already various text translation tables that come with the standard system. However, when creating your own ABAP applications, you may also have to create your own translation tables.

Translation table   A translation table must utilize a key that indicates the language and the primary key of the table, which it is describing. Figure 8.15 shows an example of such a table.

Transparent Table	ZTRANSLATE_DESC	New				
Short Description	Description Translation Table					

Attributes	Delivery and Maintenance	Fields	Entry help/check	Currency/Quantity Fields		

Field	Key	Initi...	Data element	Data Type	Length	Decim...	Short Description
MANDT	✓	✓	MANDT	CLNT	3	0	Client
LANGU	✓	✓	LANG	LANG	1	0	Language ID
UNIQUE_ID	✓	✓	INTEGER	INT4	10	0	Whole Number with +/- Sign (-2.147.483.648 .. 2.147.483.647)
DESCRIPTION			CHAR255	CHAR	255	0	Char255

Figure 8.15 Translation Table

In order to keep your database normalized, the translation should only include a unique identifier for the item you're holding translations for, the language, and the translation. Any additional details should be stored in a different table.

Translation technical settings   When you click the TECHNICAL SETTINGS button for this table, you will see a new popup asking what type of translation table you're creating. For this example, select the radio button for TRANSLATION USING STANDARD TRANSLATION PROCEDURE (see Figure 8.16).

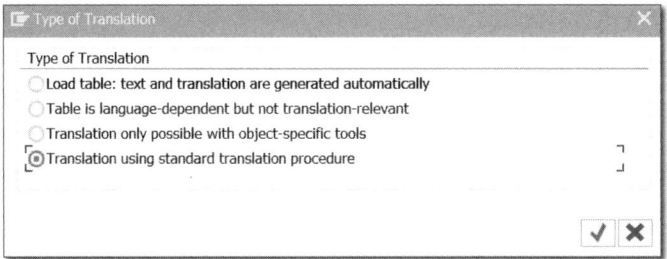

Figure 8.16 Type of Translation Popup

Translation editor (SE63)   With a table like this, you can maintain the language-specific records through an ABAP program that updates the database like we've done before, but you can also maintain the translations using Transaction SE63 the translation editor. In order to use transaction SE63 to add translated records, you must have a record in the database to be translated from the original language.

To use Transaction SE63, enter the transaction and navigate to Translation • ABAP Objects • Short Texts or click the Short Texts button. In the popup, expand the option titled 00 Meta Objects and double-click the option for TABL Tables (Meta) (see Figure 8.17).

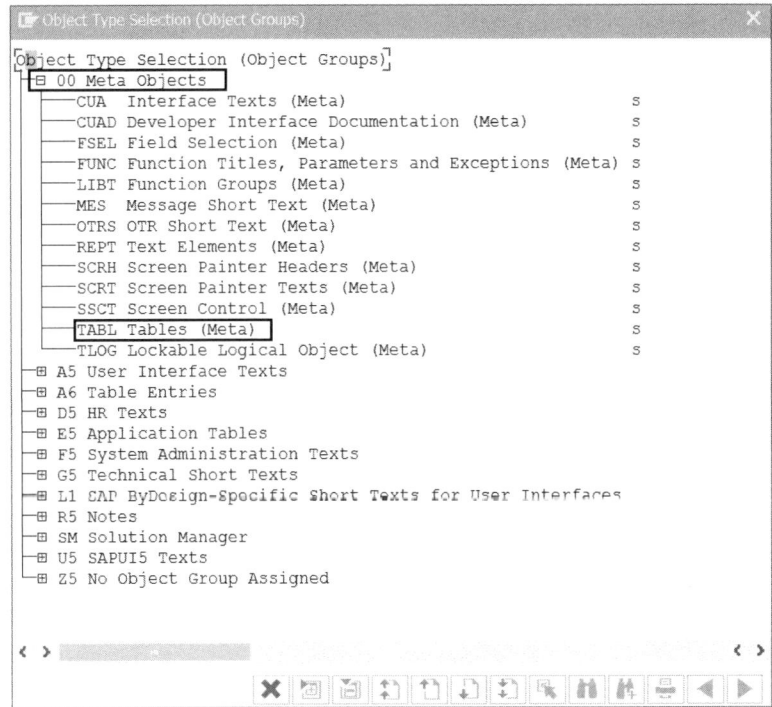

Figure 8.17 Object Type Selection in Transaction SE63

Now, you will see the Tables (Meta) screen shown in Figure 8.18. From here, you can enter the table name and the source and target languages.

After you click Edit, you can select a range of records from the key to be translated. You can leave the entries blank to select all existing records and click the Execute button. The translation screen (Figure 8.19) should look the same as other translation screens that you've seen in this chapter. Update the table by clicking the Submit Proposal button and then clicking Save.

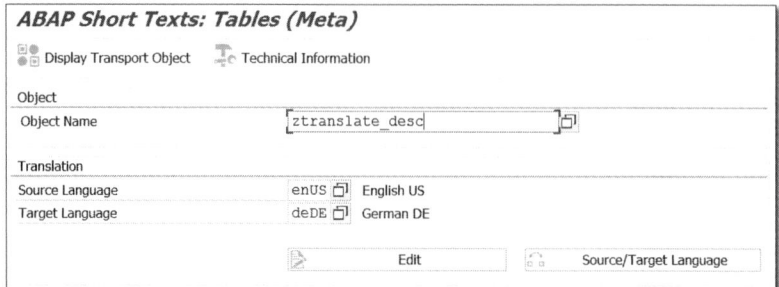

Figure 8.18 ABAP Short Texts: Tables Screen

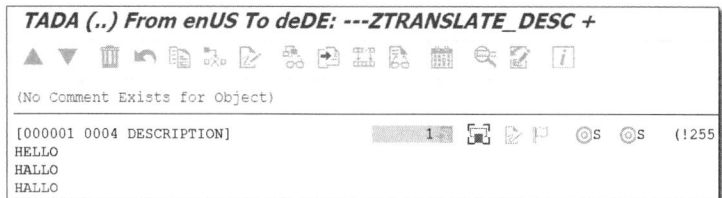

Figure 8.19 Translating Records in a Table

After saving, the table will be updated with the translated records, as shown in Figure 8.20.

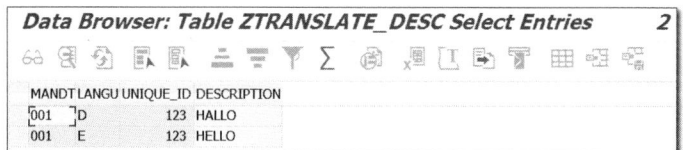

Figure 8.20 Records in Translated Table

Transaction SE63 can be used to translate all objects in the system. However, if you are only working on one program, sometimes it is easier to set the translation using GOTO • TRANSLATION.

SELECT by language

You can then select the correct translation using the logged in user's selected logon language via the `sy-langu` system variable, as shown in Listing 8.19.

```
SELECT DESCRIPTION
FROM ZTRANSLATE_DESC
```

```
WHERE UNIQUE_ID = 123
AND LANGU = sy-langu.
```
Listing 8.19 Pulling Localized Description from Translation Table

Now that you've localized the content within the table, there's also content used to create the table that can be localized. Translate a table by selecting GOTO • TRANSLATION; this will bring up the same screen that you saw when translating text symbols and table data, except that for a table the only thing to translate is the short description, as shown in Figure 8.21.

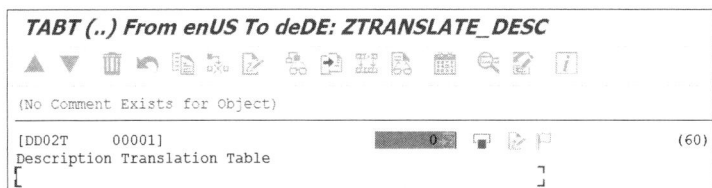

Figure 8.21 Translation Options for Tables

You can also translate the field labels defined in the data elements by opening a data element and selecting GOTO • TRANSLATION, as shown in Figure 8.22. The heading label will be listed as REPTEXT, and the short, medium, and long labels will be SCRTEXT_S, SCRTEXT_M and SCRTEXT_L, respectively.

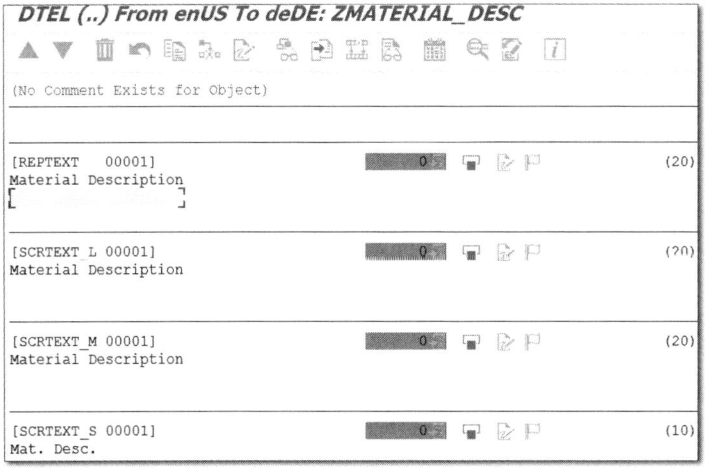

Translating field labels

Figure 8.22 Translation Options for Data Elements

Obsolete Strings and Text

CONCATENATE

Earlier in the chapter, you learned to concatenate strings using string templates. In ABAP, the old way to do this used the `CONCATENATE` keyword followed by any strings and then `INTO` followed by the string to hold the result and `SEPARATED BY` followed by a character to separate each string in the new string. An example using the `CONCATENATE` keyword and the string templates is shown in Listing 8.20.

```
DATA: d_string1 TYPE string VALUE 'one',
      d_string2 TYPE string VALUE 'two',
      d_string3 TYPE string VALUE 'three',
      d_result  TYPE string.
"old way
CONCATENATE d_string1 d_string2 d_string3
  INTO d_result SEPARATED BY ' '.
"new way
d_result = |{ d_string1 } { d_string2 } { d_string3 }|.
```
Listing 8.20 Using the CONCATENATE Keyword and String Templates

Look at Listing 8.20 and compare the `CONCATENATE` keyword with string templates. The `CONCATENATE` keyword relies more on the old style of ABAP, which is verbose instead of relying on symbols. As you learned earlier in the chapter, there are various functions that you can apply to each variable when using it in a string template, and you have more flexibility in terms of what separates each string being concatenated.

Updating the Shopping Cart Example

Now that you've learned about translating applications, let's return to the shopping cart example created in the previous chapter. There are a few areas of the example that used text without using text symbols. This section walks through updating the program to use text symbols and creating a new table to hold localized product descriptions.

Applying Text Symbols

The shopping cart class doesn't contain any strings, but if it did, you could follow the same process used for updating programs to update the class. Starting with the program zproduct_maint, we need to set any strings to be text symbols. Do so by adding parenthesis and a three-digit number after each string (remember that 001 and 002 are used by our selection screen). The updated code is shown in Listing 8.21.

```
...
IF p_upd = abap_true.
    MODIFY zproduct FROM s_product.
    WRITE: 'Update Completed'(003).
ELSEIF p_rem = abap_true.
    DELETE zproduct FROM s_product.
    WRITE: 'Delete Completed'(004).
ELSEIF p_dis = abap_true.
...
```

Listing 8.21 Code from ZPRODUCT_MAINT Updated for Translation

Now, press the ACTIVATE button to activate your code before continuing. Next, if you are using the Eclipse IDE, right click the program in your Project Explorer and select OPEN WITH SAP GUI. Then, select GOTO • TEXT ELEMENTS • TEXT SYMBOLS and click the COMPARE TEXT SYMBOLS button. Make sure that you're in edit mode so that the compare program can update the text pool. You should see that the TEXT SYMBOLS THAT NEED TO BE ADDED TO THE TEXT POOL checkbox is selected, as shown in Figure 8.23.

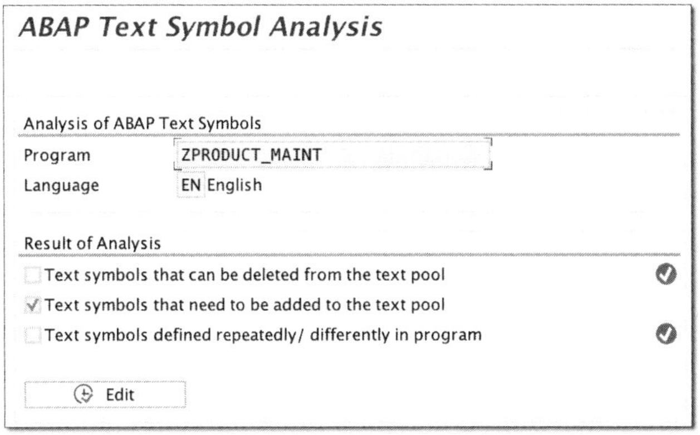

Figure 8.23 ABAP Text Symbol Analysis for ZPRODUCT_MAINT

Click the EDIT button to continue, and you should see the result shown in Figure 8.24. Ensure that both text symbols are checked, and click the INSERT TEXT SYMBOLS button at the top left of the screen highlighted in Figure 8.24 to add them to the text pool.

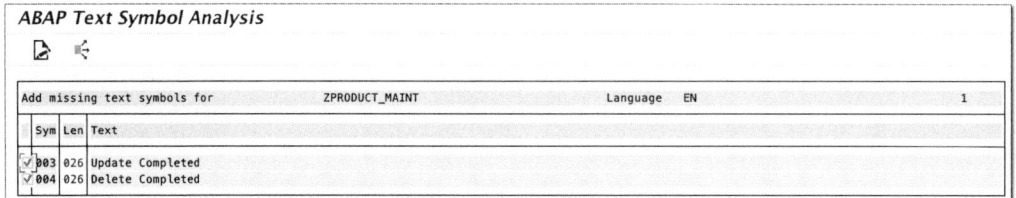

Figure 8.24 Text Symbols to Add to Text Pool

Click SAVE back on the comparison screen to save the changes, and click the BACK button. You will now see the new text symbols created in the CHANGE TEXT SYMBOLS screen, as shown in Figure 8.25.

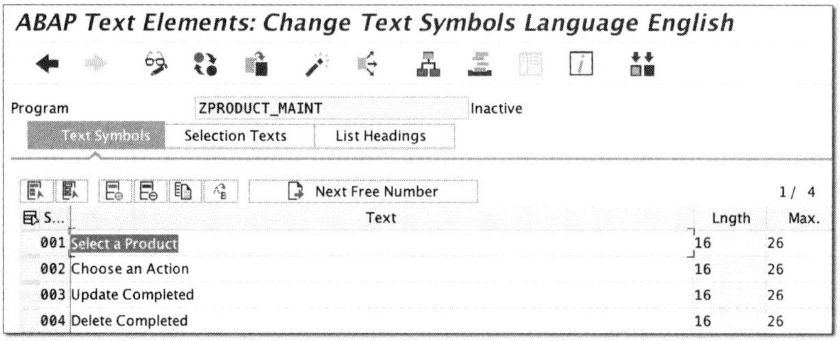

Figure 8.25 Updated Text Symbol Page with New Text Symbols Listed

Next, navigate to GOTO • TRANSLATION, add the translation for the text symbols that you just created below the original language text, and click the SUBMIT PROPOSAL button to create the translation proposal. Once completed, your screen should look like the one in Figure 8.26; click SAVE to save the translations.

Now, press the ACTIVATE button and ensure that all of your source code and texts are activated. Follow the same steps to update and translate the `zcart_maint` program.

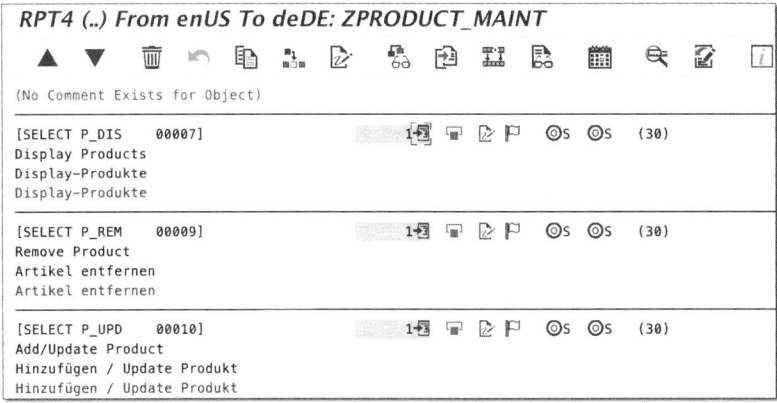

Figure 8.26 Completed Translation of the Maintain Products Program

Updating the Database

We will need to create a new table to hold the localized descriptions of the products, and then we need to update our code to get the description for the appropriate logged in language.

First, we will update the ERD to add the translatable description table, as shown in Figure 8.27. The new table ZPRODUCT_DESC has a primary key of PRODUCT and LANGUAGE. Also, table ZPRODUCT needs to be updated to remove the description that's now in table ZPRODUCT_TEXT. We will be adding more details to the ZPRODUCT table in the next chapter, so don't worry that it does not have any fields besides the key at this time.

ERD changes

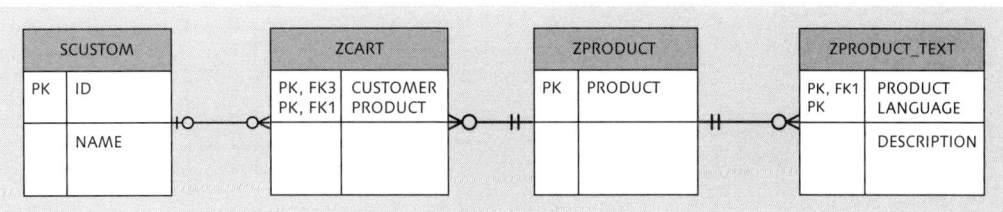

Figure 8.27 Updated ERD with Translatable Description Table

To update the table ZPRODUCT, open the transparent table using transaction SE11. Select the TRANSPARENT TABLE radio button and enter ZPRODUCT in the corresponding text box and click the CHANGE button.

Updating ZPRODUCT

Select the field DESCRIPTION and click the DELETE ROW button to remove the field. Then press the SAVE button and ACTIVATE button to activate the updated table. The updated table ZPRODUCT is shown in Figure 8.28.

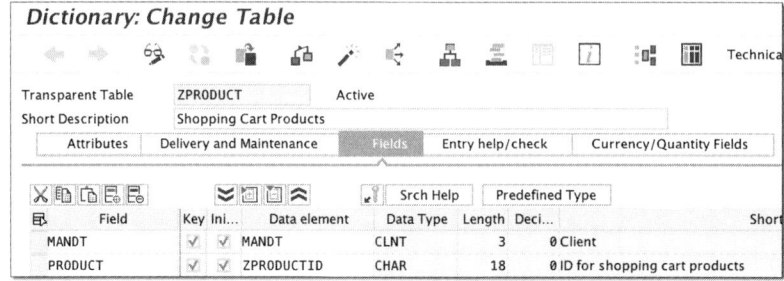

Figure 8.28 Updated Table ZPRODUCT

Next, we will create the new table ZPRODUCT_TEXT using transaction SE11. Select the radio button for TRANSPARENT TABLE and enter "ZPRODUCT_TEXT" in the corresponding textbox and click the CREATE button.

In the change table screen, add "Shopping cart product text" in the SHORT DESCRIPTION textbox. Within the DELIVERY AND MAINTENANCE tab, set the DELIVERY CLASS to "A" for MASTER AND TRANSACTION DATA and select Display/Maintenance Allowed for the DATA BROWSER/TABLE VIEW MAINT. drop down as shown below in Figure 8.29.

Figure 8.29 Delivery and Maintenance Settings for ZPRODUCT_TEXT

Next, select the FIELDS tab and add the FIELD "MANDT" with DATA ELEMENT "MANDT", FIELD "PRODUCT" with DATA ELEMENT "ZPRODUCTID", FIELD "LANGUAGE" with DATA ELEMENT "LANGU" and

Updating the Shopping Cart Example

FIELD "DESCRIPTION" with DATA ELEMENT "ZPRODUCT_DESC". The new LANGUAGE field will store what language a description is tied to. The end result should match what is shown below in Figure 8.30.

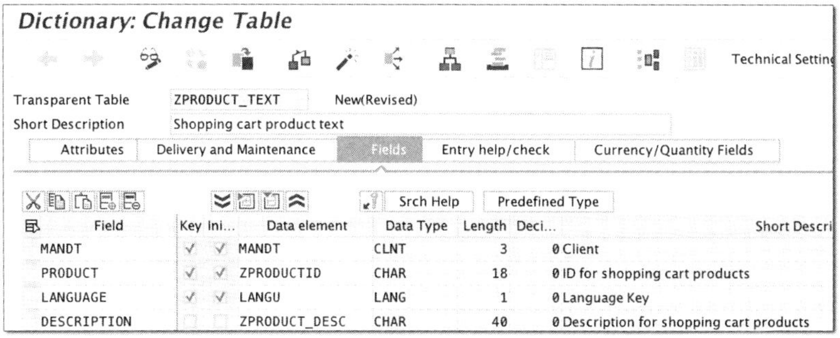

![Figure 8.30 table configuration]

Figure 8.30 New Table ZPRODUCT_TEXT Configuration

We also need to create foreign keys for some of our fields. To create the foreign key, select the field and press the FOREIGN KEY button. First, create a foreign key for the field MANDT. The system will suggest to use the check table T000, select the YES button to accept this proposal. In the CREATE FOREIGN KEY popup, select THE KEY FIELDS/CANDIDATES radio button and set the CARDINALITY to 1:CN as shown below in Figure 8.31. Then press the COPY button to save the key.

ZPRODUCT_TEXT
Foreign keys

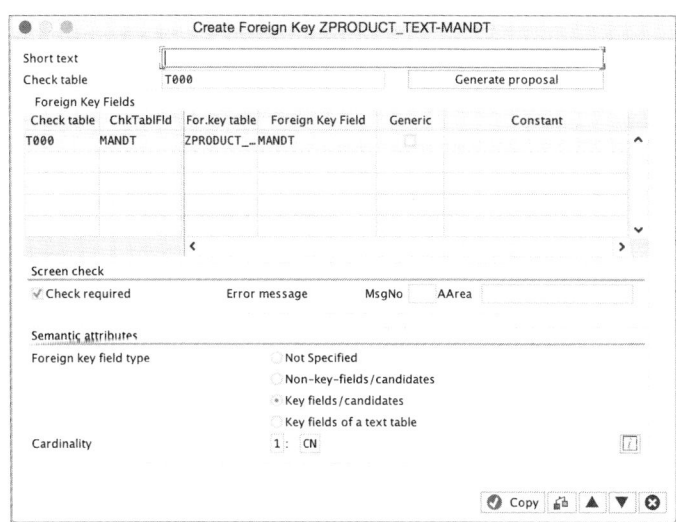

Figure 8.31 MANDT foreign key settings

Working with Strings and Texts

Next, select the FIELD PRODUCT and click the FOREIGN KEY button. The system will suggest to use the check table ZPRODUCT, select the YES button to accept this proposal. In the CREATE FOREIGN KEY popup, select the KEY FIELDS/CANDIDATES radio button and set the CARDINALITY to 1:CN as shown below in Figure 8.32. Then click the COPY button to save the foreign key.

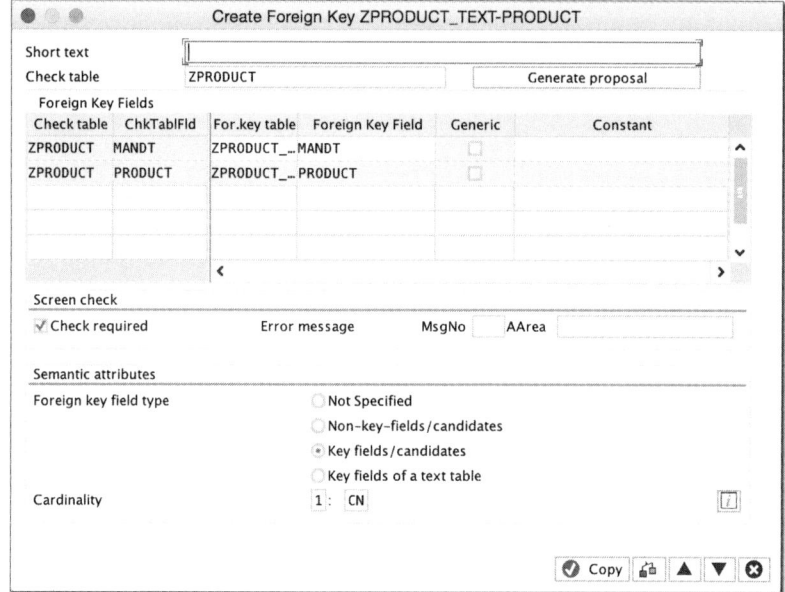

Figure 8.32 PRODUCT Foreign Key Settings

Next, select the FIELD LANGUAGE and click the FOREIGN KEY button. The system will suggest to use the check table T001, select the YES button to accept this proposal. In the CREATE FOREIGN KEY popup, select the KEY FIELDS / CANDIDATES radio button and set the CARDINALITY to 1:CN as shown below in Figure 8.33. Then click the COPY button to save the foreign key.

ZPRODUCT_TEXT technical settings

Next press the SAVE button to save what has been completed so far and then select the TECHNICAL SETTINGS button. In the TYPE OF TRANSLATION popup, select the radio button for TRANSLATION USING STANDARD TRANSLATION PROCEDURE (Figure 8.34) so that you can use Transaction SE63 to complete the translation.

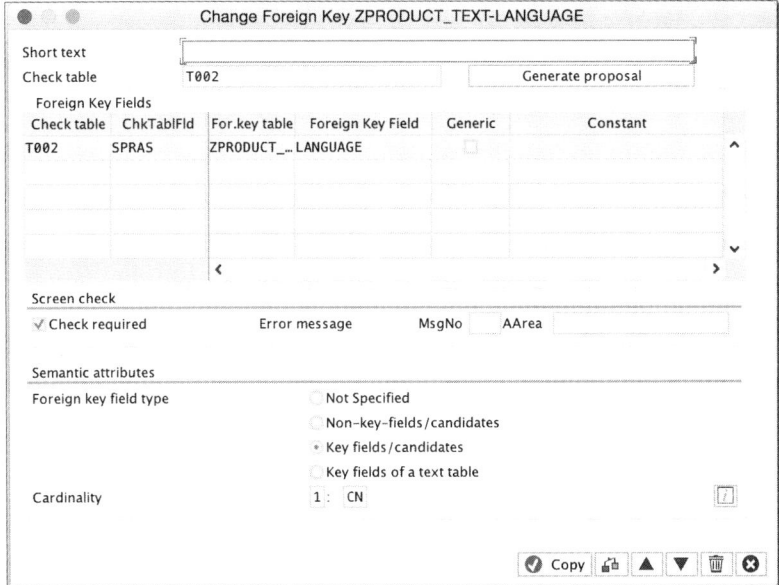

Figure 8.33 LANGUAGE Foreign Key Settings

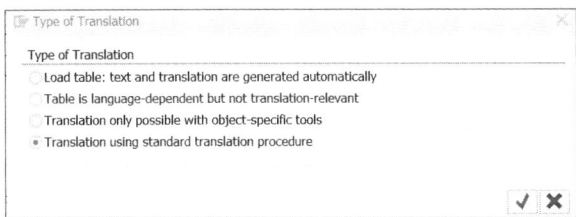

Figure 8.34 Type of Translation Selection

Next, set the DATA CLASS to APPL0 for master data and set the SIZE CATEGORY to "0" for expected 0 to 4,900 records as shown below in Figure 8.35. Then press SAVE to save the technical settings and BACK to return to the ZPRODUCT_TEXT table.

Next, set the enhancement category by selecting EXTRAS • ENHANCEMENT CATEGORY and choose the radio button for CANNOT BE ENHANCED and click the COPY button to save your choice. We are now done creating this table. Press the ACTIVATE button to activate the table.

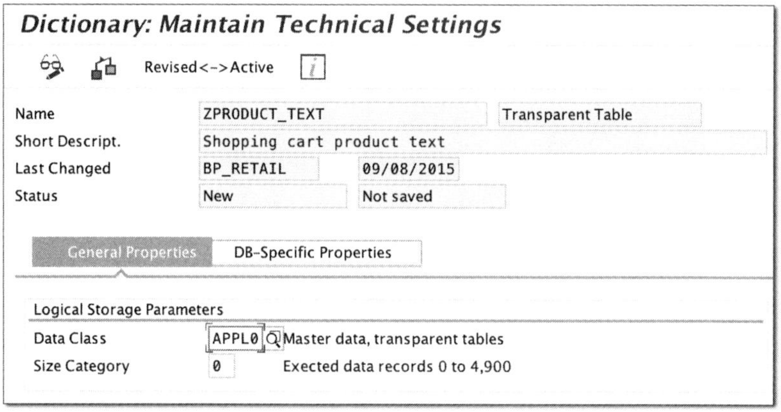

Working with Strings and Texts

Figure 8.35 ZPRODUCT_TEXT Technical Settings

Using the Translation Table

We can now update our program `zproduct_maint` to save the provided description in the translatable table. We will use the logged in user's language (sy-langu) as the language key when saving the description. In Listing 8.22 we changed the `product_maint` code to update both the `zproduct` and `zproduct_text` table. Since the `zproduct` table only contains keys, we have to use the `INSERT` Open SQL command. We also updated the description parameter, which now has to be based on the `zproduct_text` table.

```
...
    P_desc TYPE zproduct_text-description LOWER CASE.
...
DATA: s_product      TYPE zproduct,
      s_product_text TYPE zproduct_text.

s_product-product = p_prod.
s_product_text-product = p_prod.
s_product_text-language = sy-langu.
s_product_text-description = p_desc.

IF p_upd = abap_true.
    INSERT zproduct FROM s_product.
    MODIFY zproduct_text FROM s_product_text.
    WRITE: 'Update Completed'(003).
ELSEIF p_rem = abap_true.
    DELETE FROM zproduct_text WHERE product = p_prod.
    DELTE zproduct FROM s_product.
```

```
    WRITE: 'Delete Completed'(004).
ELSEIF p_dis = abap_true.
...
```
Listing 8.22 Changes to the Add and Remove Product Code in the ZPRODUCT_MAINT Program

Next, we need to update the SELECT statement used when displaying the list of products. The changes are to add an INNER JOIN to the zproduct_text table and to select only the logged in user's language (sy-langu). The example using inline data declarations is updated below in Listing 8.23.

```
...
SELECT zproduct~product, description
FROM zproduct
INNER JOIN zproduct_text
ON zproduct~product = zproduct_text~product
WHERE language = @sy-langu
INTO TABLE @DATA(t_products).
...
```
Listing 8.23 Updating the SELECT Statement in PRODUCT_MAINT using Inline Data Declarations

The example in Listing 8.24 accomplishes the same result without using inline data declarations. Notice that we need to update the type we created since description is now in a different table.

```
ELSEIF p_dis = abap_true.
    TYPES: BEGIN OF y_products,
           product TYPE zproduct-product,
           description TYPE zproduct_text-description,
           END OF y_products.

DATA: t_products TYPE STANDARD TABLE OF y_products,
      gr_alv TYPE REF TO cl_salv_table.

SELECT zproduct~product description
INTO TABLE t_products
FROM zproduct
INNER JOIN zproduct_text
ON zproduct~product = zproduct_text~product
WHERE language = sy-langu.
...
```
Listing 8.24 Updating the SELECT Statement in PRODUCT_MAINT without Using Inline Data Declarations

8 Working with Strings and Texts

Updating zcl_shopping_cart

Next, we will update the shopping cart global class to read the description from the new language-dependent table. We will also need to update the `y_cart` type to use the new `zproduct_text` table description. We will also need to update the `get_cart` method as shown in Listing 8.25, using both old Open SQL and new Open SQL.

```
...
PUBLIC SECTION.
    TYPES: BEGIN OF y_cart,
           product TYPE zproduct-product,
           description TYPE zproduct_text-description,
           END OF y_cart.
...
METHOD get_cart.
"using new Open SQL
SELECT zcart~product, description
FROM zcart
INNER JOIN zproduct
ON zcart~product = zproduct~product
INNER JOIN zproduct_text
ON zcart~product = zproduct_text~product
WHERE zproduct_text~language = @sy-langu
AND zcart-customer = @d_customer
INTO TABLE @rt_cart.

"using old Open SQL
SELECT zcart~product description
INTO TABLE rt_cart.
FROM zcart
INNER JOIN zproduct
ON zcart~product = zproduct~product
INNER JOIN zproduct_text
ON zcart~product = zproduct_text~product
WHERE zproduct_text~language = sy-langu
AND zcart-customer = d_customer.

ENDMETHOD.
```

Listing 8.25 Updating the GET_CART Method

You can now press the ACTIVATE button to activate your global class. The shopping cart program now works with multiple languages.

Summary

This chapter introduced new ways to work with strings in ABAP, including string templates and string functions. Working with strings in this way can allow your ABAP code to be more compact and easier to read and understand.

Next, we discussed different ways to translate your ABAP programs, beginning with text symbols. Many companies' ABAP standards require the use of text symbols when defining texts so that they can be easily translated, even if they do not need to be translated at the time the program is written.

Next, you learned how to create tables with translatable fields and how to use Transaction SE63 to translate the values in the table. You also discovered how to update descriptions and field labels of tables and data elements by using GOTO • TRANSLATE.

We then covered some obsolete string methods, which are much more verbose than their modern counterparts.

Finally, you updated the shopping cart example from the previous chapter to be a multilingual solution by creating a new table that contains the product description in multiple languages and by adding text symbols to your different ABAP applications.

In the next chapter we will look at dates, times, quantities and currencies and cover how to handle these special data types in our code and we will update the shopping cart example again to utilize these data types.

Working with Dates, Times, Quantities, and Currencies

Typical customers of ABAP applications are large corporations with operations spanning across the globe. As a result, ABAP programs need to be written with the expectation that they can handle working across time zones and with different currencies.

In addition, when working with any large company, the topics of inventory and quantity can be quite important. An ABAP program may need to work with converting measurements of products or keep track of how many items can fit in a given storage location for that item.

In this chapter we will cover various some key items to take in to account when calculating and converting dates and times in ABAP programs. We will also cover how quantities are handled in ABAP transparent tables and how to convert quantities between different units of measurement. Next we will cover how currencies are stored in ABAP transparent tables and how to convert amounts between different currencies. We will then update our shopping cart example program to use quantity and currency fields.

Dates

In this section we will cover the details on how the date type (d) works and some different ways that we can use dates in our ABAP programs. Chapter 2 introduced the date data type (d), showing how to define a date and that it is stored in a YYYYMMDD format, meaning that the first four digits represent the year, the second two represent the month, and last two represent the day.

9 Working with Dates, Times, Quantities, and Currencies

Date Type Basics

Using substring A date is a character string of eight characters, meaning that you can apply some of the string concepts from the previous chapter, such as using substring, to get specific year, month, and day values as shown in Listing 9.1.

```
DATA: d_date   TYPE d VALUE '20150102',
      d_year   TYPE i,
      d_month  TYPE i,
      d_day    TYPE i.
d_year  = substring( val = d_date off = 0 len = 4 ).
d_month = substring( val = d_date off = 4 len = 2 ).
d_day   = substring( val = d_date off = 6 len = 2 ).
```
Listing 9.1 Using SUBSTRING to Get Year, Month, and Day

The code in Listing 9.1 can be used regardless of the user's date format preferences; the value when working with the date data type will always be the same.

Adding days Adding days to a date data type can be done by adding an integer to the date; the date data type will handle updating the day, month, and year values, as shown in Listing 9.2, in which the new date is February 6, 2015.

```
DATA: d_date TYPE d VALUE '20150102'.
d_date = d_date + 35.
```
Listing 9.2 Adding 35 Days to Janurary 2, 2015

Adding a month to a date is not as easy. If you want to add a month to your date, you can call the RP_CALC_DATE_IN_INTERNAL function modules shown in Listing 9.3 below, which will change the date from January 1st, 2015 to February 1st, 2015.

```
DATA: d_date TYPE d VALUE 20150101.
d_date = sy-datum.

CALL FUNCTION 'RP_CALC_DATE_IN_INTERNAL'
    EXPORTING
         date    = d_date
         days    = 0
         months  = 1
*        signum  = '+'
         years   = 0
```

```
IMPORTING
    calc_date = d_date.
```
Listing 9.3 Example Adding a Month to a Date Using a Function Module

Factory Calendars

There may be a situation in which you need to write a program that will act differently based on which days are working days for a given company. Factory calendar days will take in to account any public holidays and any relevant working days, allowing you to complete date calculations based on the number of actual working days.

Factory calendars are client independent and typically created for each relevant country or region in which a company operates. This allows for a factory calendar to be created that incorporates the local public holiday schedule. To view all of the calendars in an ABAP system, enter Transaction SCAL, select the FACTORY CALENDAR radio button, and click the DISPLAY button, as pictured in Figure 9.1.

Viewing factory calendars

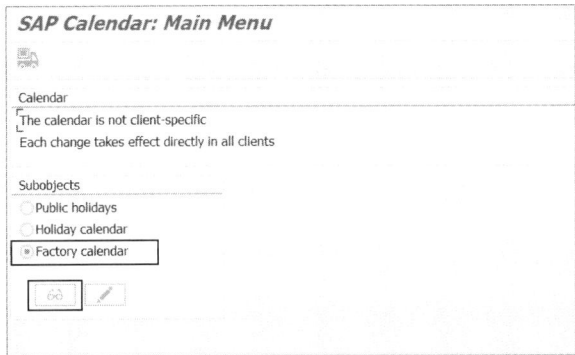

Figure 9.1 Initial Screen for Transaction SCAL

In the next screen, you'll see a list of the factory calendars defined in the system. These are usually based on country or region and will have VALID FROM and VALID TO dates. Select the calendar you're interested in viewing and click the CALENDAR button, as shown in Figure 9.2.

9 Working with Dates, Times, Quantities, and Currencies

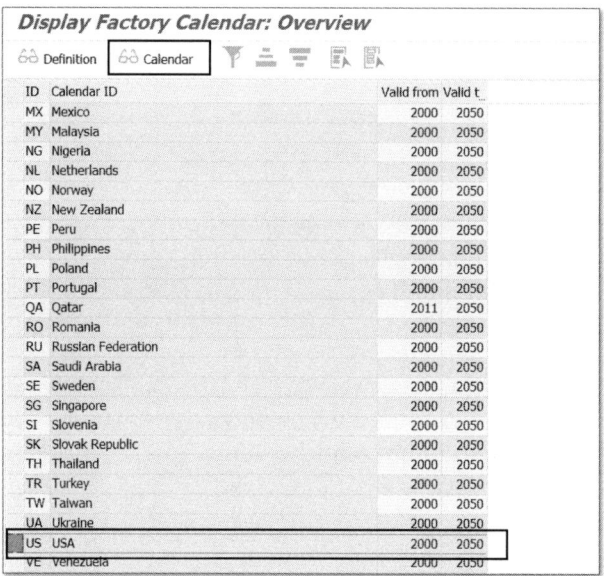

Figure 9.2 Selecting a Factory Calendar

Next, select a relevant year for the calendar that you want to view and click the DISPLAY YEAR button, as shown in Figure 9.3.

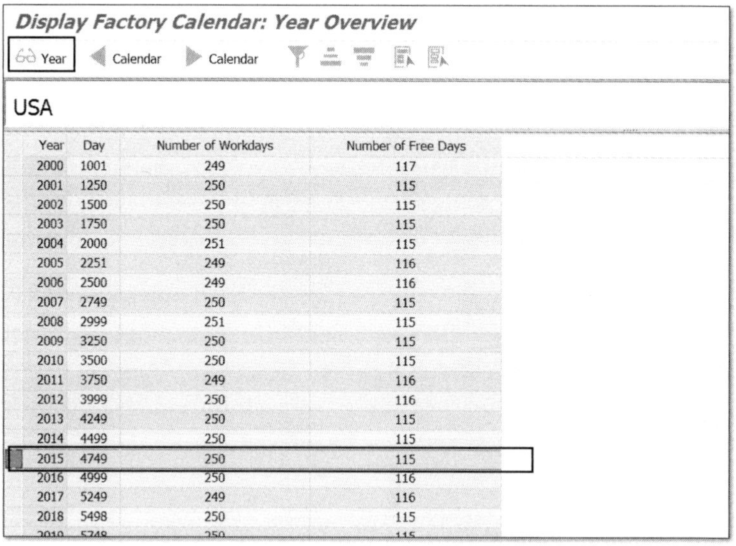

Figure 9.3 Selecting a Calendar Year in Transaction SCAL

Now, you'll see a calendar display for the selected year showing which days are considered working days and which days are non-working days, including a list of public holidays for the year (Figure 9.4).

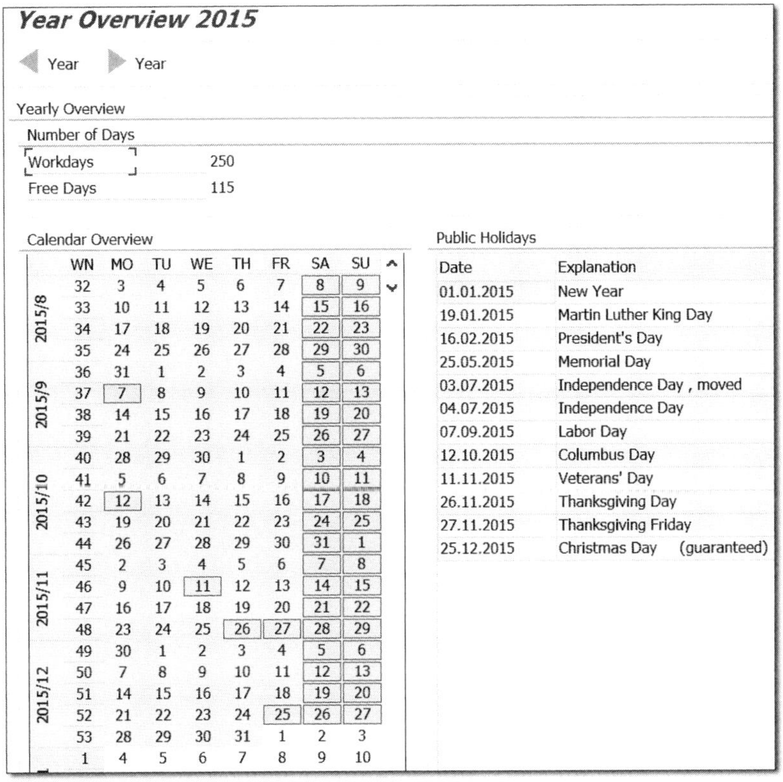

Figure 9.4 Viewing Working/Nonworking Days and Public Holidays for a Factory Calendar

Now that you understand what a factory calendar is and how to set one up, you can use factory dates in your ABAP code with the help of some standard function modules.

Converting factory dates

Use function module `DATE_CONVERT_TO_FACTORYDATE` to convert a regular date into a factory date. The factory date will be a number representing the number of working days since the factory calendar began. If you convert a date that is not a working day, the next working day will be used.

You can then perform some calculations using the factory date and convert it back to a calendar date using the function module FACTORYDATE_CONVERT_TO_DATE. An example of this is shown in Listing 9.4, which calculates a date 10 working days in the future from August 3; the result is August 17, not August 13.

```
DATA: d_date TYPE d VALUE '20150803',
      d_factory_date TYPE scal-facdate.

CALL FUNCTION 'DATE_CONVERT_TO_FACTORYDATE'
  EXPORTING
    Date               = d_date
    factory_calendar_id = 'US'
  IMPORTING
    factorydate        = d_factory_date
  EXCEPTIONS
    calendar_buffer_not_loadable = 1
    correct_option_invalid       = 2
    date_after_range             = 3
    date_before_range            = 4
    date_invalid                 = 5
    factory_calendar_not_found   = 6
    others                       = 7
    .
IF sy-subrc <> 0.
 MESSAGE ID sy-msgid TYPE sy-msgty NUMBER sy-msgno
            WITH sy-msgv1 sy-msgv2 sy-msgv3 sy-msgv4.
ENDIF.

d_factory_date = d_factory_date + 10.

CALL FUNCTION 'FACTORYDATE_CONVERT_TO_DATE'
  EXPORTING
    Factorydate         = d_factory_date
    factory_calendar_id = 'US'
  IMPORTING
    date                = d_date
  EXCEPTIONS
    calendar_buffer_not_loadable = 1
    factorydate_after_range      = 2
    factorydate_before_range     = 3
    factorydate_invalid          = 4
    factory_calendar_id_missing  = 5
    factory_calendar_not_found   = 6
    others                       = 7
    .
IF sy-subrc <> 0.
```

```
MESSAGE ID sy-msgid TYPE sy-msgty NUMBER sy-msgno
         WITH sy-msgv1 sy-msgv2 sy-msgv3 sy-msgv4.
ENDIF.
```
Listing 9.4 Using Factory Date Conversions to Complete Date Calculation

Datum Date Type

The `d` date type will output the day and month in the order matching the logged in user's preferences when using `WRITE` or an ALV grid, but it won't include slashes or dots to separate the day, month, and year (see Listing 9.5 and the resulting output shown in Figure 9.5).

```
DATA: d_date TYPE d VALUE 20150801.
WRITE: d_date.
```
Listing 9.5 Output d Date Type

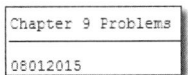

Figure 9.5 Output of Listing 9.5

Instead of using the `d` date type, you can use the `datum` date type, which will be displayed per the style of the user's date preference any time it's displayed to the user (see Listing 9.6 and the resulting output shown in Figure 9.6).

Datum formatting

```
DATA: d_datum TYPE datum VALUE 20150801.
WRITE: d_datum.
```
Listing 9.6 Output datum Date Type

```
Chapter 9 Problems
08/01/2015
```

Figure 9.6 Output of Listing 9.6

Therefore, it's better to use the `datum` date data type in your program instead of the `d` date data type whenever you'll be displaying a date to the user. The `datum` and `d` date types can be used interchangeably in your code; the underlying data will be exactly the same.

System Date Fields

There are three system date fields: `sy-datum`, `sy-datlo`, and `sy-fdayw`. All of these system dates return values related to the current date. `sy-datum` returns the current system date. The system date is dependent on the system's current time zone. If you're concerned about the date for the logged in user's time zone, you can use `sy-datlo`. Finally, `sy-fdayw` will return the factory day of week as an integer, meaning 0 for Saturday and 6 for Friday.

These system date fields can all be directly assigned to valid variables and can also be used in the variable declaration, as shown below in Listing 9.7.

```
DATA: d_today type sy-datum,
      d_today_local type sy-datlo,
      d_fday TYPE sy-fdayw.

d_today = sy-datum.
d_today_local = sy-datlo.
d_fday = sy-fdayw.
```
Listing 9.7 System Date Fields

Date-Limited Records

Dates in the database

A *date-limited record* is a record in a database with `valid_from` `valid_to` date fields indicating the dates between which the record is considered valid. There are many reasons that a table may contain date-limited records; for example, a table may contain promotional discounts that are only valid between two dates, or a table containing an employee's position in the company may be date limited so that it can contain all current and past positions.

Often, you don't know when a record will no longer be valid, in which case the `valid_to` date will be set to the latest date possible, which is December 31, 9999. An HR record displaying an employee's current position would have a `valid_to` date like that; if the employee's position changes, the `valid_to` date is updated to show the last day at that position.

Selecting a date-limited record valid today is easy. First, determine if you will be using the system date (`sy-datum`) or the local date (`sy-datlo`).

In the following example, you'll select a record from the user table USR02, which has optional VALID FROM and VALID TO fields, as shown in Figure 9.7.

Cl.	User Name	Valid from	Valid to	User Type	User Master Maintenance: User Group	Number of failed l
001	ALEREMOTE			A	SUPER	
001	BGRFC_SUPER	01/16/2014	12/31/9999	S		
001	BWDEVELOPER			A	SUPER	
001	DDIC			A	SUPER	
001	DEMO			A	SUPER	
001	DEVELOPER			A	SUPER	
001	SAP*			A	SUPER	

Figure 9.7 Table USR02 with Valid from and Valid to Fields

In order to select only the records that have a value for the date-limiting fields and that are valid for today, you need to select records with a valid from date less than or equal to today and valid to date greater than or equal to today. For this example, the valid from field is GLTGV and the valid to field is GLTGB, as shown in Listing 9.8, which will only return the record for user BGRFC_SUPER.

Using dates in SELECT

```
"New Open SQL
SELECT *
FROM USR02
INTO TABLE @DATA(t_results)
WHERE GLTGV <= @sy-datum
AND GLTGB >= @sy-datum.

"old Open SQL
DATA: t_results TYPE STANDARD TABLE OF USR02.
SELECT *
FROM UR02
INTO TABLE t_results
WHERE GLTGV <= sy-datum
AND GLTGB >= sy-datum.
```
Listing 9.8 Selecting a Record Valid for Today

Times

In this section we will cover how the time data type (t) works and some additional functions for calculating time as well as other time data types. Chapter 2 introduced the time data type (t) and that time is stored with two characters for hours, two characters for minutes, and two characters for seconds, in the format hhmmss.

If you need time that is more exact than seconds, you can also use a timestamp, which will be covered in this section. A *timestamp* will calculate time to the precision of 100 nanoseconds, which is seven decimal places, and will also include the date. The timestamp format is yyyymmddhhmmss.sssssss.

Calculating Time

Just as with dates, you can compare time using the regular comparison operators.

Timestamps

A timestamp is a combination of date and time for the UTC time zone. This can be used to record the exact date and time that an action was completed by a user without having to rely on the local time zone for the user or the server.

Creating timestamps

There are two types of timestamp data types: timestamp and timestampl. timestamp is a short-form timestamp, which represents only the date and time combined with a format of yyyymmddhhmmss. timestampl is a long-form timestamp and will include up to seven decimal places to capture the time with the precision of a microsecond using a format of yymmddhhmmss.sssssss.

You can get the current timestamp using the GET TIME STAMP FIELD function, as shown in Listing 9.9. This function will work with both timestamp and timestampl data types. If an inline data declaration is used, timestamp, not timestampl, will be used.

```
DATA: d_timestamp   TYPE timestamp,
      d_timestampl TYPE timestampl.
GET TIME STAMP FIELD d_timestamp.
GET TIME STAMP FIELD d_timestampl.
GET TIME STAMP FIELD data(d_inline_timestamp).
```
Listing 9.9 GET TIME STAMP FIELD

Comparing timestamps

The regular comparison operators can only be used between two timestamps, not between a timestamp and a date or time. The comparisons will work between a `timestamp` and `timestampl` comparison, as shown in Listing 9.10, in which the `timestampl` variable will be found to be bigger.

```
DATA: d_timestamp  TYPE timestamp,
      d_timestampl TYPE timestampl.
d_timestamp  = '20150101000000'.
d_timestampl = '20150101000000.0000001'.
IF d_timestamp > d_timestampl.
    WRITE: 'true'.
ENDIF.
```
Listing 9.10 Comparing TIMESTAMP and TIMESTAMPL Data Types

You can also convert a timestamp to a local date and time variable using the CONVERT TIME STAMP function. You'll have to specify a time zone that exists in table TTZZ. You can store the result in date and time variables or use inline declarations, which will be created as date and time variables. You also can store a Boolean value for whether or not daylight savings is in effect. The example in Listing 9.11 gets the current UTC timestamp and converts it to a PST time zone date and time. The DATE, TIME, and DAYLIGHT SAVINGS TIME additions are all optional, so you can use only the ones that you need.

Converting timestamps

```
GET TIME STAMP FIELD DATA(d_utc).
CONVERT TIME STAMP d_UTC TIME ZONE 'PST'
INTO DATE DATA(d_pst_date)
     TIME DATA(d_pst_time)
     DAYLIGHT SAVINGS TIME DATA(d_dst).
```
Listing 9.11 Converting Timestamp from UTC to PST Date and Time

You can also convert a local date and time into a timestamp using the CONVERT INTO TIMESTAMP function. A DATE and TIME ZONE are both required when using this function, but the TIME and DAYLIGHT SAVINGS TIME variables are optional. An example converting the results from Listing 9.11 back into a timestamp is shown in Listing 9.12. Remember the time zone passed is used to convert the local date and time from that time zone and into a UTC time zone.

```
CONVERT DATE d_pst_date
TIME d_pst_time
DAYLIGHT SAVINGS TIME d_dst
INTO TIME STAMP d_utc TIME ZONE 'PST'.
```
Listing 9.12 Converting PST Date and Time to a UTC Timestamp

9 Working with Dates, Times, Quantities, and Currencies

Timestamp formatting

When outputting timestamps to a string template, there are special formatting options that can be applied to display the timestamp in a more user-friendly format. Table 9.1 provides a list of all of the possible formatting options.

Timestamp Format	Output
SPACE	Based on ISO 8601. Format: yyyy-mm-dd hh:mm:ss.zzzzzzz. For example, 2015-01-01 12:00:00.0000000.
ISO	Also based on ISO 8601, but uses a "T" to separate the date and time and always uses a comma as the seconds decimal. Format: yyyy-mm-ddThh:mm:ss,zzzzzzz. For example, 2015-01-01T12:00:00.0000000.
USER	Based on the user's preferences, which can be changed by going to SYSTEM • USER PROFILE • OWN DATA under the DEFAULTS TAB. For example: 01/01/2015 12:00:00 PM
ENVIRONMENT	Based on the user's currently selected language environment and will display the default for that country, regardless of the user defaults. For example: 01/01/2015 12:00:00 PM.

Table 9.1 Timestamp Formats for String Templates

The syntax to use these different timestamp formats is simple: It's just `timestamp =` and then any of the formats listed in Table 9.1 in between the curly braces where the timestamp is added to the string template as shown in the example in Listing 9.13, which will return 2015-01-01T12:00:00.0000000.

```
DATA: d_unformatted TYPE timestamp1
  VALUE '20150101120000.0000000'.
DATA(d_string) = |{ d_unformatted TIMESTAMP = ISO }|.
```
Listing 9.13 Setting the Timestamp Format from within a String Template

You also can convert the time used in the string template to reflect a given time zone by adding `TIMEZONE =` followed by the desired time zone, as shown in Listing 9.14, which will return 2015-01-01T04:00:00.0000000.

340

```
d_string = |{ d_unformatted TIMESTAMP = ISO
                            TIMEZONE  = 'PST' }|.
```
Listing 9.14 Setting Timestamp Output and Time Zone for Output in a String Template

There are some additional timestamp-related functions that use the system class `CL_ABAP_TSTMP`. This class should be used if you want to add or subtract seconds from a timestamp, calculate the difference between two timestamps, or convert a long timestamp to a short timestamp or vice versa.

SY-UZEIT (System Time vs. Local Time)

There are a few system fields related to time. Just as with system dates, there are times based on the system time zone and times based on the logged-in user's time zone. The system time can be found with `sy-uzeit`, whereas the user's time can be found with `sy-timlo`; both will return the result in a variable of type `t`. You can also get the system time zone using `sy-tzone` or the user's local time zone using `sy-zonlo`, both of which will return a `char` variable with a length of 6.

System time fields

Just as with system dates, you can declare system variables as data types, as shown in Listing 9.15.

```
DATA: d_sys_time TYPE sy-uzeit,
      d_sys_timezone TYPE sy-tzone,
      d_loc_time TYPE sy-timlo,
      d_loc_timezone TYPE sy-zonlo.

d_sys_time = sy-uzeit.
d_sys_timezone = sy-tzone.
d_loc_time = sy-timlo.
d_loc_timezone = sy-zonlo.
```
Listing 9.15 Declaring and Getting System Time and Local Time Data

Quantities

Quantities are used to track and convert different units of measurement. Quantities include all types of measurements, ranging from lengths (e.g., meters and inches) to masses (e.g., grams and pounds).

You can see the different possible units of measurement that are set up in your ABAP environment by entering Transaction CUNI, shown

Display units of measurement

in Figure 9.8. From there, select a dimension such as length from the dropdown, and click UNITS OF MEASUREMENT.

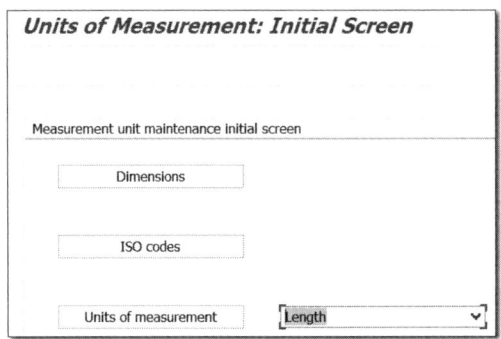

Figure 9.8 Initial Screen of Transaction CUNI

Next, you will see a list of possible measurements for that dimension, as shown in Figure 9.9.

Unit	Commercial	Technical	Meas. unit text	
CM	CM	cm	cm	
DM	DM	dm	dm	
FT	FT	Foot	Foot	
IN	"	"	Inches	
KM	KM	km	km	
M	M	m	m	SI..
MI	MI	mile	Mile	
MIM	µM	µm	µm	
MM	MM	mm	mm	
NAM	NAM	nm	nm	
YD	YD	yd	Yards	

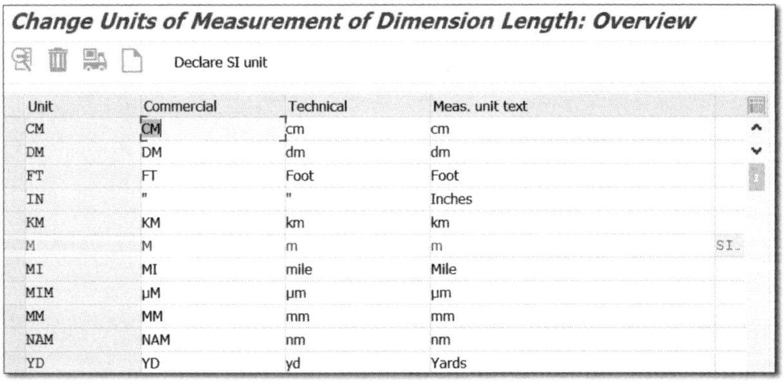

Figure 9.9 List of Length Units of Measurement from Transaction CUNI

Data Dictionary

When storing quantities in transparent tables, you need to store the quantity as a `QUAN` data type and the unit of measurement as a `UNIT` data type. Then, when creating the table using Transaction SE11, you need to relate the two fields in the CURRENCY/QUANTITY FIELDS tab.

ZQUANTITY transparent table

To demonstrate this, create the table `ZQUANTITY` shown in Figure 9.10 using Transaction SE11. The table should contain FIELD "MANDT" with DATA ELEMENT "MANDT", FIELD "ID" with DATA ELEMENT "INTEGER", FIELD "QUANTITY" with DATA ELEMENT "BASMN" (type `QUAN`) and FIELD "UNIT_OF_MEASURE" with DATA ELEMENT "CGSUNIT" (type `UNIT`). If some of the data elements do not look familiar, don't worry they are data types that should exist in any ABAP system.

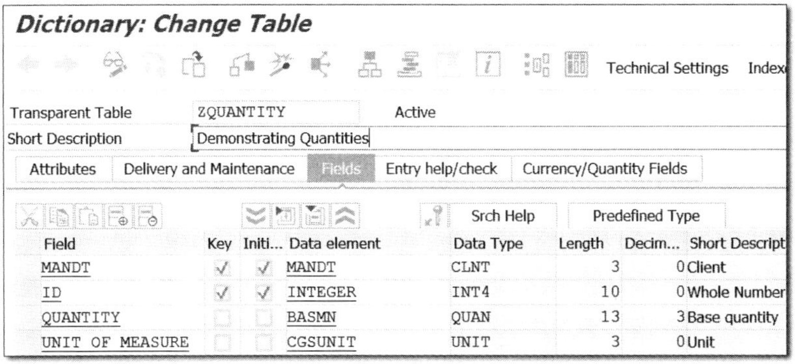

Figure 9.10 Table Containining a Quantity and Unit of Measure

Next, click on the CURRENCY/QUANTITY FIELDS tab, and you will see that only the QUANTITY field has an editable row. From here, you can add a reference to the table and field that will describe the quantity. For this example, enter the current table "ZQUANTITY" and the field "UNIT_OF_MEASURE", as pictured in Figure 9.11. Assigning a corresponding unit of measurement field for any quantity data type is required in order to activate the table.

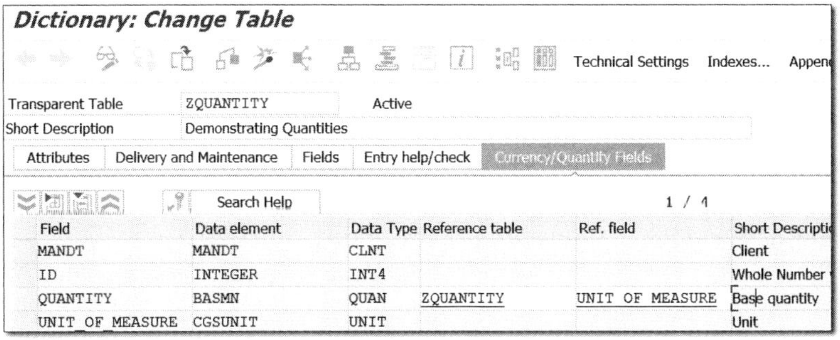

Figure 9.11 Currency/Quantity Fields Data for Assigning Units to Quantities

343

Because you store the quantity and unit in the same table, different records can have data stored in different quantities.

Converting Quantities

Within your ABAP program, you can read data stored in a certain unit of measure and then convert the value into a different unit of measure as long as the unit of measurement that you're converting from and the unit of measurement that you're converting to are both part of the same dimension.

ABAP unit conversion

You can complete the conversion using function module UNIT_CON-VERSION_SIMPLE, which will allow you to pass in a quantity with a unit to convert from and a unit to convert to. This function module will also round results if necessary, and you can optionally pass in a + or - to force it to always round up or down. Listing 9.16 demonstrates converting a quantity of 5 from meters ('M') to centimeters ('CM'). The unit of measurement used can also be seen in the length units of measurement list in Figure 9.9.

```
DATA(d_5) = 5.
CALL FUNCTION 'UNIT_CONVERSION_SIMPLE'
  EXPORTING
    input            = d_5
    unit_in          = 'M'
    unit_out         = 'CM'
  IMPORTING
    output           = d_5
  EXCEPTIONS
    conversion_not_found = 1
    division_by_zero = 2
    input_invalid    = 3
    output_invalid   = 4
    overflow         = 5
    type_invalid     = 6
    units_missing    = 7
    unit_in_not_found = 8
    unit_out_not_found = 9
    others           = 10
    .
IF sy-subrc <> 0.
  MESSAGE ID sy-msgid TYPE sy-msgty NUMBER sy-msgno
          WITH sy-msgv1 sy-msgv2 sy-msgv3 sy-msgv4.
ENDIF.
```

```
WRITE: d_5.                                                              500
```
Listing 9.16 ABAP Code for Converting Data between Measurements

Currencies

Currencies work a lot like quantities; they're used to capture both a value and a type. In today's world of global business, transactions can be captured in one currency and then transferred to another. This makes it very important to keep track of the currency being referenced in any financial transaction, which is easy with an ABAP system.

You can see a list of currencies defined in your system by entering Transaction OY03. The results will be displayed, and the key to keep track of is listed in the CURRENCY column. If you wanted to know what to use to indicate a currency as United States dollars, you could look up the currency and see that the answer is USD, as shown in Figure 9.12.

Display currencies

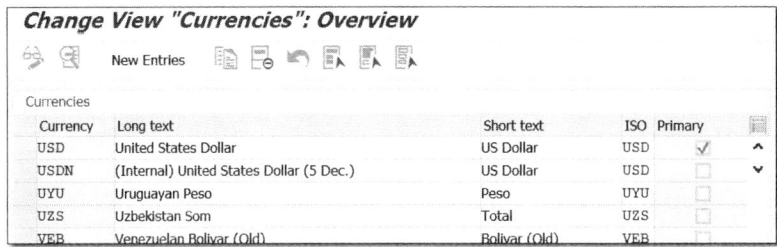

Figure 9.12 List of Currencies from Transaction OY03

When converting amounts across different currencies, the current exchange rate can be found in Transaction OB08. Because exchange rates regularly change, it's possible to have the exchange rates in your system automatically update on a daily or weekly basis, which is a topic far outside the scope of this book. Figure 9.13 shows that the currency exchange rate between the US dollar and the euro is 0.94 euros to 1 US dollar.

9 Working with Dates, Times, Quantities, and Currencies

Figure 9.13 Currency Exchange Rates from Transaction OB08

Data Dictionary

Just as currencies use a QUAN data type to keep track of the quantity and a UNIT data type to keep track of the unit of measure, a currency value requires that the amount of currency be stored in a field with a CURR data type, and the currency key needs to be stored with a CUKY data type. You can then relate the fields in the CURRENCY/QUANTITY FIELDS tab in the change transparent table screen from Transaction SE11.

Currency in a transparent table

To demonstrate this, you can create table ZCURRENCY shown in Figure 9.14 using Transaction SE11. The table should contain FIELD "MANDT" with DATA ELEMENT "MANDT", FIELD "ID" with DATA ELEMENT "INTEGER", FIELD "PRICE" with DATA ELEMENT "PREIS" (type CURR) and FIELD "CURRENCY" with DATA ELEMENT "USRCUKY" (type CUKY). If some of the data elements do not look familiar, don't worry they are data types that should exist in any ABAP system.

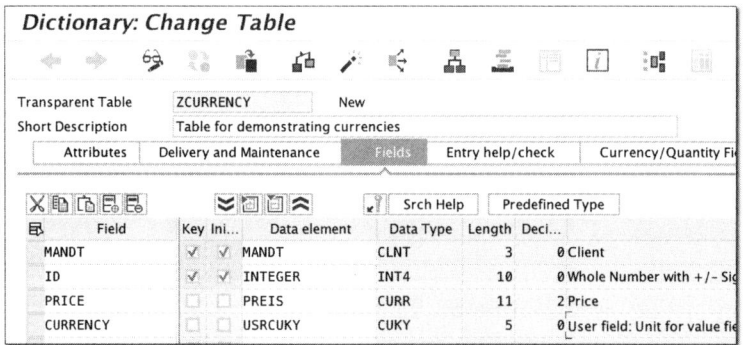

Figure 9.14 Table ZCURRENCY Using Currency Data Types

Currency/Quanitity Fields settings

You won't be able to activate table ZCURRENCY until you add a reference for the currency field. This works just as you saw with the quantity field; select the CURRENCY/QUANTITY FIELDS tab and enter

"ZCURRENCY" as the reference table and "CURRENCY" as the reference field so that the currency and currency key fields are linked as shown in Figure 9.15 below.

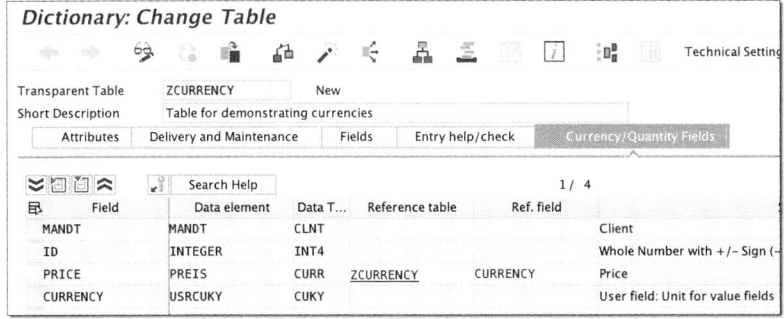

Figure 9.15 Currency/Quantity Fields Tab for Table ZCURRENCY

Because you have a field for currency in the table being used, each record in the table can have any currency denomination.

Converting Currencies

Within your ABAP program, you may want to convert currency to a different denomination, using the current exchange rates shown in Transaction OB08, and you can do so using the function module `CONVERT_TO_LOCAL_CURRENCY`.

When using `CONVERT_TO_LOCAL_CURRENCY`, you're required to pass a date that will be used to determine the exchange rate for converting `foreign_amount` from `foreign_currency` to `local_currency`. The result will be returned as `local_amount`, as shown in Listing 9.17 and you can also gather additional information from the function module, such as the exchange rate used, or you can specify an exchange rate to be used in the conversion.

Currency conversion in ABAP

```
DATA: d_amount TYPE P DECIMALS 2.

CALL FUNCTION 'CONVERT_TO_LOCAL_CURRENCY'
  EXPORTING
    date              = sy-datlo
    foreign_amount    = 100
    foreign_currency  = 'EUR'
    local_currency    = 'USD'
  IMPORTING
```

9   Working with Dates, Times, Quantities, and Currencies

```
        local_amount     = d_amount
    EXCEPTIONS
      no_rate_found      = 1
      overflow           = 2
      no_factors_found   = 3
      no_spread_found    = 4
      derived_2_times    = 5
      others             = 6.

IF sy-subrc <> 0.
  MESSAGE ID sy-msgid TYPE sy-msgty NUMBER sy-msgno
          WITH sy-msgv1 sy-msgv2 sy-msgv3 sy-msgv4.
ENDIF.
```
Listing 9.17 Currency Conversion

You should now be familiar with currencies and the aspects required for storing and converting currencies. In the next section we'll update the shopping cart example with currencies and quantities.

Updating the Shopping Cart Example

Now that you know how to use dates, times, quantities, and currencies, let's revisit the shopping cart example to take advantage of the currency and quantity features.

Shopping cart ERD

First, we need to update our ERD design to include currency and quantity values. In Figure 9.16, note the addition of PRICE and CURRENCY in table ZPRODUCT, allowing you to set a price per item for a specified currency. Also, unit of measurement (UOM) is added to table ZPRODUCT, allowing you to determine the quantity unit that the price is set for. Additionally, the quantity unit that indicates the quantity of the material in a cart.

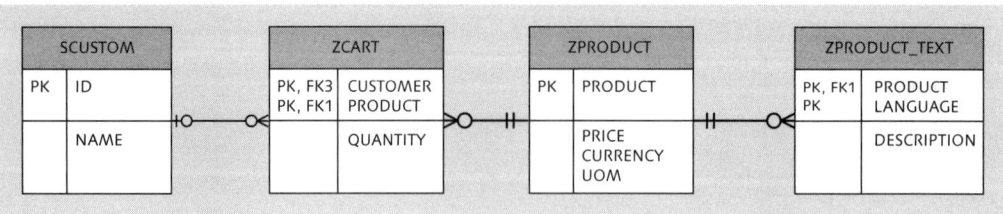

Figure 9.16 Updated ERD Diagram with Currency and Quantity Fields

348

Updating the Database

We are now ready to update the transparent tables to match our updated ERD diagram. This section will walk through the steps to accomplish that. First we will create data elements for the new fields and then add those data elements to the transparent tables.

First we will create the data element for the product price field. To begin, enter Transaction SE11 and select the DATA TYPE radio button and enter "ZPRODUCT_PRICE" in the corresponding textbox and click the CREATE button. Select the DATA ELEMENT radio button in the data type popup and click the CONTINUE button.

Price data element

In the change data element screen, enter "Product Price for Shopping Cart Example" in the SHORT DESCRIPTION textbox. Then, with the DATA TYPE tab selected, choose the ELEMENTARY TYPE radio button and the PREDEFINED TYPE radio button. Enter the DATA TYPE "CURR", LENGTH "11", and DECIMAL PLACES "2". We are using the PREDEFINED TYPE options instead of a DOMAIN in our new data elements because we do not need any of the additional settings available within a domain. Your data element should look like the one pictured below in Figure 9.17.

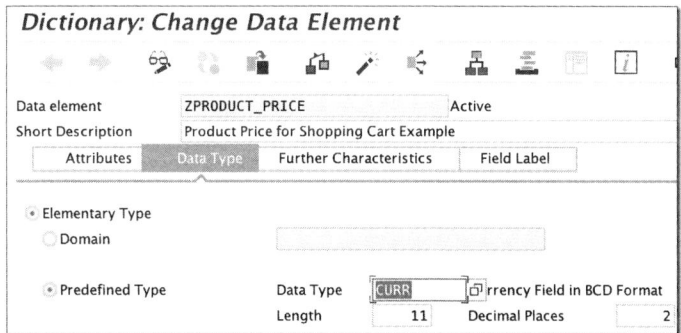

Figure 9.17 Data Type Settings for Data Element ZPRODUCT_PRICE

Next, select the FIELD LABEL tab and enter "Price" for all FIELD LABEL textboxes. Then press [Enter] and the LENGTH textboxes will be automatically populated as shown below in Figure 9.18. Press the SAVE button to save the data element and the ACTIVATE button to activate it.

349

9 Working with Dates, Times, Quantities, and Currencies

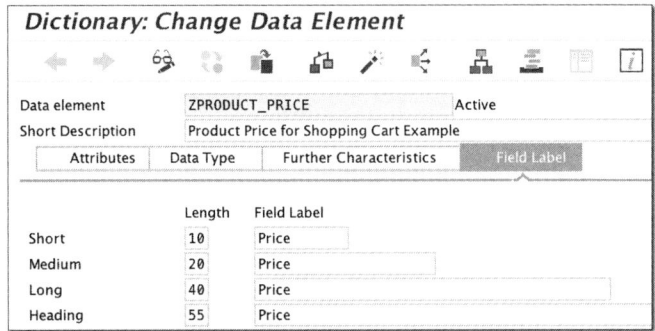

Figure 9.18 ZPRODUCT_PRICE Field Label Settings

Currency data element

Next, return to Transaction SE11 and select the DATA TYPE radio button and enter "ZPRODUCT_CURRENCY" in the corresponding textbox and click the CREATE button. Select the DATA ELEMENT radio button in the data type popup and click the CONTINUE button.

In the change data element screen, enter "Product Currency for Shopping Cart Example" in the SHORT DESCRIPTION textbox. Then, with the DATA TYPE tab selected, choose the ELEMENTARY TYPE radio button and the PREDEFINED TYPE radio button. Enter the DATA TYPE "CUKY", and LENGTH "5". Your data element should look like the one pictured below in Figure 9.19.

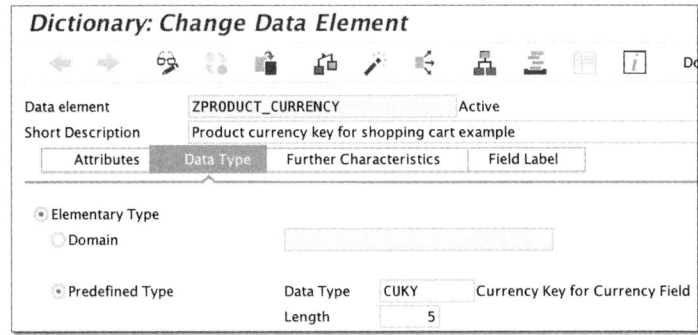

Figure 9.19 ZPRODUCT_CURRENCY Data Type Settings

Next, select the FIELD LABEL tab and enter "Currency" for all FIELD LABEL textboxes. Then press [Enter] and the LENGTH textboxes will be automatically populated as shown below in Figure 9.20. Press the SAVE button to save the data element and the ACTIVATE button to activate it.

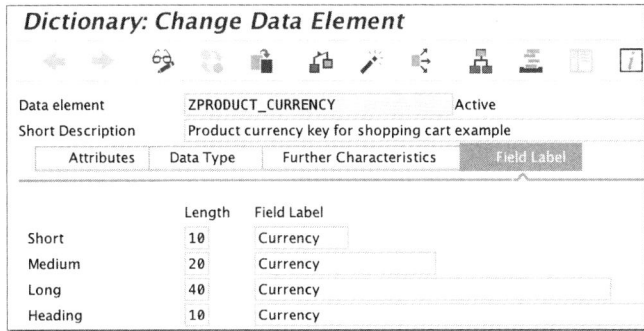

Figure 9.20 ZPRODUCT_CURRENCY Field Label Settings

Next, return to transaction SE11 and select the DATA TYPE radio button and enter "ZPRODUCT_UOM" in the corresponding textbox and click the CREATE button. Select the DATA ELEMENT radio button in the data type popup and click the CONTINUE button.

UOM data element

In the change data element screen, enter "Product UOM for the Shopping Cart Example" in the SHORT DESCRIPTION textbox. Then, with the DATA TYPE tab selected, choose the ELEMENTARY TYPE radio button and the PREDEFINED TYPE radio button. Enter the DATA TYPE "UNIT", and LENGTH "3". Your data element should look like the one pictured below in Figure 9.21.

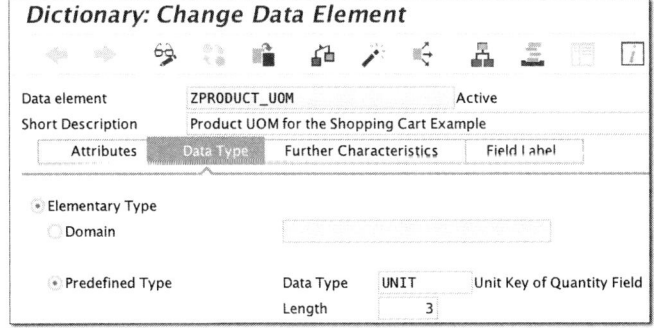

Figure 9.21 ZPRODUCT_UOM Data Type Settings

Next, select the FIELD LABEL tab and enter Unit for the SHORT FIELD LABEL text box and "Unit of Measure" for all other FIELD LABEL textboxes. Then press [Enter] and the LENGTH textboxes will be automatically populated as shown below in Figure 9.22. Press the SAVE button to save the data element and the ACTIVATE button to activate it.

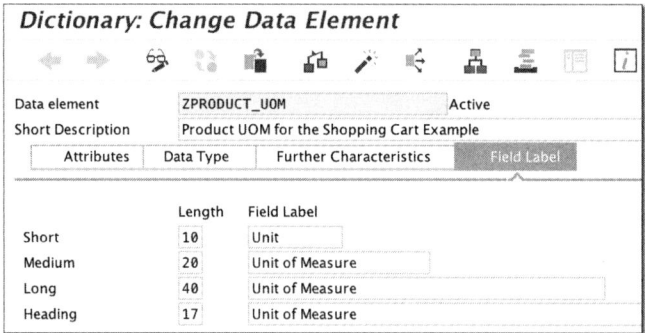

Figure 9.22 ZPRODUCT_UOM Field Label Settings

Quantity data element

Next, return to transaction SE11 and select the DATA TYPE radio button and enter "ZCART_QUANTITY" in the corresponding textbox and click the CREATE button. Select the DATA ELEMENT radio button in the data type popup and click the CONTINUE button.

In the change data element screen, enter "Cart Quantity for the Shopping Cart Example" in the SHORT DESCRIPTION textbox. Then, with the DATA TYPE tab selected, choose the ELEMENTARY TYPE radio button and the PREDEFINED TYPE radio button. Enter the DATA TYPE "QUAN", LENGTH "13", and DECIMAL PLACES "3". Your data element should look like the one pictured below in Figure 9.23.

Next, select the FIELD LABEL tab and enter "Quantity" for all of the FIELD LABEL textboxes. Then press [Enter] and the LENGTH textboxes will be automatically populated as shown below in Figure 9.24. Press the SAVE button to save the data element and the ACTIVATE button to activate it.

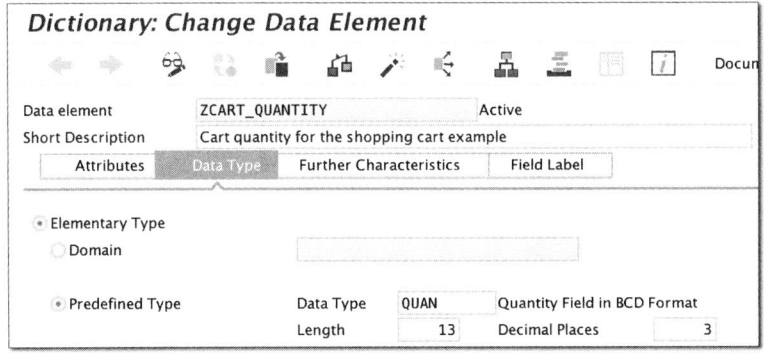

Figure 9.23 ZCART_QUANTITY Data Type Settings

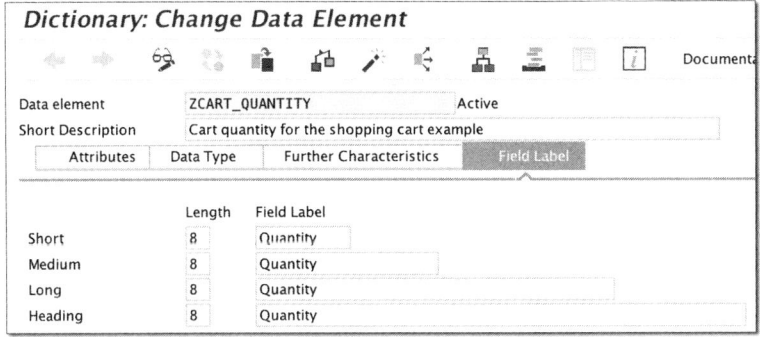

Figure 9.24 ZCART_QUANTITY Field Label Options

Now that we have created the new data elements, we can update the transparent table that use those data elements. First, we will update the transparent table ZPRODUCT. To do this, go back to transaction SE11 and select the radio button for DATABASE TABLE and enter "ZPRODUCT" in the corresponding textbox. Then press the CHANGE button.

Updating zproduct

With the Fields tab selected, add FIELD "PRICE" with DATA ELEMENT "ZPRODUCT_PRICE", FIELD "CURRENCY" with DATA ELEMENT "ZPRODUCT_CURRENCY", and FIELD "UOM" with DATA ELEMENT "ZPRODUCT_UOM" as shown in Figure 9.25 below.

353

Working with Dates, Times, Quantities, and Currencies

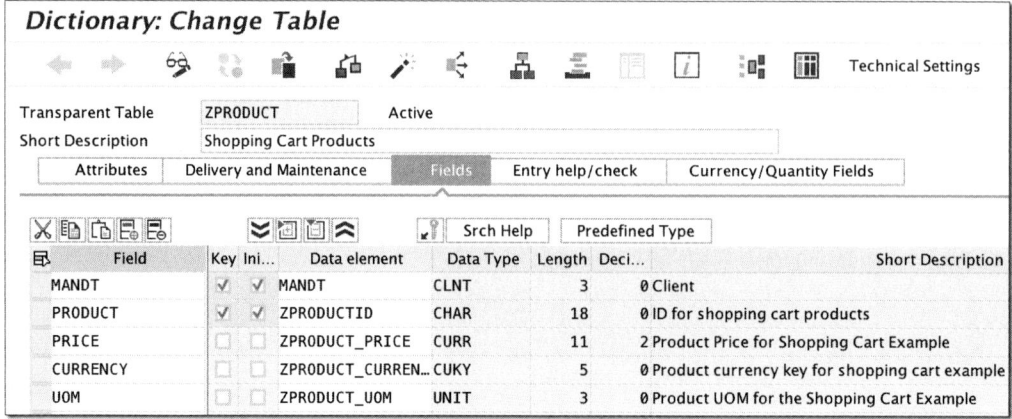

Figure 9.25 ZPRODUCT Fields Tab Settings

Next, select the CURRENCY/QUANTITY FIELDS tab and enter REFERENCE TABLE "ZPRODUCT" and REFERENCE FIELD "CURRENCY" for the FIELD "PRICE" as shown in Figure 9.26 below. This will set the field CURRENCY as the currency key for field PRICE.

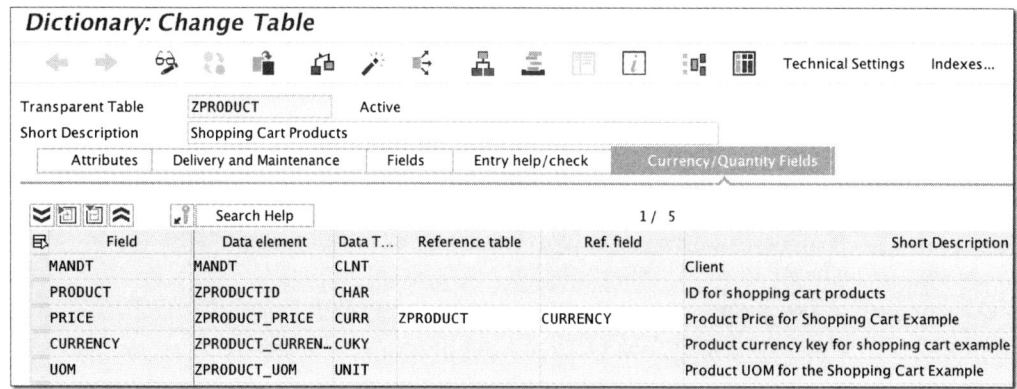

Figure 9.26 ZPRODUCT Currency/Quantity Fields Tab Settings

The ZPRODUCT table is now done, press the SAVE button and ACTIVATE button to save and activate the table.

Updating zcart — Now, go back to Transaction SE11 and select the radio button for DATABASE TABLE and enter "ZCART" in the corresponding textbox. Then press the CHANGE button.

354

With the FIELDS tab selected add FIELD "Quantity" with DATA ELEMENT "ZCART_QUANTITY" as shown in Figure 9.27.

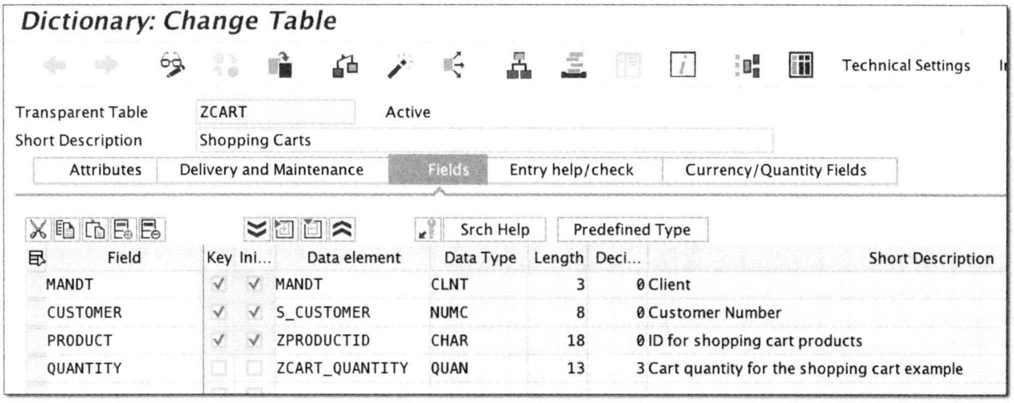

Field	Key	Ini...	Data element	Data Type	Length	Deci...	Short Description
MANDT	✓	✓	MANDT	CLNT	3	0	Client
CUSTOMER	✓	✓	S_CUSTOMER	NUMC	8	0	Customer Number
PRODUCT	✓	✓	ZPRODUCTID	CHAR	18	0	ID for shopping cart products
QUANTITY			ZCART_QUANTITY	QUAN	13	3	Cart quantity for the shopping cart example

Figure 9.27 ZCART Table Fields Tab Settings

Now, select the CURRENCY/QUANTITY FIELDS tab and enter REFERENCE TABLE "ZPRODUCT" and REFERENCE FIELD "UOM" for the FIELD "Quantity". This will set the field UOM in the ZPRODUCT table as the unit for the field QUANTITY in this table, as shown in Figure 9.28.

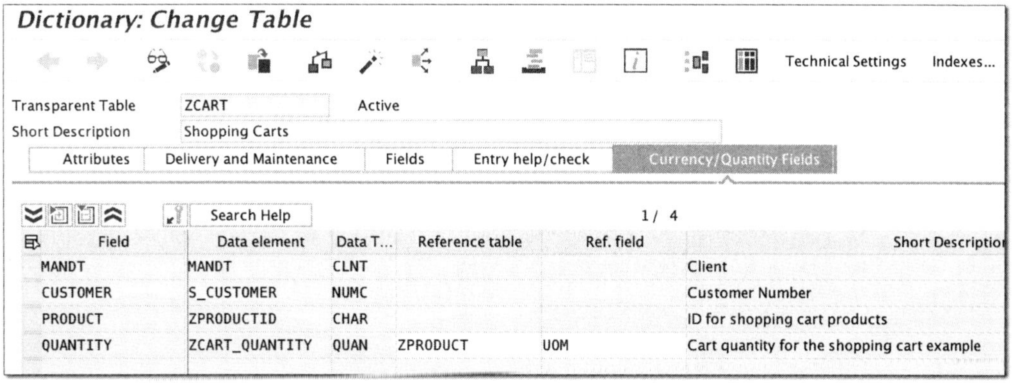

Field	Data element	Data T...	Reference table	Ref. field	Short Description
MANDT	MANDT	CLNT			Client
CUSTOMER	S_CUSTOMER	NUMC			Customer Number
PRODUCT	ZPRODUCTID	CHAR			ID for shopping cart products
QUANTITY	ZCART_QUANTITY	QUAN	ZPRODUCT	UOM	Cart quantity for the shopping cart example

Figure 9.28 ZCART Currency/Quantity Fields Tab Settings

The ZCART table is now complete. Select the SAVE button and ACTIVATE button to save and activate the table.

9 Working with Dates, Times, Quantities, and Currencies

In the next section, we will update the global class to use the new currencies and quantities.

Updating the Global Class

Now that our tables have been updated, we need to update our global class `zcl_shopping_cart` to use the new information. We will need to update the `add_product` method to take an additional parameter for quantity and we will need to update the `get_cart` method to return the quantity and unit of measurement for all of the items in the cart.

Updating add_product

First we will update the `add_product` method. To do this, update the method definition to include the IMPORTING parameter `ip_quantity` as shown in Listing 9.18 below. Additionally, we will add the new parameter as an optional parameter so other programs are not impacted by the change.

```
...
    add_product IMPORTING ip_product  TYPE zproduct-product
                          ip_quantity TYPE zcart-quantity OPTIONAL,
...
```

Listing 9.18 Updated Definition for the ADD_PRODUCT Method

Now, we can update the `add_product` method implementation. The change will be to check if `ip_quantity` has a value and if it does, to use that value for in the local structure, otherwise to set the local structure quantity to 1. We can also now change the INSERT statement to a MODIFY statement. This will allow the `add_product` method to be called to change the quantity as well as add new products. This is accomplished using the code in Listing 9.19 below, which has the specific changes in bold.

```
METHOD add_product.
    DATA: ls_cart TYPE zcart.
    ls_cart-customer = d_customer.
    ls_cart-product = ip_product.
    IF ip_quantity IS NOT INITIAL.
        ls_cart-quantitity = ip_quantity.
    ELSE.
        ls_cart-quantity = 1.
    ENDIF.
```

```
    MODIFY zcart FROM ls_cart.
ENDMETHOD.
```
Listing 9.19 Updated ADD_PRODUCT Method Implementation

Next, we want to update the `get_cart` method to return the quantity and unit of measurement. To do this, we must first update the `y_cart` definition to include a quantity and unit of measurement component as shown in bold below in Listing 9.20.

Updating get_cart

```
...
PUBLIC SECTION.
    TYPES: BEGIN OF y_cart,
              product     TYPE zproduct-product,
              description TYPE zproduct_text-description
              quantity    TYPE zcart-quantity
              uom         TYPE zproduct-uom,
           END OF y_cart,
...
```
Listing 9.20 Updates to Y_CART Definition in ZCL_SHOPPING_CART

Now in the `get_cart` method, we need to add the new fields to our SELECT statement as shown in Listing 9.21 below.

```
METHOD get_cart.
"using new Open SQL
SELECT zcart~product, description, quantity, uom
FROM zcart
INNER JOIN zproduct
ON zcart~product = zproduct~product
INNER JOIN zproduct_text
ON zcart~product = zproduct_text~product
WHERE zproduct_text~language = @sy-langu
AND zcart-customer = d_customer
INTO TABLE @rt_cart.

"using old Open SQL
SELECT zcart~product description quantity uom
INTO TABLE rt_cart.
FROM zcart
INNER JOIN zproduct
ON zcart~product = zproduct~product
INNER JOIN zproduct_text
ON zcart~product = zproduct_text~product
WHERE zproduct_text~language = sy-langu
AND zcart-customer = d_customer.
```

```
ENDMETHOD.
```
Listing 9.21 Updated GET_CART Method in ZCL_SHOPPING_CART

Now, press the ACTIVATE button to activate the ZCL_SHOPPING_CART. The class ZCL_SHOPPING_CART is now ready to use quantities. In the next section, we will update the ABAP programs to use the new price and quantity fields.

Updating the ABAP Programs

ZPRODUCT_MAINT parameters

We are now ready to update the maintenance ABAP programs. First we will update the ZPRODUCT_MAINT program. In listing Listing 9.22 below, we add the additional parameters needed for price, currency, and unit of measurement all shown in bold.

```
...
SELECTION-
SCREEN BEGIN OF BLOCK product WITH FRAME TITLE text-001.
  PARAMETERS: p_prod  TYPE zproduct-product,
              p_desc  TYPE zproduct_text-description
                LOWER CASE,
              p_price TYPE zproduct-price,
              p_curr  TYPE zproduct-currency,
              p_uom   TYPE zproduct-uom.
SELECTION-SCREEN END OF BLOCK product.
```
Listing 9.22 Adding New Parameters to the Selection Screen

Press the ACTIVATE button to activate the program so we can add the selection texts for our new parameters.

ZPRODUCT_MAINT selection text

Next, we want to add the selection text for the new parameters. If you are using the Eclipse IDE, right click the program in your PROJECT EXPLORER and select OPEN WITH SAP GUI. Select GOTO • TEXT ELEMENTS • SELECTION TEXTS. In the Change Selection Texts screen, select the checkbox for Dictionary Ref. for all of the new parameters listed. Then click the SAVE button and ACTIVATE button to activate the new texts.

We can now test the updated selection screen by running the program. It should look like Figure 9.29 below.

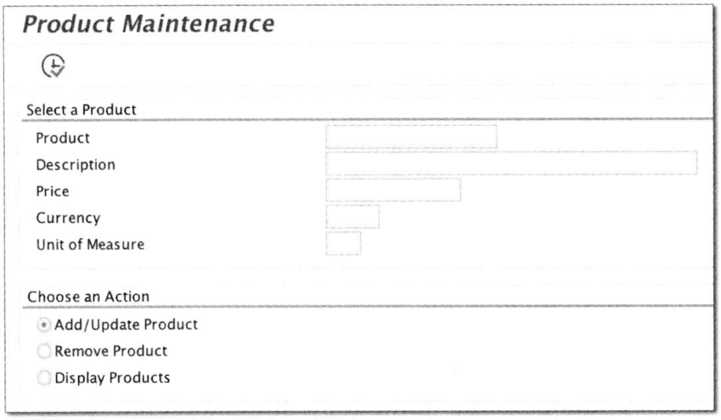

Figure 9.29 The Updated ZPRODUCT_MAINT Selection Screen

We can now update the logic in ZPRODUCT_MAINT to save the new parameters to the database. To do this, add the bold code in Listing 9.23 below.

ZPRODUCT_MAINT logic

```
...
s_product-product = p_prod.
s_product-price = p_price.
s_product-currency = p_curr.
s_product-uom = p_uom.
s_product_text-product = p_prod.
s_product_text-description = p_desc.
...
```

Listing 9.23 Updated Code to Save New Parameters Is ZPRODUCT_MAINT

When using inline data declarations, the SELECT statement is quickly updated to display the new fields as shown below in Listing 9.24.

```
...
SELECT zproduct~product, description, price, currency, uom
FROM zproduct
INNER JOIN zproduct_text
ON zproduct~product = zproduct_text~product
WHERE language = @sy-langu
INTO TABLE @DATA(t_products).
...
```

Listing 9.24 Updating the SELECT Statement with Inline Data Declations

9 Working with Dates, Times, Quantities, and Currencies

When not using inline data declarations, we need to update the type definition before we can update the select statement as shown in Listing 9.25 below.

```
ELSEIF p_dis = abap_true.
    TYPES: BEGIN OF y_products,
            product     TYPE zproduct-product,
            description TYPE zproduct_text-description,
            price       TYPE zproduct-price,
            currency    TYPE zproduct-currency,
            uom         TYPE zproduct-uom,
          END OF y_products.

DATA: t_products TYPE STANDARD TABLE OF y_products,
      gr_alv TYPE REF TO cl_salv_table.

SELECT zproduct~product description price currency uom
INTO TABLE t_products
FROM zproduct
INNER JOIN zproduct_text
ON zproduct~product = zproduct_text~product
WHERE language = sy-langu.
```
Listing 9.25 Updating the SELECT Statement without Inline Data Declarations

You can now press the ACTIVATE button to activate the program. The ZPRODUCT_MAINT ABAP program is now ready to handle currencies and quantities.

ZCART_MAINT changes

Next, we will update the ZCART_MAINT program to utilize the new currency and quantity options. In Listing 9.26 below, you can see that we added a new parameter for the quantity and added it as a parameter when calling the add_product method. Notice that we now have to indicate which parameters we are passing when calling the add_product method.

```
...
PARAMETERS: p_cust TYPE zcart-customer OBLIGATORY,
            p_prod TYPE zcart-product,
            p_qty  TYPE zcart-quantity.
...
ELSEIF p_add = abap_true.
    o_cart->add_product( ip_product = p_prod ip_quantity = p_qty ).
...
```
Listing 9.26 Updates for the Program ZCART_MAINT

Now, press the ACTIVATE button to activate these changes and make the new parameters available in the selection texts screen.

Next, we want to add the selection text for the new parameters. If you are using the Eclipse IDE, right click the program in your PROJECT EXPLORER and select OPEN WITH SAP GUI. Select GOTO • TEXT ELEMENTS • SELECTION TEXTS. In the Change Selection Texts screen, select the checkbox for Dictionary Ref. for all of the new parameters listed. Then click the SAVE button and ACTIVATE button to activate the new texts.

ZCART_MAINT selection texts

The ZCART_MAINT program is now ready to handle quantities. Add data using both programs to test the new functionality.

Summary

This chapter covered some important steps and tools for working with dates, times, and timestamps. With the information covered here, we can now create ABAP applications that can accurately calculate dates and times across various time zones and take into account only working days to calculate important dates.

We also covered how to work with quantities and currencies in both the ABAP Data Dictionary and in ABAP programs and how to read and convert quantities and currencies.

Finally, we updated the shopping cart program from Chapter 7 and Chapter 8 to use quantities and currencies.

In the next chapter, we will cover error handling in ABAP and further enhance the shopping cart example to take advantage of various error handling techniques.

Error Handling

10

Error handling is important for any ABAP programmer; it can be used to ensure data quality in an ABAP system, and when used properly it can improve the user experience and allow users to resolve issues themselves instead of requiring a call to the support team.

We have covered some basic error handling techniques in examples throughout this book, but this chapter will go into more detail about the various options for handling errors in ABAP.

SY-SUBRC

The most basic type of error handling is to check the result of the `sy-subrc` variable after completing an action. Checking if sy-subrc has a value of 0 will always mean success. When looking at the READ TABLE keyword in Chapter 5, we used sy-subrc to determine if a record was found, as shown in Listing 10.1 below. By checking the result of the `sy-subrc` variable, we are avoiding an error happening because no record was found using READ TABLE.

```
...
READ TABLE t_table ASSSIGNING FIELD-SYMBOL(<ls_table>)
INDEX 1.
IF sy-subrc = 0.
    "Do Somethint
ENDIF.
```
Listing 10.1 Using SY-SUBRC to determine if READ TABLE was successful

We can also use `sy-subrc` after an Open SQL statement to determine if the Open SQL executed successfully. For example a SELECT statement will set `sy-subrc` to 0 unless no results were returned and INSERT will set `sy-subrc` to 0 as long as the provided record was inserted successfully. An example using `sy-subrc` with Open SQL is shown below in Listing 10.2.

```
SELECT *
FROM SFLIGHT
INTO TABLE @DATA(t_flights).
IF sy-subrc = 0.
    "Do something with results
ENDIF.
```
Listing 10.2 Example demonstrating using sy-subrc with Open SQL

Now that we have covered the most basic form of error handling using the sy-subrc variable. In the next section we will cover message classes, which can be used to provide users with information of an error that has occurred.

Message Classes

A *message class* is used as a single area for success, warning, and error messages that will be displayed to users. Unlike text symbols, the messages inside of a message class can be used across multiple programs or classes. Message classes should be created for a particular department, process, or entire company, such as ZFI to cover all finance-related messages to be used for a particular company, and should never be created for a specific program or class.

Displaying a Message Class

We can display a message class using Transaction SE91. If you're using Eclipse, you can also-double click a message class under the DICTIONARY OBJECTS folder to open it or open the GUI within Eclipse and then open Transaction SE91. To examine an existing standard message class, enter "02" in the MESSAGE CLASS textbox and click the DISPLAY button, as pictured in Figure 10.1. Message class 02 was created by SAP and contains messages used by the general ABAP runtime environment.

Message Classes

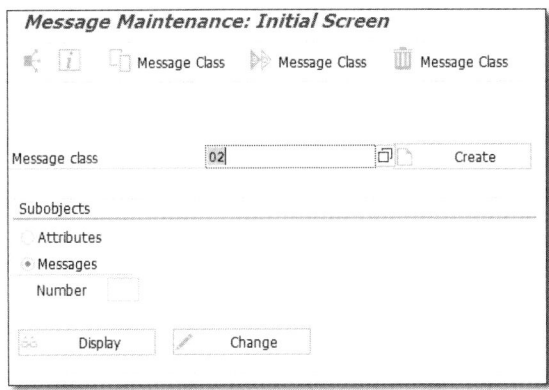

Figure 10.1 Transaction SE91

If you're using the SAP GUI, you'll see the messages as shown in Figure 10.2, and if you're using Eclipse, you'll see the messages as shown in Figure 10.3. The MESSAGE NUMBER column contains the three-digit number used to identify each message. The SHORT TEXT column displays the text of the message, which sometimes contains an ampersand (&) symbol, used to indicate that a string can be passed into the message text.

Short text

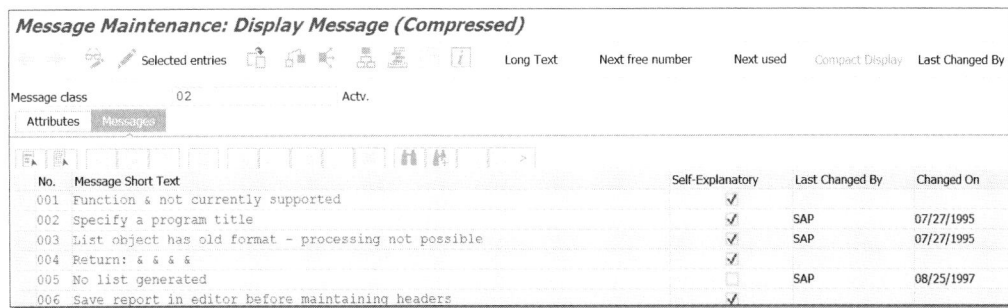

Figure 10.2 Message Class 02 Displayed Using SAP GUI

The SELF-EXPLANATORY checkbox indicates whether or not the text is self-explanatory. Messages that are not marked as self-explanatory can have long text added to allow for a more verbose explanation of the error that has occurred and possible steps to resolve the issue.

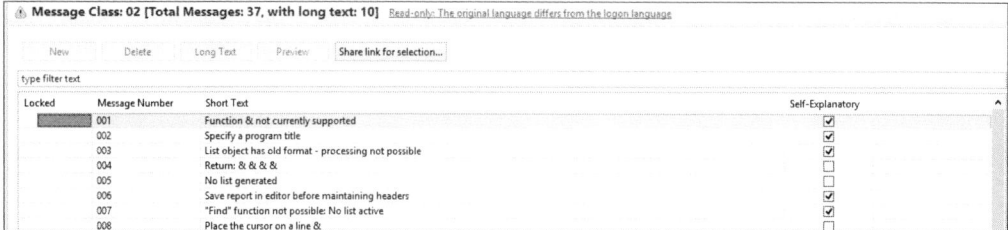

Figure 10.3 Message Class 02 Displayed within Eclipse

Long text   We can display the long text for a message that is not listed as self-explanatory by selecting it and clicking the LONG TEXT button in SAP GUI or by clicking the PREVIEW button in Eclipse. If you select message 005 in message class 02 and click The LONG TEXT or PREVIEW button, you'll see the results shown in Figure 10.4 (for SAP GUI) or Figure 10.5 (for Eclipse).

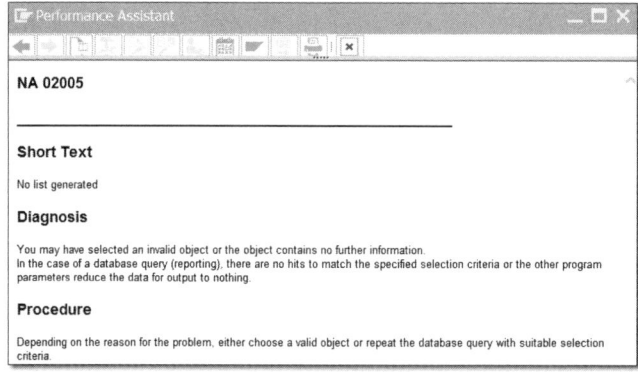

Figure 10.4 Message Long Text Displayed in SAP GUI

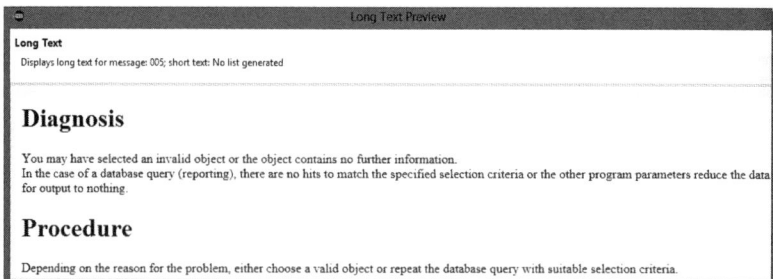

Figure 10.5 Message Long Text Previewed in Eclipse

Creating a Message Class

Create a message class in SAP GUI in Transaction SE91 by entering the desired message class name starting with "Z" and clicking the CREATE button (refer back to Figure 10.1).

From within Eclipse, you can create a message class by selecting FILE • NEW • OTHER... and then selecting MESSAGE CLASS from within the ABAP folder in the popup and clicking the NEXT button as shown in Figure 10.6 below. Then, enter a class name beginning with Z and a description.

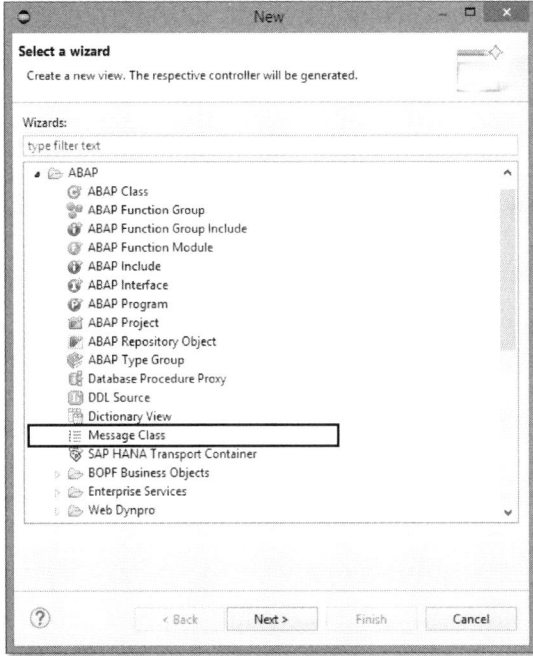

Figure 10.6 New ABAP Message Class Popup

For our example select $TMP as the package to keep it in the local system.

In the edit view, you can add the message text to the MESSAGE TEXT column and click the LONG TEXT button to add an additional explanation. Examples of a new message are shown in Figure 10.7 (SAP GUI) and Figure 10.8 (Eclipse).

Edit view

10 Error Handling

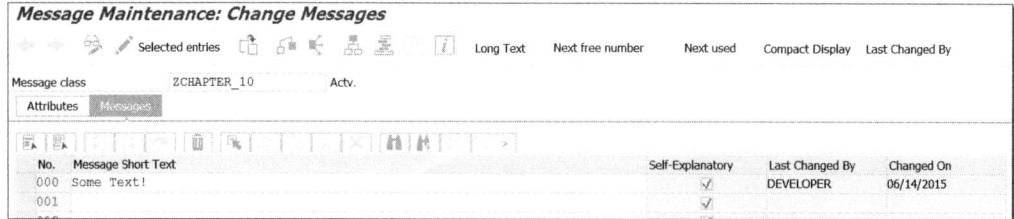

Figure 10.7 Changing Message Classs in SAP GUI

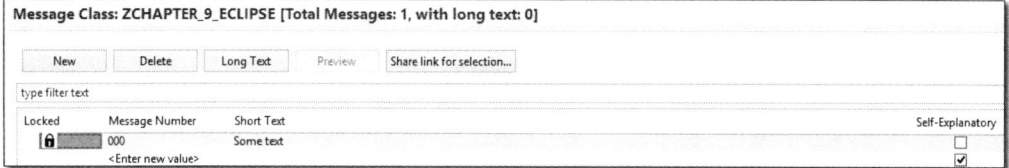

Figure 10.8 Changing Message Class in Eclipse

The message class needs to be saved and does not require activation to be used.

Using the MESSAGE Keyword

The MESSAGE keyword is used in classic ABAP programs, such as those you've used to execute programs so far in this book. You can use this keyword to display a success or error message back to the user. Web Dynpro and SAPUI5 programs may not use the MESSAGE keyword, but they can still display messages from a message class.

Syntax   The syntax for using the MESSAGE keyword is MESSAGE, followed by a message type (see Table 10.1), followed by the message number, and finally the message class in parenthesis (see Listing 10.3).

```
MESSAGE e000(ZCHAPTER_10).
```
Listing 10.3 MESSAGE Keyword

Message types

Message Type	Description
s	Success message
i	Information message

Table 10.1 Types of Messages

368

Message Type	Description
W	Warning
e	Error

Table 10.1 Types of Messages (Cont.)

A success message will be displayed with a bar at the bottom of the page, as shown in Figure 10.9, using the code in Listing 10.4.

Success message

```
MESSAGE s000(ZCHAPTER_10).
```
Listing 10.4 Success Message

Figure 10.9 Status Message Display

Double-click the message to display the long text in a popup. If there is no long text, the short description with the message class and number will be displayed, as in Figure 10.10.

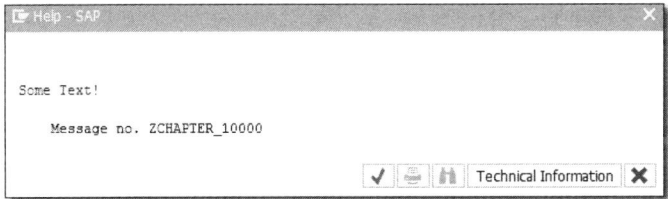

Figure 10.10 Message Long Text

An information message will be displayed as a popup with a checkmark button to continue and a question mark button to view the long text, as shown in Figure 10.11, using the code in Listing 10.5.

Information message

```
MESSAGE i000(ZCHAPTER_10).
```
Listing 10.5 Information Message

10 Error Handling

Figure 10.11 Information Message Popup

Error message An error message will be displayed at the bottom of the screen like a success message, but it will show a exclamation mark, as shown in Figure 10.12 using the code in Listing 10.6. Use the error message with caution, because it will stop the program from executing any additional code.

```
MESSAGE e000(ZCHAPTER_10).
```
Listing 10.6 Error Message

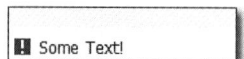

Figure 10.12 Error Message Diplay

Screen validation When used within the AT-SELECTION-SCREEN event, an error message can be used to validate the data being entered and only allow for valid entries. An example of this is shown in Listing 10.7, in which the program will stop executing and the user will never leave the selection screen if the error message is returned.

```
SELECTION-SCREEN BEGIN OF BLOCK selection.
    Parameters: p_param TYPE i.
SELECTION-SCREEN END OF BLOCK selection.

AT SELECTION-SCREEN.
    IF p_param = 0.
        MESSAGE e000(ZCHAPTER_10).
    ENDIF.
START-OF-SELECTION
WRITE: 'END'.
```
Listing 10.7 Error Message with Selection Screen

A warning message can only be used as part of the selection screen validation and will require the user to press [Enter] to continue. Listing 10.7 is updated to use a warning message in Listing 10.8 below.

```
SELECTION-SCREEN BEGIN OF BLOCK selection.
    Parameters: p_param TYPE i.
SELECTION-SCREEN END OF BLOCK selection.

AT SELECTION-SCREEN.
    IF p_param = 0.
        MESSAGE i000(ZCHAPTER_10).
    ENDIF.
START-OF-SELECTION
WRITE: 'END'.
```
Listing 10.8 Information Message with Selection Screen

The warning will be displayed at the bottom of the screen, as shown in Figure 10.13.

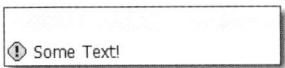

Figure 10.13 Warning Message Display

The warning can only be used as part of data validation, meaning that it must be placed after the AT-SELECTION-SCREEN event (as shown in Listing 10.7); otherwise, it will be treated as an error message and not a warning.

You can also use the WITH keyword to include your own text to be displayed as part of the message by replacing the & symbol in the message with your own text, as shown in Listing 10.9, which uses a message that only contains an & symbol as shown in Figure 10.14 using Eclipse and Figure 10.15 using the SAP GUI.

Using WITH

```
MESSAGE e001(ZCHAPTER_10) WITH 'An Error Occurred'(001).
```
Listing 10.9 Error Message Using WITH and a Text Symbol

Figure 10.14 Demonstrating Message Class with & in Eclipse

10 Error Handling

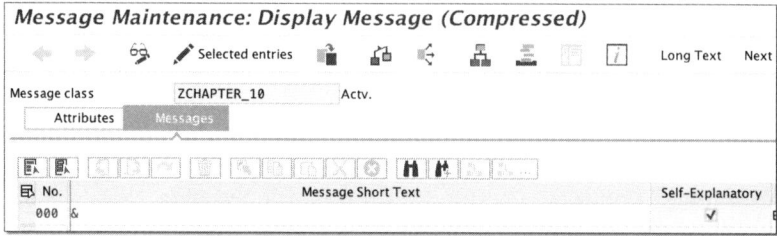

Figure 10.15 Demonstrating Message Class with & in the SAP GUI

Now that we have covered how to use the MESSAGE keyword to display messages to users and stop a running program, we will now cover exception classes.

Exception Classes

If you're new to the concept of exceptions, there are a few terms you may need to get used to: An exception is *thrown* or *raised* when it occurs, after which it can be *caught* or *handled*. After the exception is raised, it will stop executing code and start executing code within a CATCH statement, which can be in the current program or any parent calling program. Figure 10.16 illustrates how the execution of code moves from a program to a method and then back to the original program when an exception is thrown.

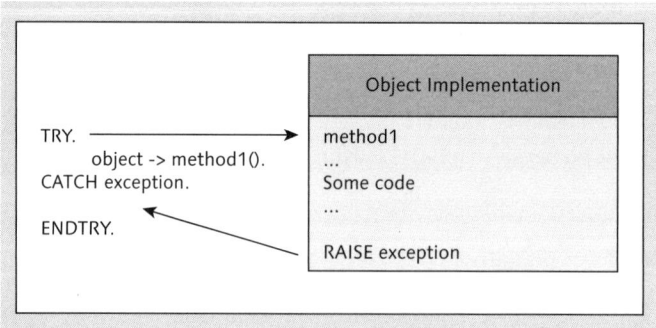

Figure 10.16 Calling and Catching an Exception

Exceptions in SAP work like exceptions in other programming languages. This section covers what happens when exceptions occur and are not handled, how to handle exceptions, and how to create your own custom exceptions.

Unhandled Exceptions

Exceptions can be handled using the `TRY` and `CATCH` statements, which will covered in the next section. However, when an exception goes unhandled, a *short dump* is created.

An example of an unhandled exception occurs if you run the code in Listing 10.10 and enter zero for the parameter. As a result, you'll get an unhandled exception for dividing by zero.

Unhandled exception example

```
SELECTION-SCREEN BEGIN OF BLOCK selection.
    PARAMETERS: p_para TYPE i.
SELECTION-SCREEN END OF BLOCK selection.
START-OF-SELECTION.
DATA: d_result TYPE i.

d_result = 10/p_param.

WRITE: d_result.
```
Listing 10.10 Code that Causes an Unhandled Exception

If users are accessing the system using SAP GUI, they'll see a short dump, like that shown in Figure 10.17. The short dump contains a lot of useful information for a developer, but it's not very user-friendly and looks like Microsoft's dreaded Blue Screen of Death.

Short dump examples

When using a Web Dynpro application, the short dump will be displayed to the user as a 500 SAP INTERNAL SERVER ERROR, as shown in Figure 10.18. The user will only see the 500 error, but the full short dump will be logged in the backend ABAP system.

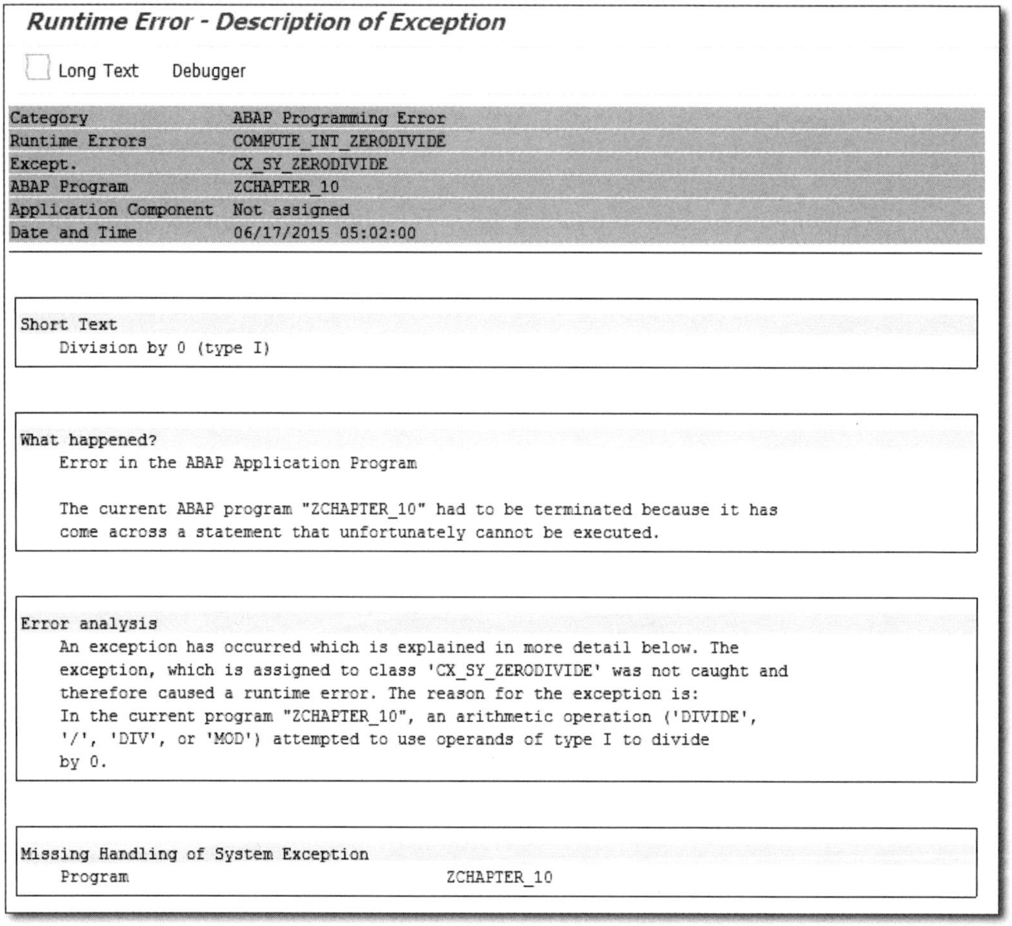

10 Error Handling

```
Runtime Error - Description of Exception

  Long Text    Debugger

Category              ABAP Programming Error
Runtime Errors        COMPUTE_INT_ZERODIVIDE
Except.               CX_SY_ZERODIVIDE
ABAP Program          ZCHAPTER_10
Application Component Not assigned
Date and Time         06/17/2015 05:02:00


Short Text
    Division by 0 (type I)


What happened?
    Error in the ABAP Application Program

    The current ABAP program "ZCHAPTER_10" had to be terminated because it has
    come across a statement that unfortunately cannot be executed.


Error analysis
    An exception has occurred which is explained in more detail below. The
    exception, which is assigned to class 'CX_SY_ZERODIVIDE' was not caught and
    therefore caused a runtime error. The reason for the exception is:
    In the current program "ZCHAPTER_10", an arithmetic operation ('DIVIDE',
    '/', 'DIV', or 'MOD') attempted to use operands of type I to divide
    by 0.


Missing Handling of System Exception
    Program                              ZCHAPTER_10
```

Figure 10.17 Short Dump in SAP GUI

500 SAP Internal Server Error

ERROR: Division by 0 (type I) (termination: RABAX_STATE)

Figure 10.18 500 SAP Internal Server Error

When using OData web services, the unhandled exception is turned in to a 500 error response, as shown in Figure 10.19, which can be handled in any way by the application using the service and will be logged in the backend ABAP system.

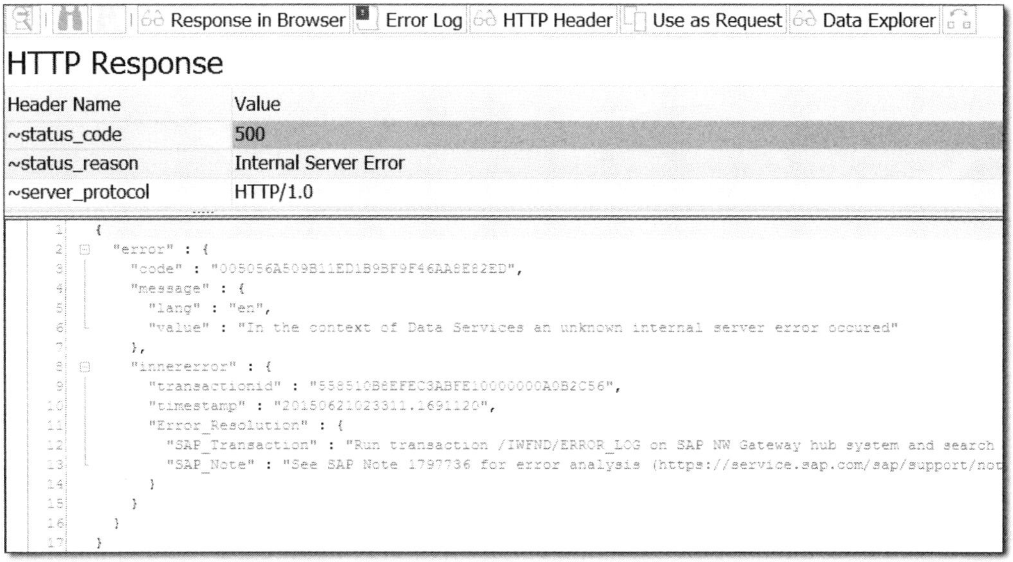

Figure 10.19 500 Error Response from OData Service

No matter which way the user was accessing the system, the short dump is logged and can be viewed by entering Transaction ST22. The selection screen is pictured in Figure 10.20, where you can see TODAY and YESTERDAY buttons, which will show all of the unhandled exceptions that occurred on the selected day. The OWN SELECTION section contains various selection options such as DATE and TIME, which can be used to search for a specific exception that occurred. Click the START button to search based on the entered selections. If a user reports that an error occurred, you can use these selections to find the exception, using the username for the user that reported the error and the day on which the user said the error occurred.

Short dump logs

The list of errors will be displayed as a list based on the selections you entered or the day that you selected (Figure 10.21). Double-click any exception to see more information about that exception.

10 Error Handling

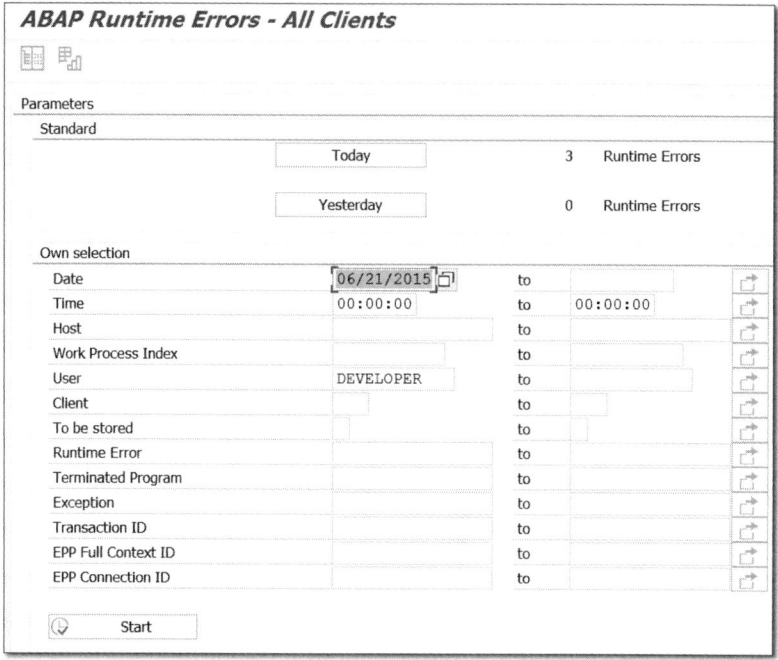

Figure 10.20 Transaction ST22 Selection Screen

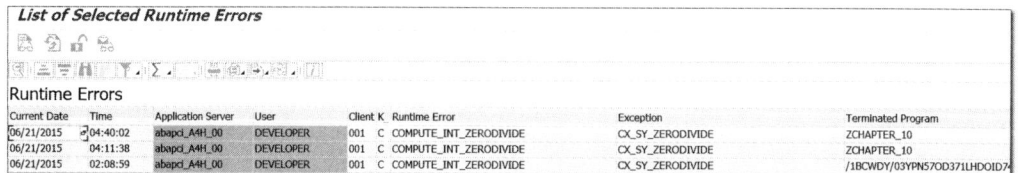

Figure 10.21 Result List of Unhandled Exceptions Selected from Transaction ST22

After opening one of the exceptions, you will be taken to a long text view of the exception, which will contain a lot of useful information. The following paragraphs go over a few of the items that are the most important to developers.

Basic information The top of the screen shows some basic information about the exception that occurred, such as the name of the program in which the exception occurred, the date and time that the exception occurred, and the type of exception. In the example in Figure 10.22, you can see that the ABAP program is ZCHAPTER_10, the exception type is CX_SY_

ZERODIVIDE, and the exception occurred on June 21, 2015, at 4:11 in the morning (system time).

```
Category              ABAP Programming Error
Runtime Errors        COMPUTE_INT_ZERODIVIDE
Except.               CX_SY_ZERODIVIDE
ABAP Program          ZCHAPTER_10
Application Component Not assigned
Date and Time         06/21/2015 04:11:38
```

Figure 10.22 Basic Information in Short Dump

There also is some additional information in the SHORT TEXT section to help you understand what the exception means. The short text shown in Figure 10.23 helps explain that the issue that occurred was caused by division by 0.

Short text

```
Short Text
    Division by 0 (type I)
```

Figure 10.23 Divide by Zero Short Dump Short Text

For a developer, the SOURCE CODE EXTRACT is usually the most useful element. The arrows boxed in Figure 10.24 show where the exception occurred; you can see that it occurred when performing a division calculation. You can double-click the source code extract to view the code in the source code editor.

Source Code Extract

```
Source Code Extract

Line   SourceCde

    1  REPORT zchapter_10.
    2
    3  SELECTION-SCREEN BEGIN OF BLOCK selection.
    4      parameters: p_param TYPE i.
    5
    6
    7  SELECTION-SCREEN END OF BLOCK selection.
    8
    9  START-OF-SELECTION.
   10
   11  data: d_result type i.
   12
>>>>>  d_result = 10 / p_param.
   14
   15  WRITE: d_result.
```

Figure 10.24 Short Dump Source Code Extract

377

10 Error Handling

Chosen variables

You can also see the values of the program's variables at the time the exception occurred in the CHOSEN VARIABLES section. In Figure 10.25, you can see that p_param was not assigned a value, and so it holds the initial value of zero; d_result was also never given a value, and so it also holds the value of zero.

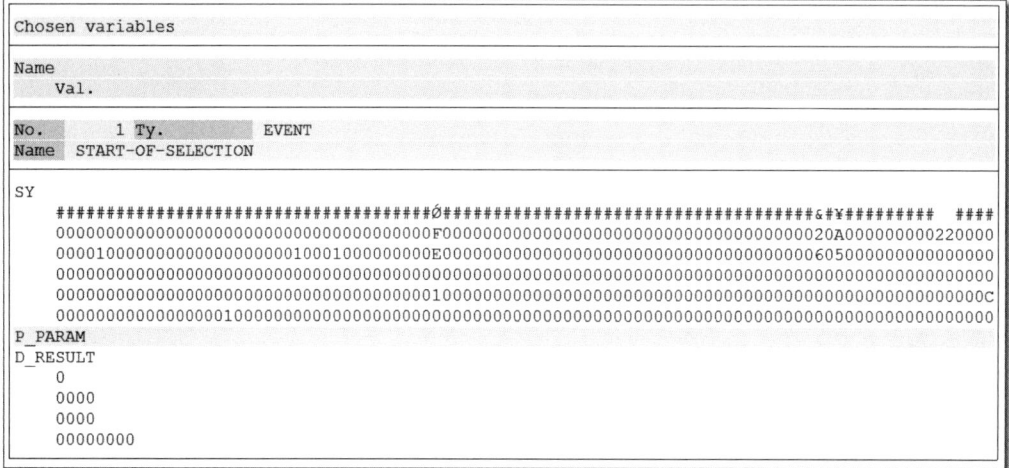

Figure 10.25 Short Dump Chosen Variables Section

Sometimes, these exceptions will occur not in your own code but in SAP standard ABAP code that may have been called when your program accessed a function module, method, or BAPI written by SAP. In this case, you can find more information or possibly a support note from SAP by entering the program where the exception occurred and the exception type in to the *http://support.sap.com* search.

TRY/CATCH Statements

Now that you understand what happens when exceptions go unhandled, I'll cover how to use TRY...CATCH statements to handle exceptions.

Syntax

The syntax for a TRY...CATCH statement is easy. Begin with the keyword TRY, followed by some code that could throw an exception. Next, add the keyword CATCH with an exception class that should be caught, followed by some code to execute if the specified exception occurs, and ending with the keyword ENDTRY. Listing 10.11 applies a TRY...CATCH statement to the program introduced in the last section so that if an exception of type `CX_SY_ZERODIVIDE` is thrown, the program will write CAUGHT! to the screen.

```
SELECTION-SCREEN BEGIN OF BLOCK selection.
    PARAMETERS: p_para TYPE i.
SELECTION-SCREEN END OF BLOCK selection.
START-OF-SELECTION.
DATA: d_result TYPE i.
TRY.
    d_result = 10/p_param.
CATCH cx_sy_zerodivide.
    WRITE: 'Caught!'.
ENDTRY.

WRITE: d_result.
```
Listing 10.11 Adding a TRY...CATCH Statement

 Catch All Exceptions

Listing 10.11 specifically catches the exception of type `CX_SY_ZERODIVIDE`, but you may want to catch all exceptions, no matter what the type is. To do so, catch the exception `CX_ROOT`, which is the super class for all other exceptions and thus will catch all exceptions that can occur.

You can access the exception that occurred using the `INTO` keyword to save the exception details into an object of the exception type that you're catching or a super class of that exception. You'll need to declare the object you're using with the `INTO` keyword. This will allow you to access additional attributes of the exception that occurred, as shown in Listing 10.12, which displays the short text of the exception in an error message.

Using INTO

```
SELECTION-SCREEN BEGIN OF BLOCK selection.
    PARAMETERS: p_param TYPE i.
SELECTION-SCREEN END OF BLOCK selection.
START-OF-SELECTION.
DATA: d_result TYPE I,
      o_exception TYPE REF TO cx_sy_zerodivide.
TRY.
    d_result = 10/p_param.
CATCH cx_sy_zerodivide INTO o_exception.
    MESSAGE e001(zchapter_10)
  WITH o_exception->get_text( ).
```

ENDTRY.

WRITE: d_result.

Listing 10.12 Extending the Divide by Zero Exception Example to Use the INTO Keyword

When using the `INTO` keyword, you don't need to use the `CREATE OBJECT` keyword, because the exception was already created when it was thrown; you're just copying it into a local object that you can access with your code.

Cleanup You also can add a `CLEANUP` code block, which can be used to roll back database changes or clear parameters used elsewhere in the program. You can also have this type of code in your `CATCH` code block, but if you have multiple `CATCH` statements for different types of exceptions, you can use the `CLEANUP` code block so that this type of code is only entered once. Listing 10.13 expands on the running example to include a `CATCH` statement for the `cx_root` exception and adds a `CLEANUP` code block that will be executed if either `CATCH` statement is executed.

```
SELECTION-SCREEN BEGIN OF BLOCK selection.
    PARAMETERS: p_param TYPE i.
SELECTION-SCREEN END OF BLOCK selection.
START-OF-SELECTION.
DATA: d_result TYPE I,
      o_exception TYPE REF TO cx_sy_zerodivide.
TRY.
    d_result = 10/p_param.
CATCH cx_sy_zerodivide INTO o_exception.
    MESSAGE e001(zchapter_10) WITH o_exception->get_text( ).
CATCH cx_root.
CLEANUP.
 WRITE: 'cleanup executed'(001).
ENDTRY.

WRITE: d_result.
```
Listing 10.13 Using the CLEANUP Code Block

Raise exception You can raise any standard or custom exception in your own code by using `RAISE EXCEPTION TYPE` followed by the exception class that you want to raise. Listing 10.14 shows an example of raising the system exception `cx_sy_zerodivide` using this syntax.

```
RAISE EXCEPTION TYPE cx_sy_zero_divide.
```
Listing 10.14 RAISE EXCEPTION Syntax

Exceptions can also be raised as *resumable*, meaning that after being caught within a program or method, the program can decide to continue the execution after the exception was thrown. To raise a resumable exception, the syntax `RAISE RESUMABLE EXCEPTION TYPE` must be used. The `CATCH` statement also must use `CATCH BEFORE UNWIND` in order to use the `RESUME` keyword, as shown in Listing 10.15, in which the program will output the text RESUMED even though the related WRITE statement occurs after an exception is raised.

Resumable exceptions

```
TRY.
    RAISE RESUMABLE EXCEPTION TYPE cx_sy_zerodivide.
    WRITE: 'resumed'.
CATCH BEFORE UNWIND cx_sy_zerodivide.
    RESUME.
ENDTRY.
```
Listing 10.15 Resumable Exception

Custom Exception Classes

You've seen existing exception classes, such as `CX_SY_ZERODIVIDE`, which is triggered by dividing a number by zero. You can also create your own custom exception classes. This section covers how to create custom exception classes and how to throw an exception using the `RAISE` keyword.

Before you create a new exception class, you need to determine the category of the exception. The options are `CX_STATIC_CHECK`, `CX_DYNAMIC_CHECK`, or `CX_NO_CHECK`. The exception categories are all exception classes themselves, so the exception class you create is assigned to one of these categories by using the appropriate category as the super class to your custom exception class.

Exception categories

With an exception that's a child of `CX_STATIC_CHECK` or `CX_DYAMIC_CHECK`, the exception must be declared in the method definition where it's raised using the `RAISING` keyword or must be handled within the method. If the `RAISING` keyword is used, the method that calls the method should catch the exception or use the RAISING keyword to pass the exception to its caller. If the exception is not listed as RAISING in the method definition or caught using a handler, the exception CX_SY_NO_HANDLER will be thrown. Listing 10.16 demonstrates using a raising exception in method1 and then catching the exception in method2.

```
CLASS zcl_global_class DEFINITION
  PUBLIC
  FINAL
  CREATE PUBLIC .
  PUBLIC SECTION.
    DATA d_i TYPE i .
    METHODS: method1
      IMPORTING
                !ip_parameter    TYPE i
      RETURNING
                VALUE(rp_value) TYPE i
      RAISING   zcx_exception,

      method2.

  PROTECTED SECTION.
  PRIVATE SECTION.
ENDCLASS.

CLASS zcl_global_class IMPLEMENTATION.
  METHOD method1.
    RAISE EXCEPTION TYPE zcx_exception.
  ENDMETHOD.
  METHOD method2.
    TRY.
        me->method1( 5 ).
      CATCH zcx_exception.
        "Handle exception
    ENDTRY.
  ENDMETHOD.
ENDCLASS.
```
Listing 10.16 Using RAISING

When using CX_STATIC_CHECK as the custom exception's super class, the compiler will return a warning if the exception is not handled by each method or passed to the calling method using the RAISING keyword in the definition. The CX_DYNAMIC_CHECK exception type will act in the same way, except that a compiler warning will not be issued.

> **Resumable Exceptions in Method Definition**
>
> When using resumable exceptions of type cx_static_check or cx_dynamic_check, they must be listed in the method differently than normal exceptions; that is, they must be defined as resumable exceptions. For example:
>
> METHOD method1 RAISING RESUMABLE(zcx_exception).
>
> Otherwise, the exception CX_SY_ILLEGAL_HANDLER will be raised when trying to resume the exception.

The third type of exception is CX_NO_CHECK, which cannot be passed using RAISING in any method definition but can still be handled using a TRY...CATCH block from either the method that throws the exception or a method that calls that method.

You typically use CX_NO_CHECK when the exception can occur almost anywhere. In general, this type of exception cannot be handled cleanly, so you're not concerned with warning the developer to include a check for the exception.

The CX_STATIC_CHECK exception type should be used when the exception should be handled by the method where it can occur or by a method calling the method where it occurs. The compiler warning for these types of exceptions will help to ensure that the exception is handled cleanly.

The CX_DYNAMIC_CHECK type of exception should be used when the exception can be avoided by checking a precondition—for example, checking if the denominator in a division method is zero before using it to divide a number. You may want this type of exception to go unhandled because the code being used should have handled the precondition and should be updated.

Once you've decided on the category of your exception, you can create the exception class as a global or local class that inherits from the class that you decided to use as your category. When creating a global class, you still need to prefix the name of the class with z, and to indicate that it's an exception class, you should use zcx instead of zcl. Listing 10.17 creates a new exception class called zcx_custom_exception by creating a new class with the super class cx_static_check.

```abap
CLASS zcx_custom_exception DEFINITION
  PUBLIC
  INHERITING FROM cx_static_check
  FINAL
  CREATE PUBLIC .

  PUBLIC SECTION.
    INTERFACES if_t100_message .
    METHODS constructor
      IMPORTING
        !textid   LIKE if_t100_message=>t100key OPTIONAL
        !previous LIKE previous OPTIONAL .
  PROTECTED SECTION.
  PRIVATE SECTION.
ENDCLASS.

CLASS zcx_custom_exception IMPLEMENTATION.
  METHOD constructor.
    CALL METHOD super->constructor
      EXPORTING
        previous = previous.
    CLEAR me->textid.
    IF textid IS INITIAL.
      if_t100_message~t100key =
        if_t100_message=>default_textid.
    ELSE.
      if_t100_message~t100key = textid.
    ENDIF.
  ENDMETHOD.
ENDCLASS.
```
Listing 10.17 Creating Custom Exception Class

If you want additional custom attributes stored in your exception, you can add them to the new exception class here. You can also use the exception created in Listing 10.17 just as shown. Listing 10.18 adds an additional attribute called custom_data, which is a string, and then sets that value in the constructor.

```abap
CLASS zcx_custom_exception DEFINITION
  PUBLIC
  INHERITING FROM cx_static_check
  FINAL
  CREATE PUBLIC .

  PUBLIC SECTION.
    DATA: custom_data TYPE string.
    INTERFACES if_t100_message .
```

```abap
    METHODS constructor
      IMPORTING
        !textid        LIKE if_t100_
message=>t100key OPTIONAL
        !previous      LIKE previous OPTIONAL
        ip_custom_data TYPE string.
  PROTECTED SECTION.
  PRIVATE SECTION.
ENDCLASS.

CLASS zcx_custom_exception IMPLEMENTATION.
  METHOD constructor.
    CALL METHOD super->constructor
      EXPORTING
        previous = previous.
    CLEAR me->textid.
    IF textid IS INITIAL.
      if_t100_message~t100key =
        if_t100_message=>default_textid.
    ELSE.
      if_t100_message~t100key = textid.
    ENDIF.
    me->custom_data = ip_custom_data.
  ENDMETHOD.
ENDCLASS.
```
Listing 10.18 Adding CUSTOM_DATA Attribute to Custom Exception Class

Now, you can set the custom data value when raising the exception and then retrieve the value when you catch the exception, as shown in Listing 10.19.

```abap
DATA: o_custom_exception TYPE ref to zcx_custom_exception,
      d_string TYPE string.
TRY.
    d_string = |More Information|.
    "Do Something
    RAISE EXCEPTION TYPE zcx_custom_exception
      EXPORTING ip_custom_data = d_string.

    CATCH zcx_custom_exception INTO o_custom_exception.
      WRITE: o_custom_exception->custom_data.
ENDTRY.
```
Listing 10.19 Setting and Retriving an Attribute from Custom Exception Class

It's important to use exceptions that make sense for the error that occurred; you shouldn't reuse exceptions created for other, unrelated purposes. This means that you even can create an exception that just inherits from an exception class but is given a name that is descriptive for its purpose in your application.

We have now covered error handling using MESSAGE and class based exceptions. Next, we will cover some obsolete error handling techniques.

Obsolete Exceptions

When possible, we should use the class based exceptions introduced in the last section. However, there are still many function modules that use non-class based exceptions, so we should know how they work to be familiar with them.

Non-Class-Based Exceptions

Existing function modules will typically use non-class-based exceptions, but a class-based exception can still be thrown from inside a function module. A particular function module can only use either class-based or non-class-based exceptions, not both. This section covers how to raise and handle non-class-based exceptions, which must be handled by the calling program or method and will not bubble up past the calling program or method.

Type of exceptions used

When using the SAP GUI to maintain function modules, you'll see a EXCEPTN CLASSES checkbox in the EXCEPTIONS tab that will indicate whether you are using class-based or non-class-based exceptions. Figure 10.26 highlights the exception classes checkbox, which is unchecked, indicating non-class-based exceptions. Because the exception in Figure 10.26 is non-class-based, it can have any name, and there is no corresponding class.

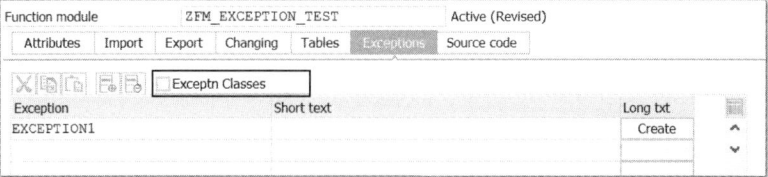

Figure 10.26 Using Non-Class-Based Exception

When using ABAP in Eclipse, you can define non-class-based exceptions using the keyword EXCEPTIONS in the function module parameter signature, as shown in Listing 10.20.

```
FUNCTION ZFM_EXCEPTION_TEST
  IMPORTING
    VALUE(IP_STRING) TYPE STRING
  EXPORTING
    EP_STRING TYPE STRING
  EXCEPTIONS
    EXCEPTION1.
```
Listing 10.20 Defining Non-Class-Based Exceptions in Eclipse

For non-class-based exceptions, use the keyword RAISE without the addition of EXCEPTION TYPE, as shown in Listing 10.21, which can be entered in the SOURCE CODE tab when using SAP GUI or after the parameter definition when using Eclipse.

Raising exceptions

```
RAISE EXCEPTION1.
```
Listing 10.21 Using RAISE with Non-Class-Based Exception

When calling a function module that uses non-class-based exceptions, you need to declare the exceptions when you call the function module and assign a numeric value to the exceptions that can occur, as shown in Listing 10.22. This will set the value of the system variable sy-subrc to the value of the exception that occurred or to 0 if no exception occurred. You should always include handling for the OTHERS exception in case a new exception is added at a later point.

```
DATA: d_string TYPE string VALUE 'string'.

CALL FUNCTION 'ZFM_EXCEPTION_TEST'
  EXPORTING
    ip_string = d_string
  IMPORTING
    ep_string = d_string
  EXCEPTIONS
    exception1 = 1
    OTHERS     = 2.
```
Listing 10.22 Calling a Function That Uses Non-Class-Based Exceptions

To handle the exception that occurred, check the value of the system variable sy-subrc after calling the function module. You can catch all

Handling exceptions

10 Error Handling

exceptions by checking if the value of sy-subrc is not zero, or you can add specific error handling per possible exception, as shown in Listing 10.23.

```
DATA: d_string TYPE string VALUE 'string'.

CALL FUNCTION 'ZFM_EXCEPTION_TEST'
  EXPORTING
    ip_string  = d_string
  IMPORTING
    ep_string  = d_string
  EXCEPTIONS
    exception1 = 1
    OTHERS     = 2.
IF sy-subrc = 1.
  "exception exception1 was raised
ELSEIF sy-subrc = 2.
  "Another exception was raised
ENDIF.
```
Listing 10.23 Adding Exception Handling to Function Call

Preferred method for exceptions

The preferred method for exceptions and exception handling in function modules is to use class-based exceptions, the same exception classes covered earlier in the chapter. In the function module, ensure that the EXCEPTN CLASSES checkbox (highlighted in Figure 10.26) is checked, and you can add existing global exception classes to the selections on the EXCEPTIONS tab, as shown in Figure 10.27.

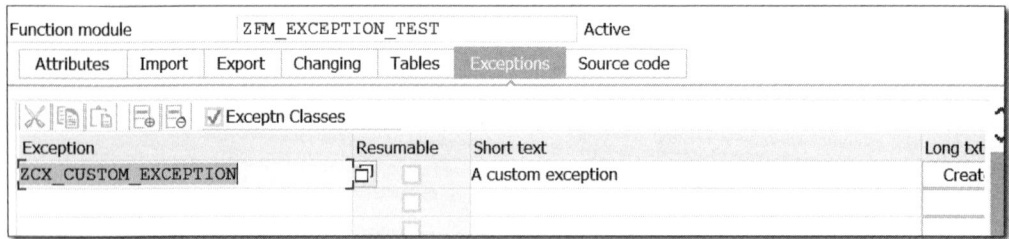

Figure 10.27 Adding Exception Classes to Function Module Definition

Then, raise and catch the class-based exceptions using the same code covered earlier in the chapter. Just like we can't declare exceptions derived from the CX_NO_CHECK type in a class method, you also can't declare those exceptions in the function module definition; however, you can still raise them in the code.

In the next section, we will apply some of the techniques covered in this chapter to the shopping cart example.

Updating the Shopping Cart Example

Now that we have covered some additional methods for error handling in ABAP, we can now update the shopping cart example to use some of these techniques.

First, we will create an exception class that we can raise when errors occur in our class `zcl_shopping_cart`. The new class will inherit from the super class `cx_static_check` so that the calling method or program must be updated handle the exception. The new class `ZCX_SHOPPING_CART` is shown below in Listing 10.24. The code displayed is the default code added when creating a class with `cx_static_check` as its superclass.

Custom exception class

```
CLASS zcx_shopping_cart DEFINITION
  PUBLIC
  INHERITING FROM cx_static_check
  FINAL
  CREATE PUBLIC .
  PUBLIC SECTION.
    INTERFACES if_t100_message .
    METHODS constructor
      IMPORTING
        !textid   LIKE if_t100_message=>t100key OPTIONAL
        !previous LIKE previous OPTIONAL .
  PROTECTED SECTION.
  PRIVATE SECTION.
ENDCLASS.

CLASS zcx_shopping_cart IMPLEMENTATION.
  METHOD constructor.
    CALL METHOD super->constructor
      EXPORTING
        previous = previous.
    CLEAR me->textid.
    IF textid IS INITIAL.
      if_t100_message~t100key =
        if_t100_message=>default_textid.
    ELSE.
      if_t100_message~t100key = textid.
    ENDIF.
```

10 Error Handling

```
    ENDMETHOD.
ENDCLASS.
```
Listing 10.24 Custom Exception Class zcx_shopping_cart

We can now press the ACTIVATE button to activate the class zcx_shopping_cart.

Constructor changes Next, we will update the constructor method to raise the exception zcx_shopping_cart if the provided customer does not exist. To do this, we need to update the constructor method definition to add a RAISING parameter as shown in Listing 10.25 below.

```
METHODS:
    constructor IMPORTING ip_customer TYPE scustom-id
                RAISING zcx_shoppping_cart,
```
Listing 10.25 Updating the Constructor Method Definition

Next, we will update the constructor method to SELECT the provided ID from the table SCUSTOM to determine if the provided customer exists. In Listing 10.26, we use sy-subrc to determine if a result was found and raise the exception zcx_shopping_cart if it was not.

```
METHOD constructor.
"new Open SQL
    SELECT SINGLE id
    INTO @d_customer
    FROM scustomer
    WHERE id = @ip_customer.
    IF sy-subrc <> 0.
        RAISE EXCEPTION TYPE zcx_shoppping_cart.
    ENDIF.

"old Open SQL
    SELECT SINGLE id
    INTO d_customer
    FROM scustomer
    WHERE id = ip_customer.
    IF sy-subrc <> 0.
        RAISE EXCEPTION TYPE zcx_shoppping_cart.
    ENDIF.
ENDMETHOD.
```
Listing 10.26 Updated Constructor Method Using Error Handling

Next, press the ACTIVATE button to activate the updated class.

Now, we need to update the ABAP program `zcart_maint` to handle this new exception. To do this, we moved the `o_cart` declaration to an `INITIALIZATION` section, so that we can use o_cart in both `AT SELECTION-SCREEN` and `START-OF-SELECTION`. Next, we moved the `CREATE OBJECT` call to the `AT SELECTION-SCREEN` section and added a `TRY/CATCH` block around it to catch the `zcx_shopping_cart` exception. We then added an error message to display that a customer was not found as shown in Listing 10.27 below.

Zcart_maint changes

```
...
SELECTION-SCREEN END OF BLOCK action.
INITIALIZATION.
    DATA: o_cart TYPE REF TO zcl_shopping_cart.

AT SELECTION-SCREEN.
    TRY.
        CREATE OBJECT o_cart EXPORTING ip_customer = p_cust.
    CATCH zcx_shopping_cart.
        MESSAGE e000(38) WITH 'Customer not found'(006).
    ENDTRY.
START-OF-SELECTION.
    IF p_view = abap_true.
...
```

Listing 10.27 Updating zcart_maint to Handle the New Exception

We can now press the ACTIVATE button to activate the program. If we test the program, we will see that the message in Figure 10.28 will be shown if we try to use the program with a bad customer number (such as 99999).

> ❗ Customer not found

Figure 10.28 Customer Not Found Error Message

We have now successfully updated the shopping cart example to use class based exceptions. For more exercises, think of other areas in the shopping cart solution that could use additional error handling.

Summary

Errors can occur in a program for any number of reasons. What's important is how you handle those errors, especially ones that can be corrected by the user. Including proper error handling will make users feel better about the system and will give them the opportunity to resolve errors on their own instead of calling on the developer or support team.

This chapter covered various ways to handle errors, including message classes that are used to let users know what error occurred and possibly how to resolve the error on their own. You also explored the MESSAGE keyword, which is used in classic Web Dynpro screens to display error, warning, success, and informational messages to users.

The chapter also covered class-based exceptions, which allow you to handle errors that occur in a modern way. Using TRY and CATCH statements, you can catch and handle problematic situations, no matter where in the call stack the exception occurred.

We also learned about the obsolete exception format of non-class-based exceptions, which are still regularly used in many function modules in ABAP systems. We covered how to declare and handle these types of exceptions.

Finally, we updated the constructor method of the shopping cart example that began in Chapter 7 to raise a custom exception class when incorrect data is passed to the constructor method.

We have now completed the entire book! In the next appendices, we will cover how to set up a development system and provide some additional resources that can help you continue your ABAP learning career.

Appendices

A **Preparing your Development Environment** 395

B **Modern UI Technologies** 431

C **Other Resources** 439

D **The Author** 443

A   Preparing your Development Environment

This appendix will cover both how to set up a trial system using SAP's cloud application library and how to set up a development environment for connecting to an on-premise ABAP system. This process is fairly easy, and you can find lots of help online through the forums at *http://scn.sap.com*.

This appendix will also cover some basics of ABAP in Eclipse as well as some of the Integrated Development Environments (IDEs) built in to the ABAP system. I recommend that you use ABAP in Eclipse, but the contents of this book support either solution.

A.1   Setting Up a Cloud Trial System

The thought of having a trial or development ABAP system is something fairly new to the SAP world. Many people within SAP worked very hard to make this a possibility, and with the integration with cloud hosting providers, it's easier now than ever before to set up a system and start writing ABAP code on a trial system.

A trial system does not contain a full SAP ERP or SAP CRM solution; it only includes the base ABAP system. Therefore, you can write your own programs and create database tables, but you can't access the many modules that are part of a full SAP ERP solution. For an additional cost, you can activate an IDES solution, which contains a full standard SAP ERP solution with test data.

Even if you already have access to an ABAP system, you may want to consider setting up a trial system to experiment with some of the new language features in an ABAP 7.4 SP8 system or newer if your system is not yet on the latest version of the ABAP stack.

The steps and screenshots in this section are current as of the time of writing in 2015; since they're using cloud systems, the steps may change slightly over time. If you get stuck, try the forums at *http://scn.sap.com*.

Using the SAP Cloud Appliance Library (CAL), you can deploy an SAP trial system to a virtual machine hosted by either Amazon Web Services (AWS) or Microsoft Azure. You'll need to create an account for either before starting:

> Amazon Web Services signup: *http://aws.amazon.com*
> Microsoft Azure signup: *http://azure.microsoft.com*

 Cloud Costs

Although SAP doesn't charge for the trial system software, the cloud providers charge for hosting the server.

Pricing will change depending on the hosting service; SAP CAL will provide an estimate of what the cost will be when setting up the system.

I'll provide some tips later in this section for how to control costs when hosting an ABAP trial system in the cloud.

If you don't already have an SAP ID (S-user), you can register for one at *http://cal.sap.com*. Click on LOGIN, and then click the REGISTER button to register a new account.

Once you have an account with one of the supported cloud hosting providers, you'll need to provide some information required to connect SAP CAL to your cloud hosting account.

A.1.1 Preparing an AWS Environment

The following steps will walk you through how to prepare an Amazon Web Services (AWS) environment.

AWS users will need to provide an *access key* and *secret key* in order for SAP CAL to access your system. The following steps will allow you to find this information:

1. Log on to your AWS account at *http://aws.amazon.com*.

    Select SERVICES • ADMINISTRATION & SECURITY • IAM, as highlighted in Figure A.1.

Setting Up a Cloud Trial System

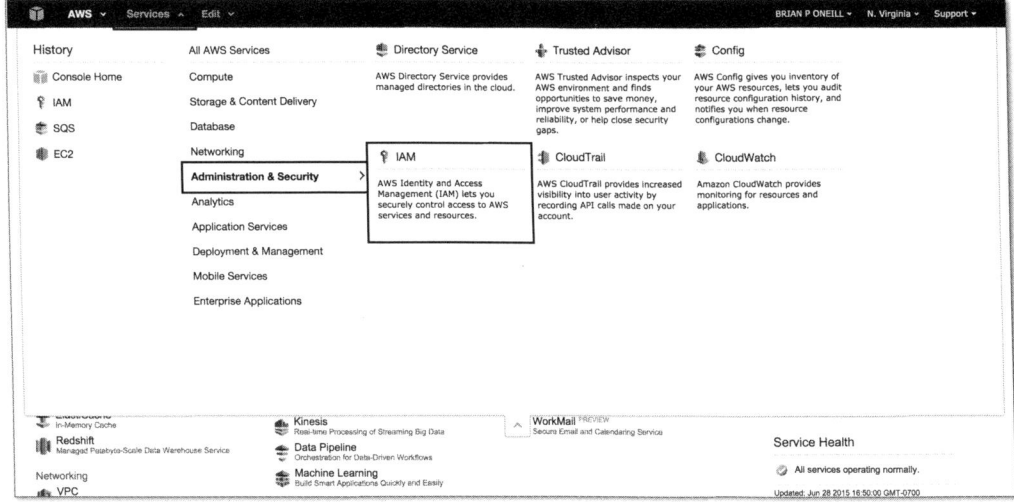

Figure A.1 Entering AWS Identity and Access Management (IAM)

2. Select USERS from the navigation area on the left side of the screen.
3. Click the CREATE NEW USERS button, as shown in Figure A.2.

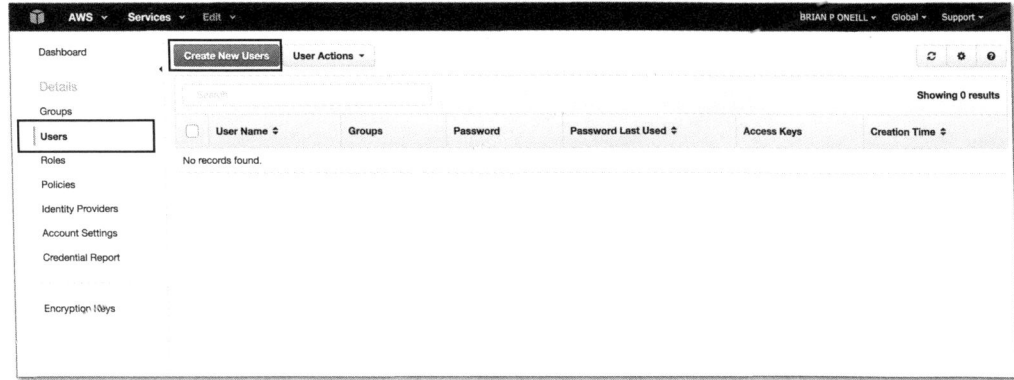

Figure A.2 Creating New Users in AWS

4. Enter the username "SAP_CAL_USER", and leave the checkbox for GENERATE AN ACCESS KEY FOR EACH USER selected.
5. Click CREATE, as shown in Figure A.3.

397

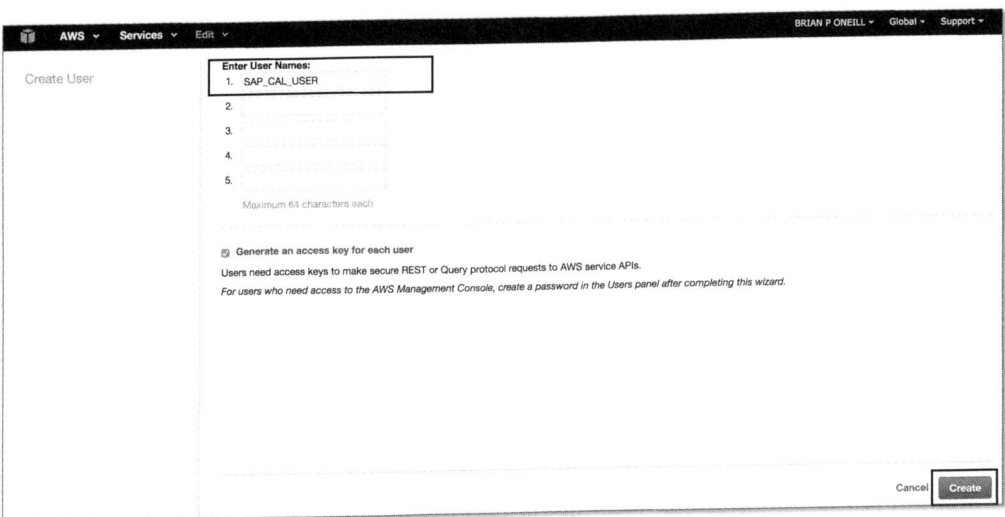

Figure A.3 Creating SAP_CAL_USER in AWS

6. Click DOWNLOAD to store the access key ID and secret access key in a .csv file, as shown in Figure A.4. You'll use this information later to give SAP CAL access to AWS.

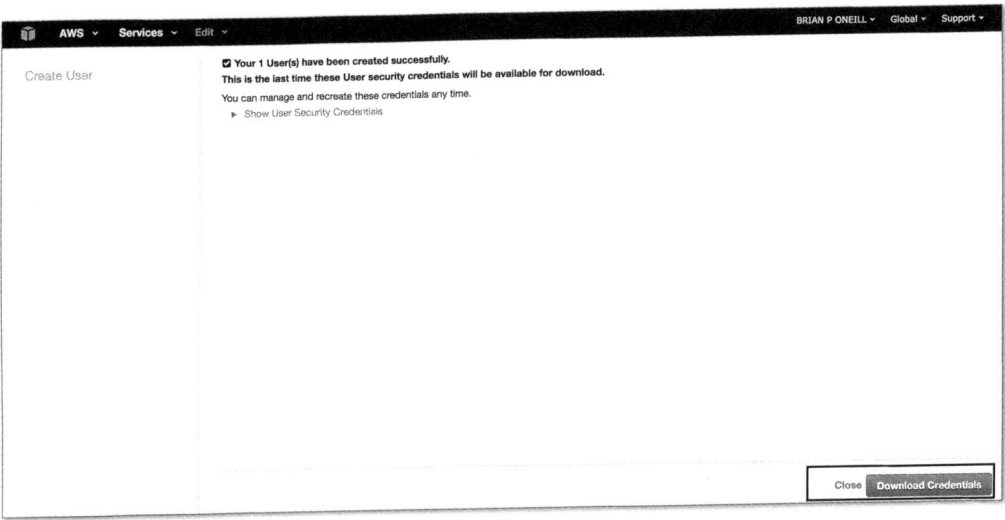

Figure A.4 Downloading Credentials for New User in AWS

7. Click CLOSE to return to the USERS page.
8. Select GROUPS from the navigation area on the left side of the screen.
9. Select the CREATE NEW GROUP button, as shown in Figure A.5.

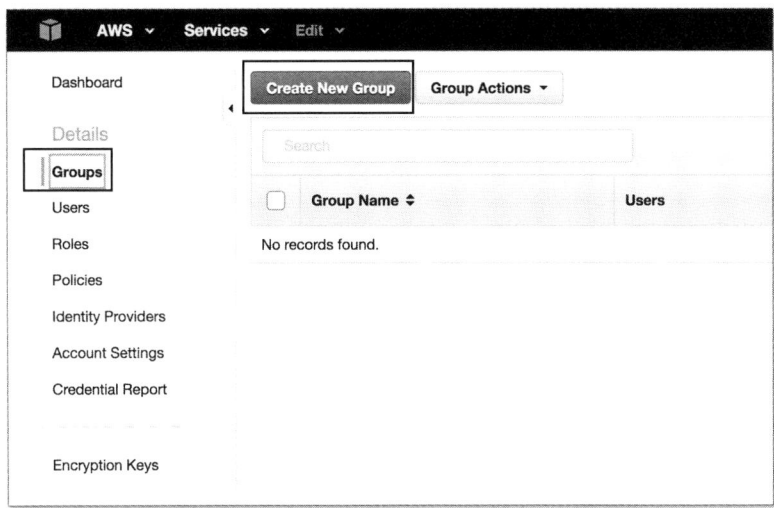

Figure A.5 Creating New Group in AWS

10. Set the group name to "sap_cal_group" and click the NEXT STEP button.
11. Select the checkbox next to the policy for ADMINISTRATORACCESS and click the NEXT STEP button, as shown in Figure A.6.
12. On the review screen, click the CREATE GROUP button to create the group.
13. Now, select your new group and then select GROUP ACTIONS • ADD USERS TO GROUP, as shown in Figure A.7.

Preparing your Development Environment

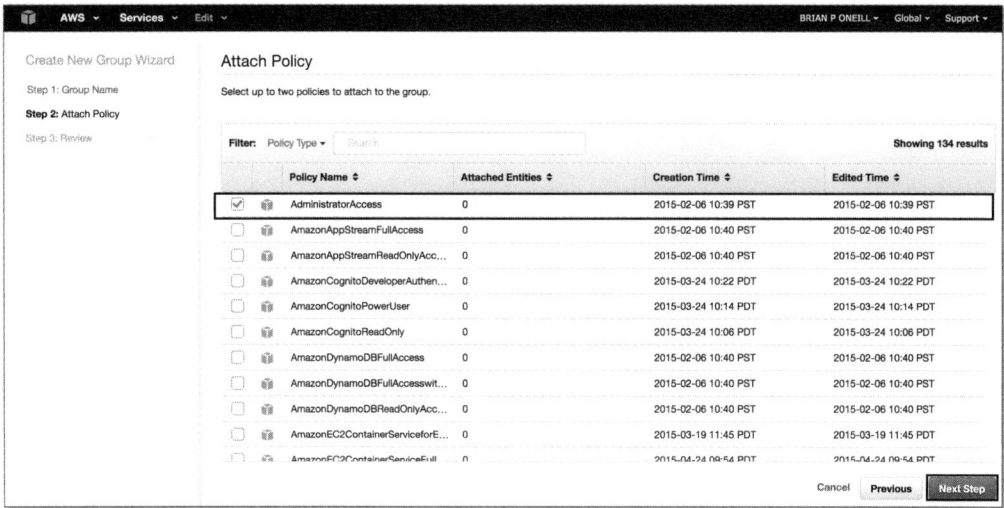

Figure A.6 Attaching the Adminstrator Access Policy to New Group

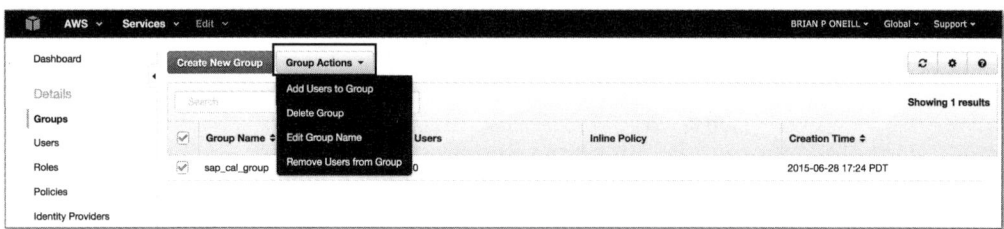

Figure A.7 Adding Users to New Group in AWS

14. Select the checkbox for the SAP_CAL_USER and click the ADD USERS button.
15. Log on to your SAP CAL environment at *http://cal.sap.com*.
16. Select the ACCOUNTS tab and click the CREATE ACCOUNT link, as shown in Figure A.8.

Figure A.8 Creating New Account in SAP CAL

17. Give the account a relevant name, such as "AWS_Cloud", and a relevant description if necessary, then click the NEXT button.

18. Select AMAZON WEB SERVICES from the CLOUD PROVIDER dropdown, enter the ACCESS KEY and SECRET KEY for the user you created earlier, and then click the NEXT button, as shown in Figure A.9.

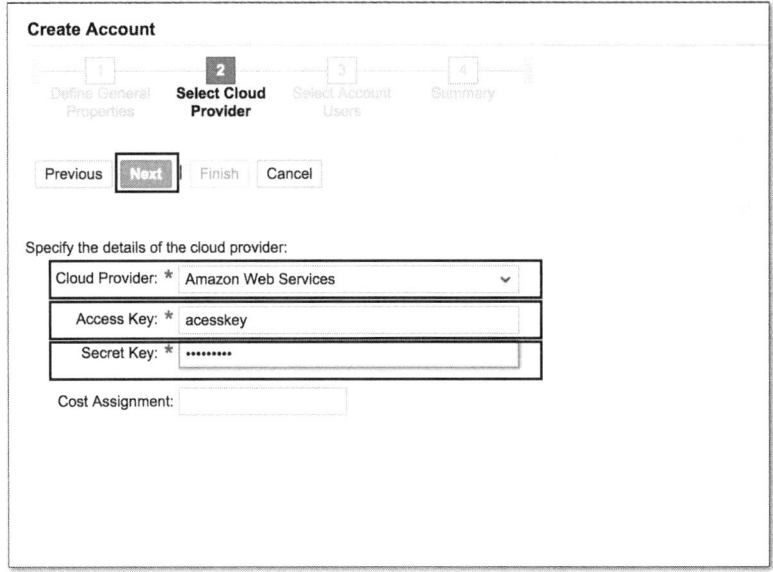

Figure A.9 Adding AWS Cloud Provider Account

19. Add any additional users other than yourself that should be able to use this account, or click NEXT if you are the only user for this account.

20. Click the FINISH button on the SUMMARY screen.

You can now connect to your AWS environment from SAP CAL, allowing SAP CAL to create, terminate, start, and stop virtual machines in your AWS environment.

A.1.2 Preparing an Azure Environment

The next section will cover how to set up an environment using Microsoft's Azure platform.

Preparing your Development Environment

1. Go to *http://azure.microsoft.com* and click the MY ACCOUNT link at the top of the page, as shown in Figure A.10.

Figure A.10 Selecting My Account Information for Azure

2. Click the option to view USAGE AND BILLING, as shown in Figure A.11.

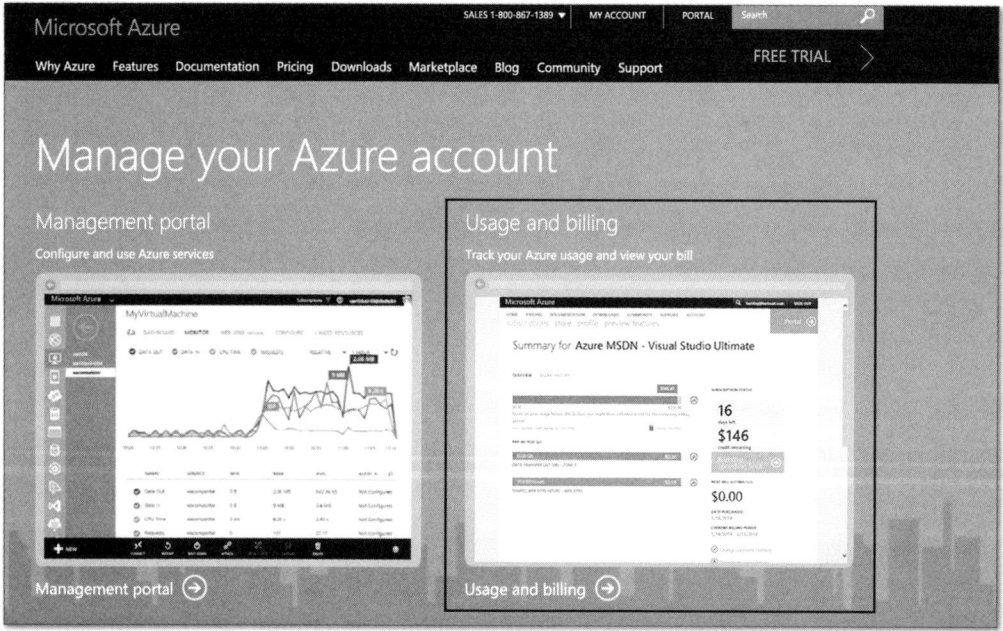

Figure A.11 Selecting Usage and Billing Information for Azure

3. Log in using your Azure account credentials.
4. Select an existing subscription that you want to host your ABAP system on, or choose to add a new subscription.

5. In the bottom right of the screen, you will see a subscription ID, as shown in Figure A.12. Write that number down; you'll need it to set up SAP CAL access.

Figure A.12 Azure Subscription ID

6. Go to *http://cal.sap.com* and log in using your SAP ID credentials.
7. Click on the ACCOUNTS tab and click the CREATE ACCOUNT link, as shown in Figure A.13.

Figure A.13 Adding Accounts in SAP CAL

8. Give the account a relevant name, such as "Azure_Cloud", and a relevant description if necessary, then click the NEXT button.
9. Select MICROSOFT AZURE from the CLOUD PROVIDER dropdown, enter the relevant SUBSCRIPTION ID, and click the NEXT button, as shown in Figure A.14.

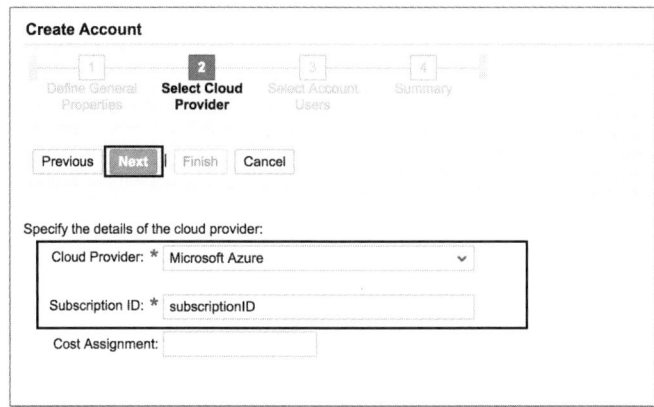

Figure A.14 Adding an Azure Account in SAP CAL

10. On the next screen, you can add any additional users that have access to your SAP CAL, or just click NEXT if you are the only user that will have access to this account.

11. Click FINISH in the SUMMARY section to continue to the next step.

12. You will see a popup to download a management certificate. Select the checkbox and click the DOWNLOAD button, as shown in Figure A.15.

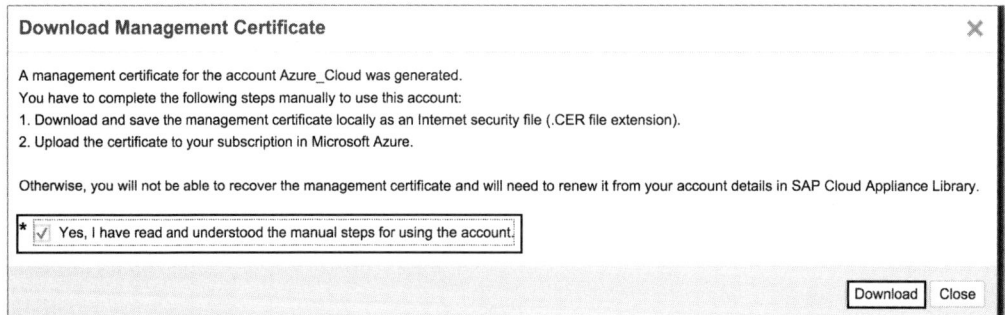

Figure A.15 Download Management Certificate

13. Log on to your azure account at *http://manage.windowsazure.com*.

14. Select SUBSCRIPTIONS • MANAGE SUBSCRIPTIONS/DIRECTORY, as shown in Figure A.16.

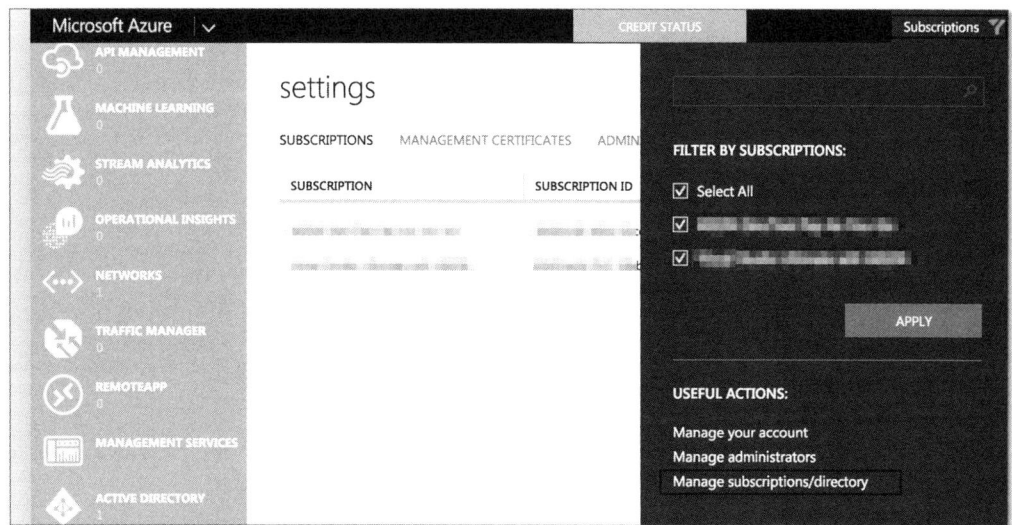

Figure A.16 Subscription Settings from Azure Portal

15. Select the MANAGEMENT CERTIFICATES tab and click the UPLOAD button, as shown in Figure A.17.

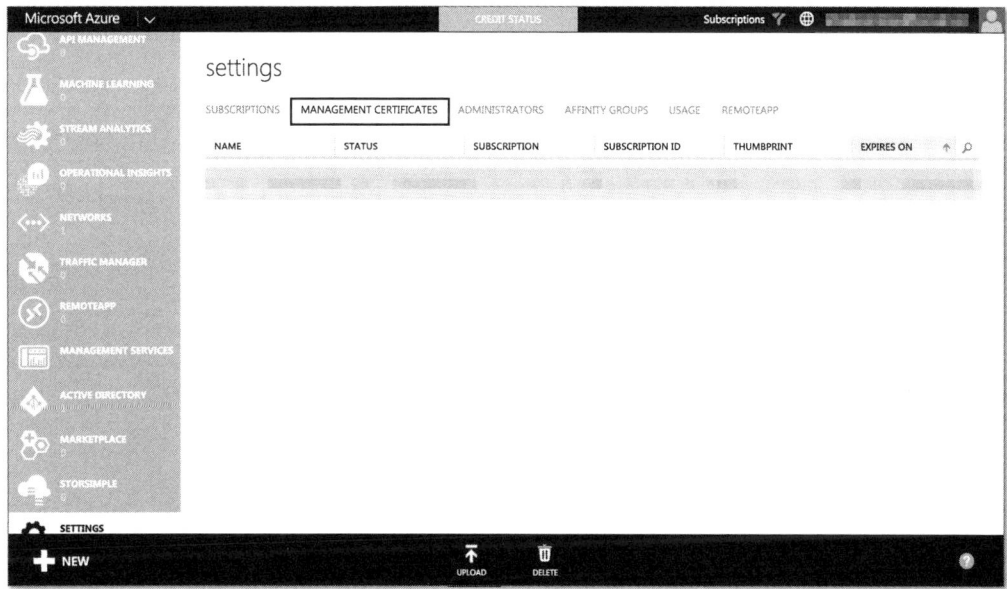

Figure A.17 Azure Portal Management Certificates Settings

Preparing your Development Environment

16. In the UPLOAD A MANAGEMENT CERTIFICATE popup, select the management certificate downloaded from SAP CAL, then select the corresponding subscription from the SUBSCRIPTION dropdown, as shown in Figure A.18.

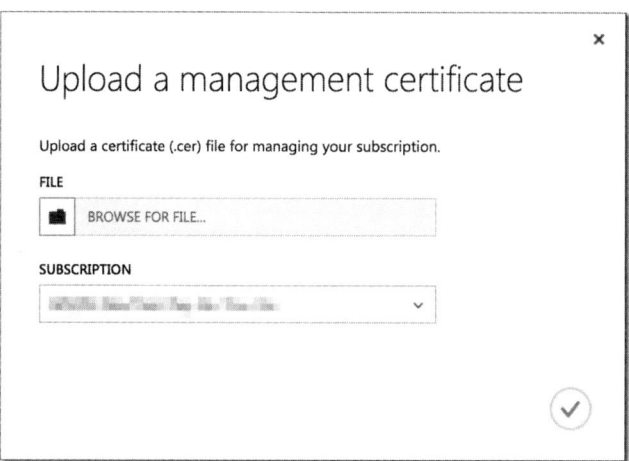

Figure A.18 Upload Management Certificate Popup

17. Back in SAP CAL, click on the account that you created, and select the CLOUD PROVIDER tab in the popup.
18. Select the TEST CONNECTION button under the MANAGEMENT CERTIFICATE section to ensure that the account is set up correctly, as shown in Figure A.19.

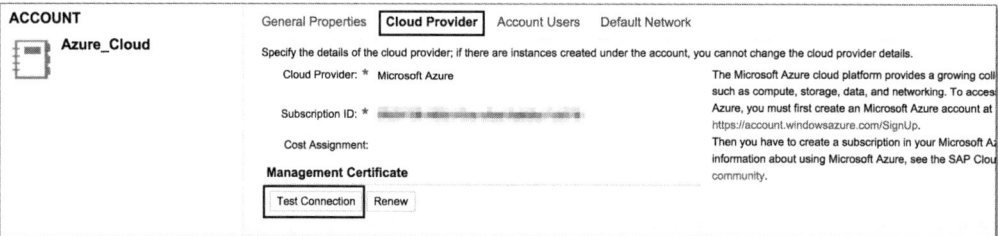

Figure A.19 Account Cloud Provider Settings

If you receive a successful message, your Azure/SAP CAL account is now set up.

You can now connect to your Azure account from SAP CAL, and SAP CAL has permission to create, terminate, activate, and suspend virtual machines in your Azure cloud environment.

A.1.3 Creating a New Cloud-Hosted Instance

Now that you have a connection to your cloud provider set up, you can create an instance of the ABAP trial system to be hosted on the cloud provider. The following steps will create a new instance of an ABAP trial system:

1. Log in to the SAP CAL at *http://cal.sap.com*.

2. Select the SOLUTIONS tab, and click the TRY NOW link corresponding to the system that you want to create, as shown in Figure A.20. I recommend activating any SAP NetWeaver 7.4 SP 08 or higher developer edition system. All systems with a lock icon in the STATUS column require additional licenses to be activated, and all systems with a green circle are available to be activated.

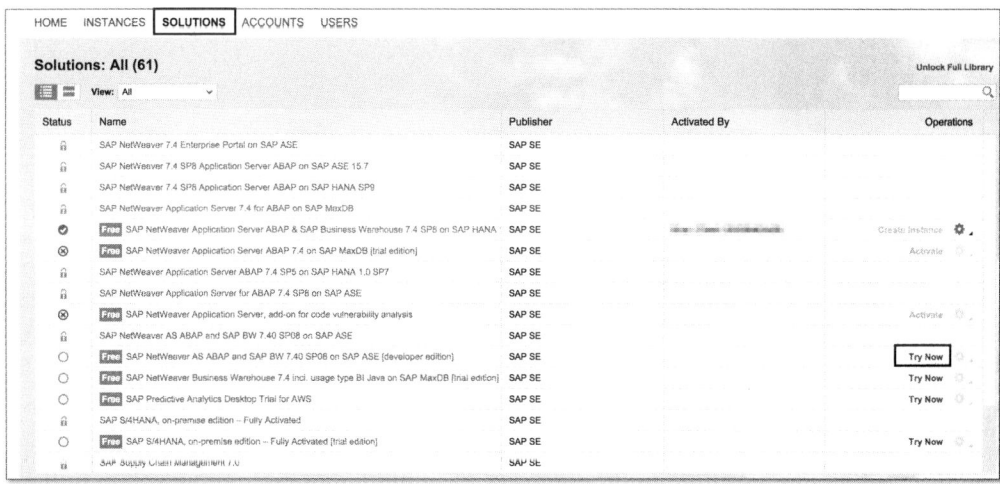

Figure A.20 Activating an SAP CAL Solution

3. Scroll to the bottom of the TERMS AND CONDITIONS page presented, and click the I ACCEPT button to accept the terms.

4. In place of the TRY NOW link, you will see an ACTIVATE link; click it. You may not be able to activate certain solutions that are not available for all cloud providers.

5. Once activated, you will see a CREATE INSTANCE link; click it.

6. A popup will appear to create the instance. This popup shows the estimated cost per hour and code over 30 days. Enter a name, relevant description, and account provider. You can also choose whether to use the default network for your cloud provider or a private network already set up within your cloud provider. You can choose to use a static IP address, but doing so will result in additional costs. An example is shown in Figure A.21. Once completed, click the NEXT button.

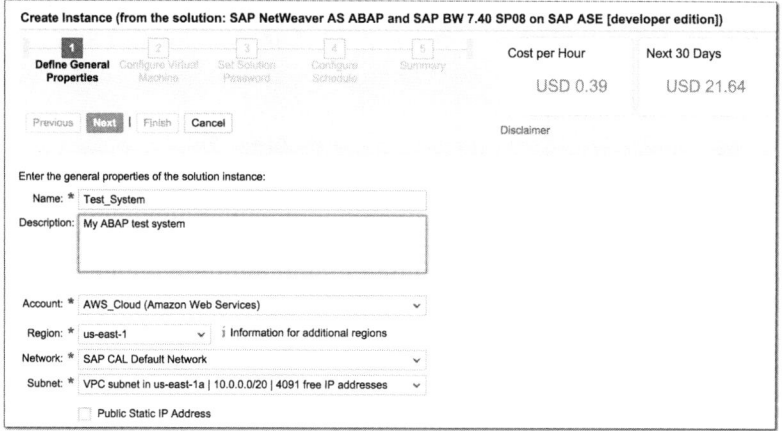

Figure A.21 Create Instance Popup

7. On the next screen, you can configure your virtual machine(s). We recommend leaving the options set to their defaults. Changes that affect price, such as virtual machine size, will update the cost estimates in the top right of the screen, as shown in Figure A.22. For advanced users, you can look up required ports to open in the ACCESS POINTS section to connect without using a frontend server. Click the NEXT button when you're ready to continue.

8. The solution password will be used to log into the virtual machine frontend and to log into the ABAP system itself. Enter a valid password in the provided textbox, and click the NEXT button to continue.

Setting Up a Cloud Trial System

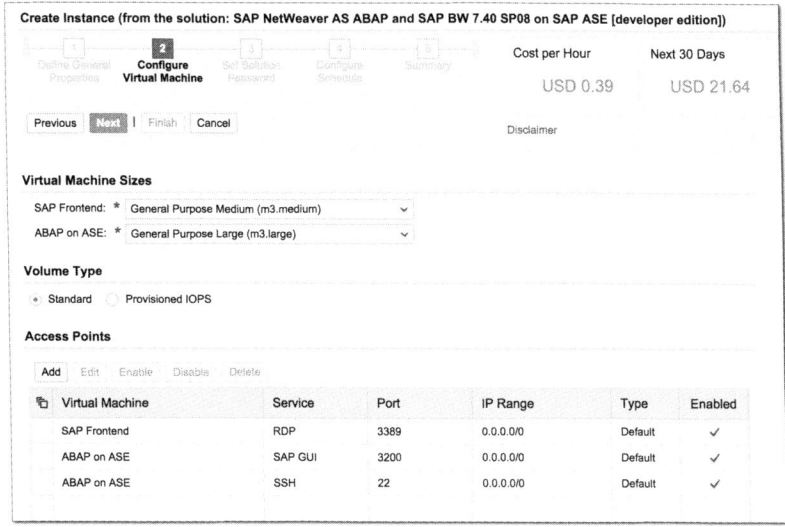

Figure A.22 Configure Virtual Machine Options

9. In the CONFIGURE SCHEDULE section, you can choose to have the system active until a specified point in time, to have it automatically turn on and off on a schedule, or to manually activate and suspend the solution. The estimated cost will update accordingly. We recommend choosing MANUALLY ACTIVATE AND SUSPEND, and only turn it on when you need it and off when you're done if you're using the system for learning purposes. The 30-day cost estimate assumes that the system will be on for the full 30 days. An example of this setting is shown in Figure A.23. Once you've made your selection, click the NEXT button.

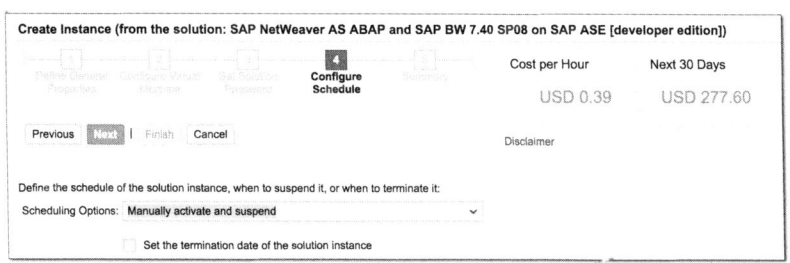

Figure A.23 Configuring the Schedule for New Instance

A Preparing your Development Environment

10. You'll see a summary of the chosen setup, as shown in Figure A.24; click the FINISH button to create the instance.

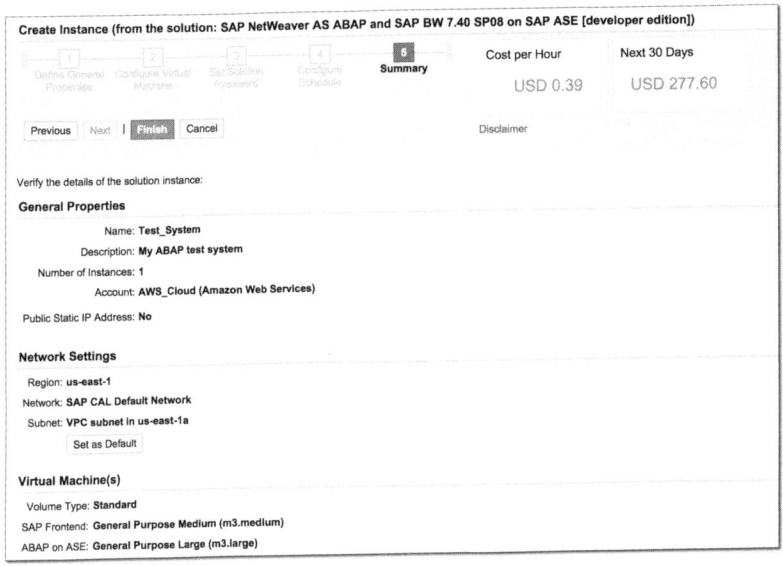

Figure A.24 Create Instance Summary

You'll now be brought to the INSTANCE screen while the new instance is set up. The process to create the new instance can take at least an hour to complete.

From the INSTANCES tab, you can choose to ACTIVATE or SUSPEND your solution at any time. For learning and testing ABAP, we recommend only keeping the system active when needed. When activating the system, you'll be prompted to activate it for a limited time, as shown in Figure A.25; always enter some number of hours so that you don't accidentally leave the system running while you're being charged. You can suspend the system before that time or extend it to last longer if needed.

Once the system is activated, you can change the date and time for when it will automatically be suspended by selecting your instance from the INSTANCES tab and then selecting SCHEDULE CONFIGURATION in the popup. Then, click the EDIT button and change the suspend date and time as you prefer.

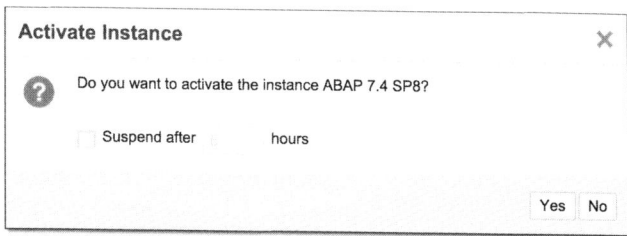

Figure A.25 Activate Instance Popup

You can also activate and suspend your system by clicking on the ACTIVATE or SUSPEND link in the INSTANCES tab.

A.1.4 Connecting to the Instance Frontend

Your trial system will typically have both a frontend instance and a server instance. The frontend instance will have all of the software required for you to access the system already installed.

You can connect to your frontend instance via a Remote Desktop connection, which will already be installed if you're on Windows, or you can download Microsoft Remote Desktop from the Mac app store if you're on a Mac.

Ensure that you have a remote desktop tool installed, and then follow these steps to log in:

1. Login to *http://cal.sap.com*.
2. Select the INSTANCES tab.
3. Click on the instance that you want to connect to and copy the FRONTEND EXTERNAL IP ADDRESS, as highlighted in Figure A.26.
4. Enter the frontend external IP address in your remote desktop product of choice and connect to the server.
5. Login using the username "Administrator" and the master password that you set when creating the instance.

Preparing your Development Environment

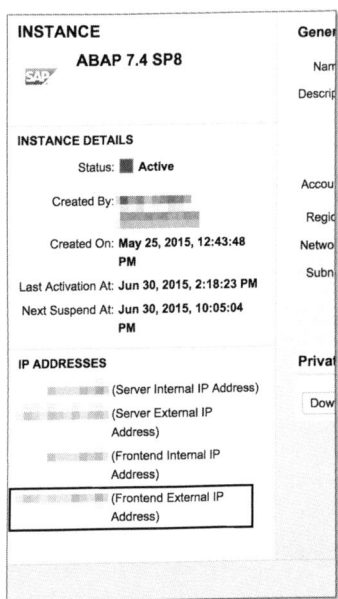

Figure A.26 Getting the Frontend External IP from SAP CAL

You'll now see the SAP Logon application, which is typically referred to as SAP GUI, and SAP Dev Tools for Eclipse, also referred to as ABAP in Eclipse, as shown in Figure A.27.

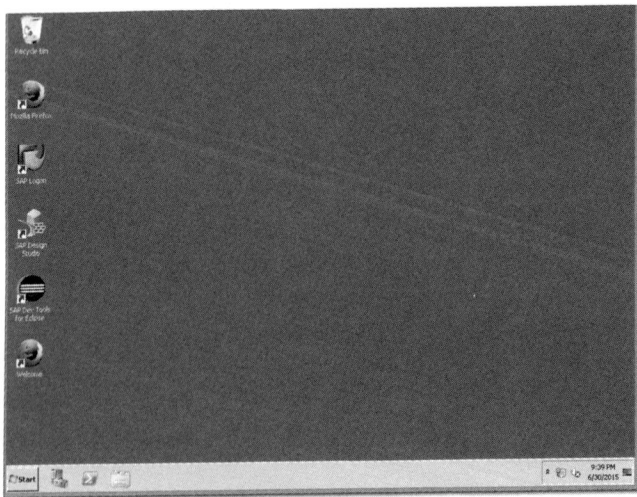

Figure A.27 Example Frontend Server

When using SAP GUI or Eclipse, you can use the user ID DEVELOPER with the password that you set up as your master password to log on to client 001 on your system.

A.1.5 Updating the License

Before you can start developing on your ABAP system, you need to install a 90 day MiniSAP license. The following steps will cover how to get and set your 90 day MiniSAP license:

1. Log in to your SAP system in client 000 using SAP GUI with the username SAP* and your master password, as shown in Figure A.28.

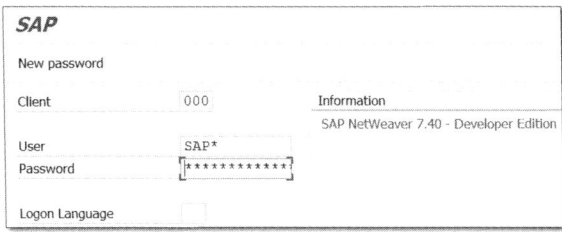

Figure A.28 Logging On Using SAP GUI

2. Enter Transaction SLICENSE by entering the transaction name in the textbox in the top left of the screen and either pressing [Enter] or clicking the checkmark.
3. Copy the ACTIVE HARDWARE KEY shown in the top left of the screen.
4. Go to the URL *http://www.sap.com/minisap*.
5. Fill out the requested information; make sure you select the system ID for the system instance that you created and enter the hardware key that you obtained from your system.
6. You will receive the license key in an email.
7. Back in Transaction SLICENSE, select EDIT • INSTALL LICENSE.
8. You will be prompted to upload a file. Upload the license file you received in an email from SAP.

Following these steps, you can log out.

After your license expires, you will need to delete your instance, create a new one, and request a license for the new system.

A.1.6 Connecting Using Your Own System

You can also choose to connect to your trial system using software installed locally on your machine. This will allow you to save money from your cloud provider by shutting down the provided frontend instance. Before connecting using your own system, log on to the frontend system and ensure that you are able to log on to the trial system from there.

First, you must open up access to various ports on the server so that you can access the SAP system from your own computer. To do so, log on to *http://cal.sap.com*.

Then, follow these steps to open the required ports:

1. Click on the INSTANCES tab.
2. Click on the system name that you want to open.
3. Select the VIRTUAL MACHINE tab from the popup.
4. Click the EDIT button.
5. Click the Add button.
6. Set the SERVICE dropdown and PORT textbox, as listed in Table A.7.
7. Click the Add button.
8. Repeat steps 1 to 7 for all ports listed in Table A.7.

Protocol	Port	Description
Custom TCP	3200	SAP dispatcher
Custom TCP	3601	Message server
HTTP	50000	HTTP
HTTPS	50001	HTTPS

Table A.7 Ports to Open on Server to Connect from Your Computer

You may need to suspend and activate your instance before the change can take effect.

Follow the steps in the next section if you need to install ABAP in Eclipse to access the system.

Once you've confirmed that you can access your system from your computer, you can shut down the frontend server by logging on to your cloud provider and shutting down the virtual machine labeled frontend. You will need to do this every time that you activate your ABAP instance.

A.2 Setting Up ABAP in Eclipse for an Existing System

ABAP in Eclipse is the new IDE for writing ABAP code. This section will cover the steps to install Eclipse on your local machine. You will need an ABAP 7.31 or higher system in order to use Eclipse.

First, you need to install SAP GUI. You can find a download link for the latest version at *http://scn.sap.com/docs/DOC-25456*. You'll need a SAP Service Marketplace account to download SAP GUI.

Next, you'll need to download Eclipse from *http://www.eclipse.org/downloads/packages/release/Luna/SR2*. It's important that you download the Luna release of Eclipse, because as of the time of writing, ABAP tools are not available in the latest release of Eclipse (Mars).

The package you select isn't important, because you'll be installing the ABAP add-in. Eclipse IDE for Java EE Developers or Eclipse IDE for Java Developers will work fine.

Once downloaded, there is no install process for Eclipse. Eclipse is contained in the downloaded ZIP file and just needs to be extracted somewhere, such as the root of the C drive. You can then execute Eclipse by running the Eclipse executable file.

If Eclipse does not run, you may need to install the Java Runtime Environment (JRE) from *http://java.com*.

To install the ABAP tools, open Eclipse, select HELP • INSTALL NEW SOFTWARE..., and then click the ADD... button in the popup.

You'll then see an ADD REPOSITORY popup. Here, you can add any name, such as "SAP Eclipse Tools"; the location should be *https://tools.hana.ondemand.com/luna*, as shown in Figure A.29.

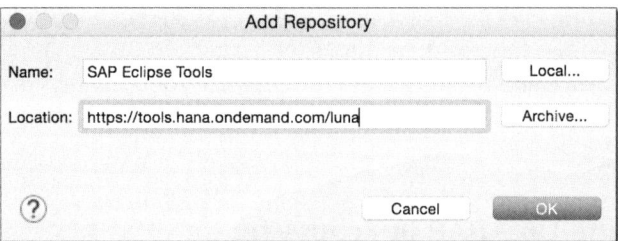

Figure A.29 Eclipse Add Repository Popup

You'll then see a selection of tools from SAP available in Eclipse, as shown in Figure A.30. Select the checkbox for ABAP DEVELOPMENT TOOLS FOR SAP NETWEAVER and then choose any additional items that you may need.

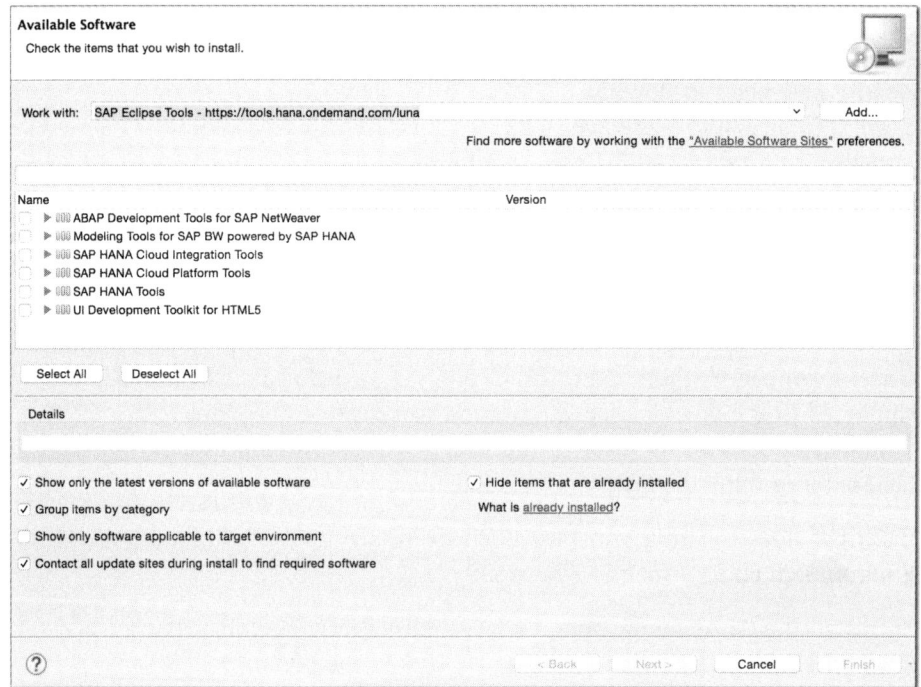

Figure A.30 Installing SAP Tools in Eclipse

To continue, click the NEXT > button, accept the relevant terms in the next screen, and click FINISH.

During the install process, you will likely see the error shown in Figure A.31. This message is not an issue; just click OK to finish the installation.

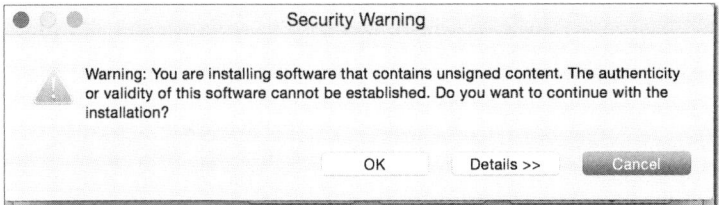

Figure A.31 Security Warning during ABAP in Eclipse Installation

Once completed, you'll be prompted to restart Eclipse. Click YES.

A.3 Getting Started with ABAP in Eclipse

This section will cover the basics of using the Eclipse IDE for anyone new to Eclipse. Eclipse's initial release was in 2001, and new versions of the IDE are released in an alphabetical order. The latest version of Eclipse currently supported by SAP's Eclipse development tools is Luna. As of this writing, the latest release of Eclipse is Mars, and the next release after that will be a name beginning with a N.

Although Eclipse is probably most popular with Java programmers, it can be used with a variety of languages, such as ABAP, C, C++, JavaScript, Ruby, and more. Eclipse is a versatile IDE because of its use of plug-ins, such as the SAP-provided plug-ins that we discussed how to install in the previous section. Just as SAP released plug-ins for working with ABAP and SAPUI5, anybody can release additional plug-ins to help with the development of ABAP programs.

A.3.1 Eclipse Workspaces

When you first start Eclipse, you'll be prompted to select a workspace in a popup window like the one shown in Figure A.32.

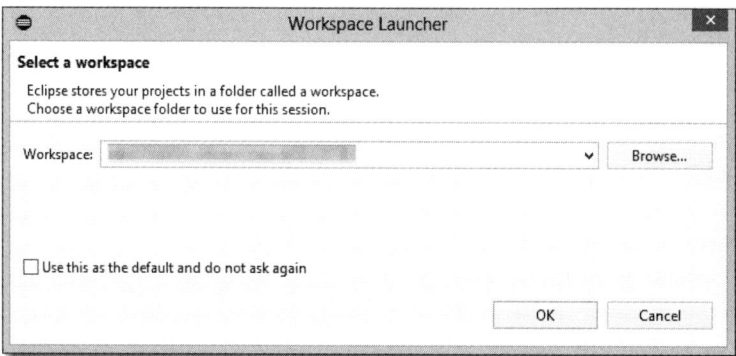

Figure A.32 Select Eclipse Workspace

An Eclipse workspace is a collection of metadata about your Eclipse setup, such as a list of projects, perspectives, and settings. For most people, it's easiest to use one workspace and set it as the default by using the checkbox shown in Figure A.32. Also, ABAP projects are created per system, so you may only have one project for the development system that you typically work on.

A situation in which you might use multiple workspaces is if you have a collection of work that you're doing as part of a work project and a collection of work that you're doing as part of a hobby project. By switching workspaces, you can see only the projects and perspectives related to what you're currently working on.

A.3.2 Eclipse Perspectives

Perspectives in Eclipse are a collection of views and additional settings that may be shown or hidden depending on the selected perspective. For the purposes of this book, we use either the ABAP perspective or the debug perspective.

Within Eclipse, there are multiple perspectives, which you can change by selecting WINDOW • OPEN PERSPECTIVE and selecting a perspective of your choice or choosing OTHER... to select a nonlisted perspective. You can also change your perspective by selecting a new option from the top-right side of the screen (see Figure A.33).

Getting Started with ABAP in Eclipse

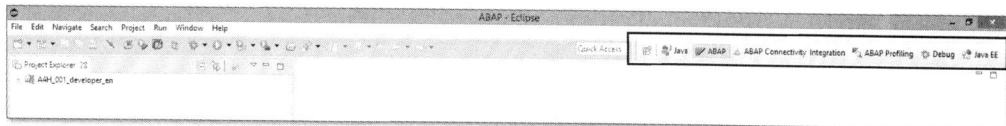

Figure A.33 Perspective Options in Eclipse

The ABAP perspective includes various views, such as the FEATURE EXPLORER window on the right side of the screen, which is a quick tutorial covering some features of ABAP in Eclipse. There's also a PROBLEMS window on the bottom of the screen that will list syntax warnings or errors when you're writing ABAP code. In addition, there's a useful TRANSPORT ORGANIZER window that can be used to view and release any transports that need to be sent to other systems.

Each Eclipse view can be maximized, minimized, dragged to another location in Eclipse, dragged out of Eclipse, or even closed. Figure A.34 shows the default ABAP perspective, and Figure A.35 demonstrates some of the changes you can make to Eclipse views.

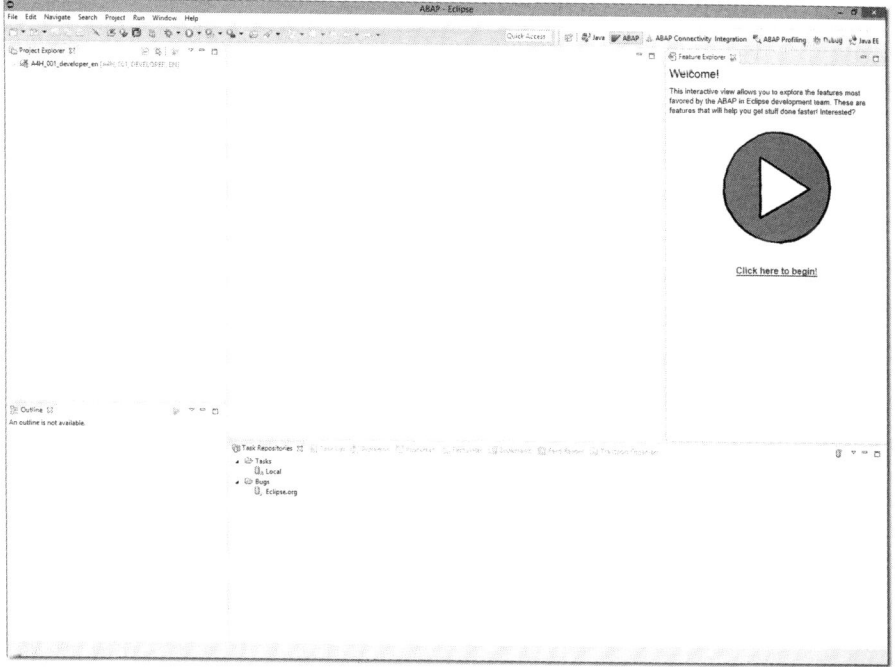

Figure A.34 ABAP Perspective Default

419

A Preparing your Development Environment

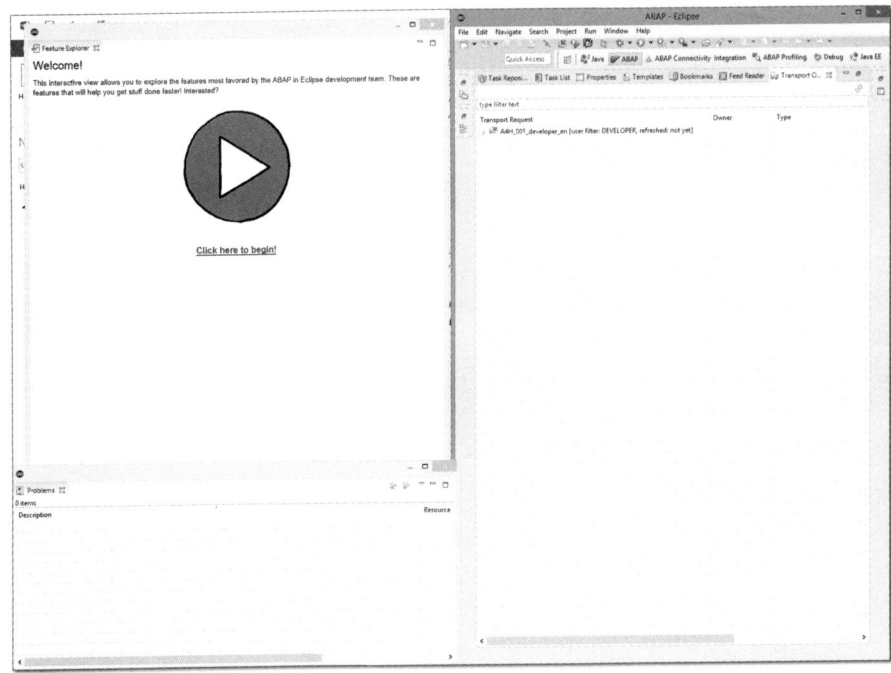

Figure A.35 Modified ABAP Perspective

You can add a view by selecting WINDOW • SHOW VIEW and then selecting a view of your choice. The full list of views is under the OTHER... option.

You can always revert back to the original layout of the perspective by selecting WINDOW • RESET PERSPECTIVE... or by right-clicking the perspective in the top-right of your screen and choosing RESET. This will hide, show, and resize all of your changed views.

You can also make changes to the views in your perspective and then save your changes in a new perspective. To do so, make your changes, select WINDOW • SAVE PERSPECTIVE AS..., and enter a new name for your perspective in the NAME textbox, such as "myABAP" (see Figure A.36).

Creating your own perspective will allow you to make changes to the views in the perspective and then reset to your preferred default instead of to the standard default.

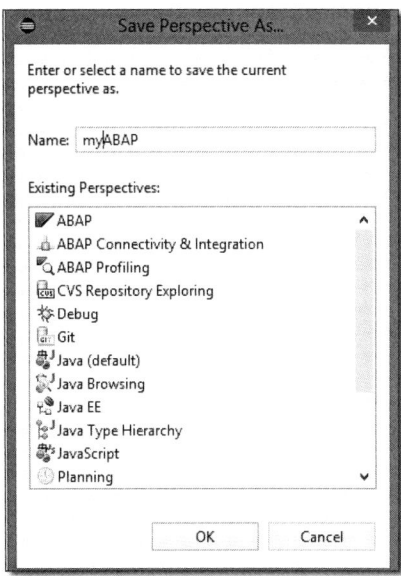

Figure A.36 Creating New Eclipse Perspective

A.3.3 ABAP Projects in Eclipse

To add an ABAP project in Eclipse, you should be in the ABAP perspective (or a copy of that perspective). Select FILE • NEW • ABAP PROJECT. You can then click the BROWSE... button to select a system defined in your SAP GUI and click NEXT. You will need to enter the client and credentials required to connect to the system and click FINISH.

If you're unable to connect to an ABAP system using Eclipse, it's possible that the system has not yet been prepared to use Eclipse. For advanced users, you can find backend configuration steps at *http://help.sap.com/download/netweaver/adt/SAP_ADT_Configuration_Guide_Backend_en.pdf*. Your system also must be an ABAP 7.31 or higher system.

After creating a new ABAP project, you'll see the system listed in the Project Explorer, which can be expanded to show the different packages within the system and expanded further to show the ABAP programs and objects within that package (Figure A.37). Double-click any object to edit it in the workbench view, and right-click any package listed under SYSTEM LIBRARY and select ADD TO FAVORITES to add the package to the list of favorite packages.

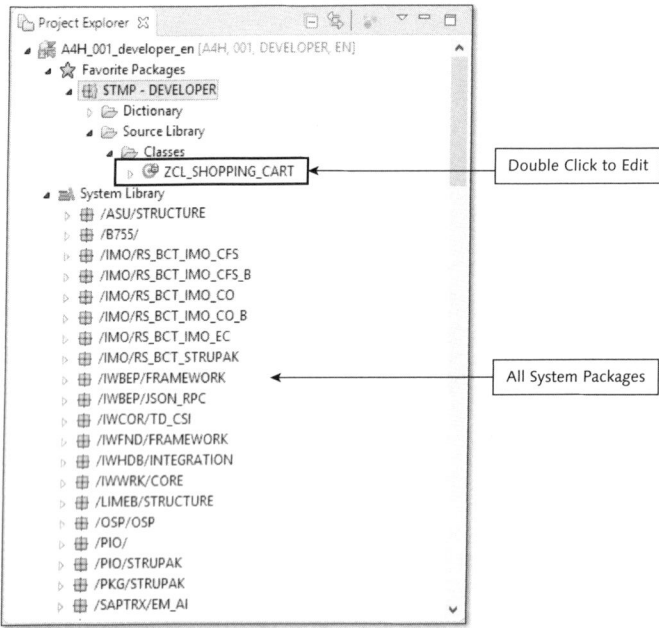

Figure A.37 The Project Explorer Window in Eclipse

As you write ABAP, the system will automatically complete syntax checks and will underline your code in red if an error is detected and display a red X or underline your code in yellow if a warning is detected. The details for the any syntax errors or warnings will be shown in the problems view (Figure A.38).

As you add more code to the program or class in the Eclipse workbench, the outline view will update with a list of methods, subroutines, and global data variables for the program or class that you're currently editing (Figure A.39). Double-click any item listed in the outline view to jump to the method or subroutine implementation or global data variable definition.

Getting Started with ABAP in Eclipse

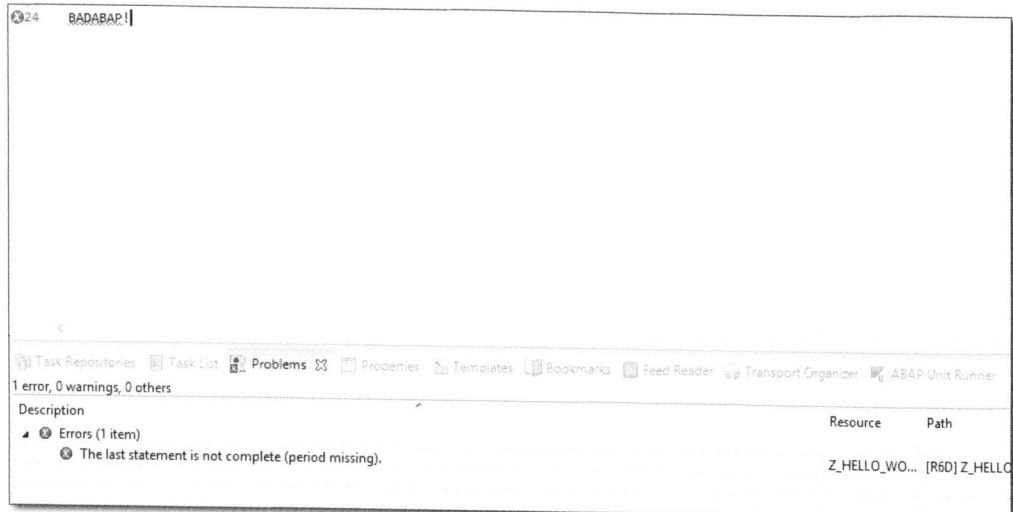

Figure A.38 Syntax Error

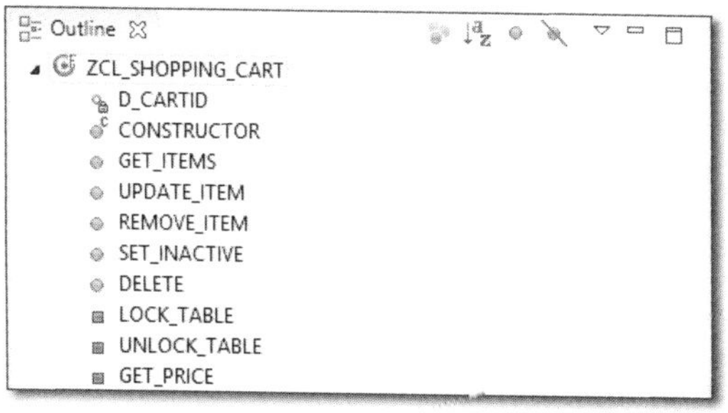

Figure A.39 Outline View Displaying Global Class Attributes and Methods

The same outline is also displayed in the Project Explorer after expanding the class or program as shown in Figure A.40. This outline will act just like the outline view, allowing you to double-click any listed item to jump to its definition or implementation.

You should now be able to comfortably navigate Eclipse. In this section, you learned how to personalize Eclipse by adding and removing different views. You may not know exactly how you want it set up until you've spent some time working in Eclipse, so experiment to find which views you find useful and which can be removed or moved.

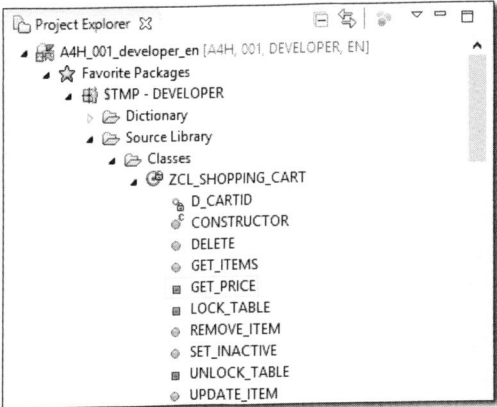

Figure A.40 Outline View Information Shown in Project Explorer

A.4 ABAP-Based IDEs

Some people may choose not to use Eclipse as their preferred IDE due to company policy or a system that is not up-to-date enough to allow it or maybe simply because they prefer ABAP-based IDEs. Whatever the reason, it's important to be familiar with ABAP-based IDEs, even if your preferred IDE is Eclipse.

A.4.1 Transaction SE80

Transaction SE80 in SAP is named the ABAP workbench. Prior to SE80, there were multiple individual ABAP editors (SE37, SE38, and others) used depending on the object that was being edited. With the ABAP workbench, the relevant editor will open based on the object that is being edited.

From within the transaction, the left side of the screen is a navigation pane used for navigating to different editable objects, whereas the right side of the screen is the workbench that will be populated with the relevant program for editing the selected object.

The left navigation pane is shown in Figure A.41. Here, focus on the default REPOSITORY BROWSER option, selected in the figure. The Repository Browser will allow you to search through various types of objects to find what you need to edit, including packages, programs, function groups, and classes, among others. In Figure A.41, you can see folders for all of the local objects for the user DEVELOPER, meaning all of the objects in the $TMP package created by DEVELOPER.

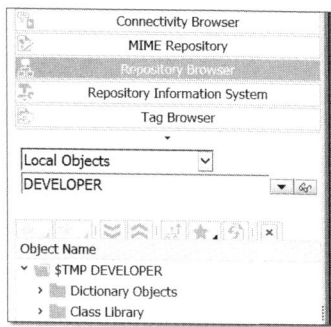

Figure A.41 Transaction SE80 Navigation Pane

Beginning in ABAP 7.31 systems, when you start to enter a value in the textbox under the REPOSITORY TYPE dropdown, the system will automatically search through the selected repository types to find the entered value and will present results below the textbox. An example of this is shown in Figure A.42, the system presents have the class ZCL_SHOPPING_CART as an option in a new selection box below the search textbox after selecting CLASS / INTERFACE from the dropdown and entering only "ZCL_sh" in the textbox. You can also use a wildcard asterisk (*) in your entry to search for results.

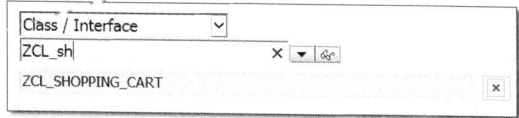

Figure A.42 Autosearch of Repository Objects in Transaction SE80

You can also complete a selection by pressing the down arrow button to open the INPUT HELP popup. If you see previous search results, you can click the INFORMATION SYSTEM button to see the input help options shown in Figure A.43, showing a search for a class beginning with ZCL.

Preparing your Development Environment

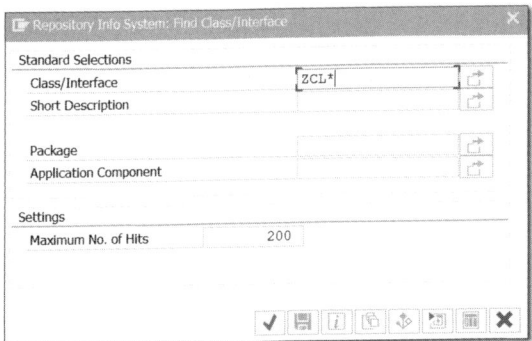

Figure A.43 Completing Input Help Search for Class/Interface

Once a program or class is selected, you can see navigation options for that class or program in the bottom half of the navigation pane by double-clicking the organizational folders to expand them. An example of this is shown in Figure A.44, in which we opened a class called ZCL_SHOPPING_CART and expanded all of the organizational folders within that class. You can double-click the class name to open it or click on any of the listed attributes or methods to open their implementations.

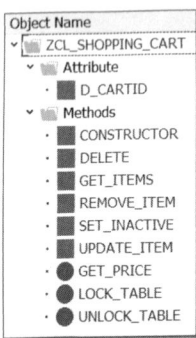

Figure A.44 Navigating through a Class in SE80

After selecting PACKAGE in the dropdown box and opening a package, you can easily navigate between objects stored within that package. In Figure A.45, the package $TMP contains database tables, views, and a class, and you can navigate to any of those items by double-clicking them.

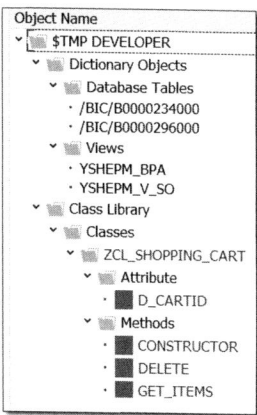

Figure A.45 Package with All Organizational Folders Opened

When you double-click any editable object, such as a table or method, the relevant editor will open in the workbench section, as shown in Figure A.46, in which the Class Builder (Transaction SE24) was opened to edit a class. Don't worry for now if this screen doesn't make sense; other chapters of this book cover how to edit classes and programs.

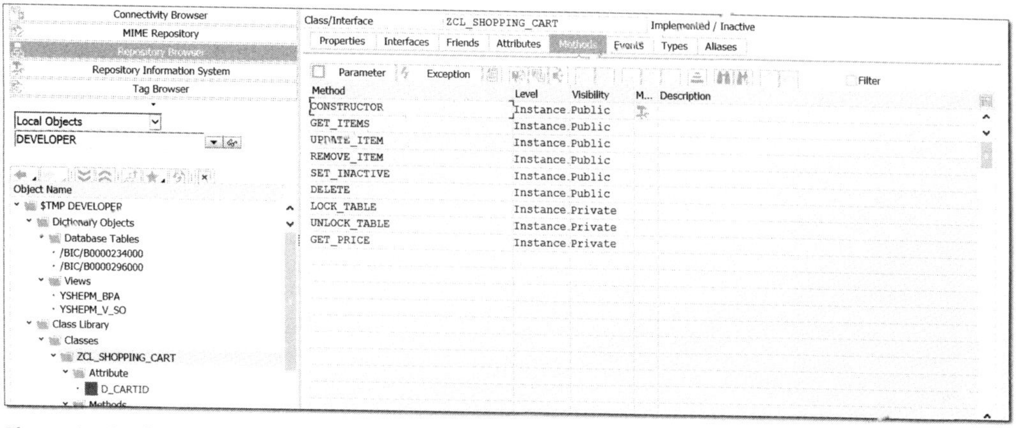

Figure A.46 Editing a Class while Viewing the $TMP Package

Each object also has additional options that can revealed by right-clicking the object you want to change. Options include creating variants for an ABAP program, reassigning a function module to a different function group, deleting an object that's no longer needed, and more.

A.4.2 Other ABAP IDE Transactions

The last section covered the basics for navigating Transaction SE80. Transaction SE80 loads other programs in to the workbench section of the transaction, but you can also open objects in their editors without using Transaction SE80 at all. In this section, we will introduct those other transactions.

Transaction SE38 is the ABAP Editor, which can be used to view, edit, create, delete, or execute an ABAP program. Transaction SE38 was the only way to edit ABAP code before the introduction of Transaction SE80, and it opens in the workbench section of SE80 anytime an ABAP program is opened.

The functionality for editing code will be identical to SE80, and the main screen for the transaction is shown in Figure A.47.

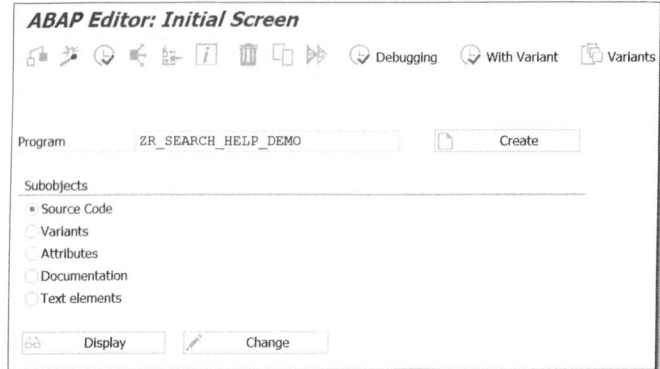

Figure A.47 Transaction SE38 Main Selection Screen

You can also use Transaction SE37 to view, edit, create, delete, or execute a function module, as shown in Figure A.48. This is the same editor that opens when editing a function module using Transaction SE80.

ABAP-Based IDEs

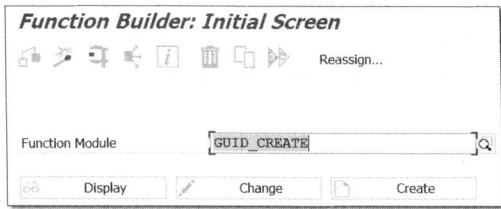

Figure A.48 Accessing Function Module Using Transaction SE37

When editing, viewing, changing, or testing classes, you can use Transaction SE24. This is the same editor used when accessing classes through Transaction SE80. The selection screen for Transaction SE24 is shown in Figure A.49.

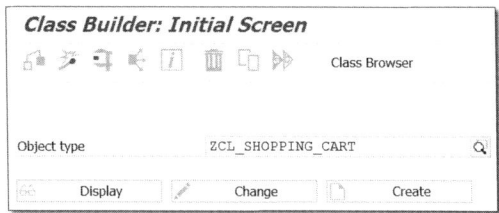

Figure A.49 Selection Screen for Transaction SE24

B   Modern UI Technologies

Throughout this book, you've used classic ABAP selection screens to interact with users. Although this method may be used regularly, its use is also a point of contention among users, because it's not considered very user-friendly. In fact, the entire SAP GUI has not been considered user-friendly for a long time.

As a result, SAP has released new UI technologies to improve the way users interact with the system. Covering how to create interfaces with these technologies is out of the scope of this book, but this appendix will serve to introduce them.

SAP's current user experience (UX) strategy is called "new, renew, and enable" and is based on the following points (quoted from *http://experience.sap.com/ux-strategy/2015*):

- Provide a consumer-grade UX for **new** applications
- **Renew** existing applications by improving the UX for the most commonly used business scenarios
- **Enable** customers to improve the UX of the SAP software with tools

New SAP applications are being written using the SAP Fiori style with the SAPUI5 JavaScript library or using web-based Web Dynpro. Also, SAP is using an "SAP Fiori First" approach to new functionality in S/4 HANA.

Even though SAP is creating new applications and renewing existing applications with Web Dynpro and SAPUI5, some customers are not ready to start creating new interfaces for their custom programs or for existing transactions that have not been renewed by SAP. This is where SAP Screen Personas can enable customers to renew classic ABAP screens. The screens can be redesigned with SAP Screen Personas to hide unnecessary options and even automate some screen inputs.

This appendix will briefly review the different available UI technologies. To learn more about these technologies, I recommend researching online and purchasing SAP PRESS books on these topics.

B.1 Web Dynpro

Web Dynpro is a web-based ABAP UI available since SAP NetWeaver Application Server version 7.0, which is based on a model-view-controller (MVC) paradigm. To create Web Dynpro applications, you don't write HTML and JavaScript; instead, you define a screen using metadata, and the system is able to generate the HTML and JavaScript for the final product. The only language required to know is ABAP, and the applications can be written using Transaction SE80 or the Eclipse IDE.

If you have experience with Microsoft Active Server Pages (ASP) or with JavaServer Pages (JSP), you will notice that Web Dynpro applications work in a similar way. These are all stateful web pages that are generated from the server. When you interact with the application, it will send data to the server and redraw the page. The statefulness allows you to lock an object being edited for however long the user is making changes to that object.

A Web Dynpro ABAP page can be viewed using an HTTP browser, the SAP NetWeaver Business Client (NWBC), or from within an iView in an SAP Enterprise Portal.

The basic structure of a Web Dynpro application is a Web Dynpro component containing a component controller and one or more windows containing one or more views. Each view also contains its own controller. Custom code only exists in the controllers, and data is shared between the view controllers and the component controller. The model can be a functional module or a BAPI for accessing data from the system. A drawing of this architecture is shown in Figure B.1.

An example of a Web Dynpro application that comes with sample flight data is shown in Figure B.2. In this application, clicking SEARCH will display a list of flights for the provided departure and arrival cities.

Web Dynpro B

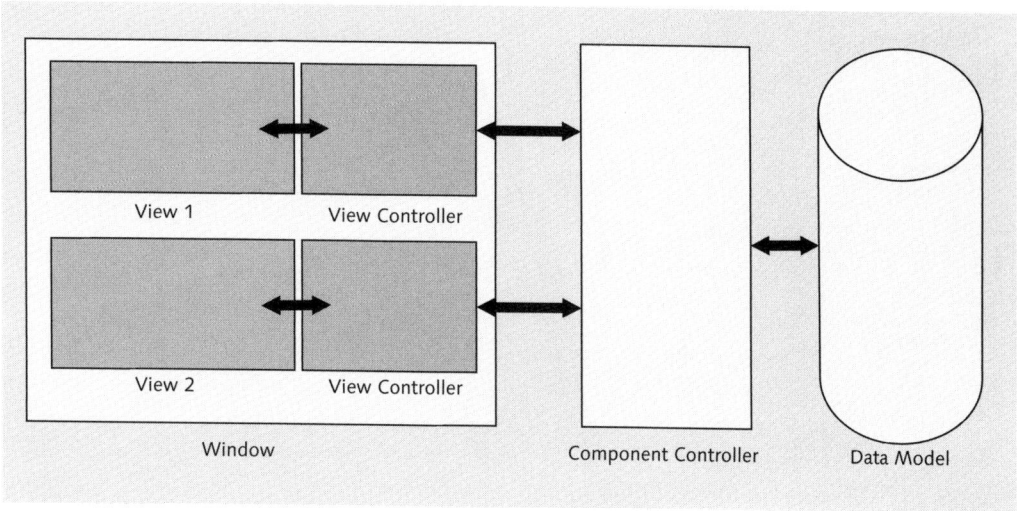

Figure B.1 Architecture of a Web Dynpro Component

Figure B.2 Web Dynpro Flight Data Application

In order to launch the Web Dynpro application shown in Figure B.2 you must first activate the service using Transaction SICF. From that transaction, search for the service name "WDT_FLIGHTLIST"; you should see the results shown in Figure B.3. From there, right-click the node named WDT_FLIGHTLIST and click ACTIVATE SERVICE. Once activated, the node's text should be black instead of gray. You can then right-click WDT_FLIGHTLIST and select TEST SERVICE to open the Web Dynpro application.

433

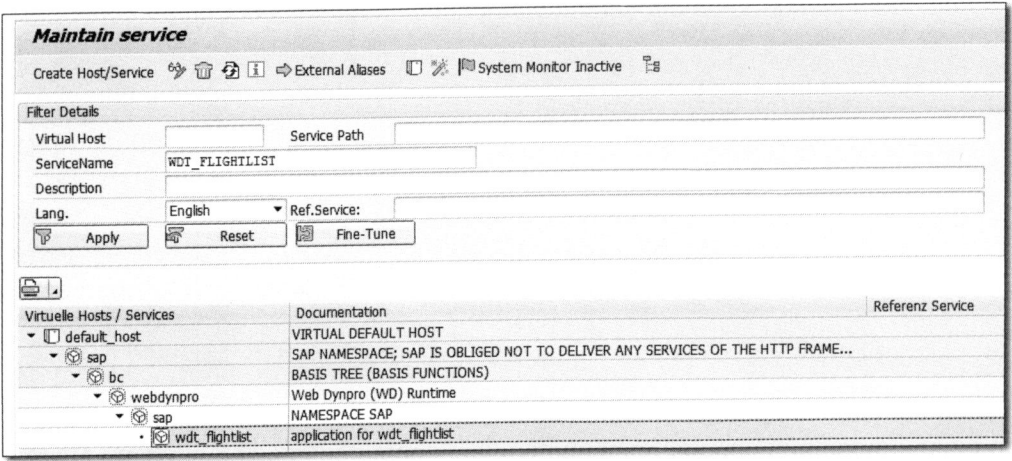

Figure B.3 Activating Web Dynpro Service

B.2 SAP Gateway and SAPUI5

Writing applications that utilize SAP Gateway and SAPUI5 is a newer method for writing web-based ABAP interfaces. When creating applications with this method, you'll be writing backend services in ABAP and a frontend UI in HTML and JavaScript. This is the method used for SAP Fiori-style applications and will most likely become the preferred method for accessing ABAP systems.

The SAP Gateway system creates OData REST web services that can be consumed by any client application, whether an HTML5 application or any type of native mobile application. SAP Gateway is typically set up as a hub system connecting to one or more ABAP-based systems through an RFC connection. An overview of the SAP Gateway architecture is shown in Figure B.4.

Services are generated based on metadata in a model provider class and on ABAP logic stored in a data provider class that will be created inside the ABAP backend system. Because REST services that are generated follow the OData standard, SAPUI5 and other libraries are able to easily consume such services. You can learn more about the OData standard at *http://www.odata.org*.

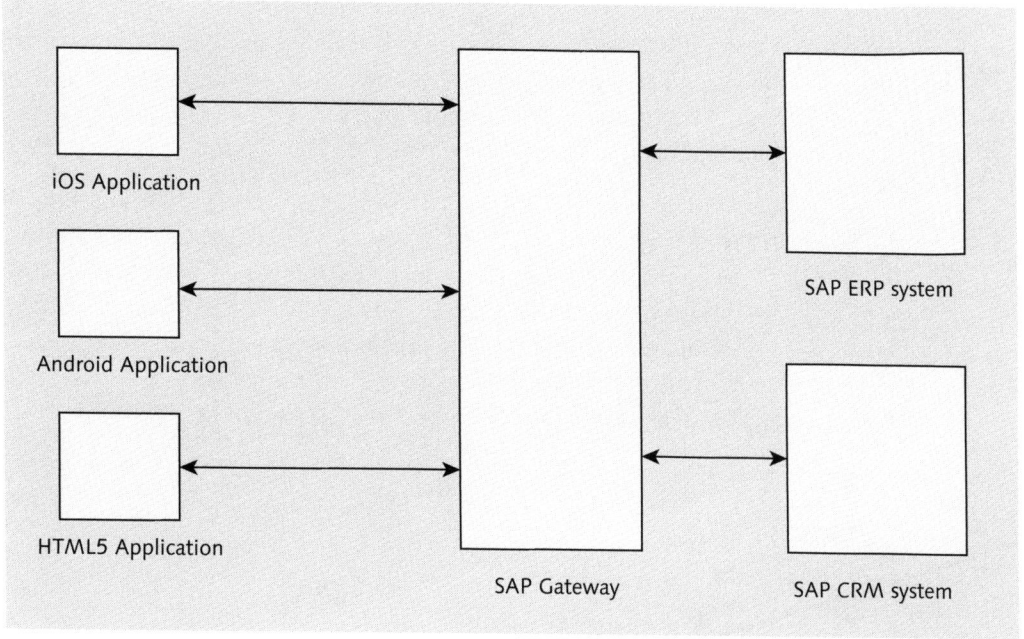

Figure B.4 Overview of SAP Gateway Architecture

The services that are created can be consumed in a JSON, XML, or Atom format. An example OData response using JSON is shown in Listing B.1, with a result list of three customers.

```
"d" : {
    "results": [
        { "id" : 1,
          "CustomerName" : "Customer 1" },
        { "id" : 2,
          "CustomerName" : "Customer 2" },
        { "id" : 3,
          "CustomerName" : "Customer 3" }
    ]
}
```
Listing B.1 OData Response in JSON Format

When accessing an ABAP system using OData services, you're creating a stateless application, unlike the stateful applications created using Web Dynpro. This is because once the system returns data from a service that was called, the system no longer knows what's happening on the UI or when the user will respond. As a result, you should be careful not to lock objects being called from an OData service unless you're doing so before making a change and then unlocking it before returning results to a user.

One option for building a UI for OData services is to build an HTML5-based application that uses the SAPUI5 JavaScript library. These applications will follow the MVC paradigm, like you saw with Web Dynpro applications. In SAPUI5 applications, the model will be the OData service that is being called, and the controller will be JavaScript code that binds the data to the view. An example of a SAPUI5 application utilizing the SAP Fiori style is shown in Figure B.5.

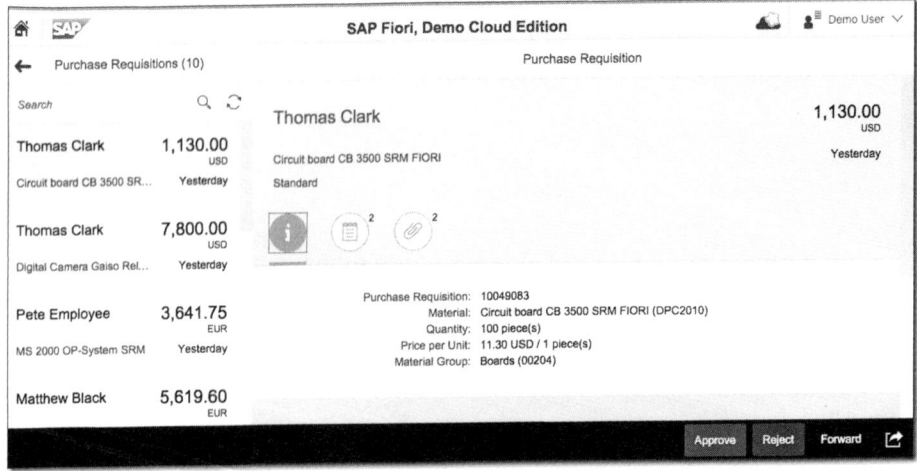

Figure B.5 SAPUI5 Application Using SAP Fiori Style

When users run an SAPUI5-based application, they can do so on any device; the HTML5 and JavaScript code is all executed within the browser. This allows the application to connect to the ABAP backend asynchronously, and it should also only contain code related to the UI and no business logic. Instead, all of the business logic should be located within data provider classes located in the backend systems.

Keeping business logic outside of the UI makes it easy to determine whether an issue is caused as a result of frontend code or backend code.

B.3 SAP Screen Personas

Converting custom applications to a new web-based interface can be a lot of work, and customers may also have old transactions that have not yet been made available in one of the new web-based interfaces. As a result, some customers may want to simplify their old classic ABAP screens without writing entirely new applications. This is where SAP Screen Personas can be used.

SAP Screen Personas allows customers to hide unused items from the screen and even add new items to the screen to create an entirely new-looking interface for a classic ABAP screen. You can also populate different values without showing anything to the user and use scripting to automate steps in a process. This can greatly improve the user experience and speed up the amount of time required to complete transactions in an ABAP system.

SAP Screen Personas has adopted many recent improvements, such as no longer relying on Microsoft Silverlight and allowing scripts to be written using JavaScript.

Although SAP Screen Personas is generally touted as a "drag and drop" and "no developer needed" type of solution, it's much more powerful when developers are able to write scripts that can automate steps in a given transaction.

B.4 What User Interface Should You Use?

After reviewing the different options for modern ABAP UIs, you may be wondering, "Which one should I use?" It depends. When possible, it's always best to use SAPUI5 or Web Dynpro, but it's important to factor in what's currently used and supported within your organization.

As a developer, it's a good idea to learn these technologies even if you aren't currently using them; eventually, you'll need to know them.

C   Other Resources

Hopefully, this book will be a great resource for you to begin your ABAP journey. There are various other resources available for you to continue your journey. Remember that the ABAP language is constantly changing and evolving, so in order to stay on top of the latest changes and enhancements to the language, you need to continue to learn or your skills may soon be outdated.

C.1   SAP PRESS Books

We assume that you are familiar with SAP PRESS books already, since you purchased this one. SAP PRESS continually releases new books on ABAP and other SAP topics.

This book is intended to be an introduction to the ABAP language, and you should consider reading *ABAP to the Future* by Paul Hardy, which will cover some more advanced and various new ABAP topics. You may also consider getting a book on ABAP for SAP HANA. Especially if working on S/4 HANA is in your future, you may want to learn more about how to optimize your ABAP code to run on an SAP HANA database system.

You can also look into the SAP PRESS offerings related to learning Web Dynpro, SAPUI5, and SAP Gateway to learn about the various modern interfaces that were only lightly introduced in this book.

C.2   SAP Community Network

A great and free way to keep up-to-date with the ABAP language and SAP products is to sign up for the SAP Community Network (SCN) at *http://scn.sap.com*.

SCN is an incredible resource. The forums are a channel outside of SAP support in which all members of the SAP community can help to solve a problem you may have, and you can help others who have had a problem that you know the answer to.

Once you are registered, you can choose to follow people and spaces on the site. A *space* is a location where people can post blogs or post questions for help. There is an entire space dedicated to ABAP development, which can be found at *http://scn.sap.com/community/abap*. This is a great location to visit frequently in order to keep up with the latest ABAP developments.

I most frequently read and post on SCN, though I have found the ABAP Help Blog at *http://zevolving.com* to be a great resource as well.

C.3 SAP Certifications

The purpose of this book was not to prepare you for an ABAP certification exam, but there are other books from SAP PRESS that do offer such preparation.

Once you have some more experience as an ABAP developer, you should consider applying to get an SAP certification in ABAP. Certifications can make it easier to get a job or client in the SAP field. SAP offers certifications in various functional and technical areas.

You can find more information about SAP certifications from SAP's training and certification site at *https://training.sap.com/shop/certification*.

C.4 SAP TechEd Conferences

SAP TechEd conferences are held in various cities across the world. The 2015 conferences will be in Las Vegas, Barcelona, and Bangalore.

These conferences are a great way to learn about some of the changes to the ABAP language and to learn more about the direction of SAP and its products from some of the people involved in such areas. Many of the lectures are also hosted online, so if you're unable to attend, you can still watch the lectures from your home.

The most beneficial session I ever attended was a hands-on workshop called "Modernizing ABAP Development," which was led by Horst Keller. Horst is in charge of creating SAP's ABAP documentation. In his sessions, he covers the latest ABAP developments. Every year, there are more improvements to the language, and his sessions are a great way to stay on top of those improvements so you can write robust and easily understandable code.

D   The Author

Brian O'Neill has worked in various IT positions over the past 10 years, starting as a help desk support worker, then moving into SAP support, and then to ABAP development while working in the IT department of SAP customer IGT (International Game Technology).

More recently, Brian has focused on mobilizing SAP environments and is currently a SAP mobility senior consultant with IBM.

Brian has a bachelor's degree in Computer Information Systems from California State University, Chico and a master's degree in Information Systems from the University of Nevada, Reno.

Brian has been a speaker at multiple SAP Technology conferences, including the Mastering SAP Technologies conference in Melbourne, Australia, in 2014 and SAP TechEd in Las Vegas in 2015. Brian was also featured in the 2011 Demo Jam at SAP TechEd in Las Vegas and was part of the SAP TechEd UpClose video series in 2011.

Brian has also been featured as a background actor in the 2008 film *Four Christmases* and the 2008 film *Milk* and was a featured actor in the 2011 three-minute short film *9 Pound Trout*.

Index

$TMP, 43

A

ABAP
  backward compatibility, 34
  code updates, 34
  modern syntax, 36
  obsolete code support, 35
  system implementation, 35
ABAP and screen stack, 86
ABAP clients, 23
  SAP Fiori, 23
  SAP GUI, 23
  SAP NetWeaver Business Client, 23
ABAP Perspective
  select, 38
ABAP systems
  client/server architecture, 29
  program status, 30
abap_false, 61
abap_true, 61
Activation log
  warnings, 122
Aliases, 161
ALV, 213
  cl_salv_table, 214
  SALV_OM_OBJFCTS, 214
ALV Grid Display, 117
Append Structure
  create, 119
Application table, 110
Arithmetic operations, 52
AS, 161, 169
AT SELECTION-SCREEN, 75
  event, 75
Attributes, 131
Authorization group, 141

B

b, 47–48
BEGIN OF SCREEN, 66
BETWEEN .. AND, 57

Binary floating point, 49
Binary logic, 56
BLOCK, 65–67
  NO INTERVALS, 67
  WITH FRAME, 67
  WITH FRAME TITLE, 67, 287
Boolean, 61
  yes/no user response, 72
Breakpoint, 77, 80
  create, 84
  remote, 85
  remove, 80
Buffering, 179
  options, 116

C

CALL SELECTION-SCREEN, 66
Cardinalities, 104, 125
CASE statements
  WHEN, 59
  WHEN OTHERS, 59
Chained statements, 45–46
Character-based data types, 49
Check Table, 112
Class
  definition, 280
  implementation, 283
Classic selection screen
  programming, 65
Client, 29
Cloud application library, 395
Clustered Tables, 108
Comments, 63
  ", 63
  *, 63
  mistakes, 64
  use in programming, 64
Constructor, 281, 284
Crow's foot notation, 103
Currencies, 345
  CONVERT_TO_LOCAL_CURRENCY, 347
  CUKY, 346

Currencies (Cont.)
  CURR, 346
  exchange rates, 345
Currency/quantity, 114
Custom Exception classes
  CX_DYNAMIC_CHECK, 383
  CX_NO_CHECK, 383
  CX_STATIC_CHECK, 381–382
  CX_SY_ILLEGAL_HANDLER, 383
  CX_SY_NO_HANDLER, 382
Customizing table, 110

D

DATA, 46, 53–54, 57–61, 63, 72, 77
Data class, 127
  types, 115
Data Dictionary, 97, 99
  Activation Log, 121
  Data Element, 183
  Data elements, 99
  documentation, 140
  domain, 99, 183
  table field, 183
  translation, 312
  transparent table, 98, 184
Data element, 97, 99, 112, 130–131, 266
  create new, 133
  predefined type, 131
  redundant, 102
  search help, 132
Data type, 112, 131
  numeric, 47
  structure, 186
Database
  definition, 98
  normalization, 101–102
Date
  CL_ABAP_TSTMP, 341
  CONVERT TIME STAMP, 339
  DATE_CONVERT_TO_FACTORYDATE, 333
  date-limited record, 336
  datum, 335
  Factory Calendars, 331

Date (Cont.)
  FACTORYDATE_CONVERT_TO_DATE, 334
  GET TIME STAMP FIELD, 338
  public holiday, 331
  RP_CALC_DATE_IN_INTERNAL, 330
  sy-datum, 336
  sy-fdayw, 336
  sy-timlo, 341
  sy-tzone, 341
  sy-uzeit, 341
  sy-zonlo, 341
  timestamp, 338
  timestampl, 338
  type, 50
  valid_from/valid_to, 336
Deadlock, 170
Debugging, 76
  execution stack, 229
decfloat, 47–49, 53–54, 77
Decimal floating point numbers, 48
Decimal places, 48
DELETE, 159, 284, 289
  FROM...WHERE, 285
DELETE ADJACENT DUPLICATES
  FROM, 204
  COMPARING, 204
  COMPARING ALL FIELDS, 204
DELETE TABLE, 197, 210
  hashed table, 208
  sorted table, 202
  WHERE, 199
  WITH TABLE KEY, 198
Deletion anomaly, 102
Delivery and maintenance, 110
DEQUEUE, 172, 175, 178
DIV, 53
Documentation, 140
Domain, 97, 135, 268, 270, 274
  BOOLEAN, 136
  create new, 138
  range, 137
Dynamic breakpoints, 82

E

Eclipse
   ABAP perspective, 38
   Create program, 37
   create project, 40
   format code, 61
   open project, 38
   SQL console, 149, 152
E-commerce, 22
ELSE, 58
ELSEIF, 58
ENDDO, 60
Enhancement category, 120, 127
ENQUEUE, 175
Entity, 101
Entity Relationship Diagrams R ERD
Entry help/check, 127
ERD, 101, 263, 319, 348
   crow's foot notation, relationship indication, 103
   normalized, 102
Exception, 372
   500 SAP internal server error, 373
   CATCH BEFORE UNWIND, 381
   CATCH...INTO, 379
   categories, 381
   CLEANUP, 380
   custom exception classes, 381
   function modules, 386
   non-class based exceptions, 386
   RAISE EXCEPTION TYPE, 380
   resumable exceptions, 381
   RESUME, 381
   short dump, 373
   ST22, 375
   TRY...CATCH, 378
   unhandled, 373
Exclusive lock, 171
Execution stack, 81
EXIT, 60

F

Field, 111
   label, 132, 134
   symbols, ASSIGN, 187

Flight data
   model, 105
   view, 116
Flight model
   load data, 118
FLUSH_ENQUEUE, 177
FOR ALL ENTRIES IN, 165
Foreign key, 103, 112, 273
   cardinality, 125
   create, 125
   set, 124
Format your code, 61
Fully Buffered, 180
Function
   ceil, 55
   floor, 55
   frac, 55
   ipow, 55–56
   sign, 55
   trunc, 55
Function group, 141, 250, 254
Function modules, 249, 255
   CALL FUNCTION, 257
   parameters, 253

G

Generic area buffered, 180
GETWA_NOT_ASSIGNED, 187
Global class, 262

H

Hash board, 205, 210
Hello World
   add user input, 71
   chained statements, 45

I

Identifying relationship, 103
IF Statement Operators, 56
   AND, 57–58
   OR, 57, 59
Initial value, 46, 111, 156
INITIALIZATION, 75

Inline data declaration, 51, 153, 289, 293
INNER JOIN, 160, 163, 285
INSERT, 156, 195, 210
  hashed table, 207
  INDEX, 195
  LINES FROM, 195
  sorted table, 201
Insert anomaly, 102
Integrated development environments, 395
Internal tables, 183, 208
  hashed table, 205, 209
  key, 189
  SORT, 200
  sorted table, 199, 208
  standard table, 188, 208
INTO, 170
IS NULL, 156
ITAB_ILLEGAL_SORT_ORDER, 200

J

Joins, 179
Junction Table, 105

K

Key, 111
Key fields/candidate, 125

L

LEFT OUTER JOIN, 163
LENGTH, 50, 68–69
Lifecycle event, 75
LIKE, 184, 189
  LINE OF, 184
LOAD-OF-PROGRAM, 75
Lock
  mode, 172
  objects, 174
  parameter, 173
Log data options, 116
Logical storage parameters, 115

Loop, 60
  infinite, 60
LOOP AT, 193
  BINARY SEARCH, 202
  hashed table, 207
  WHERE, 194

M

Maintenance dialog, 141
MANDT, 106, 124, 126, 157, 189
Many-to-many relationship, 105
Message class, 364, 371, 392
  &, 371
  create, 367
  long text, 369
  MESSAGE, 368
  WITH, 371
Method, 300
MOD, 53
Modalities, 104
MODIFY, 158, 210, 284, 289
  hashed table, 207
  sorted table, 201
MODIFY TABLE, 196
  INDEX, 197
  WHERE, 196
Modularize ABAP, 217
MOVE, 52
MOVE-CORRESPONDING, 212

N

New Open SQL, 169
Nonidentifying relationship, 104
NoSQL, 100
NULL, 111
Numeric data types, 47

O

Object, 293
Object-oriented programming, 220
  attributes, 225
  CHANGING, 230, 235
  class, 222–224

Object-oriented programming (Cont.)
   class definition, 223–224
   class implementation, 223–224
   CONSTRUCTOR, 236
   CREATE OBJECT, 224
   CREATE PUBLIC, 243
   EXPORTING, 230, 234
   FINAL, 243
   global classes, 241–242, 263
   IMPORTING, 230, 233
   INHERITING FROM, 239
   method, 221, 226, 228
   method chaining, 232
   object, 221
   OO-ABAP, 220
   OPTIONAL, 233
   private section, 225
   protected section, 225, 240
   public section, 225
   READ-ONLY *attributes*, 226
   recursion, 237
   REDEFINITION, 240
   RETURNING, 230–231
   returning parameters, 236
   subclass, 239
   superclass, 239
   TYPE REF TO, 224
One-to-many relationship, 104
One-to-one relationship, 104
Open SQL, 149
   MODIFY, 184
Optimistic lock, 171
Origin of the input help, 112

P

Package, 109
Packed numbers, 48
PARAMETER, 65–66, 69
   AS CHECKBOX, 70
   AS LISTBOX VISIBLE LENGTH, 70
   LOWER CASE, 287
   OBLIGATORY, 70, 291
   RADIOBUTTON GROUP, 70, 287, 291

Parameter ID, 132
Pooled tables, 108
Primary key, 101, 111, 282
Procedural programming, 218
Program attributes
   authorization group, 42
   editor lock, 42
   fixed point arithmetic, 42
   logical database, 42
   selection screen, 42
   start using variant, 42
   status, 42
   unicode checks active, 42
Program lifecycle events, 75
Promote optimistic lock, 171
Pseudocode, 283

Q

Quantities, 341
   QUAN, 342
   UNIT, 342
   UNIT_CONVERSION_SIMPLE, 344

R

RAISE, 387
RAISING, 381–382
Ranges, 168
READ TABLE, 190, 210
   ASSIGNING, 190–191
   BINARY SEARCH, 202
   hashed table, 206
   INDEX, 191
   INTO, 190–191
   WITH KEY, 207
   WITH TABLE KEY, 192
Relational Database Management System (RDBMS), 100
REPORT, 40, 44, 75, 77

S

S/4 HANA, 22
SAIRPORT, 106

SAP BASIS, 28, 34
SAP Cloud Application Library, 396
  Amazon Web Services, 396
  Microsoft Azure, 396
  trial system, 395
SAP ERP, 21
SAP Fiori, 27
SAP GUI, 23
  application toolbar, 24
  breakpoints, 83
  developer user menu, 26
  favorites menu, 25
  system information, 26
  toolbar, 24
SAP HANA, 22, 27
SAP NetWeaver, 22
SAP NetWeaver Business
  Client, 23, 27
SAP Transport Management
  System, 31
SAPBC_DATA_GENERATOR, 118
SAPBC_DATAMODEL, 106
SBOOK, 107
SCARR, 107
Scope, 171
SCUSTOM, 106
Search help, 113
SELECT, 151, 179, 285
  *, 152
  INTO TABLE, 151
SELECT SINGLE, 153
SELECT...UP TO n ROWS, 155
SELECT...ENDSELECT, 181
Selection screen, 167, 291
Selection screen keywords, 65
Selection text, 74, 287, 292
SELECTION-SCREEN, 65
  BLOCK...WITH FRAME TITLE, 291
SELECT-OPTIONS, 65–66, 72, 112, 167
  High, 168
  Low, 168
  Option, 168
Separation of concerns, 217
Sessions, 24

SFLIGHT, 107, 109
  append structure, 119
  primary key, 111
  view data, 116
Shared lock, 171
Short form
  [], 215
  LOOP AT, 215
  OCCURS, 215
  READ TABLE, 215
  WITH HEADER LINE, 215
Short form open SQL, 181
Sign, 168
Single quotes, 44
Single records buffered, 179
Size category, 127
Space category, 116
SPFLI, 107
START-OF-SELECTION, 75
  Event, 76
String, 49–51, 66, 68–72, 75
  ALIGN, 301
  chaining strings, 301
  concat_lines_of, 303
  CONCATENATE, 316
  CONDENSE, 303
  DECIMALS, 302
  SIGN, 301
  string functions, 302
  string literals, 299, 305
  string template, 300
  strlen, 302
  substring, 303, 330
  substring_before, 303
  substring_from, 303
  substring_to, 303
  timestamp formatting, 340
  WIDTH, 301
Structure, 143, 156, 188–189
Subroutines, 257
  Form, 257
  parameters, 258
  PERFORM, 257
sy-subrc, 193, 363, 387
sy-tabix, 193–194

T

Table
  custom transparent, 122
  normalized, 107
  technical settings, 114
  view single row, 153
Table column, 111
Table configuration, 109
Table locks, 170
Table type, 143, 153, 186, 210
TABLES, 181
Technical settings, 115, 127, 274, 279
Text symbols, 67, 287, 292, 304, 317
  comparison, 305
  translation, 309, 318
Third normal form, 102
  table, 103
Transactions, 24
  OB08, 345, 347
  OY03, 345
  SE11, 109, 117, 122, 136, 138, 141, 143, 145, 172, 174, 210, 266, 268, 271, 274, 276, 319–320, 342, 346, 349
  SE16, 116
  SE38, 118
  SE63, 322
  SE63 Translation editor, 312
  SE80, 280
  SE80 ABAP Workbench, 40
  SE80, create new program, 40
  SE80, create program, 40
  SE80, format code, 62
  SE80, form-based view, 245
  SE80, IDE settings, 44
  SE80, source code view, 245
  SE91, 364
  SM30, 141, 143
  SM37, background job selection, 30
  ST22, 375

Transactions (Cont.)
  STMS, transport management system, 32
Transparent Table, 97–98, 101, 108, 122, 156, 188–189, 262–263
  create data element, 133
  Currency/Quanity Fields, 342, 346
  data elements, 130
TYPE, 46, 53–54, 57–61, 63, 66, 68–72, 75, 77, 185

U

UML, 264, 280
UPDATE, 158
User Interface (UI), 65

V

Value range, 137, 139
Variable, 46
  assign value to, 52
  chain together, 46
  naming, 47

W

Watchpoints, 77, 88
WHERE, 155, 165
WHERE IS NULL, 165
WHERE..IN, 167
WHILE Loops, 60
Whitespace, 53
Wireframe, 264, 286, 290
WRITE, 44, 57–61, 72, 76, 78
  Hello World, 44

Z

ZBOOK, 107
Zero-to-many Relationship, 104
Zero-to-one Relationship, 104
ZSBOOK_SFLIGHT, 107

- Discover the latest and greatest features in the ABAP universe
- Explore the new worlds of SAP HANA, BRFplus, BOPF, and more
- Propel your code and your career into the future

Paul Hardy

ABAP to the Future

ABAP has been around for a while, but that doesn't mean your programming has to be stuck in the past. Want to master test-driven development? Decipher BOPF? Manage BRF+? Explore ABAP 7.4? With clear explanations, engaging examples, and downloadable code, this book is your ride to the future. After all: If you're going to build something with ABAP, why not do it with some style?

727 pages, 2015, $69.95/€69.95
ISBN 978-1-4932-1161-6

www.sap-press.com/3680

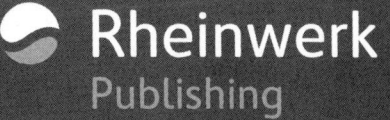

- ▶ Make the move from procedural to object-oriented programming
- ▶ Learn from conceptual explanations and practical examples
- ▶ Download sample code that you can use to put your skills to the test

James Wood, Joseph Rupert

Object-Oriented Programming with ABAP Objects

There's more to ABAP than procedural programming. If you're ready to leap into the world of ABAP Objects—or are already there and just need a refresher—then this is the book you've been looking for. Thanks to explanations of basic concepts, practical examples, and updates for AS ABAP 7.4, you'll find answers to questions you didn't even know you had.

470 pages, 2nd edition, 2015, $69.95/€69.95
ISBN 978-1-59229-993-5
www.sap-press.com/3597

- Learn about the ABAP certification test structure and how to prepare
- Review the key topics covered in each portion of the exam
- Test your knowledge with practice questions and answers

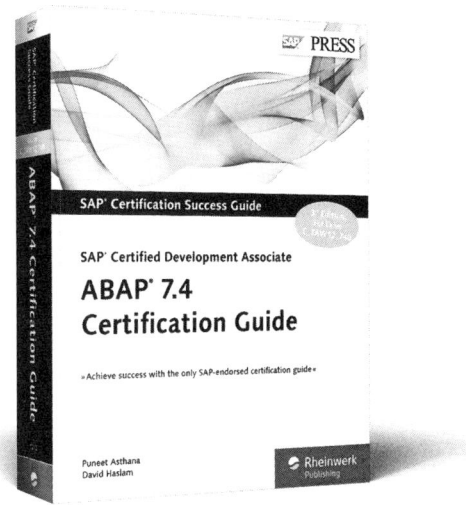

Puneet Asthana, David Haslam

ABAP 7.4 Certification Guide—SAP Certified Development

Getting ready to take your ABAP certification exam? Find everything you need to ace the test in this helpful resource! In or out of the classroom, you'll find comprehensive coverage of topics on the 7.4 test. Review your knowledge of the test material by answering sample questions, revisiting key terminology, and implementing recommended test-taking strategies. Soothe your pre-exam jitters and make the grade!

663 pages, 3rd edition, 2015, $69.95/€69.95
ISBN 978-1-4932-1212-5
www.sap-press.com/3792

- ► Understand the impact of SAP HANA on ABAP application development
- ► Learn how to develop applications for SAP HANA with SAP NetWeaver AS ABAP 7.4
- ► Work with advanced functions such as fuzzy search and predictive analysis

Thorsten Schneider, Eric Westenberger, Hermann Gahm,

ABAP Development for SAP HANA

They say there's nothing new under the sun—but every once in a while, something novel comes along. With SAP HANA, even the most seasoned ABAP developers have some learning to do. Newbie or not, this book can help: install the Eclipse IDE, brush up your database programming skills, perform runtime and error analysis, transport old ABAP applications to HANA—and more. Expand your horizons!

609 pages, 2013, $69.95/€69.95
ISBN 978-1-59229-859-4

www.sap-press.com/3343